GUARDIANS OF TRADITION

There is probably no better place than a schoolroom to judge of the character of a people, or to find an explanation of their national peculiarities. Whatever faults or weaknesses may be entailed upon them, will show themselves there without the hypocrisy of advanced age, and whatever virtue they may possess is reflected without admixture of vice and corruption. In so humble a place as a schoolroom may be read the commentaries on the past, and the history of the future development of a nation.

Francis J. Grund, 1837

Guardians of Tradition

American Schoolbooks of the Nineteenth Century

RUTH MILLER ELSON

UNIVERSITY OF NEBRASKA PRESS · LINCOLN

Chapter 7 first appeared in somewhat different form as "American Schoolbooks and 'Culture' in the Nineteenth Century" in the *Mississippi Valley Historical Review*. The Section on Germany and the Germans is a revision of "Deutschland und die Deutschen in amerikanischen Schulbüchern des 19. Jahrhunderts", which appeared in *Internationales Jahrbuch für Geschichtsunterricht*.

Library of Congress Catalog card number 64-17219

Most recent printing shown by first digit below:
3 4 5 6 7 8 9 10

Manufactured in the United States of America

To Robert and Elizabeth

PREFACE

To discover what ideas were held by the ordinary man in any period of history is one of the persistent problems of intellectual history. The ideas and ideological development of literary men can be analyzed; recent work in intellectual history has presented us with analyses in abundance. But the ordinary man, unliterary by nature, left no direct expression of the concepts he accepted. His household furniture and artifacts offer source material for social history, but his intellectual furniture rarely appears in a form capable of surviving him.

What the averbal man of the past thought about anything is probably lost forever to historical research, but one can at least discover those ideas to which most Americans were exposed by examining the books they read. Apart from the Bible, the books most widely read in nineteenth-century America were not those written by intellectuals, but schoolbooks written by printers, journalists, teachers, ministers, and future lawyers earning their way through college. The selective process by which these people decided what political, economic, social, cultural, and moral concepts should be presented to American youth undoubtedly helped to form the average American's view of the past, the present, and the possible future of man. However ill qualified to do so, the authors of schoolbooks both created and solidified American traditions. Their choice of what they admired in the past and the present, and what they wished to preserve for the future, was likely to be the first formal evaluation of man and his works to which an American child was exposed. The schoolbooks delineated for him an idealized image both of himself and of the history that had produced the admired American type. They were a compendium of ideas popularly approved at the time, and they offer an excellent index of concepts considered "proper" for the nineteenth-century American.

To what extent an individual may be influenced by concepts implicit in his schoolbooks is a question that needs the attention of the psychologist as well as of the social scientist. The frequent attacks on current schoolbooks in the United States today, and the publicly sponsored revisions of schoolbooks, indicate that popular opinion still accepts without question the importance of schoolbooks in forming public opinion. Books used in the nineteenth-century school were undoubtedly more influential in this respect than are those of the twentieth century. Today's texts must compete for the child's attention with an abundance of reading material as well as with radio and television. Not only did the nineteenth-century child read little besides his schoolbooks, but the schoolbook itself occupied the central position in most public schools throughout the century. Educational theories, as well as the scarcity of highly trained teachers, required that most of the textbook be memorized word for word.

This study is based on more than a thousand of the most popular textbooks used in the first eight years of schooling, since high school was not then a normal part of the education of most Americans, and even the eight-year span did not become standard until the end of the century. It assumes that the first presentation of a concept to the child, with the authority of the school behind it, probably makes a greater impression than subsequent presentations. Obviously the beliefs and concepts held later by adults are not entirely the product of schoolbooks used in childhood. It seems safe to say, however, that the child more readily adopts those attitudes from his first formal study of society that are not contradicted by his own immediate experience. He may be drilled in school to absolute truthfulness, but if this directive is contradicted by the behavior of his parents or someone whose authority is of primary importance to him, the precept of the school is not likely to be effective. Conversely, schoolbook attitudes toward ideas and people remote to his experience probably influence his thinking more strongly on these subjects, and it is likely that the cluster of concepts associated with other nations in his schoolbooks would have an effect on the formation of his adult attitudes toward these nations. What the generations that faced the problems of the Civil War and Reconstruction learned in their schoolbooks of the problems of the Negro, slavery, American economic development, and American federalism would predispose them to certain views on these public issues. What the child learned of the national character of other nations could influence his attitude toward immigrants from these countries, and toward foreign affairs in general.

In a sense this is a study of attitudes which make up the lowest common denominator of American intellectual history. The ideas of the major intellectuals are familiar to us, but to what extent did they penetrate to the ordinary man of that period? We can discover the reception in cultivated circles of Darwin and Marx and of Romantic, Realist, and Naturalist writers, but when and in what form did these ideas reach the public at large?

I have tried to let the textbooks speak for themselves as much as possible, in the hope that their charm as well as their diction and sentiments will interest the reader.

Ruth Miller Elson

CONTENTS

LIST OF ILLUSTRATIONS

I. Introduction

Chapter 1

THE SCHOOLBOOK AND THE SCHOOL

The history of schoolbooks as a part of the history of education—curriculum, child psychology, and administration—in this country is an interesting subject in itself, but one that is ancillary to this discussion.[1] In this study only those aspects of schoolbooks related to their social and cultural content and to their impact on the child will be considered.

The purpose of nineteenth-century American public schools was to train citizens in character and proper principles. Most textbook writers had an exalted idea of their function; almost all made statements such as the following: "The mind of the child is like the soft wax to receive an impression, but like the rigid marble to retain it."[2] They were much more concerned with the child's moral development than with the development of his mind. The important problem for nineteenth-century American educators was to mold the wax in virtue rather than in learning. Noah Webster advocated the use of his book on the grounds that it would enable teachers "To instil into their [the children's] minds, with the first rudiments of the language, some just ideas of religion, morals and domestic economy."[3] The textbook was to be a compilation of the ideas of the society. In

[1] For a detailed and comprehensive examination of the form, history, authors, and place in the curriculum of American schoolbooks, there are two excellent books: Clifton Johnson, *Old Time Schools and Schoolbooks* (London: Macmillan, 1917), and the more recent work by Professor John A. Nietz of the University of Pittsburgh, *Our Textbooks* (Pittsburgh: University of Pittsburgh Press, 1961). For an equally good study of changing attitudes toward child psychology see Monica Kiefer, *American Children Through Their Books, 1700–1835* (Philadelphia: University of Pennsylvania Press, 1948).

[2] S 1799 Fenning, p. 157.

[3] S 1810 Webster, p. vi; see also R 1796 Bingham, pref.; R 1797 Alexander, pref.; S 1847 ASDUK, p. vi; S 1859 Ormsby, Cushing and Farnham, p. 94; et al.

1789 he stated his purpose in writing a schoolbook: "To refine and establish our language, to facilitate the acquisition of grammatical knowledge and diffuse the principles of virtue and patriotism is the task I have labored to perform."[4] There was no doubt in the minds of the authors that the books used in public schools were important for the future of the Republic. They saw their function as the creation of an American nationality, the formation of a "National Character."[5] Most of them believed that as European educators sponsored children's books which "are calculated to impress on their youthful minds a prejudice in favor of the existing order of things," so American educators must inculcate "American principles."[6] The ideas taught in the nineteenth-century school were not necessarily universal truths, but national truths. It was the national prototype that was to be embodied in American schoolbooks. Dissent appeared in only one book, an 1832 Reader: "The effort has been made to select such articles as men of a truly catholic spirit, in all countries may regard with approbation, rather than those of a patriotic or national character."[7]

Spellers and Arithmetics were the first books presented to the child entering school. After introducing the child to the alphabet, the Spellers offer long lists of letter combinations to be memorized. These nonsense syllables were probably of slight educational value. The Spellers also include lists of words to be memorized. In the early books, those before 1830, there was little attempt to confine the first of these words to concrete objects familiar to the child. Such words as "heresy," "popery," "republic," "kingdom" appear in most of the early lists, and always without definition. Presumably these represented words needed by the child to get along in his society, but what meaning they carried to the young is indeed a dubious matter. Although the vocabulary presented in the Spellers and Readers throughout the century was a more varied and sophisticated one than is offered in present-day schoolbooks, one cannot conclude that children learned more or faster than children of today. In introductions or prefaces or

[4] R 1789 Webster, pref. [5] G 1825 Butler, p. 32.

[6] R 1803 Carey, pp. iv–xii. This sentiment was universal from Webster's 1783 Speller through the nineteenth century.

[7] R 1832 Edwards, p. 4.

sections entitled "Hints to Teachers" one often finds such statements as the following: "A leading object of this work is to enable the scholar while learning to *read*, to *understand*, at the same time, the meaning of the words he is reading."[8] Apparently teaching the child the meaning of the words he had learned to read or spell was not standard practice. Perhaps such a complex vocabulary offered more than the present ones to the bright child with outside resources, but most of it must have been incomprehensible to the ordinary student. In any case the principles used in the selection of such word lists are interesting as clues to the interests of the society. The Spellers also present disconnected sentences for practice in the use of words on the lists. The social and cultural values embodied in these sentences are of great value in determining what concepts the child was expected to accept as of value to society.

A study of the Arithmetics was not fruitful enough to warrant a thorough survey. They were sampled from the beginning, middle, and end of the century. The subjects of the problems clearly mirrored the broad economic situation of America in this period. Most of these books were designed for a practical end. Each author stated on his title page or in his introduction that his book would give the American child all he needed to know of accounting and calculating to enter business. Indeed, many of the Arithmetics were addressed to the merchant and mechanic as well as to the child. Almost every book also included a section on surveying, a subject obviously useful in a country engaged in the process of agricultural expansion. For this study the major interest in these books was in the subject matter used as a framework for the problems. Did the nature of the problems accustom the child to the shift from an agricultural and mercantile economy to an industrial one? Were such controversial matters as slaves, rum, and tobacco included as terms in the problems? How frequently did military problems appear?

The Readers were the most numerous class of books examined. Until about 1830 the Readers for all grades were compilations of

[8] R 1828 Putnam, p. 3; see also S 1799 Fenning, p. 58; R 1803 D. Adams, title page; S 1820 Kneeland, pref.; S 1821 Hull, intro.; Warren Burton, *The District School As It Was by One Who Went to It* (Boston: Phillips Sampson, 1833), pp. 29, 54, 57.

pieces selected from diverse sources, and the Readers for more advanced classes continued to be of this sort throughout the century. In the first two decades considered in this study the selections were usually excellent from the point of view of literary style. These books were made up of discrete fragments chosen from such authors as Cicero, Livy, Molière, Shakespeare, Sheridan, Sterne, and always Poor Richard. They were evidently chosen by the English authors of the first textbooks used in the United States as samples of the best in literature. The motive was an admirable one, but it left much to be desired from the pedagogical point of view. The scenes were plucked from the middle of a play, story, or essay and presented with no introduction. Sometimes the particular pieces selected had no unity of any kind and made little sense when taken out of context. Furthermore the vocabulary as well as the concepts were far beyond the grasp of any but the most advanced students. Gradually these literary fragments were replaced by excerpts selected for their moral content, aesthetically a dubious change. It was not until the 1830's that better pedagogical techniques began to produce books for beginners centered around things familiar to the child. Moral and religious essays and pieces on such Romantic subjects as death, disease, scenic wonders, patriotism, and heroism dominated all of the Readers from this time on.

Geographies and Histories were valuable not only because they embodied political and social concepts but also because they evaluated the civilization of the United States in relation to other countries. The Geographies present surveys of each country in the world, and, in the United States, of each section and each state. They were astonishingly resistant to change for schoolbooks of a country subject to great and visible changes during the period. Much of the space devoted to each country was taken up by a description of what was considered to be the inherent mental and personality characteristics of that nation. This was also often true of the space devoted to each section and to each state of the United States. The Histories of the United States were especially useful in sorting out what of the American past was considered worthy to be included as part of the American tradition.

Because this study is concerned with the cultural concepts to which the child was introduced early in his school career, the books used have been limited to those of the first eight years of schooling. The grading of books by age was at first, however, nonexistent; the lessons were merely graded within each book. Grading among books began to appear near midcentury, but without any uniformity among publishers and without any external standards. Thus a third Reader in one series may bear little relationship in degree of difficulty to a third Reader in another series, nor may either have anything to do with the third grade in school. In each case the third Reader may simply be the third in point of difficulty in that particular series of Readers. In this study, therefore, the judgment of the writer, based on internal evidence in the books themselves, has been the final criterion for grading in most of the century. Near the end of the century professional educators took an increasing interest in such matters, and grading became more uniform. By this time too the hand of the professional educator can be clearly discerned in the simplification of vocabulary and the introduction of pedagogical aids of all sorts.

The elementary school curriculum at the time of the Revolution consisted of reading, writing, and arithmetic, all strongly permeated with religion. By 1825 grammar and geography were added in many schools. The history of the United States appeared as a separate subject in some schools by the 1830's, but it was not generally a required subject until after the Civil War.[9] This does not mean that the child of this period was unaware of American history. Although it was a required subject only in Vermont and Massachusetts before the Civil War, American history made up much of the material in the textbooks in other fields.

Not only was the curriculum expanding, but the number of Americans who attended school increased tremendously during this century. The public school movement gathered momentum with the abolition of a property requirement for voting, with the advent of an increasing number of immigrants, and with the need for an educated labor force in a growing economy. A free

[9] Ellwood P. Cubberley, *Public Education in the United States* (Boston: Houghton Mifflin, 1934), pp. 219–222. Otis W. Caldwell and Stuart A. Courtis, *Then and Now in Education, 1845–1923* (Yonkers-on-Hudson, N.Y.: World Book, 1924), p. 119. Paul Monroe, *The Founding of the American Public School System* (New York: Macmillan, 1940), I, 346. R. Freeman Butts, *A Cultural History of Education* (New York: McGraw-Hill, 1947), p. 503.

school system was set up in Massachusetts in 1827, in Delaware in 1829, in Pennsylvania in 1834, in Vermont in 1850, in Indiana in 1851, in Ohio in 1853, and in Iowa in 1858.[10] And in 1852 Massachusetts adopted the first compulsory school attendance law. Not only did more people attend school, but they remained in school for a longer period of time. According to the United States Bureau of Education the time spent by the average American in school increased from four months and two days in 1800 to ten months and eight days in 1840 to twenty-two months and ten days in 1850.[11] Thus schools, and therefore schoolbooks, were used by an increasing number of children for a longer period of their lives as the century advanced.

Many of the early American schoolbooks were unrevised English books. American cultural independence might be declared by a Morse or a Webster shortly after American political independence, but for physical and economic reasons cultural independence took longer to achieve. English books continued to be used well into the nineteenth century, even though they embodied British nationalism. The Grammars and Readers of Lindley Murray were among the most popular of all textbooks.[12] As late as 1849 American authors of schoolbooks were complaining of the constant reissue of Murray's works in America.[13] Many such books were issued in pirated copies, but they were gradually superseded by books written or compiled by Americans. Even the first of these were strongly dependent on English works. Often those extracts most flagrantly representing British nationalism

[10] Monroe, *op. cit.*, p. 332. [11] Cubberley, *op. cit.*, p. 253.

[12] Lindley Murray was by birth an American and a Quaker. During the American Revolution he gave up his business in New York City and moved to Long Island to hunt and fish. In 1794 he went to England for his health and remained there until his death in 1826. Whether he regarded himself as English or American is difficult to discover, but his schoolbooks embody no hint of American nationalism. He is considered English by other writers of schoolbooks. His American origin may have been unknown to these colleagues, or, as is more likely, they may have been using this characterization in order to persuade school administrators to discard Murray's books in favor of their own. For examples of other books written by Englishmen but used in American schools, see: S 1789 Perry; R 1793 Moore; A 1797 Milns; R 1798 Enfield; G 1804 Goldsmith; A 1806 Vyse; S 1824 Guy; G 1825 Butler; S 1836 Brandreth; R 1854 Pycroft.

[13] R 1827 Pierpont, p. iii; R 1843 Cobb, pref.; R 1849 Leavitt, p. 41.

were deleted in favor of American speeches, but the basic structure remained the same.

From internal evidence in the books themselves one must conclude that most of them were written by New Englanders, a fact borne out by their profound New England bias as well as by an investigation of their authors' lives. A Phi Beta Kappa oration at Harvard, July 19, 1849, seems to give further support to this inference: "Nearly all of our teachers, with the authors of our schoolbooks, and a very large proportion of our preachers, as well as our editors (the classes which have the greatest control over the growing character of our youth) come from, or receive their education in New England."[14] Certainly, with the notable exception of McGuffey, the most popular authors of nineteenth-century American schoolbooks were from that section: Noah Webster, Jedidiah Morse, S. G. Goodrich, C. A. Goodrich, S. Augustus Mitchell, Jesse Olney, and Emma Willard were all born in Connecticut; Lyman Cobb, William Woodbridge, Richard Parker, and Salem Town were products of Massachusetts; John Frost was from Maine and Benjamin D. Emerson from New Hampshire. In this period New England can justly be termed the schoolmaster of the nation. Cubberley also observes that the educational leaders of the West were originally from New England.[15] The public school was the product of New England Puritanism, and it should occasion no surprise that textbook authors were a by-product.

According to Edgar Knight, the pre-Civil War South reluctantly but necessarily relied on schoolbooks written in the North. At a convention of administrators and teachers in Augusta County, Virginia in 1853, the following authors were suggested as the best in their fields: for spelling, Webster (Connecticut); for reading, McGuffey (Ohio, though born in Pennsylvania), and Mandeville (New York); for geography, Mitchell (Connecticut) and Smith (Connecticut); for arithmetic, Davies (Connecticut).[16] Southern authors frequently complained of this situation; an

[14] George W. Bethune, "The Claim of our Country on Its Literary Men" (Cambridge: John Bartlett, 1849), p. 21. See also Dixon Wecter, *The Hero in America: A Chronicle of Hero Worship* (New York: Charles Scribner's Sons, 1941), pp. 45–46.

[15] Cubberley, *op. cit.*, pp. 170–171.

[16] Edgar W. Knight, *Public Education in the South* (Boston: Ginn, 1922), p. 271.

article in *De Bow's Review* in 1861, noticing the New England monopoly, demanded that Southern textbooks be written to supplant those then in use in the South because some presented an unfavorable view of slavery.[17] Largely for economic reasons such requests met with very limited success even under the Confederacy. The few texts issued under the Confederacy were badly edited and printed. In the post-Civil War period Northern books were still used in Southern schools, often with offensive pages pinned together at the request of the teacher.

The classroom method of the period made the textbook peculiarly important in the school. Because the teachers were relatively untrained, letter-perfect memorization without particular attention to meaning was the basic method of common, or public, school education.[18] Few teachers outside of the large cities had much education beyond that of the schools in which they taught. When examined for the position their moral character was considered more important for teaching than any technical training.[19] A nineteenth-century work on the theory and practice of teaching suggests that teachers be better prepared; the author believed that this could be accomplished if the teacher would read over the textbook before class.[20] Apparently even this would have constituted a reform. The subject of professional training for teachers increasingly absorbed educational leaders from the 1830's on. In 1839 Massachusetts established the first public normal school, but by 1860 there were only twelve such schools in the United States. One half of these were in New England; the others were distributed one in New York (1844), one in Michigan (1849), one in New Jersey (1855), one in Illinois (1857), one in Pennsylvania (1859), and one in Minnesota (1860.)[21] Four of the pre-

[17] J. W. Morgan, "Our School Books," *DeBow's Review*, XXVIII (1860), 434–440. See also Knight, *op. cit.*, pp. 291–292. Merle E. Curti, *The Social Ideas of American Educators* (New York: Charles Scribner's Sons, 1935), pp. 73–74. R 1862 Sterling and Campbell, pref., p. iv (Confederate textbook) states that this is probably the first series of schoolbooks produced wholly by Southern industry.

[18] Monroe, *op. cit.*, I, 344–345.

[19] Cubberley, *op. cit.*, p. 243.

[20] David P. Page, *Theory and Practice of Teaching* (New York: A. S. Barnes, 1885), originally published in 1847, pp. 141–143.

[21] Cubberley, *op. cit.*, p. 293.

Civil War normal schools were in one state, Massachusetts. These were reinforced by six private normal schools, but it is obvious that although the situation was improving, the day of the teacher trained for his profession was still in the future for most American schools.

The Pestalozzian method, antithetical to memorization, became known here after 1835 with the publication of a translation of Victor Cousin's report to the French government on the schools of Prussia, Calvin Stowe's report in Ohio in 1837 on Prussian schools, and Horace Mann's Seventh Report on European education. The educational journals, particularly those of William Woodbridge, published between 1831 and 1839, and the later ones of Mann and Henry Barnard introduced their readers to this method. But such reports and journals obviously reached only a small fraction of the teaching population and had relatively little effect on the schools of the nineteenth century.

In many classrooms the memorization technique was reinforced by the monitorial system, whereby older students were designated to hear the recitations of the younger ones. It was a method attractive to taxpayers, since one teacher with the aid of monitors could handle an enormous class of many grades. But the monitor could be trusted only to see whether the student's memorization of the schoolbook was letter perfect. Questions given as teaching aids in the books themselves clearly expect this method. The typical form of question is: "What is said of . . . ?" Memorizing the sentiment or value judgment was quite as often required as memorizing the fact. For example, a textbook in the history of the United States requires that the child: "Mention any other things in our national history which should excite our gratitude."[22] A list of these "other things" appears in the text above.

Such classroom methods required absolute uniformity of texts to make mass recitation or recitation before an untrained teacher possible. This system remained in the realm of the ideal during the first part of the century, because the children used the schoolbooks of their parents, neighbors, or relatives to save money. In 1846 the state of Connecticut discovered that there were two hundred and fifteen different texts in use in its schools, although

[22] H 1843 Hall and Baker, p. 244.

an official text had been chosen by each district board.[23] But the method apparently conditioned the writers of textbooks effectively. Many of the books were written wholly in the catechism form.[24] In order to assure boards of education that a new issue of an older textbook could be used in the same classroom with the original work, many of the Histories retained the old copyright date and added more recent material at the end of the book. A History ostensibly published in 1881 might include material through 1888.[25] Many gave such assurance of stability as the following: "Teachers may rest assured, that all future editions of this work will be printed page for page with the present."[26] This often produced strange anachronisms: the 1862 and 1865 editions of Mitchell's Geographies follow previous editions so closely that no word of secession or the Civil War appears, although both contain extensive treatments of the Southern states. When a revision of an older text was published, the publisher often made some such promise as the following: "This revision can be used in class with the older edition as the pages correspond throughout."[27] As a result of this effort at uniformity the textbooks were singularly resistant to change.

Furthermore the basic material of many of the textbooks was in previously published schoolbooks; the essential method of composing a schoolbook was often one of compilation and plagiarism. Throughout this study such similarities will be manifest; word order was left unchanged in many cases where no authority was cited, and where the last authority was clearly another textbook author. This is true even in the Geographies, where one would expect recent expert knowledge to be vital. The method of compilation itself, then, produced a startling similarity and time lag. It is well to keep in mind that experts in

[23] Monroe, *op. cit.*, pp. 345–346; see also Alonzo Potter, *The School and the Schoolmaster* (Boston: W. B. Fowle and N. Capen, 1843), pp. 228–229.

[24] For examples see: G 1796 Dwight; G 1806 Cottineau; G 1824 Fowle; G 1825 Butler; G 1827 C. Goodrich; G 1832 Olney.

[25] H 1881 Thalheimer; see also H 1885 Donnelly (contains material to 1897); H 1889 Chambers (contains material to 1892); H 1897 McMaster (contains material to 1900); H 1899 Morris (contains material to 1904).

[26] S 1826 Alden, p. vi; see also R 1812 Daggett, p. 4; R 1819 Strong, p. 5; R 1834 Angell, p. iii; G 1848 Smith, pref.

[27] H 1889? Steele, back of title page.

the particular fields did not enter the textbook writing arena until almost the end of the century, and that even then they accounted for a very small minority of schoolbooks.

Schoolbooks, central to the curriculum of the nineteenth-century school, offered both information and standards of behavior and belief that the adult world expected the child to make his own. What these standards were will be examined in the following pages.

II. God and Nature

Chapter 2

NATURE

Belonging to a frontier civilization, the American has always been acutely conscious of himself as an agent of change in his natural environment.[1] The nineteenth-century American inhabited a world which had developed spectacular new scientific methods for the control of nature; this circumstance enabled him to incorporate into his civilization a vast amount of land at an astonishingly rapid pace. While creating his own urban and industrial environment sometimes seemed to involve penalties, its accomplishments had an obvious value that seemed limitless. But, proud of his increasing dominion over nature, he was suddenly brought to face a theory backed by overwhelming empirical evidence that man is himself a creature of nature, limited in his potentialities by his own animalistic qualities. The idea that man was subject to natural law and conditioned by his natural environment was not new, but Darwinian evolution seemed to reveal man to himself as a creature developed almost accidentally through natural selection by a neutral and unpredictable natural process. Whether nature as viewed by the Romanticists was benign or malign, it was always purposefully related to man as a spiritual being; now it seemed devoid of moral meaning. The nature that allowed the senseless destruction of Stephen Crane's open boat was far removed from the nature that led Emerson's free spirit to transcendental truth.

In this chapter, then, we shall consider how man's relationship to nature was evaluated by schoolbooks in a period when that relationship was subject to fundamental re-examination. We shall examine such problems as these: When and how was the child introduced to new scientific hypotheses about the origins of

[1] David M. Potter, *People of Plenty* (Chicago: University of Chicago Press, 1954). Henry Nash Smith, *Virgin Land* (Cambridge: Harvard University Press, 1950).

the natural world? How much control can and should man exercise over nature? Does man make nature or does nature make man?[2] Was man's avid conquest of nature in the nineteenth century a fulfillment or a violation of natural processes? Was nature distinctive in America?

To an American of 1859, whose knowledge of the earth and its history was derived mainly from his schoolbooks and the Bible, the *Origin of Species* came as a shock—because of both its philosophical bases and its particulars. No hint of the discoveries of the remains of prehistoric monsters, found some fifty years before, had yet entered schoolbooks. Schoolbook authors seemed equally innocent of any knowledge of the theories and discoveries of the geologist Sir Charles Lyell. Universally they upheld the belief that the true history of the earth comes from *Genesis*: "The Bible contains the only rational and authentic history of the creation of the world which took place, as we are there informed, 4004 years before the commencement of the Christian era. At that period the visible universe was called into being, by the word and power of God."[3] Bishop Ussher's date for the Creation, accepted as unquestionable fact, is used in arithmetic problems: How long was the interval from the Creation to the birth of Christ? How many seconds have passed since the creation of the world?[4] In only one case are new geological hypotheses noticed, but then only to be refuted: S. Goodrich in 1853 rejects the theory of the great age of the earth because the Bible asserts that present continents and oceans were created six thousand years ago.[5] One Speller of 1826 offers to shield the child from possible clashes between new scientific discoveries and the Bible's descriptions of nature by explaining that the Bible is designed for the unlearned as well as the learned, and it therefore speaks of things as they appear to our senses rather than to our minds. When the Bible states that the sun moves, although we know it does not, there is no real contradiction—science and the Bible operate on different

[2] For an interesting discussion of this question in the nineteenth century see David Lowenthal, *George Perkins Marsh* (New York: Columbia University Press, 1958), especially chapter 13.

[3] G 1831 Blake, p. 10.

[4] First problem: A 1795 Root, p. 45; second problem: A 1810 Hendrick, p. 70.

[5] G 1853 S. Goodrich, p. 18.

planes of human experience.[6] Obviously this author is concerned rather with the Copernican theory than with later doctrine, but his general precept could be useful to the nineteenth-century child. These are the only suggestions of a gap between scientific thought and revealed religion; schoolbooks before the Civil War accept without question the Biblical history of the world and the creation of man. The Garden of Eden and its inhabitants are as real as the Appalachians.

After the publication of the *Origin of Species*, as well as before, schoolbooks assumed that the earth was created for man: "The Earth was formed by the Creator to be the abode of man during a short life, and the school in which he is to prepare for a life that will never end." [7] Not only was the earth created as a training ground for the human soul, but all parts of the earth serve man. God stocked the rivers with fish "for the benefit of man"; he even made the sky blue and the grass green because "these colors are most agreeable to the eye." [8] The professional geographer, Arnold Guyot, in his schoolbooks announces such a pattern: "We thus learn the wisdom and goodness of the great God, who not only made man, but, in preparing the earth to be his home, placed all those things most needful to him so abundantly in that climate in which it is best for him to live." [9] Even the evolution that does appear in certain books in the latter half of the century is not by natural selection; it is a teleological evolution instituted by God to perfect man's world. "Man is made the central object and the adaptation of the earth to his wants is clearly shown." [10] This fundamental assumption, perhaps more than particular contradictions between the Bible and the new science, would inhibit the acceptance of the Darwinian view of the evolution of man. The nineteenth-century child was left in no doubt that the world was created for man, and man for God.

[6] S 1826 Alden, p. 162.

[7] G 1845 Woodbridge, p. 45; see also *Ibid.*, p. 67; G 1828 Adams, p. 98; G 1853 S. Goodrich, p. 14; G 1866 Woodbridge, p. xviii; G 1887 Warren, p. 13, *et al.*

[8] G 1851 Smith-G, pp. 13, 18; see also G 1866 Woodbridge, p. 247; R 1873 American, p. 116; R 1895 Hazen, p. 212.

[9] G 1866 Guyot-C, p. 95.

[10] G 1891 Morton, pref.; see also G 1872 Hall, p. 15.

In the beginning of the century, order in the universe is used to prove the existence of God. Among the many illustrations, one of the most popular shows George Washington's father planting his son's name in seeds to show that only an intelligent being can create design in nature.[11] In our own time the same anecdote appears now and then in children's books, but in a secular form, a mere garden game.[12] After the first few decades of the nineteenth century, schoolbooks take the existence of God for granted; design in the world is evidence of God's faultless planning. Throughout the century, nature is studied to reveal the glory of God by understanding the perfection of his creation: "What an august, what an amazing conception, do the works of creation give us, of the greatness, power, wisdom and goodness of the Creator!"[13] Geography is particularly recommended:

> The study of geography may lead your mind to pious reflections by bringing to your view the power, wisdom, and goodness of God . . . all these are the workmanship of His Hands, whose creatures we are. When we consider the power which He has displayed in their creation, the wisdom which He has fitted them to their variousness, and the goodness with which He has adapted them to the wants of His living creatures, while we contemplate *them*, we shall learn to adore Him.[14]

Most nature lessons end in the idea that every leaf, every flower shows us God's love by "its use of beauty."[15] Several McGuffey Readers use a poem by John Keble called "The Creator" to point out that though the rose is beautiful, He who made it is infinitely more so; though the lion is strong, He who made it is more so; though the sun is glorious, He who made it is more so.[16] Most nature lessons that show the adaptation of animals to their environment have nothing to do with evolution; they illustrate the harmony of God's universe. The thick fur of the polar bear

[11] R 1866 McGuffey-4, pp. 69–74; R 1899 Judson and Bender, pp. 168 ff.

[12] For example: Bella Koral, *George Washington* (New York: Random House, 1954).

[13] G 1789 Elements, p. 5.

[14] G 1826 E. Willard, pp. 11, 12.

[15] R 1870 Sanders, p. 261; see also *Ibid.*, pp. 95–96; R 1866 McGuffey-4, pp. 244–248; R 1867 Edwards-5, pp. 95–96; R 1872 Osgood-5, pp. 284–288; R 1873 American, frontispiece.

[16] R 1866 McGuffey-4, pp. 30–37; R 1879 McGuffey, pp. 126–127.

1. The study of nature is important because it reveals the glory of God. This print is from the fifth Reader of *The American Educational Readers,* 1873.

protects him from the cold; the feathers of the ostrich protect him from the sun, etc.[17] Even such unpleasant inhabitants of the plant world as nettles have a purpose; "God makes nothing without its use."[18] After indicating that lightning is useful because it rids the atmosphere of noxious vapors, McGuffey continues, "All the works of God are founded in wisdom and are intended for some benevolent purpose." To wish it otherwise "is a very wrong and wicked wish."[19] The man who thinks it would have been more logical if the large oak tree bore large fruit, such as the pumpkin, sees the Creator's wisdom in arranging things as they are after he is hit on the head by a falling acorn. "God has made the whole world in wisdom and in love; and where we cannot understand the uses of things, we should believe that God who sees their beginnings and ends, is the best judge."[20] Even when natural phenomena are explained in natural terms, they are ultimately ascribed to the perfection of God's plan for man. Nature lessons are most frequently religious lessons. And nature is never neutral. Although man's limited comprehension may not always be able to encompass every instance of the fact, nature is always benevolently related to the final ends of man. By analogy, nature is also used in many of these stories for moral instruction. The industry of the ant and the bee and the feckless-ness of the grasshopper are ever present on the pages of nine-teenth-century schoolbooks. The coming of spring is a metaphor for life after death. Pure joy in the sun, flowers, and grass, un-mixed with a moral lesson, is met so rarely[21] that one is startled to find it at all; such an attitude seems indeed to be so alien to these books that it could be called "pagan."

Expository descriptions of the natural world, devoid of moral and supernatural meaning, increase significantly toward the

[17] G 1869 Warren-C, p. 13; R 1873 Monroe-2, p. 73; R 1895 Hazen, pp. 188, 212; G 1898 Payne, p. 56.

[18] R 1866 McGuffey-4, pp. 167–170; R 1879 McGuffey, pp. 121–124; see also R 1868 Parker and Watson, pp. 50–52, 52–54; R 1885 Monroe-3, p. 12; R 1895 Hazen, pp. 243–244.

[19] R 1866 McGuffey-4, p. 181.

[20] R 1866? Sargent-2, p. 38; see also R 1873 Hillard and Campbell-3, pp. 34–37; R 1881 Monteith, pp. 199–200; G 1891 Morton, p. xxxi.

[21] See, for example, R 1866 Sargent-3, p. 21.

end of the century.[22] Lessons in science also become more frequent, usually side by side with moral lessons from nature.[23] Throughout the century the practical application of a scientific knowledge of nature is much praised: "In our own day, one of the most striking features of civilization is the rapid progress in discovery and invention. Especially is this true in the application of science to the practical affairs of life. At no other age in the history of the world has the knowledge of nature's laws been so rapidly and widely diffused."[24] Furthermore, penetration of nature for practical purposes is a distinctive American talent; "the best American ideas are often said to be those of our inventors."[25] There is nothing impious in penetrating the secrets of the universe; the more one knows of nature, the more one appreciates the power and wisdom of God. Only one book, using a part of Carlyle's *Heroes and Hero Worship*, warns against possible dangers in science, and then only when scientific knowledge is misused: "Science has done much for us; but it is a poor science that would hide from us the great, deep, sacred infinitude of nescience, whither we can never penetrate, on which all science swims as a mere superficial film."[26] Another, after telling of Newton's discovery of gravity by the falling apple, advises the reader in a footnote that natural laws are secondary, for: "The only ultimate reason we can give for anything is *God wills it*."[27] Man's control of nature through science is the triumph of a God-given human spirit, and part of God's plan. The world was made for man, and science simply allows man to make even better use of God's creation.

From the above it is clear that the American familiar with the interrelationships of God, nature, and man that are explicit and implicit in nineteenth-century schoolbooks would be profoundly disturbed by the theories of Darwin, and even those of Lyell. How much the writers of schoolbooks knew of these hypotheses is a question. They were, on the whole, relatively innocent of expert knowledge in other fields. They were more likely to know

[22] See, for example, R 1895 Todd and Powell; R 1899 Holmes and Hill; R 1900 Demarest and Van Sickle.

[23] See, for example, R 1872 Monroe, pp. 181–183, 185–187, 199.

[24] H 1885 Ridpath, p. 491.

[25] H 1881 Eliot, p. 488; see also H 1881 Thalheimer, p. 361.

[26] R 1884 Campbell-5, pp. 347–349.

[27] R 1872 Willson, p. 126.

the Christianized versions of John Fiske, and other popularizers who maintained teleological evolution, than Darwin's own writings. Certainly they must have known of some of the spectacular discoveries, made in the beginning of the century, of dinosaur remains. Charles Willson Peale's painting of 1806, for example, of the excavation of mastodon bones had considerable fame. But the *Book of Genesis* did not encompass such revelations, and perhaps it was thought wiser to wait until an authoritative doctrine did. There are some modifications in describing the history of the world. Adam and Eve continue to inhabit the Garden, but the date of Creation recedes in most books from the previously accepted 4004 B.C. Only books for Catholic parochial schools, and one other, still stand firm with Bishop Ussher.[28] The rest push back the Creation into an indefinite past.

The preface to Tarbell's 1899 *Geography* defines for the teacher the "'New Geography' . . . the product of the doctrine of evolution. Its fundamental ideas are of processes, quite as much as of conditions. It views the earth as now in progress, with results slowly modifying both." General as this statement is, it is still a clear indication that the science of geography was in a revolutionary state of change. This book is one of the very few that clearly accept the challenge of this change. But whatever new concepts are offered to the child, evolution is always teleological and God's creation. An 1885 Geography, containing quite specific definitions of prehistoric ages and descriptions of the changes wrought by time as evidenced by fossils in different geological strata, has as its frontispiece a sunset over a mountain, and the caption "In the Beginning God Created the Heaven and the Earth."[29] Often what appears to be a statement of evolution becomes, on closer examination, a great chain of relationships in the structure of all living things rather than a single development through time from the same sources.[30] God has used the same model, but He has brought it nearer and nearer perfection

[28] See H 1868 Kerney, pp. 15–16; G 1876 Comprehensive, p. 13; G 1878 Catholic, p. 13. The non-Roman Catholic G 1891 Morton, p. xix offers a diagram of the history of the world to be copied on the blackboard with the 6000 years of the world's existence clearly drawn.

[29] G 1885 Houston, frontispiece, and see pp. 31–32, 34.

[30] G 1870 Cornell-P, p. 74.

with the creation of man. The first hints of a history of the world that differs in any respect from that in the Bible come late in the century. Not until the 1870's, and after that more commonly, is there mention of discovery of fossilized remains of mammoths and dinosaurs which are now extinct but which are related in structure to living animals—although these remains had been brought to light almost seventy years before. They are sometimes described as comparable to the mythical monsters in fairy tales. An ice age is also first mentioned in the 1870's.[31] And finally, in the 1880's, in discussions of the earth anterior to man, the age of the earth is pushed back: "All of these changes must have taken place thousands, and perhaps millions of years ago."[32] This evidently mirrors the concurrent assimilation by the general culture of the Christianized version of Darwinism. Perhaps such startling discoveries could not appear in schoolbooks until there was some generally accepted theory to explain them. That the earth has changed continuously in the past, and is still changing all the time, is finally accepted. A few books at the end of the century mention the evolution of plants and animals from lesser to more complex forms, usually as evidence of the wonderful order of the universe: "Investigation of the earth's crust not only teaches us that a mighty chain of living links stretches down from the first plants and animals to those of our day, but it shows the exact order in which these plants and animals succeeded each other. The resemblance between the old forms and those now in existence proves the relationship which all living things bear to each other."[33] Darwin is somewhat mysteriously referred to by name in a piece by Charles Kingsley, "The Coral Reef," included in an 1897 Reader: "Mr. Darwin was the first to guess the answer, as he had guessed many an answer besides."[34] Unless he read this book, the nineteenth-century child would be unaware of Mr. Darwin's existence.

[31] R 1873 American, p. 273; H 1875 Higginson, pp. 1–3; H 1879 Quackenbos, p. 7; R 1883 Swinton-5, p. 186; R 1900 Aldrich and Forbes-I, pp. 179–181; R 1896 Holmes and Hill, pp. 157–160; G 1898 Redway and Hinman, p. 30.

[32] R 1884 Campbell-4, p. 241; see also R 1885 Monroe-3, pp. 149–152; G 1885 Houston, pp. 31–32; G 1900 Tarr and McMurry-1, p. 5.

[33] R 1900 Aldrich and Forbes-I, p. 175; see also G 1885 Houston, p. 32; G 1899 Fairbanks, p. 192.

[34] R 1897 Arnold and Gilbert-5, p. 207.

2. From Houston's 1885 Geography. Throughout the century it is the Biblical story of the creation of the world that is accepted. When evolution appears at all it is teleological and God's creation. The world was made for man.

Only two books in the post-Darwinian period take note of any conflict between the new theories and the Bible. One simply records the reconciliation: "Geology, which has brought to light a vast number of facts hitherto unknown, has convinced men of science that the earth is much older than heretofore supposed, and most learned Christian divines interpret the Mosaic account of the Creation in such a manner as to be entirely in accordance with the revelations of this science."[35] The other, a long piece called "The Mosaic Vision of Creation," by Hugh Miller, describes the creation day by day through the creation of man "formed in God's own image . . . [when] the work of creation ceases forever upon earth." The days, however, are "unreckoned ages, condensed in the vision into a few brief moments." He finally evaluates the Mosaic Creation ". . . rightly understood, I know not a single scientific truth that militates against even the minutest or least prominent of its details."[36] In all other books the issue is avoided; the Mosaic Creation and scientific geology are assumed to be compatible, and the child is informed about the former more than the latter.

The reader of these schoolbooks could suppose, then, that God created processes by which our present animals developed from His original material—but what of man? His own creation may also have been by evolution, but with a difference that is prominent in the books that include man at all in the evolutionary process: "In the arrangement of his organs and the general structure of his body, Man resembles the other mammals; but, made in the image of his Creator and endowed with dominion over the brutes, he stands alone in his spiritual expression, his power of articulation, and above all in the possession of reason and an immortal soul."[37] In books that recognize evolution, the creation of the world is the establishment of processes which in time produced the perfect environment for man; but man's soul seems to have been complete in a single creation, which distinguishes him from the general process. One Geography, after describing in scientific terms the prehistoric changes in the earth and its inhabitants,

[35] H 1893 Creery, p. 8 footnote.

[36] R 1894 Columbian, pp. 169–174.

[37] G 1870 Cornell-P, p. 74; see also G 1866 Woodbridge, p. 302; G 1869 Warren-E, p. 86.

defines the present age as: "when man was created, and our present animals and plants introduced."[38] A Reader at the end of the century uses an extract from Kingsley's *Water Babies* to show man's participation in evolution, as well as his superiority to other subjects of the process: "If the changes in the lower animals are so wonderful, and so difficult to discover, why should not there be changes in the higher animals far more wonderful, and far more difficult to discover? And may not man, the crown and flower of all things, undergo some change more wonderful than all the rest?"[39] Only two Geographies indicate that man first appeared in a state very different from his present one. One author, who gives the only general account of the development of the world that is also entirely secular, reassures his readers with the observation that prehistoric man "is believed now represented by the Finns and Lapps."[40] The other says: "In an early part of his history man lived in a savage state. . . . But all through the long dreary ages man steadily grew wiser. . . . In time, as man learned to use better the senses that God had given him, he came to love right, justice and peace. He associated with other men in classes and tribes which were always ruled by the strongest and bravest."[41] The thorny problem of savage man, made in the image of God, does not mar the pages of these books.

Apart from this exception, then, evolution, when it appears in schoolbooks at all, is a process of development instituted by God to provide the perfect environment for His supreme creation—Man. It is the evolution of Fiske and other popularizers rather than that of Darwin. Nature is still the benefactor of man; its processes are seen to be more intricate, and therefore more wonderful, than they had been thought before. There is increasing discussion of natural causes, but the First Cause is present in all discussions of nature, as He is in all lessons throughout these books. Even at the end of the century an Emersonian nature is confidently presented to the child, not the neutral nature of Darwinism or of the Realists in literature. The shock of the latter was still in the future for the readers of these books.

[38] G 1885 Houston, p. 34.

[39] R 1897 Arnold and Gilbert-4, p. 213.

[40] G 1887 Quackenbos, p. 15.

[41] G 1888 Redway, p. 28.

Although man's scientific penetration of nature, and his use of this knowledge, produced laudable industrial progress, the environment most suitable for man is nevertheless the one he has least disturbed. Throughout the century, side by side with unstinted praise of industrial progress, there is an immense literature in these schoolbooks contrasting city life unfavorably to country life. Man's ideal environment is not what he has created, but what God has created; men live best in harmony with natural phenomena. Although one McGuffey Reader, in a selection from Parkman, suggests a trip to the wilderness for the physical and spiritual renewal of the urban dweller,[42] primitive or untouched nature is not generally advocated, but a nature cultivated, though not violated, by men. Admiration for rural life is based not on the ideology of the Physiocrats or the Jeffersonians, but on a description of American life in the pre-Civil War period. Throughout the century the typical American is shown to be an independent farmer, which, in the first half of the century and most of the second, he was. Morse, who bitterly opposed everything Jeffersonian and who early advocated the protective tariff, describes Connecticut:

> The bulk of the inhabitants are husbandmen. Their farms furnish them with all the necessaries, most of the conveniences, and but few of the luxuries of life. They of course must be temperate, and if they choose can subsist with as much independence as is consistent with happiness. The subsistence of the farmer is substantial, and does not depend on incidental circumstance like that of most other professions. There is no necessity of serving an apprenticeship to the business, nor of the large stock of money to commence it to advantage. Farmers, who deal much in barter have less need of money than any other class of people.[43]

Probably rural life was seen as more godly because there man lived in a God-given environment. And in contrast to Europe, American nationalism required, even at the end of the century, the idealization of an American society which was still predominantly rural. In any case, throughout the century most of the vocabulary and reading selections, even in the Primers, reflect farm life or life in a rural community. Major American

[42] R 1888 McGuffey, pp. 121–123.
[43] G 1791 Morse, p. 117.

heroes are all independent farmers, and Uncle Sam retains a rustic quality. A great deal of space is given to explicit discussions of the superiority of country life and rural occupations. In the first part of the century these pieces are relatively straightforward and unsentimental, and the usefulness of agriculture is stressed. An agricultural occupation is believed to be the "*noblest*, because it is the most useful of all, and that which is the foundation of the rest."[44] One author implies that it is the occupation God meant us to consider primary: in discussing metallic ores, he asks the question: "Why are all these under the surface of the earth?" and answers: "That they may not occupy our attention too much and prevent our cultivation of the soil."[45] Many books in the period before the Civil War describe a game called "The Colonists," designed to show which professions are most useful to man:[46] as each child chooses a profession, he is told by the moderator whether he will be useful, and therefore welcome, in a new colony. The most acceptable is the farmer: "Farming is the chief thing we have to depend upon, so we cannot have too much of it." The soldier is allowed to go only if he will be a farmer as well; the lawyer cannot go at all. It is interesting that although many of the leaders of the American Revolution were lawyers, throughout the textbooks lawyers as a class are looked on with suspicion. The law is regarded generally as a parasitic occupation, engaged in too frequently by unscrupulous and avaricious people in service to the rich, and the lawyer is particularly contrasted to the farmer:

> To fit up a village with tackle for tillage
> Jack Carter he took to the saw.
> To pluck and to pillage, the same little village
> Tim Gordon he took to the law.[47]

[44] R 1835 Merriam, p. 24; see also G 1800 Smith, p. 139; S 1815 Picket, p. 207; S 1826 Alden, p. 143; S 1826 Principal, p. 9; R 1835 Webster, p. 17; S 1845 Bentley, p. 150.

[45] S 1815 Bradley, p. 128.

[46] S 1826 Kelley, pp. 149–151; R 1828 Robbins-A, p. 124; R 1830 Frost, pp. 53–57; R 1833 Leavitt, pp. 95–99; R 1835 Pierpont-Y, pp. 43–48; R 1838 Blake, pp. 128–133; R 1843 McGuffey, pp. 59–63; R 1859 Sargent, pp. 130–133; R 1866 McGuffey-4, pp. 86–91.

[47] R 1844 Smith, p. 134; see also G 1784 Morse, pp. 81–82; S 1825 Torrey, p. 105; S 1827 Webster, p. 98.

Agriculture is not only the solid basis of all prosperity, but it is also a nursery of virtue: "As a profession it strengthens the mind without injuring the body; and tends to increase virtues, without introducing vice; as it naturally inspires us with pious sentiments, and a dependence on Providence, without a tincture of infidelity."[48] Another author expresses this sentiment even more positively: "*Agriculture* and the *Gospel* are the two great instruments of Divine Providence to check the voluptuousness and exercise the virtues of man."[49] Another proves the same hypothesis by the lesson of history: "Corruption of morals, in a man of cultivation, is a phenomenon of which no age or nation, has furnished an example."[50] In trade, on the other hand, vice, in the form of misrepresentation, is often regarded by businessmen as nothing but a good business technique.[51]

In the second half of the century, although schoolbooks neglect the theme of the usefulness of the farmer, they are in hearty agreement with the idea that the cultivator of the soil is at the same time a cultivator of virtue. The independent farmer is "nature's nobleman in life."[52] But now enters a strong element of nostalgia, of looking back to a simpler, more rural, and more virtuous America. At the same time, vast pride in America's increasing industrial progress characterizes these books. America must do well in the economic trend of the times, but the values of the old rural America must be retained. The simple, honest, hardworking, ingenious American, who developed from a life close to nature, has been the foundation for American growth in the past and will be the basis for a new industrial development. The industrial revolution offers adventure and opportunity for power, but it also presents perils as man leaves farther behind his natural environment, close to the soil. A poem by Richard Henry Stoddard, "When This Old Flag Was New," looks back with yearning:

[48] R 1810 Alden, p. 138; see also R 1811 Chandler, pp. 168–170; R 1813 New York, p. 113; R 1823 N. Worcester, pp. 138–139; R 1828 Putnam, pp. 70–74; R 1853 Webb, pp. 52–54; R 1856 Sanders-4, pp. 182–184.

[49] R 1824 D. Adams, p. 31.

[50] R 1839 Sigourney, p. 175.

[51] S 1819 Alden, p. 138; G 1826 Blake, p. 100; R 1843 Olney, pp. 132–133; R 1850 Hall, p. 313; R 1853 Mandeville, pp. 99–100; R 1859 Sargent, pp. 73–75.

[52] R 1871 Hillard, p. 189–190.

A brave old race they were,
Who peopled then the land,—
No man of them ashamed
To show his horny hand;
Hands that had grasped the sword,
Now drew the furrow true;
For honored was the plow,
When this old flag was new.[53]

In those days everyone lived "the plain old-fashioned way." In such selections the independence of the farmer, his close family ties, and his nearness to nature and nature's God all sponsor virtue. These later schoolbooks offer nostalgia for the simpler rural ways *ad nauseam*. "Woodman, Spare That Tree," by George P. Morris, who wants to return to the old tree under which his mother kissed him, appears in seven Readers; Longfellow's "Village Blacksmith" in eight Readers; Whittier's "Barefoot Boy" in six Readers. Almost every book in the last thirty years of the century includes some object symbolizing the yearning for the simple days of the past: "The Old Arm Chair," "The Old Oaken Bucket" (this poem by Samuel Woodworth appears in nine Readers), "The Old Homestead," "The Old Barn," "The Cider Mill," etc. Also ever present are descriptions of haying, going to fetch the cows, or other farm chores seen through a haze of sentimentality. The lost innocence of the individual and of society are recalled in remembering childhood on the farm—a memory possible to many late nineteenth-century American urban dwellers. A piece called "Old Times" by Gerald Griffin sadly notes that though the author is older, the wisdom he has gained is full of woe, and the knowledge he has acquired is mixed with care.[54] Thomas Hood's poem, "I Remember, I Remember," used many times, recalls how as a child he could appreciate nature's beauties. Virtue and wisdom are combined in the child, who is untutored except by nature.[55] Childhood and the life close to nature, then, are frequently identified, a process natural in a society in transition from a rural to an urban life. The simpler

[53] R 1875 Sheldon, pp. 118–120; see also R 1888 McGuffey, pp. 39–41, 212, 215; R 1898 Williams G-2, pp. 75–81.

[54] R 1873 Progressive, pp. 78–79.

[55] See R 1866 McGuffey-4, p. 223; R 1874 Hillard, pp. 74–82.

3. "Village Blacksmith"

In Baldwin's fifth reader (1897), as in all schoolbooks of the late nineteenth century, nostalgia for a simpler past makes village life idyllic.

past of the individual was consonant with a simpler past of the society.

Another constant theme, especially in the later books, is embodied in the sentence, "The city for wealth, the country for health."[56] As early as 1813 the unhealthy effect of city life is discussed; city artisans are "pale, thin and emaciated" in contrast to the robust health of the farmer.[57] After the 1830's, contrasts between city and country abound. There are innumerable tales of pale, wan city people who, after moving to the country, recover their health and joy in life. Conversely:

> From Munster Vale they brought her,
> From the pure and balmy air,
> An Ormund peasant's daughter,
> With bright eyes and golden hair.
> They brought her to the city,
> And she faded slowly there.[58]

The life of the farmer is an idyllic one that sweetens his rest and food. "City and Country," a poem by Oliver Wendell Holmes, recalls to the country those "who have wandered, like truants, for riches and fame!"

> Though not at the "Astor," we'll give you at least
> A bite at an apple, a seat on the grass,
> And the best of cold water—at nothing a glass![59]

Another poet rejects the wealth of the city in favor of the healthier, more natural life in the country:

> Let vapid idlers loll in silk
> Around their costly board;
> Give us the bowl of samp and milk,
> By homespun beauty poured![60]

The country is not only healthier but safer. In "A Picture of Broadway," N. G. Shepherd describes factory workers at the end

[56] S 1869 Day, p. 163.

[57] R 1813 New York, p. 109; see also R 1830 Bartlett, pp. 28–30; R 1856 Sanders-4, p. 49; R 1875 Sheldon, p. 208.

[58] R 1873 Progressive, pp. 255–257.

[59] R 1871 Hillard, p. 185–188.

[60] R 1884 Campbell-5, p. 208.

of the day coming out into "squalid, narrow, and gloomy streets." One of their number is callously run down by the coach of a "haughty millionaire," and, after miserable sufferings alone in a dismal hospital, he dies.[61] The picture of the city as an unsafe, unhealthy place to live, as contrasted to the country, probably described the actual situation with some accuracy, if also with an excess of sentiment.

Unquestioned throughout the century is the idea that happiness as well as health is much more prevalent in the country than in the city. "The man who stands upon his own soil, who feels that he is the rightful owner of the land which he tills, feels more strongly than another the character of a man, as the lord of the lower world."[62] The artificial life of the city is lonely and sordid, hardly conducive to the happiness of man. In 1842 one author announces in his preface that he will deliberately try to show the pleasure of rural life as a brake on the mass migration of young people to the city, where they are most likely to be miserable.[63] For the rich the city is an attractive place: "They can go to the stores and get anything they want."[64] But the poor, told that the streets of Boston are "paved with gold," find themselves doomed to misery and disappointment.[65] McGuffey tells of a poor lame girl forced to live in the city at the top of a "dingy staircase" in a "rickety old house" because her father died, and her mother could find work more easily in the city.[66] According to these schoolbooks people come to the city for two reasons: they are forced by economic necessity, or they come to make a fortune. Most of the latter are unsuccessful and lead pitiable lives, returning to the country if they can; if they are successful, they retire happily to the country. For whatever reasons, however, all who come suffer from the artificialities of city life. Particularly to be pitied is the city child without grass and trees to play in, and, even more important, without nature as a teacher. One such child, taken to a park, thought a dandelion a star: "Poor

[61] R 1872 Willson, p. 208.
[62] R 1860 McGuffey, p. 28.
[63] R 1842 Palmer, p. v.
[64] R 1900 Collard-II, p. 80.
[65] R 1844 Smith, p. 23–25.
[66] R 1879 McGuffey, pp. 35–38.

little girl, not even to know what a dandelion is!"[67] In the city one's standard of living deteriorates: "Many live in the midst of conditions that can scarcely be described,—filth, vice and crime of all kinds prevailing."[68] The city slicker who takes advantage of the country visitor appears often. He sells razor blades that are good to look at but do not shave.[69] He makes fun of the countryman, though sometimes rustic wisdom is too much for city cleverness in the end.[70] Innocence and virtue prevail in the country, artificiality and vice in the city: "The town for manners, the country for morals."[71] That city life is inimical to enjoyment of the senses is strikingly illustrated in a poem, "Pan in Wall Street" by Edmund C. Stedman, in which the great Pan is chased by the police from Wall Street as he is "a-strolling through this sordid city."[72] (It should be noted here, however, that the joys of the senses, symbolized by Pan, are pleasures usually disapproved of in these books.) Reformers attempt to bring country joys to the city by establishing parks, but these are poor substitutes for the real thing; nature cannot be successfully imitated. "Nice fingered art must emulate in vain."[73] One boy complains that Central Park is kept "so very nice, that a beetle would hardly dare crawl there."[74] Clearly such an artificial environment is not likely to produce a healthy, happy, virtuous population.

Those who speak from experience—country people who have lived in the city—often appear in these pages after they have returned with relief to their old country homes. A very popular poem, "Farmer John" by J. J. Trowbridge, recounts the reactions

[67] R 1878 Harris, Rickoff, Bailey-2, pp. 72–73; see also R 1871 Monroe, pp. 160–162; S 1890 Kupfer, pp. 68–69; R 1900 Demarest and Van Sickle, pp. 21–26.

[68] G 1900 Tarr and McMurry-2, p. 190.

[69] R 1883 Swinton-5, pp. 451–452.

[70] R 1881 Willson, p. 236–238; R 1883 Swinton-5, pp. 454–455.

[71] S 1843 Fowle, p. 17; see also R 1803 Murray, p. 38; R 1807 Bingham, pp. 289–293; R 1813 New York, pp. 80–81; R 1816 Staniford, p. 233; S 1836 Brandreth, p. 73; R 1843 Pippin, p. 43; R 1860 McGuffey, pp. 98–99; S 1866 Swan, p. 51; S 1874 Worcester, p. 53.

[72] R 1898 Williams I-2, p. 221.

[73] Cowper quoted in R 1888 McGuffey, pp. 165–166; see also S 1896 Dutton, pp. 14–15; R 1900 Williams, p. 74.

[74] R 1885 Monroe, p. 109.

of a farmer to such a return. He would not trade his farm for all of Paris or Rome, nor

> These hills for the city's stifled air,
> And big hotels and bustle and glare;
> Land all houses and road all stones
> That deafen your ears and batter your bones!
>
> . . . .
>
> Where money is king and fashion is queen
>
> . . . .
>
> The town is a perfect Babylon.

He concludes that wealth is not all in gold

> But in simple ways and sweet content,
> Few wants, pure hope and noble ends,
> Some land to till and a few good friends
>
> . . . .
>
> And a happy man is Farmer John—
> Oh, a rich and happy man is he![75]

A piece called "The Young Shepherd" by Fénelon describes a shepherd, adopted by a king and living a life of luxury, who yearns for the simple life of his past. When he dies he leaves just enough money to his relatives to "maintain them in the station of shepherds, which he always thought the safest and most happy."[76]

The stability of natural things, as opposed to man-made, also appears often in the later books. And of all natural things, the soil is most durable. Two Histories point to the Indian mounds: "It is a singular fact that banks of earth grassed over are more enduring than any other work of man." "Structures of hardest stone decay and crumble into dust, but an earth mound retains its shape indefinitely."[77] Likewise in farm life, not only are you fanned by God's breezes, bemused by the music of His birds,

[75] R 1871 Monroe, pp. 146–148; R 1871 Sargent and May-5, pp. 139–141; R 1881 Willson, pp. 356–358; R 1884 Campbell-4, pp. 96–99; R 1899 Holmes and Hill, pp. 126–128; and part of this in S 1900 Bowen, p. 34.

[76] R 1872 Willson, pp. 189–193; R 1873 Progressive, pp. 72–77; see also R 1879 McGuffey, pp. 88–89.

[77] These two quotations are from the following in that order: H 1881 Steele, p. 10 footnote; H 1889 Chambers, p. 86.

and rewarded by the harvest of the soil, but you know that your farm is certain and secure: "In panics you feel no alarm; *wheat* is as good as gold."[78] This is the answer of an old man to a young boy who wants to go to the city, "where wealth is gained by *play*."

This stability makes the farmer particularly patriotic. Many authors observe that Washington, the greatest national hero and patriot in these books, was a farmer. "The cultivator of the soil is indeed a *patriot*. . . . The very trees and rocks among which he has grown up, are objects of his affection."[79] The same author also believes that the trader can have no patriotism; he is concerned only with making money wherever he can. Talk to a trader about "*love of country* and he will think you mad. He has no country." The farmer is naturally loyal to the land he has struggled with, and therefore to his country. In one instance, diversity of population in a city is pointed out as a bar to nationalism: "It is difficult for a people thus made up to take the same fixed and abiding interest in their country as is felt by men whose forefathers have for generations lived on the same soil."[80]

In the early books emphasis is put on the idea that the farmer, who by virtue of his occupation is full of the spirit of independence, is the backbone of free government. All will be well in the United States:

> Long as our hardy yoemanry command
> The rich *fee simple* of their native land.[81]

Several authors point a lesson from antiquity: "In the most glorious times of Greece, and in the most virtuous period of the Roman republic, agriculture flourished and was held in great estimation," but with the decline of agriculture came "idleness, despotism, and superstition."[82] Another contrasts the high degree of independence felt by the farmer with the high degree

[78] R 1881 Willson, pp. 154–155.

[79] R 1810 Alden, p. 140; see also R 1824 D. Adams, p. 29; S 1824 Bentley, p. 168; R 1831 Cheever, pp. 19–21; R 1835 Merriam, p. 28.

[80] H 1876 Doyle, p. 388.

[81] R 1797 Thomas, p. 214; see also R 1811 Chandler, pp. 160–171; R 1813 New York, p. 113; G 1818 Morse, p. 91; R 1855 New York, pp. 105–110.

[82] G 1826 Blake, p. 95; see also: R 1810 Alden, p. 140; R 1810 Thomson, p. 158.

of dependence of the trader and manufacturer, and he considers this to have much national significance.[83] Goldsmith's *Deserted Village* is cited innumerable times, lamenting the displacement of the farmer by a new civilization "where wealth accumulates and men decay." Mrs. Sigourney adds Washington's prestige to this concept: he knew, she says: "that nations which despise the simple pursuits of agriculture and rush onward to sudden wealth and luxury, degenerate and decline quickly."[84]

The statement that American prosperity, independence, and happiness are directly dependent on its rural condition appear in some form in many of these books.[85] One author suggests that the farm may redeem us from the potential evils of industrialization: "If our teeming manufactories should send forth an enervated or uninstructed race,—and our cities foster the growth of pomp, or the elements of discord,—we hope that from those peaceful farmhouses, will go forth a redeeming spirit, to guard and renovate the country of their love."[86] Another warns:

> COLUMBIA'S SONS spurn not the rugged toil,
> Your nation's glory is a CULTUR'D SOIL.[87]

It is important to note that the agricultural society exalted here is not the agricultural society described as that of the South. The ideal is a society of small, independent farmers, in direct contrast to the large plantation owners described as typical of the South. The latter, though living in the country, lead as artificial a life as the city dweller. They are not as close to a redeeming nature as the man who actually tills his own soil.

It seems to be a contradiction in terms that these authors, most of whom came from New England, the least agricultural part of the United States, should so consistently express admiration for an agricultural society. Throughout the century most of the authors came neither from the old commercial groups nor from the newer industrial ones, but were teachers or clergymen who

[83] R 1810 Alden, p. 136.

[84] R 1839 Sigourney, p. 174.

[85] R 1813 Richardson, pp. 151–153; R 1824 D. Adams, pp. 30–31; G 1826 Blake, p. 95; R 1845 Goldsbury and Russell, pp. 249–250; R 1854 Mandeville, p. 165; R 1854 Pierpont-N, p. 123; R 1856 Sargent-4, p. 167.

[86] R 1856 Sanders-4, p. 49.

[87] R 1845 D. Adams, p. 202.

GENERAL GAGE AND THE BOSTON BOYS.

4. General Gage, of the British army, discovers that the boys of Boston " 'draw in a love of liberty with the air they breathe.' " This print is from the 1875 American History by Thomas Wentworth Higginson.

did not participate directly in the mercantile and industrial prosperity of New England. Most of them came from rural or semirural backgrounds. Perhaps then it was easy and natural for them to follow the Romantic trend by glorifying the man closest to nature and probably to their own backgrounds, the farmer. In the first part of the century the glorification of the farmer was simply an exaltation of the American population, in contrast to the rest of the world:

> Hail, happy states! thine is the blissful seat,
> Where nature's gifts and art's improvements meet.
> Thy temp'rate air breathes health; thy fertile soil,
> In copious plenty pays the laborer's toil.
> Ask not for mountains of Peruvian ore,
> Nor count the dust that shines on Afric's shore.
> The plough explores for thee the richest mine;
> Than autumn's fruit, no goodly ore can mine.[88]

In the first part of the century, all assume that the American is a farmer. In the second part, American rural society of the past is the ideal, though present-day actuality may require a more urban society in the future. The virtues developed in the early period should uphold us in the later. The symbols of American nationalism remain largely rural; Uncle Sam is no city dweller. The impossible ideal of the American schoolbooks in the late nineteenth century would be a nation made up of a combination of independent farmers with great industrial power.

Because God-given nature is superior to the creations of man, love of country is to be generated by a loving exposition of the geographical features of the land. Most of the abundant descriptions of the natural features of America are in the form of either tender lyrics or defensive panegyrics. Several authors state as a principle to be followed in the education of the child that love of the United States will be developed by observation of nature in this country,[89] and all authors write as though they had some special motive in glorifying physical America. In an age when Romanticists admired nature in a wild state rather than

[88] R 1807 Bingham-C, pp. 237–239; R 1815 R. Adams, p. 132.
[89] R 1834 Emerson, pp. 192–194; R 1840 Snow, pp. 112–115.

in man-made cultivation, American scenery had a special claim to beauty. It is celebrated here both as unique and as superior to all other natural scenes. What are the man-made structures of Europe compared to the divinely created beauties of nature in America:

> What, though we boast no ancient towers,
> Where ivied streamers twine;
> The laurel lives upon our shores;
> The laurel, boy is thine.[90]

Several Readers take note of the European criticism that nature has operated on a smaller scale in America, and deny it vociferously and indignantly.[91] A History admits that although most American animals are smaller than their European counterparts, the deer and the bear are largest here.[92] A Reader, written in 1815, at a time when such transatlantic arguments were legion, advises American authors: "It is time for our literary characters (of whom it will hereafter appear we have a phalanx, numerous and refined, brilliant and powerful) to put forth their might, and vindicate their own and their country's reputation." Later he complains that every insignificant feature of Britain's landscape, "Her bare bleak heaths and brooks of half a mile," are all celebrated in literature, whereas:

> Our western world, with all its matchless floods,
> Our vast transparent lakes and boundless woods,
> Stamp'd with the traits of majesty sublime,
> Unhonored weep the silent lapse of time.[93]

Even when European critics are not mentioned, European scenery is compared with American in every book, much to the advantage of American. For example, American trees are not only larger than those of Europe, but they turn more colors in autumn than do those of Europe, giving to America "autumns of unrivalled beauty, magnificence and abundance."[94]

[90] R 1855 Burleigh, p. 122.

[91] R 1815 Dickinson, pp. 77–78; R 1844 Goldsbury and Russell, pp. 323–324.

[92] H 1879 Quackenbos, p. 7.

[93] R 1815 Dickinson, pp. 78 and 187.

[94] R 1839 Sigourney, pp. 75–76; see also R 1828 Robbins-P, p. 354; R 1831 Cheever, pp. 209–215; R 1834 S. Worcester, pp. 297–302; R 1875 Sheldon, p. 169.

The most common bases, however, for boasting about American landscape are its magnificent size and its future possibilities. Its raw grandeur is expressed poetically in a Geography:

> Having crossed the Pacific, we'll now take our stand
> On this happy, prolific and wide-spreading land,
> Where nature has wrought with a far bolder hand.
> No more let the *Old World* be proud of her *Mountains*,
> Her *Rivers*, and *Mines*, of her *Lakes*, and her *Fountains*,
> Though great in themselves, they no longer appear
> To be great, when compar'd with the great that are here.[95]

The vastness of our forests, lakes, and mountains is individually and collectively extolled. Morse says of American lakes, "Those of second or third class in magnitude are of larger circuit than the greatest lakes in the eastern continent."[96] One Reader contains a dialogue between an American boy and a European boy in which the American replies to the criticism of the European: "Well, if your mountains are a *little* higher than ours, they are not half as *long;* and ours too are constantly covered with snow and ice, even under the equator; . . . as to your great Vesuvius, we have a Niagara that would put it out in half a minute."[97] Two authors use a piece by Timothy Flint in which he finds compensation for all the ruins we lack in the potential use of American land: "The English, when they sneer at our country, speak of it as steril [*sic*] in moral interest. 'It has,' say they, 'no monuments, no ruins, none of the remains of former ages; no castles, no mouldering abbeys, no baronial towers and dungeons; nothing to connect the imagination and the heart with the past; no recollections of former ages, to associate past with future.'" But, according to Flint, our scenery more than makes up for this lack; it has unique possibilities for firing the imagination.[98] Whatever the scenery was to the eye, it was more to the American imagination which saw in it unlimited potentialities for the future

[95] G 1800 Davidson, p. 48; see also G 1813 Nichols, p. 17; G 1814 O'Neill, p. 65; G 1819 Adams, p. 92; G 1825 Butler, p. 27; G 1828 Woodbridge, p. 53; G 1828 J. Worcester, p. 11; G 1830 Bazeley, p. 13; S 1843 Fowle, p. 69; G 1848 Smith, p. 94; H 1851 Guernsey, p. 17; G 1898 Carpenter, p. 14.

[96] G 1784 Morse, pp. 112–113.

[97] R 1853 Sanders, pp. 171–172.

[98] R 1827 Pierpont, pp. 43–45; see also R 1852 Brothers, pp. 352–353.

development of American civilization. American schoolbooks indeed exhibit what Henry Nash Smith calls "the myth of the garden."[99] They saw the vast lands of the West not just as they were but as they would be under cultivation. The future agricultural development of the continent is as real to them as the physical landscape. Furthermore, they believed this vast landscape and this dream were unique to America. Undoubtedly such a vision helped to perpetuate the ideal of agrarianism still prominent in a rapidly industrializing America.

Descriptions of individual scenic wonders in the Geographies are really Romantic hymns of praise rather than descriptions. Emphasis is less on the appearance of the object than on its emotional impact on the observer. A typical example is the following comment on the Natural Bridge of Virginia: "This grand and awful prospect inspires the spectator with rapturous emotions almost indescribable"; and: "It is impossible for the emotions arising out of the sublime to be felt beyond what they are here—. . . the rapture of the spectator is really indescribable."[100] The Natural Bridge is soon supplanted in interest, however, by Niagara Falls, which offers "the most romantic and awful prospects imaginable."[101] Every Reader after the 1820's includes a description of the falls couched in the above terms. In the 1880's the most popular piece on the falls is a poem by John Brainerd, "Falls of Niagara," which points up how insignificant is man-made strength to that of nature and God. What is our power compared to Niagara? What is its power compared to God's?

Western scenery enters the Readers in the 1820's. The Mississippi River takes a prominent place; it is assessed in many different ways, all ending in superlatives. "If there by any ground of complaint, it is that so much gorgeousness offends good taste."[102] Even when it is not considered beautiful, it still, in a period that enjoyed "pleasing awfulness," has much to recommend it. One

[99] Smith, *op. cit.*

[100] These two quotations are from the following in that order: G 1814 O'Neill, p. 137; G 1826 Blake, p. 81.

[101] R 1796 Bingham, pp. 169–171; see also R 1873 American, p. 293; R 1884 Barnes, p. 351.

[102] R 1828 American-R, p. 247; see also R 1834 S. Worcester, pp. 11–13; R 1839 S. Goodrich, pp. 165–167.

Reader notes that Mississippi scenery has been accused of "wanting grandeur and beauty. Most certainly it has neither. But there is no scenery on earth more striking."[103] The prairies and their herds of buffalo are also popular subjects. Some description of prairie fires appears in almost every Reader between the 1840's and the end of the century; such a scene has everything; color, drama, dread. Even the dreary solitudes of American swamps may have an awesome effect on the observer.[104] America may offer little classical beauty, but in a period that admired extremes, whether pleasant to the human being or not, it can be said with pride: "Nowhere is the calm more divinely fair; nowhere is the storm more awfully sublime. . . ."[105]

Finally, it should be noted, a mystical relationship is often assumed between nature in America and American freedom. Some books plant freedom in the soil: "The *principle* of free government adheres to the American soil. It is bedded in it: immovable as its mountains."[106] Many more, however, find it in the atmosphere. One of the favorite quotations concerning the American Revolution is from General Gage, commenting that the children of Boston "draw in a love of liberty with the air they breathe."[107]

Thus the nineteenth-century child was taught that nature is animated with man's purposes. God designed nature for man's physical needs and spiritual training. Scientific understanding of nature will reveal the greater glory of God, and the practical application of such knowledge should be encouraged as part of the use God meant man to make of nature. Besides serving the material needs of man, nature is a source of man's health, strength, and virtue. He departs at his peril from a life close to nature. At a time when America was becoming increasingly industrial

[103] R 1856 Sargent-4, p. 213.

[104] R 1826 Greenwood and Emerson, pp. 145–147; R 1851 Swan-L, pp. 334–338.

[105] R 1856 Osgood, p. 259.

[106] R 1828 Hopkins, p. 136; see also R 1826 American-S, pp. 240-246; R 1827 Pierpont, pp. 250–254.

[107] R 1853 Sanders, pp. 109–110; H 1856 First Lessons, pp. 76–77; H 1857 Lossing, p. 113; R 1873 Hillard, p. 60; H 1875 Higginson, pp. 166–167; H 1879 Quackenbos, pp. 132–133; H 1889 Monroe, p. 195; R 1895 Hazen, p. 165; R 1897 Baldwin-4, p. 144.

and urban, agrarian values which had been a natural growth in earlier America became articles of fervent faith in American nationalism. The American character had been formed in virtue because it developed in a rural environment, and it must remain the same despite vast environmental change. The existence of a bounteous and fruitful frontier in America, with its promise not only of future prosperity but of continued virtue, offers proof that God has singled out the United States above other nations for His fostering care. The superiority of nature to man-made things confers superiority on the American over older civilizations. That Uncle Sam will sooner or later have to become a city dweller is not envisaged by these schoolbook writers, although their almost fanatical advocacy of rural values would seem to suggest an unconscious fear that this might be so. In an even more striking anachronism than in late nineteenth-century schoolbooks, the association of the distinctively "American" with a life close to the American soil still seems to be operative in present-day popular thought. James Fenimore Cooper and Robert Frost are often believed to represent "The Real America" more than F. Scott Fitzgerald or Henry James. Perhaps the idea of living close to nature is a fundamental human aspiration.

Chapter 3

GOD AND MAN

Just as God appears to be the final cause in nature, so He is also the final cause in human history. The last sentence in a History published just after the Civil War expresses the universal sentiment: "We cannot but feel that God has worked in a mysterious way to bring good out of evil. It was He, and not man, who saw and directed the end from the beginning."[1] Although religious emphases change during the century, none of these books is secular; a sense of God permeates all books as surely as a sense of nationalism. All of the early Readers and Spellers devote the greater part of their space to the subject of God's relationship to the universe, to man, and to the child himself.[2] Gradually more secular interests are asserted, but a religious tone is evident throughout the century. In the early period most Spellers use the Bible for basic reading material, and several recommend the New Testament as a Reader.[3] By the 1830's nonbiblical stories begin to outnumber those from the Bible, although many Readers and Spellers maintain passages from the Bible throughout the century.[4] As late as 1880 the extraordinarily popular Webster Speller includes at least one sentence on religion in every group of practice sentences: "The Holy Bible is the Book of God." "God created heaven and earth in six days." "We go to church on the first day of the week." "The devil is the great adversary of man."[5] Emphasis on the Christian story appears extensively

[1] H 1867 Willson, p. 434.

[2] For a discussion of the relationship between religion and child psychology up to 1835 see Monica Kiefer, *American Children Through Their Books, 1700–1835* (Philadelphia: University of Pennsylvania Press, 1948), pp. 28–68.

[3] S 1814 Pike, p. viii; S 1821 Hull, pref.

[4] For examples: R 1866 Sargent-3, pp. 132–133; R 1867 Edwards-5, pp. 133–136; R 1866 McGuffey-4, pp. 216, 223; S 1874 Worcester, pp. 178–179; R 1897 Baldwin-5, pp. 45–47.

[5] S 1880 Webster, pp. 26, 29, 30, 34, 52, etc.

even in arithmetic problems: "How many days is it since the birth of Our Savior?"[6] Most Spellers, whether or not they devote themselves primarily to scriptural lessons, prepare the child to read Scripture by giving a list of individuals mentioned in the New Testament to be memorized by the student.

It was evident in the previous chapter that God is the creator and ruler of the world. His benevolence in this role may not always be immediately obvious, but the child is assured that His love and mercy are present in the very structure of the world. As the benevolent ruler of human history He is also the supreme judge of human actions. If in this role His benevolence is not always patent, belief in His absolute justice, rendered in love and mercy, nevertheless is enjoined on the child. Although God is omnipotent and omniscient, and one must obey His laws as revealed in Scripture, He is a benevolent despot. The Calvinist Jehovah is often present in the earlier books, but as the century goes on He is increasingly a deity who tempers His justice with loving kindness. By the second half of the century, although the child is told now and then to fear God,[7] it is more often love that is demanded of the reader.

Throughout the century values and actions approved by the textbook writers are assumed to be blessed by God; conversely, disapproved values and actions are cursed by God. Unethical behavior is not only socially undesirable but sinful. God is a firm and inexorable judge who not only metes out punishment after death, but who gives earthly rewards and earthly punishments for men's actions on earth. Thus a small boy in one story leaves his companions for fear "that some of them would drop down dead" as punishment for their constant swearing.[8] Death, ever present in these books, is a punishment to the guilty but a release to the innocent. To the twentieth-century reader such constant concern with death may seem morbid, but the nineteenth-century child witnessed death more frequently than does his twentieth-century American counterpart. Although the descriptions are sentimental, they realistically reflect high rates of

[6] A 1808 Thompson, p. 43; see also A 1795 Root, p. 45; A 1809 Grout, p. 15; A 1810 Hendrick, p. 70; A 1863 Lander-P (Confederate), pp. 32, 38, 49, 52, 115.

[7] R 1866 McGuffey-4, p. 81.

[8] R 1830 Putnam-I, pp. 46–47. For an extended discussion of this see pp. 252 ff, below.

child mortality. The death of the innocent appears in countless tear-evoking scenes: "Mother, how still the baby lies!"; "There's but one pair of stockings to mend tonight." "Put away the little playthings that the darling used to wear."[9] Deathbed scenes written by Charles Dickens are most popular; Little Nell or Paul Dombey expire in almost every Reader from the late 1860's on. The death of the innocent is their gate to everlasting life, and contemplation of such transmigration a spur to good behavior on earth. The viewer should not mourn, but should use the occasion to ponder the weakness of man in the eyes of God as well as his own transgressions. Often such lessons to the living become painfully vivid; the small reader is warned that a few days before, the dying child was as well as the reader is at this moment.[10] Whether by earthly or heavenly rewards, God is the sole support of the ethical system; moral behavior is necessary because God demands it. As systematized theology, religion almost disappears from the later books, but it always maintains a prominent place with regard to man's moral behavior. It has become a religion of ethics rather than one of theology.

Usually it is assumed that everyone performs Christian rites and duties naturally and unself-consciously. But in three popular books in the second half of the century an extract from *Tom Brown's Schooldays* by Thomas Hughes indicates that in some circumstances the performance of religious rites may lead to social embarrassment. A new boy at Rugby is ridiculed when he gets on his knees to pray. He persists and Tom Brown supports him; finally, it becomes the thing for all boys to pray on their knees. "Manly piety" has triumphed.[11] This is the only explicit recognition that the devout Christian is surrounded by an increasingly secular civilization.

Like the later books, those in the beginning of the century are concerned with God as the creator of nature and moral law, but they also evidence a much greater interest in theology than do the later schoolbooks. Probably as a reaction to the deism, agnos-

[9] The preceding three quotations are from the following in that order: R 1866 McGuffey-4, pp. 109–110; R 1869 Wilson, pp. 21–23; R 1867 Edwards-4, 244–245.

[10] R 1864 Moore (Confederate), pp. 38–39.

[11] R 1874 Hillard, pp. 141–146; R 1879 McGuffey, pp. 183–189; R 1896 Holmes and Hill, pp. 185–189.

ticism and atheism of the Enlightenment, they frequently offer proofs of the existence of God. One author warns of too great an interest in philosophy. Those who have pushed farthest in that study, the Greeks, Hindoos, and Romans, "have departed most from the pure faith and worship of the one true God."[12] Atheists, deists, and free-thinkers, who hardly ever appear in the later books except in connection with the French Revolution, are lumped together and, although vaguely defined, vociferously denounced. Webster in 1836 identifies the latter two in his definition: "Infidel, Deist—one who disbelieves revelation, or the divine origin of the Christian religion."[13] Such a relatively clear definition occurs in only two other instances.[14] Although all denounce such groups, schoolbooks at the beginning of the nineteenth century do so in greater detail, offering intellectual arguments to prove the existence of God in opposition to the arguments of the atheist. As the nineteenth century advanced, deism retreated before the religious revivals in all sects. By the mid-nineteenth century the child is prepared to thank God for His goodness and to follow the morals of Christianity, but not to refute the apparently moribund issues of deism and atheism.

The arguments against deism appear mainly in the form of arguments against Thomas Paine and Voltaire. The assumption throughout the books is that both men denied the existence of God. Two books quote part of the speech of Thomas Erskine at the trial of the publisher of *The Age of Reason* to the effect that the whole of government and society rests on the Bible; therefore, any denial of revelation is shocking and subversive of the social order.[15] The structure of the globe and the beauties of nature "convict the infidel of his errors, and the visionary philosopher of his folly in attempting to account for creation without the mighty hand of a Deity."[16] Deism and atheism are assumed to be illogical as well as sinful. They are also believed to be a fertile source of immorality and depravity.[17]

[12] R 1813 Richardson, p. 100. [13] S 1836 Webster, p. 25.

[14] S 1815 Picket, p. 218; G 1818 Morse, p. 4.

[15] R 1811 I. Cooke, p. 253; R 1826 American-S, pp. 160–162; see also R 1814 Alden, pp. 53, 84–85, 93–96; R 1823 Richardson, p. 179.

[16] G 1806 Webster, p. 294.

[17] R 1801 Heaton-P, p. 64; R 1811 Lyman, pp. 176–184; R 1819 Strong, p. 69.

But the major point made against the deist is his denial of personal immortality. By this the individual loses hope and cannot be cheerful.[18] The argument against the denial of revelation is enforced by fear. Many scenes are set at the bedside of the dying infidel whose sufferings are horrible to contemplate as he realizes his foolhardiness too late for redemption.[19] One author asks rhetorically what good will fame do for the historian Gibbon when he faces his Maker: "I would not, for the richest mitre in the kingdom, be a Gibbon in my latest moments."[20] To prove that science and religion cannot be antithetical, Newton, Boyle, and Locke are used as examples of scientists and philosophers who were also Christians. One author asks if the reader considers himself more intelligent than Newton, Locke, Milton, and George Washington, who were all sound Christians.[21] The hallowed name of Washington is often evoked on this subject; one of the major characteristics assigned to Washington is that he was and always felt himself to be guided by God. Several Spellers at the time of the Civil War suggest discrimination against atheists in job opportunities: "If there is a vacancy, though the atheist is capable, do not give him the agency."[22]

Most of the Geographies introduce the subject of religion by dividing the religions of the world into two basic categories—true and false. True religion consists in "worshipping God, according to His revealed will."[23] That there can be only one true belief is assumed: "Every *belief* cannot be equally true."[24] And true religion is limited only to Christianity: "*It is found in its truth and purity* only where it is derived from divine revelation. This was given to our first parents, and again to Noah. . . . It was renewed in the Mosaic or Jewish religion, and was developed in its perfect form in the Christian religion."[25] Some Geographies,

[18] R 1803 Murray-S, p. 53; R 1802 Alden, p. 56; S 1802 Snowden, pp. 128–130; R 1839 S. Goodrich, pp. 283–284; R 1840 Snow, pp. 181–182.

[19] R 1811 I. Cooke, p. 180; R 1811 Lyman, p. 202; R 1823 Morrill, p. 220; R 1823 Richardson, p. 179; R 1848 Tower, pp. 96–99.

[20] R 1797 Alexander, p. 110.

[21] R 1803 D. Adams, pp. 131–132.

[22] S 1857 Parker and Watson, p. 87; S 1866 Watson, p. 86.

[23] G 1843 Mitchell, p. 49.

[24] S 1843 Fowle, p. 29; see also S 1819 Pike, p. 154.

[25] G 1866 Woodbridge, p. 312.

especially in the 1830's, would specifically limit true religion to the Protestants, who "take the Bible only for their guide in religious matters," whereas the Catholics are guided also by the pope.[26] In all books published between 1776 and the Civil War, even when such flat statements as the above do not appear, anti-Catholic feeling is strong and universal, as will be seen below.

All the books identify virtue only with Christianity: "There never was any system besides that of Christianity, which could effectively produce in the mind of man, the virtues I have hitherto been speaking of." Religion is "the only basis of society."[27] Furthermore, Christianity is necessary for civic progress: "Where-ever the Gospel has been received, there civilization, industry, morality, knowledge and happiness have prevailed."[28] Proof is offered by the observation that "Christianity is the prevailing religion of the leading nations of the world."[29] Their power has spread their virtues to the rest of the world in a process confidently expected to continue well into the future: "Christian nations are more powerful, and much more advanced in knowledge than any others. Their power is continually increasing. They have colonies in many Pagan countries. . . . They establish schools and other useful institutions: and there is no doubt that in the course of a few generations the Christian religions will be spread over the greater part of the earth."[30] Humanitarianism is also associated with Christianity: "*Those nations are most distinguished for justice and kindness* in which the Bible is best known, and Christianity most pure."[31] In the Geographies Christianity is, indeed, one of the criteria used to evaluate the degree of civilization attained in each country. All address their readers as Christians and assume the virtuous to be Christian. This produces a problem in dealing with the heroes of classical Greece and Rome,

[26] G 1830 Smiley, pp. 29–30; see also G 1827 C. Goodrich, pp. 19–20; G 1833 Clute, p. 308; G 1839 J. Worcester, p. 7.

[27] First quotation is from R 180? Murray, p. 67; second is from R 1866 McGuffey-5, p. 306.

[28] G 1807 Parish, p. 119; see also G 1793 Workman, p. 57; G 1820 Darby, p. 135; G 1824 Woodbridge and Willard, p. 211; R 1827 Pierpont, p. 186; G 1828 J. Worcester, p. 143; G 1830 Bazeley, p. 174; G 1848 Mitchell, p. 162; G 1843 Mitchell, p. 50; G 1878 Swinton, p. 20.

[29] G 1899 Tarbell, p. 19; see also G 1869 Warren-C, p. 15.

[30] G 1887 Warren, p. 16.

[31] G 1866 Woodbridge, p. 326.

who often appear as illustrations of such particular virtues as patriotism. These books abound, for example, in descriptions of the death of Socrates, illustrating the nobility imparted to the soul by belief in its own immortality; here Socrates is actually used as an argument for Christianity. But such illustrations nevertheless contradict the general tone of the books, which finds virtue only in conjunction with Christianity. Some authors apologize for the use of such examples: "The time, however, is coming when profane poetry will give place to the songs and devotions of the blest—when our earthly Parnassus will bow in submission to Mount Zion above."[32]

In this period true religion is patently limited to Protestantism. Catholicism is depicted not only as a false religion, but as a positive danger to the state; it subverts good government, sound morals, and education. Condemnation is usually vociferous when dealing directly with the Roman Catholic religion, and in the treatment of Catholic countries as well. From the 1870's to the end of the century such harsh condemnation is softened, but it is continuously violent up to that time, heightened a bit, perhaps, during the period of Nativism.

Several authors specifically blame the Roman Catholic Church for the decline of the Roman Empire: "The Roman Catholic religion completed their degeneracy and ruin."[33] Most of the textbooks hold the church accountable for the superstition they find rampant in the Middle Ages. Church doctrine itself became mere superstition: "And the Christian world was distinguished by little more than *name* from pagans and idolaters."[34] Several make this a charge against the church in all ages by stating: "They worship before images."[35] One suggests that the conversion of the idolatrous natives of Paraguay by the Jesuits was "an

[32] R 1825 A. Cook, p. 168; see also R 1804 Peirce, p. 21; R 1811 Hubbard, p. 45; R 1831 Harrod, p. 62.

[33] G 1817 Cummings, p. 168; see also G 1818 Mann, p. 340; G 1825 Butler, p. 251.

[34] R 1845 D. Adams, p. 146; see also R 1803 Murray-S, p. 113; R 1811 Lyman, p. 255; R 1826 Greenwood and Emerson, p. 385; R 1828 Robbins-P, pp. 190–191; G 1837 Book of Commerce, p. 154; G 1853 S. Goodrich, p. 183; S 1862 Watson, p. 86; G 1866 Woodbridge, p. 314.

[35] G 1828 Smiley, p. 29; see also G 1807 Parish, p. 154; G 1824 Woodbridge and Willard, p. 174; G 1833 Clute, p. 251; G 1866 Woodbridge, p. 314.

exchange not much for the better."[36] Thus missionary activity, highly praised in Protestantism, is often disapproved in Roman Catholicism.

The power of the papacy is the most severe point of attack in portraying the Reformation and the organization of the Catholic Church. The institution of the papacy is regarded as a gigantic hoax and conspiracy. One Speller sees fit to ask the question, "Is papacy at variance with paganism?"[37] And in the context of these books one would expect a negative answer. A typical treatment is the following: "For many ages the Popes not only pretended to be infallible, but exalted themselves above all the kings of the earth, to the very throne of CHRIST; assuming the right of pardoning sin, and of giving or rather selling the liberty of indulging in every species of wickedness and corruption."[38] The papacy is generally referred to as a "usurpation,"[39] and it is always described as a form of tyranny. In one case it is compared to the tyranny of the British before the American Revolution: "He [Samuel Adams] would have suffered excommunication rather than have bowed to papal infallibility, or paid the tribute to St. Peter."[40] The indulgence is described as an invention by the pope, who "very wickedly pretends to pardon for money people who have sinned, and tells them that God will not punish them."[41] Here the abuse of the doctrine is described as the doctrine itself. All descriptions of Catholic doctrine are most unfavorable.

The Roman Catholic Church and its clergy are pictured as greedy for money. The Readers and Spellers contain many pictures of clergymen begging for money but refusing to use it for charitable purposes.[42] The wealth of the church is the subject of frequent comment. One Geography analyzes the cost of

[36] G 1784 Morse, p. 134; see also G 1824 Woodbridge and Willard, p. 183; G 1826 Blake, p. 156.

[37] S 1866 Watson, p. 86. [38] R 1828 Willard-G, p. 94.

[39] R 1823 Blake, p. 131; see also R 1789 Webster, p. 167; R 1794 Burgh, pp. 88–91; S 1824 Guy, p. 25; G 1825 Butler, p. 216; R 1826 Greenwood and Emerson, pp. 81–83; R 1832 Edwards, p. 215; G 1853 S. Goodrich, p. 185.

[40] R 1826 Frost, p. 73.

[41] G 1837 Village, p. 81; see also R 1823 Blake, pp. 128–129; R 1828 Robbins-P, p. 200; R 1828 S. Willard-G, p. 94; R 1834 S. Willard-P, p. 64.

building St. Peter's: "It would take a person from the age of twenty-one to the age of seventy years, to count over this enormous sum, provided he counted three thousand dollars an hour, and was employed twelve hours in the day for the whole time."[43] The surveys of Roman Catholic countries in the Geographies always present great contrasts between the poverty of the people and the vast wealth of the clergy.

Religious persecution is the favorite theme. Anglican persecution of the Pilgrims is assumed to be the reason for their migration to America. But they were not forced out of England: they came of their own free will, to establish the principle of religious freedom in America. The only persecutions that are fully described are Catholic persecutions of Protestants. These appear in abundant detail from the picture in the *New England Primer* of the burning of John Rogers by Queen Mary of England, to Samuel Goodrich's description of the St. Bartholomew massacre, which the pope "deemed . . . glorious events."[44] The Inquisition is mentioned in many Readers and in all of the Geographies until near the end of the century. The following is a typical description: "The unhappy victims were either strangled, or committed to the flames, or loaded with chains, and shut up in dungeons during life, their effects confiscated and their families stigmatized with infamy. . . . Nothing ever displayed so fully to the eyes of mankind the spirit and temper of the papal religion."[45] The Spanish Inquisition with its more effective means and methods is always identified with the Inquisition of the central church. Because the texts depend heavily on English literature, they have a convenient villain for Catholic persecution of Protestants—Mary Tudor of England. In most of the Readers she appears in the act of creating Protestant martyrs. A softening of hostility toward Catholics in the later part of the century is suggested by a lessening of attention on Mary; in one view of her, in 1866, she is still quite as cruel as heretofore, but the author goes on to say that there are

---

[42] R 1792 Dana, pp. 153–156; S 1809 Perry, p. 117; S 1857 Parker and Watson, p. 78; see also G 1837 Book of Commerce, p. 166.

[43] G 1831 Blake, p. 60; see also R 1797 Alexander, pp. 187–188; G 1837 Village, p. 81.

[44] R 1785 New England Primer, p. 13; G 1853 S. Goodrich, p. 202.

[45] R 1825 Blake, pp. 228–230.

good and bad Catholics as there are good and bad Protestants, "but Mary was a bad one."[46]

The character and learning of the Catholic clergy are severely criticized throughout. In 1784 Morse says of the German clergy: "The Protestant clergy are learned and exemplary in their deportment, the popish ignorant and libertine"; and of the Polish: "The popish clergy are said to be in general, illiterate bigots; and the monks the most profligate of mankind."[47] The regular clergy are most violently and consistently attacked, mainly on the grounds of hypocrisy, personal immorality, and greed. These charges appear in such forms as the following: "The monks and ecclesiastics themselves, who today will pardon your sins for a groat, tonight will become defiled with your bosom-companion in her marriage-bed. And the daughter on whom you dote, while saying her mass, will become debauched by a pretending saint!"[48] Such criticisms of the morals of the clergy occur even in the practice sentences on the Spellers: "The controversy at the monastery with regard to the profligacy of the clergy encouraged proselytism."[49] At best the regular clergy are portrayed as slothful parasites living on the hard labor of the poor. The fruits of the labor of the Italian peasant enter either the coffers of a rich landlord "or the overflowing treasury of some church or convent—the abodes of sloth and vacuity."[50] One of the most popular single selections on this subject disclosed the judgment of a magic philosopher's scale which weighs true worth: the heart of the English philanthropist Howard far outweighs a socially useless "monk, with austerities bleeding and rare."[51] In several cases the Catholic clergy is depicted as using the most dastardly means to acquire possession of the souls and bodies of those of another religion.[52] The Jesuit order is the embodiment

[46] H 1866 Lossing, pp. 41–42. [47] G 1784 Morse, pp. 166, 172.

[48] G 1818 Mann, p. 293; see also R 1828 Robbins-P, p. 192; R 1828 Willard-G, p. 182; R 1831 Cheever, pp. 430–434.

[49] S 1857 Parker and Watson, p. 145; see also S 1824 Guy, p. 14.

[50] R 1826 Frost, p. 196; see also R 1827 Pierpont, p. 175; R 1828 Willard-G, pp. 181–183; R 1831 Smiley, p. 108; G 1835 Huntington, p. 138; R 1853 Mandeville, pp. 19–20.

[51] R 1828 Putnam-A, pp. 46–51; R 1843 Olney, p. 206; R 1841 Merriam, p. 213; R 1844 Smith, p. 164; R 1851 ASDUK, p. 117; R 1851 Tower, p. 140.

[52] R 1796 Bingham, p. 184; R 1830 Hughs, pp. 15–17.

of such unscrupulousness; their behavior in such circumstances is anti-Christian. One selection in several Readers personifies a family Bible and describes its adventures: "[I] had some hopes that I might have been able to infuse a spark of Christian charity into the Jesuit's heart," but these hopes are quite in vain.[53]

Catholicism is believed to have deleterious effects other than impoverishment on the general population. By a curious juxtaposition of clauses used to describe the people of Catholic countries, the reader is left with the impression that the Roman Catholic religion induces both ignorance and indolence. It is said of the French in Canada: "Perhaps nothing tends more to brutish ignorance and depravity of manners, than a religion so much made up of mere external ceremonies"; of the Irish: "The greater proportion of the inhabitants are Papists, and many of them live in the most abject poverty and ignorance"; or of Europe in general: "In the Protestant countries, and in those favored with a mild and liberal form of government, the mass of the people are more enlightened and better informed, than in those where the Roman Catholic is the prevailing religion"; of Ecuador: "The Roman Catholic religion prevails, and ignorance and indolence pervade the great mass of the people."[54] Even when no specific charge is made that Catholicism produces an ignorant population, the implication is clear. A few authors make unqualified statements that the Catholic Church has deliberately attempted to maintain ignorance: "The perusal of the *Scriptures* is also forbidden to the people in most Catholic countries; and in this way one of the most important sources of knowledge and one of the strongest motives to its acquisition is taken away."[55] One of these authors puts great emphasis on the lack of scientific and educational advance in Catholic countries and blames it specifically on the church; later—and, one suspects, inadvertently—he notes the eminence of the French in scientific

[53] R 1801 Heaton-P, p. 63; see also G 1784 Morse, p. 106; R 1823 Blake, pp. 138–147; S 1863 W. Adams, p. 86.

[54] Of the French in Canada, G 1818 Mann, p. 168; of the Irish, G 1833 Clute, p. 239; of Europe in general, G 1835 Huntington, p. 146; of Ecuador, G 1853 S. Goodrich, p. 165; and see section on Southern Europe in this study.

[55] G 1824 Woodbridge and Willard, p. 188; see also G 1818 Smith, p. 79; G 1866 Woodbridge, p. 314.

discoveries.[56] One book mentions that the Catholic Church provided the only facilities for education in the Middle Ages, but this is described as a conspiracy to keep knowledge from the people in order to keep power for the church: "They added their own cunning devices, further to render obscure their own teaching. The more mystery they could weave into every science, and, the more perplexing the labyrinth into which they could lead their pupils, the better it suited their purpose."[57]

Only books designed for use in Catholic parochial schools deal favorably with the Catholic religion and Catholics. In the others, stories of individual Catholics in a favorable context do occur, but they are rare, and they are lost in the vehemence and reiteration of condemnations that are stated and implied in the rest of the same schoolbook. The humanitarianism of the Bernardine monks is an oft-told tale in the Readers. It would seem hard to dissociate their work from the Catholic Church, but this is achieved in several cases: in five instances before 1865, they are identified as Catholic monks; in three other instances, all after 1850, they are individual humanitarians with no visible relationship to the Catholic Church.[58] In all the Readers and Spellers before the end of the Civil War there are only eleven other instances where individual Catholic benevolence is mentioned; all occur before 1840. It seems safe to conclude that echoes of the Nativist movement at this time created a heightened awareness and fear of Catholicism and forced the rejection of any stories that treated identifiable Catholics sympathetically. One author seems to illustrate such a change: in 1839 S. Goodrich offers a pleasant picture of life in a convent, and a story of a monk heroically offering his own great artistic talent to God. In 1853 the same author presents a violently biased picture of the Catholic Church in which he accuses it of approaching idolatry.[59]

[56] G 1824 Woodbridge and Willard, compare 188 with 190.

[57] A 1846 Mix, pp. 7–8.

[58] In the following they are identified as Roman Catholics: R 1832 Progressive, pp. 99–100; R 1834 S. Worcester, pp. 179–181; R 1838 Blake, pp. 93–94; R 1840 Angell-3, pp. 114–115; R 1850 Swan, pp. 58–61. In the following they are not identified as Roman Catholics: R 1850 Webb, pp. 58–60; R 1851 Swan-P, pp. 56–59; R 1853 McGuffey E-1, pp. 52–55.

[59] R 1839 S. Goodrich, pp. 201–203, 41–44 compared with G 1853 S. Goodrich, p. 183.

It is clear, however, that although some of the stories depicting Catholics favorably are deleted in the Nativist period, this indicates no dramatic change in bias. In the earlier period just as in the later, and coexistent in the same books with the favorable stories, the Catholic Church is heartily condemned. No theme in these schoolbooks before 1870 is more universal than anti-Catholicism. To come across a description of an earthquake by an observer named Father Kircher, obviously a Catholic but one who is treated noncommittally, is not only startling;[60] it is also unique. With these few exceptions, Catholics, clergy and laymen, appear in an unfortunate light. Throughout the period the Spellers offer in the lists of words to be memorized many terms referring to Catholicism, such as "nunnery, abbot, monastick, papist, papal." Such words need not suggest condemnation of the religion they represent but in the context of the textbooks it becomes clear that they are needed only to understand the literature of anti-Catholicism. The texts themselves certainly offer no other use.

It is evident, then, that schoolbooks in use in the United States from 1776 through the Civil War provided fertile soil for the anti-Catholic agitators of the Nativist period.[61] It is also clear that the many Catholic immigrants arriving in America in this period would face strong hostility for their religion as well as for their foreign birth. The school child in this period would associate Catholicism only with unpleasant behavior and subversive beliefs. He would imbibe not only the idea that its theology is false, but that it is inimical to industry, prosperity, knowledge, and freedom—concepts considered basic to all civilization. According to those schoolbooks published before 1870, Catholicism has no place in the American past or future, nor in the economic and political climate of the United States.

In books published after 1870 anti-Catholicism is muted. Here, with few exceptions, the courage and self-sacrifice of the French Catholic missionaries is admired. The monks of St. Bernard are described in many Readers and praised for their

[60] R 1803 Murray, pp. 123–126.

[61] For extensive treatment of this movement see Ray Billington, *The Protestant Crusade, 1800–1860* (New York: Macmillan, 1938); Sister M. L. Fell, *Foundations of Nativism in America* (Washington, D.C.: Catholic University of America, 1941).

work. One exception is an 1896 McGuffey Reader, where they are referred to only as "the good men," with no suggestion of their connection to the Catholic Church.[62] On the whole, the ameliorated attitude in the second part of the century is more negative than positive: the United States remains a Protestant nation founded on Puritan principles, but the stream of anti-Catholic invective present from 1776 through the Civil War disappears, probably underground. The child would still know of Protestant rather than Catholic contributions to American culture, but at least he was not being taught about positive dangers in the Catholic religion. The decline of Catholic countries is still remarked, but it is attributed to degeneration rather than to superstitious religious institutions. Several elements in late nineteenth-century American culture probably contributed to this mitigation of anti-Catholic sentiment. Religion in the schoolbooks lost its earlier doctrinal content in the second part of the century. Man and his civilization are just as dependent on God as they were in the earlier books, but God is now shown to be the creator of the world and the founder and executor of the ethical system on which our civilization rests—although religion is still basic to life, religious institutions are much less prominent. Whose interpretation of Scripture as authoritative becomes less important. Probably interest in the developments and problems of this world—the Civil War and its aftermath, industrialization, and the movement west—absorbed energies that had once centered on sectarian controversy. America was more self-confident and more secular. Furthermore, probably some of the earlier Catholic immigrants had now a respectable middle-class position in their communities, and they carried enough political power to influence textbook content directly or indirectly. By the end of the century, for whatever reasons, questions of race and nationality occupy the schoolbooks more than does that of religion. The stratification of men by religious sect is largely superseded by national or racial classification. Certainly the later schoolbooks use the categories of race and nationality as the most prominent way of making significant statements about men. This change is visible in the treatment of the Jews as well as the population of Catholic countries.

[62] R 1896 McGuffey-2, pp. 109–112.

It should be unnecessary to add that texts used in Catholic parochial schools are an exception to all of the foregoing. Throughout the century these books maintain their sectarian point of view: "There can be but one true religion," whose benign influence is the basis of civilization.[63] They show Catholicism as the foundation of national independence: "Scotland retained its faith and its independence until the Protestant Reformation. It then lost the faith of St. Columba and soon afterwards its national independence."[64] In a piece from Chateaubriand the teachings of Jesus are asserted to be the basis of patriotism: "In Him the love of country may find a model."[65] Denial of the pope led to the destruction of Napoleon, and in a larger sense the Protestant Reformation threatened European society with anarchy and despotism.[66] What was to Protestant books the Dark Ages, in which monks kept knowledge from the people, becomes in these books the age of Charlemagne and St. Louis, wherein science and learning were preserved by the clergy. The discovery of America is the direct result of the Catholic piety of Columbus and Queen Isabella.[67] Now and then they sound a defensive note. After a description of the selfless clergy of the Middle Ages, one Reader asks how could these be called "victims of a slavish superstition."[68] Catholic schoolbooks retain throughout the century the same kind of sectarian religious zeal exhibited by Protestant books in the first part of the century, but it is Catholicism rather than Protestantism that is the foundation of civilization and American independence.

Throughout the century toleration in matters of religion is explicitly advocated as a desirable goal for the individual and the nation. But except for those books published in the last three decades of the nineteenth century, this liberal attitude is contradicted by the rest of the book and extends only to Protestant sects. Several early Readers try to bring the logic of toleration to the child by the tale of a father who takes his sons on Sunday morning to the services of three different sects, explaining that God meant men to differ in forms of religious observance. After

[63] G 1878 Catholic, pp. 13, 66.
[64] G 1876 Comprehensive, p. 85.
[65] R 1873 Progressive, p. 53.
[66] G 1876 Comprehensive, p. 91.
[67] G 1876 Comprehensive, pp. 13, 91; R 1873 Progressive, p. 287.
[68] R 1873 Progressive, p. 288.

the services a man on the street becomes ill, and people of all creeds stop to help him as they return from their various services.[69] A common humanity nullifies ritualistic differences; differences in doctrine are not noticed in the story. But from the picture presented in these same books of the Catholics and the Jews, not to mention more remote sects, one wonders how much force such a lesson would have. One Speller, apparently in reaction to recent overt anti-Catholicism in the United States, includes the practice sentence: "The burning of a church is a sacriligious [*sic*] act."[70] These are the only notices of religious toleration that are given a contemporary illustration or a concrete example in the schoolbooks published before the Civil War.

Most of the pleas for religious toleration are quite abstract; "Nothing is more unmannerly than to reflect on any man's profession, sect, or natural infirmity."[71] The most popular illustration of toleration in practice comes from the pen of Benjamin Franklin: Abraham ejects a guest from his tent who refuses to join in his own religious rites. Later Abraham is rebuked by God, who calls this action a sin.[72] It is interesting to note that in one version God's rebuke is omitted, and its moral becomes inverted into approval of religious intolerance.[73] But toleration as a virtue must surely have been negated in the child's mind by the attitude toward non-Protestant sects in the rest of the book. A typical case is that of an 1804 Reader by Peirce: on page 102 he recommends tolerance of all who differ in religious opinions, but the rest of the book is full of the horrible deeds of the Catholics.[74]

[69] R 1799 New Pleasing, pp. 66–67; R 1803 Biglow, pp. 62–65; R 1828 Robbins-A, pp. 137–139; see also R 1823 Pierpont, pp. 358–362.

[70] S 1843 Fowle, p. 78.

[71] R 1802 Alden, p. 32; R 1814 Alden, p. 29; see also R 1794 Guide, pp. 167–168; R 1798 Enfield, pp. 162–163; R 1801 Heaton-P, pp. 218–234; R 1810 Thomson, pp. 94–95; S 1823 Marshall, pp. 110–111; R 1826 American-S, pp. 52–55; R 1852 Sweet, p. 179.

[72] R 1792 Dana, pp. 156–157; R 1809 Picket, pp. 71–72; R 1821 Bingham, p. 13; R 1830 Bartlett, p. 233; R 1838 Blake, pp. 74–75; R 1843 Olney, pp. 21–22; R 1852 Sweet, pp. 70–71; R 1856 Hillard, p. 504; R 1873 American, pp. 106–108.

[73] R 1804 New Introduction, pp. 16–17.

[74] R 1804 Peirce: compare p. 102 with pp. 273, 274, 275, 278.

That Americans enjoy the unique distinction of having religious liberty is always mentioned proudly, even when in Connecticut and Massachusetts church and state were not yet separated.[75] Roger Williams is believed by some to have introduced the principle of separation of church and state to America. In the earlier textbooks this is not an unmixed blessing. Morse, for example, says of Rhode Island: this is probably why "the Sabbath and all religious institutions have been more neglected in this than in any other of the New-England States."[76] This serious indictment is typical of the general treatment accorded this state in the earlier books. Always it is the pariah of New England. Some of the histories published in the 1860's see Williams' opinions accompanied by others less desirable: "But with these doctrines of religious tolerance he united others that were deemed subversive of good government and opposed to the fundamental principles of civil society."[77] Finally, by the end of the century, Williams receives hearty approval as a pioneer in religious freedom, and Rhode Island loses its classification as substandard, although one of the Catholic Geographies indicates that Williams was merely "following the example of Maryland," the Catholic colony.[78]

In the early books the introduction of religious toleration in Catholic Maryland often escapes mention. But after the late 1860's the change in religious attitudes in schoolbooks is fully evident as the Catholic founder of Maryland is given credit for this act. Indeed, all of the Histories from that period on observe with disapproval and wonder that the Protestants, when they wrested political control of that colony from the Catholics, did away with the Catholic toleration act. The terms of religious toleration in colonial Pennsylvania, on the other hand, are generously acclaimed throughout the century. William Penn, unlike Roger Williams or George Calvert, is universally accorded heroic stature for his contributions to toleration and for his Indian policy. The rapid settlement of his colony is often ascribed

[75] For examples: R 1806 Peirce, p. 82; G 1820 Darby, p. 90; G 1833 Clute, p. 177; G 1836 Smith, p. 81; G 1840 Olney, p. 64.

[76] G 1791 Morse, p. 104; see also G 1784 Morse, p. 35.

[77] H 1867 Goodrich, p. 41; H 1867 Willson, p. 75.

[78] G 1876 Comprehensive, p. 32.

to his religious policy. Penn is often called "the father of religious liberty in the Western World."[79] There must have been a good deal of confusion in the minds of the children who read these books on this subject, however, since regardless of what is said about Rhode Island, Pennsylvania, or Maryland, the child was taught throughout the century that the Pilgrims and Puritans (identical in most of these books) came to America to establish religious freedom, and that the initial glory is theirs. Much is made of the persecution they suffered in England, very little of the persecution meted out by the Puritans to those who differed with them on religious matters. Very few indicate that religious freedom in colonial Massachusetts was confined to Puritans.[80]

In the charts of the religions of the world, that of the United States is always listed as Protestant, although there is no indication whether this is based on number of adherents or on more mysterious criteria.[81] And in America religion is assumed to be most perfectly understood in two states, Massachusetts and Connecticut, states that did not completely disestablish the church until well into the nineteenth century, although the child is not so informed. Morse asserts that the religion of Connecticut is "the best in the world, perhaps, for a republican government."[82] In consequence of its excellent religious system Connecticut, in specific contrast to Rhode Island, is assumed to have the purest morals in the United States, and, of course, in the world as well.[83] By the last three decades of the century ambivalence toward religious freedom is gone, and the United States is proudly described as Christian, but: "There is no established religion in the United States. Every man may worship God according to the dictates of his own conscience. But Christianity is the basis of the government and institutions, and public opinion is enlisted in its favor."[84] Whereas in the earlier books specific preachments on religious toleration could hardly be effective in the face of the

[79] R 1803 Carey, p. 163.

[80] H 1866 Lossing, p. 65; H 1869 Quackenbos, p. 67; H 1875 Higginson, p. 60.

[81] R 1806 Peirce, p. 82; G 1804 Goldsmith, p. 52; G 1817 Cummings, p. 197; G 1835 Huntington, p. 45; S 1846 Leonard, p. 165.

[82] G 1791 Morse, p. 109.

[83] See below p. 172 ff.

[84] G 1892 Mitchell, p. 31.

intolerance exhibited toward all but Protestant sects, the context of the later books is much more in harmony with lessons in toleration. Indeed these later books often look smugly back to the uninformed days of the past, proud of the superior morals that have since evolved. Intolerance in colonial Massachusetts is deplored; "People had not then learned to leave one another free to worship in their own way."[85]

The quality of this new toleration is a bit strained, however, in facing a new sect, the Church of Latter-Day Saints. To Willard "This is the most extraordinary imposture of the age.... Mormonism gives its followers license to commit every crime which may be sanctioned by the leading prophet," and she hopes that they will disappear with the Indian, "overwhelmed by the resistless wave of civilization."[86] The limits of toleration seem evident in such a statement as the following: "I expect there will be much trouble yet on their account, because they allow things to be done which the people of the United States do not like."[87] Some books note with approval the intervention of the United States government to suppress their "vicious" practices.[88] Books published later in the 1880's and 1890's often forget their disagreeable practices in admiration for their contributions in settling the West: "They converted a desert spot into a garden."[89] In such books polygamy goes unmentioned. Since the Mormons are succeeding in one of the major tasks and accomplishments of the Americans, they are admitted into American society.

Sponsoring true religion and religious freedom, Americans are distinguished as the chosen people of God. God led Columbus to believe in the existence of another continent because Europe needed room to establish a freedom unattainable in its crowded quarters.[90] The analogy of the Americans to the ancient Hebrews, the chosen people of God, is used in many circumstances. The

[85] R 1883 Swinton-4, p. 192.

[86] H 1868 Willard, pp. 337–338, 504; see also H 1872 Venable, p. 184; H 1874 Scott, pp. 288–289; H 1879 Quackenbos, p. 244; H 1879? Campbell, p. 159.

[87] H 1866 Lossing, p. 219.

[88] H 1889 Chambers, p. 337; see also H 1869 Quackenbos, p. 190.

[89] H 1894 Fiske, p. 321; see also G 1872 Hall, p. 79; G 1887 Warren, p. 57; G 1887 Redway, p. 72.

[90] H 1889 Monroe, pp. 79–82.

first American settlers were led from Europe to America just as the Hebrews were led to the Promised Land.[91] "His hand was scarcely more conspicuous in bringing Israel out of Egypt, than in providing for the settlement of the Pilgrims in the New World. Hardly more conspicuous to the sons of Jacob were the pillars of cloud and fire, than have been the dispensations of His providence in establishing and defending His American Israel."[92] Washington on his deathbed remembers (according to Parson Weems) "how God, by a mighty hand and by an outstretched arm, brought their fathers into this good land, a land flowing with milk and honey!"[93] The same concept is used to describe the American Revolution, with America compared to David, "the stripling of Israel, with scarcely a weapon to attack," arrayed against the British Goliath.[94] Following the Revolution:

> The savage Canaanites have left our soil,
> We the true Israel taste the wine and oil.[95]

The American Constitution is compared with the Mosaic code in one instance; it too is apparently of divine inspiration.[96] The western migrant setting up a wilderness homestead is, like the Hebrew migrants to Egypt, under the direct protection of God.[97] The most popular conception within this analogy compares Washington to Moses.[98] Thus the premise of the founders of New England themselves—that New England was the New Zion and they the New Hebrews—is thoroughly accepted in these schoolbooks for the entire United States.

Innumerable instances of God's direct interposition in favor of

[91] R 1826 American-S, p. 92; R 1830 Bartlett, pp. 209–210; R 1835 Porter, pp. 215–217.

[92] H 1843 Hall and Baker, p. 4.

[93] R 1811 Chandler, p. 146.

[94] Speech by John Quincy Adams, July 4, 1793, quoted in R 1796 Bingham, p. 144; R 1826 American-S, p. 123.

[95] R 1806 Staniford, p. 231; S 1824 Bentley, p. 170; see also R 1810 Thomson, p. 15.

[96] R 1811 Hubbard, pp. 52–55.

[97] R 1823 Pierpont, pp. 244–245; R 1831 Bailey, p. 316; R 1845 Goldsbury and Russell, p. 37; R 1856 Hillard, p. 356.

[98] R 1806 Staniford, p. 85; R 1807 Bingham-C, pp. 281–284; R 1810 Alden, pp. 215–216; R 1809 Picket, pp. 188–191; R 1811 Chandler, p. 145; R 1826 American-S, pp. 121–122.

the American people are given to support the idea that Americans are the people chosen by God in the modern world for a special destiny. In all books America is assumed to be particularly blessed by Providence. In one book this becomes evidence of the beneficence of God in general: "The predominant tendency of His providence towards us as a nation, evinces His benevolent designs."[99] Conversely, it is sometimes urged that: "The marks of divine favor shown to our nation, the striking interposition of divine PROVIDENCE in our behalf, cannot fail to enliven the patriotic sentiments of a pious mind."[100]

The literal intervention of the Deity in American affairs is illustrated throughout our history. Columbus is guided by God through great difficulties; His intervention is not by inspiration but by miracles.[101] The planting of the Pilgrims was "ordained by Providence to reform the world."[102] Specific examples of supernatural use of, or interference with, the laws of nature in our behalf appear in almost every schoolbook. In all the Histories and some Readers God sent a plague on the Indians of Massachusetts to make room for the settlement of the Pilgrims. They came as "The chosen servants of the Lord, to open the forests to the sun-beam, and to the light of the Sun of righteousness; to restore man, oppressed and trampled on by his fellow, to religious and civil liberties and equal rights."[103] The American Revolution in its inception and its course was also directed literally by God: "The great parent of the universe has peculiarly distinguished the Americans in encouraging them to defend their rights."[104] Many instances are given of the protection of God in the midst of battle. In one case God sends a fog to protect the retreat of the

[99] R 1810 Alden, p. 126.

[100] R 1834 S. Willard-P, p. 250.

[101] G 1818 Mann, p. 47; R 1819 Strong, p. 45; R 1852 Sweet, p. 302.

[102] R 1826 American-S, p. 221; see also R 1806 Peirce, p. 78; R 1826 Greenwood and Emerson, p. 102; R 1835 Pierpont-Y, pp. 103–107; H 1851 Guernsey, pp. vi, 102; H 1852 E. Willard, p. 175; R 1852 Sweet, pp. 302, 303, 304.

[103] R 1831 Cheever, p. 335.

[104] R 1797 Thomas, p. 208; see also R 1830 Emerson, pp. 170–171; R 1830 Practical-R, p. 70; H 1833 C. Goodrich, p. 195; R 1835 Pierpont-Y, p. 107; R 1835 Porter, pp. 282–284; H 1836 Olney, pp. 138–139; R 1852 Gilder, pp. 96–98; H 1852 E. Willard, p. 175.

American army from the British: "But for the interposition of a *cloud* of darkness the Egyptians would have overwhelmed the Israelites upon the sea shore."[105] Thus God both decreed and directed the American Revolution.

Washington was expressly commissioned by heaven to deliver the Americans. God trained him before the Revolution and protected him for its duration: "Everywhere we see the hand of God conducting him into danger, that he might extract from it the wisdom of an experience not otherwise to be attained, and develop those heroic qualities by which alone danger and difficulty can be surmounted,—but all the while covering him, as with a shield."[106] Many instances show the divine protection hovering over Washington: in one, at the defeat of Braddock's troops, "I expected every moment to see him fall; nothing but the superintending care of Providence could have saved him from the fate of all around him."[107] The writing of the American Constitution also exhibits "the finger of that Almighty Hand, which has been so frequently and signally extended to our relief in the critical stages of the revolution."[108]

Thus the United States is a Protestant nation with a divinely appointed mission. As the modern Chosen People its inhabitants have a special motive for piety, and concomitantly they have a special motive for patriotism. American nationalism and religion are thoroughly interwoven; love of the American nation is a correlative of love of God.

[105] R 1831 Lowe-Second, p. 49; see also R 1830 Practical-R, pp. 71–72.

[106] R 1845 Swan, p. 421; see also R 1789 Webster, p. 114; R 1810 Alden, p. 119; S 1815 Bradley, p. 146; G 1818 Morse, p. 104; S 1824 Bentley, p. 170; R 1852 Brothers, p. 374.

[107] R 1824 Lowe, p. 13; see also R 1813 Richardson, p. 117; R 1852 Brothers, p. 374; H 1855 Berard, p. 92.

[108] R 1831 Cheever, p. 221; see also H 1857 Lossing, p. 169.

III. The Nature of Man

Chapter 4

RACES OF MAN

The century that produced the racist theories of Joseph Gobineau, Houston Stewart Chamberlain, John Calhoun, and George Fitzhugh showed increasing interest in shouldering the white man's burden and raised racism to the status of scientific doctrine. In the beginning of the century the cosmopolitanism of the Enlightenment had begun to disintegrate under the ideological implications and international activities of the French Revolution. Romanticism, with its stress on local color, particularity, and the national soul, saw the individual not as a specific form of universal man, nor even as a member of a particular class, but as a creature innately conditioned by his membership in a particular race and nationality group. If medieval man had found his milieu in a local manor and a universal church, nineteenth-century man increasingly found his fulfillment as part of a race and nationality. The doctrine of race as a method of classifying men was singularly rigid: it assumed that biologically inherited traits—physical, mental, and moral—are immutable. Church and class affiliations are theoretically changeable, but biologically inherited characteristics are not. By the end of the century it was widely assumed that nature had conferred specific characteristics on each member of a racial group throughout historical time. Furthermore races could be classified according to the desirability of their traits.

In the United States popular ideas of race and of the racial inheritance of the individual came to have far-reaching importance in the generations that decided the issues of the Civil War, Reconstruction, and the place of Negroes, Indians, and immigrants in American society. These concepts are latent in all the schoolbooks, in stories, descriptions, even arithmetic problems, and most important of all in the Geographies. Here the child was formally presented with the idea of race and with the various races of the world and their characteristics. In their surveys of each country the Geographies are often more specific about the inherent characteristics of the inhabitants as a group than about the natural resources of the country. In all but the most experimental schools of the time the child was generally required to memorize such characteristics and the rank of each race in the accepted racial hierarchy.

Authors of nineteenth-century schoolbooks never questioned nature's division of mankind into separate unalterable races defined by inherent physical, intellectual, and spiritual qualities. "Nature has formed the different degrees of genius, and the characters of nations, which are seldom known to change."[1] The original historical unity of mankind is also unquestioned. Throughout the century Adam and Eve rather than any Darwinian progenitors retain their identity as the common ancestors of men; with the dispersion of the sons of Noah, environmental factors and "other causes" created separate branches of the human race. "The great family of mankind—although descended from Adam and Eve,—by being spread over the surface of the earth and subjected to the varieties of climate, and from other causes, has been divided into several distinct races, differing in color, form, and features and in mental characteristics also."[2] Differences in climate receive the most prominent etiological position, but just as invariably, mysterious "other causes beyond the reach of our investigation"[3] are also mentioned. With an evolutionary foundation for the establishment of races, a hint of the possibility of future development might be expected. But the races are regarded as fixed for most of the past, the present, and the future. Guyot, one of the few authors of schoolbooks who was a professional geographer, agrees with the rest: "Certain physical features and mental characteristics . . . have remained unchanged from a time anterior to all history."[4]

All of the Geographies divide mankind into distinct if increasingly elaborate racial categories. In the first half of the century the normal division is: Eskimo, Tartar, East Indian, Negro, American Indian, and European. In the latter part of the century the categories adopted are usually those of Blumen-

[1] R 1793 Moore, p. 300.
[2] G 1892 Mitchell, p. 8.
[3] G 1866 Woodbridge, p. 303.
[4] G 1866 Guyot, p. 114.

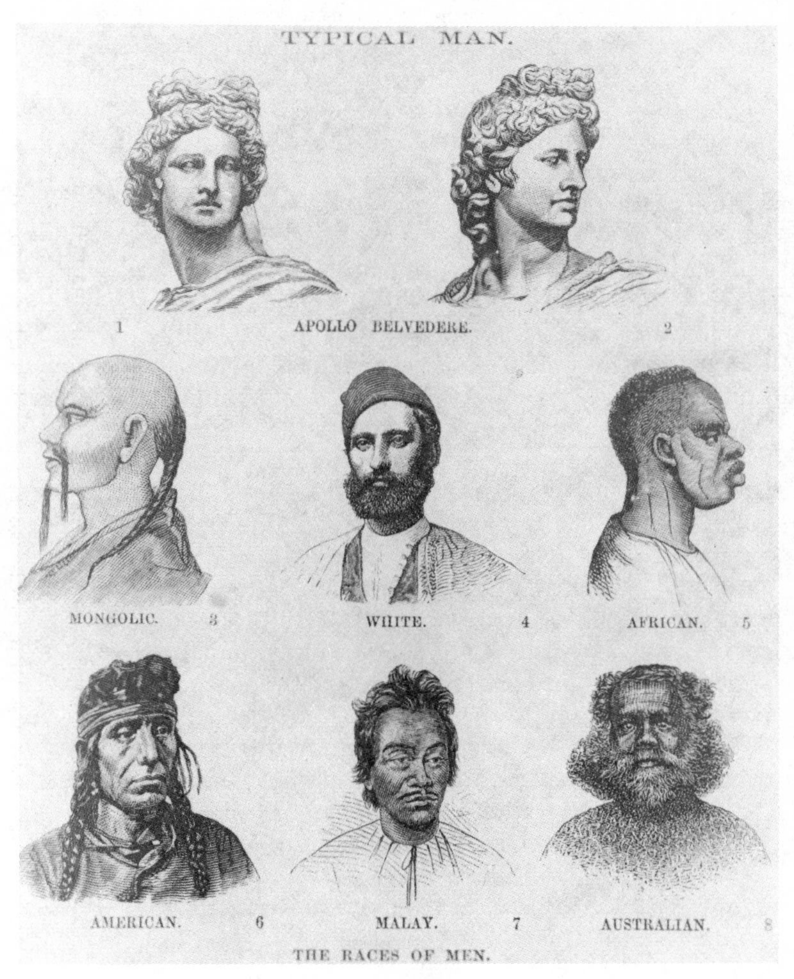

5. Arnold Henry Guyot, in his book *Physical Geography,* 1866, divides the races of man. To him the white race is "the normal or typical race" whose best representative is to be seen "in the unrivalled works of the ancient sculptors."

6. In this picture of representatives of the races of man, from the 1878 Geography of Von Steinwehr and Brinton, the white race appears in the guise of a lovely woman. In all such pictures of the races of man, the representative of the white race is a particularly handsome specimen.

bach[5]: Caucasian, Mongolian, Malayan, Negro, and American Indian. But whatever the racial subdivisions, throughout the century whites are ranked at the top and Negroes at the bottom. Guyot's is the most original theory to explain this hierarchy: in a section entitled "The White Race the Normal or Typical Race," he develops the idea that the typical man is to be seen "in the unrivalled works of the ancient sculptors."[6] "A comparison of the different tribes and races of men, reveals the fact of a *gradual* modification of types, on every side of the central or highest race, until by insensible degrees, the lowest or most degraded forms of humanity are reached."[7] The white is then the normal race from which others have deviated. The degree of degeneration from the typical race is directly dependent on geographical distance from the original habitat of the normal race: "*The degree of perfection of the type* is therefore proportioned, not to intensity of material agencies but to distance from the central or highest race irrespective of climatic conditions. The degree of culture of the races also varies in the same order. The central race is the race of culture and progress, both now and in all ages past."[8] The perfect man from whom all others are deviants was the inhabitant of the mountains of Iran. All schoolbooks imply that the white was the original race and the pattern for all others; Adam and Eve were Caucasian.[9]

The superiority of the white race is also taken for granted. Physically "they furnish the greatest number of beautiful figures."[10] They are, in addition, "superior to all others in intellectual and moral development, and are the leaders of Christian civilization."[11] Their initiative and energy are singled out as distinctive features. At the end of the chapter on race some question like the following is often asked: "Which is the most intelligent race?"[12] When pictures are used to show a typical member of each race, the cards are usually stacked in favor of the whites. Guyot uses the idealized head of the Apollo Belvedere

[5] For example, see G 1818 Morse, pp. 44–45. In the latter part of the century the categories adopted were usually those of Johann F. Blumenbach, an early German anthropologist who died in 1840.

[6] G 1866 Guyot, p. 115.

[7] G 1866 Guyot, p. 118.

[8] *Ibid.*

[9] For example, see G 1885 Houston, p. 126.

[10] G 1826 Blake, p. 103.

[11] G 1892 Mitchell, p. 111.

[12] G 1887 Warren, p. 13.

as an example of the white race, but quite ordinary specimens for the others.[13] Other Geographies display the face of a lovely white woman with refined and delicate features surrounded by rather swarthy unpleasant types to exemplify other races.[14] In the Readers, now and then, an imaginative piece of writing illustrates the superiority of the white race. One Reader at the end of the century includes an essay by Washington Irving, "Origin of the White, the Red and the Black Men":[15] the Great Spirit first made black men, saw he had bungled, and so made red men. He liked red men better, but only when he had finally made white men was he satisfied. In the context of these books Irving's whimsy becomes an anthropological statement. Several books assume that the white race is superior in quantity as well as quality.[16] In only one book does the white race as a whole assume the white man's burden: "To the Caucasian race by reason of its physical and mental superiority, has been assigned the task of civilizing and enlightening the world."[17] But the child with a social conscience, influenced by any of these books, could easily be persuaded that white superiority requires the performance of such a task.

In the latter part of the century refinements of the white race appear. Woodbridge offers a typical example of the process of subdivision. He divides the white race into the Celts (British, French, Portuguese, Spanish, Italians, and Greeks), who have "strong passions and lively dispositions; and all except the Spanish, Portuguese and Italians are conspicuous for activity, ingenuity, vivacity and enterprise"; and the Gothic or German family (Germans, Danes, Dutch, Swedes, Norwegians, and Icelanders), who are "ingenious, but usually phlegmatic, and most distinguished for patient, persevering industry."[18] By the 1860's all the best qualities of the Caucasians are centered in the western Aryans (American, British, Germans, French, Italians, Spanish, Russians, Poles)—Gobineau has been nationalized. To the Aryans now belongs the task of carrying on culture. They "are the most prominent actors in the great drama of history, and have carried

[13] G 1866 Guyot, p. 114.

[14] G 1878 Steinwehr and Brinton, p. 13; G 1878 Colton, p. 16.

[15] R 1898 Williams G-1, pp. 115–117.

[16] G 1875 Swinton, p. 29.

[17] S 1896 Dutton, p. 114.

[18] G 1866 Woodbridge, p. 353.

to their fullest growth all the elements of active life with which nature is endowed. They have perfected society and morals, literature and art, the principles of philosophy. They have become the rulers of history, and it seems to be their mission to link together all parts of the world by the chains of civilization." [19]

At the other end of the racial scale are the Negroes, usually characterized as gay, thoughtless, unintelligent, and subject to violent passions. This race has not produced a single example of a civilized nation, and it is "the least civilized of all the races." [20] The American Indians are regarded as brave and warlike, but fond of cruelty, and having "little capacity for civilization." [21] Mongols are depicted as mild but "cunning and knavish, readily sacrificing their principles and feelings to considerations of gain." [22] Later in the century they are described as "mild and timid, and make few improvements in knowledge and arts, but are skillful artists especially in imitation." [23]

The concept of racial superiority leads to interesting and somewhat contradictory results when two races contend for the same land. The history of this contention in English America is presented as an illustration of "a well-established law of nature, that causes an inferior race to yield to a superior when one comes in contact with the other." [24] In the earlier books, contemplation of this inevitable process is recommended to inspire a pleasing melancholy: "What can be more melancholy than their [the American Indians'] history? By a law of nature they seem destined to a slow but sure extinction. Everywhere at the approach of the white man they fade away." [25] The manifest destiny of the

[19] G 1869 Warren-E, p. 92. The publishers note in the preface that Warren includes some of the results of the new study of comparative philology. See also G 1878 Steinwehr and Brinton, p. 13; G 1885 Houston, p. 128; G 1887 Redway, p. 20; G 1888 Redway, pp. 28–29, 94.

[20] G 1898 Redway and Hinman, p. 34; see also discussion of Negro below.

[21] G 1878 Swinton, p. 35.

[22] G 1826 Blake, p. 103; see also G 1784 Morse, p. 211.

[23] G 1866 Woodbridge, p. 353.

[24] H 1889 Chambers, p. 83; see also H 1900 Channing, p. vii.

[25] Excerpt from a speech by Justice Story in R 1830 Emerson, pp. 68–70; R 1831 Bailey, p. 129; R 1831 Harrod, pp. 301–303; R 1832 Cobb, pp. 72–74; R 1844 Goldsbury and Russell, pp. 320–322; R 1845 Swan, pp. 66–68; R 1852 Tower and Walker, pp. 227–229; R 1856 Osgood, pp. 229–231; R 1856 Sanders-4, pp. 144–146; see also section on Indian below.

superior race to conquer the inferior is an accepted axiom throughout the period, specifically and abundantly illustrated. Although they do not set it down as a law of nature, these authors clearly believe that a superior race is bound to degenerate if it does not maintain racial purity. As in most racist doctrines, the superiority of a race does not extend to its dilution; in any racial mixture the characteristics of the inferior race dominate. A 1900 Geography, noting that more than half of the population of Spanish America is made up of descendants of Spanish-Indian marriages, ascribes to this racial mixture the primary reason why Spanish America progressed less rapidly than English America: "These half breeds are an ignorant class, far inferior to the Spaniards themselves. . . ."[26] In a child's mind, such strictures against intermarriage might be outweighed by the union of Pocohontas and a white man, from which "some of the principal families in Virginia are descended." This marriage is mentioned with approval in most books. Perhaps she was exempt from the ordinary laws of nature as a heroine of American nationalism who had saved John Smith, himself the savior of the Virginia colony. Washington and other heroes of American nationalism also found natural laws at times suspended in their favor. It is particularly interesting that a Southern history of the late nineteenth century includes the story of this marriage, and a similar complimentary comment on the ancestry of the eminent families of Virginia.[27]

The child influenced by these books probably viewed any new acquaintance in the light of his race and its characteristics as memorized from his schoolbooks. As part of nature's law, progress is possible only with the conquest and subordination of inferior races; the child would question the wisdom of indiscriminate immigration to the United States; he would not expect the Negro to take an equal place in American civilization; he would expect race to be a determining factor in the development of the individual. Nor would he think the American melting pot

[26] G 1900 Tarr and McMurry-2, p. 100; see also G 1878 Swinton, p. 92.

[27] The quotation about the descendants of Pocohontas is from H 1893 Creery, 25. Something of the same sort is said in most books that consider the subject including the Southern histories: H 1889 Chambers, 115 and H 1898 Chambers, 83.

capable of amalgamating racial traits into a homogeneous whole.

In the ensuing sections specific attitudes toward American racial minorities—Indians, Jews—who came to be regarded during this century as a racial rather than a religious or cultural minority—and Negroes will be examined.

THE AMERICAN INDIAN

In nineteenth-century schoolbooks the American Indian occupies a unique position among American minorities. He is described as a savage, but American nationalism required that he have qualities superior to other savages because he was the original occupant of the American continent. Although classified as barbarian, he comes out well in the early books: "At a time when barbarous nations elsewhere had lost their primitive purity, we find the American Indian the only true child of nature,—the best specimen of man in his native simplicity."[28] In later books, when classification of men by race was emphasized rather than by degree of civilization, one finds the Indian race described as inferior only to the white: "In symmetry of form, the Americans rank next to the Caucasians."[29] On the other hand the Indian afforded the most serious barrier to American continental expansion. Unlike the natives of Mexico and Peru, the Northern Indians' semi-nomadic civilization did not encompass the skills and the potentialities for forced labor so useful to Europeans. Their one desirable possession in English eyes was the land, which the English settlers could acquire best by eviction rather than amalgamation. To possess the land without its native inhabitants became the ambition of the colonists. No serious attempt was made to incorporate the American Indian into the English civilization developing on these shores. Instead the settlers instituted a process of forcing the Indians to move to land considered undesirable at the time for European settlement. Because the frontier was a dynamic one the whites' definition of "un-

[28] R 1852 Town, p. 274; see also G 1818 Morse, p. 56; G 1845 Woodbridge, p. 165.

[29] G 1870 Cornell-P, p. 81.

desirable" was fluid; warfare was local but constant during most of the nineteenth century. In the 1830's, by a series of treaties over which the Indian had little control, the eastern Indians were removed beyond the Mississippi. Not until the Dawes Act of 1887 did the Federal government seriously undertake to provide for the future of the Indian as a part of American civilization.

Throughout the century the image of the Indian in schoolbooks is that of the "noble savage." His inherent nobility is detailed as eloquent, extraordinarily brave, persevering, and able to withstand the most excruciating tortures without flinching. Typical descriptions of the Indians of North America are the following: "They are quick of apprehension, and not wanting in genius. At times they were friendly, and even courteous. In council, they were distinguished for gravity and eloquence; in war, for bravery and address. They were taciturn and unsocial, except when roused by some strong excitement. When determined upon revenge, no danger would deter them, neither absence nor time could cool them"[30] "These savages, though ignorant, cruel and treacherous, were remarkable for a peculiar dignity and courtesy of manner and were highly poetic in their language and perceptions."[31] The individual Indian chief is glorified as a Romantic figure. He appears not only as a personification of the noble savage, but as a great patriotic hero. Phillip, "was a patriot, attached to his native soil; a prince true to his subjects, and indignant of their wrongs; a soldier, daring in battle, firm in adversity, patient of fatigue, of hunger, of every variety of bodily suffering, and ready to perish in the cause he espoused."[32] Tecumseh is described in a piece from the *New York Statesman*:

> He fought in defence of his kindred and king,
> With a spirit most loving and loyal,
> And long shall the Indian warriors sing
> The deeds of Tecumseh, the royal.[33]

[30] H 1867 Goodrich, p. 21.

[31] G 1872 Hall, p. 34.

[32] Washington Irving, quoted in the following: R 1830 Emerson, pp. 183–184; R 1836 Cobb-N.A., pp. 130–131; see also G 1824 Woodbridge and Willard, p. 206; G 1831 Blake, p. 19; G 1833 Clute, p. 56; R 1834 Emerson, pp. 51–53; H 1869 Quackenbos, pp. 56–59; H 1873 Anderson-R, pp. 79–81.

[33] R 1827 Pierpont, p. 39.

Two Readers use a particularly interesting poem by Fitz-Greene Halleck containing these lines:

> We, the democratic,
> Outrival Europe; even in our kings.[34]

Under Romantic influence American nationalism required that the native Americans be assigned traits superior not only to those of other savage groups, but in some cases to those of more complex societies. Their very opposition to white expansion is described in heroic terms. Although it hindered the westward movement, it did so in the service of a virtue much admired in the schoolbooks—patriotism.

On the other hand the Indians who hampered the westward movement were as savage as they were noble. Without question the former portrayal is more prominent in these books than the latter. Inherent cruelty is their major trait; they are a "savage foe, whose delight was cruelty."[35] They "listened to the cries of their victims with pleasure,"[36] while they exhibited their "diabolical thirst of blood"[37] and fulfilled their "lust of murderous deeds."[38] Practice sentences in the Spellers abound with such phrases as: "a gory scalp,"[39] "Indians are sometimes very cruel."[40] Every Reader includes at least one detailed account of gory Indian warfare. Indians are frequently identified as merciless savages "whose only occupation was shedding the blood of their fellowman."[41] One 1888 Speller would allow citizenship to Negroes more easily than to Indians.[42] The same book notes, "It was a favorite amusement among the Indians of New York to burn the soles of the feet of the faithful missionaries, whose sole object was to save their souls."[43] Another Reader describes the American forest at the time of the American Revolution: "where wild beasts and scarcely less savage Indians roamed in their freedom."[44]

In the Histories and Geographies the cruelty of Indian warfare is abundantly illustrated; indeed the entire colonial period is

[34] R 1830 Hughs, p. 48; R 1843 Griswold, pp. 27–30.
[35] G 1831 Blake, p. 19. [36] R 1804 Webster, p. 49.
[37] R 1815 R. Adams, p. 59; R 1828 Pierpont-I, p. 78.
[38] R 1815 Dickinson, p. 178. [39] S 1863 Willson, p. 39.
[40] S 1851 Northend, p. 15. [41] R 1828 Putnam, p. 76.
[42] S 1888 Shoup, p. 57. [43] *Ibid.*, p. 110.
[44] R 1895 Hazen, p. 97.

treated largely as a detailed chronicle of the evil deeds of the Indians. It is not so much the proliferation of statements that the Indians were cruel which would appeal to the imagination of the child reading these books as the profuse illustrations of their cruelty in highly dramatic tales of Indian warfare. No child familiar with any of these books would be unfamiliar with the details of the major Indian massacres. Only two books point out that Indian love of bloody warfare can be matched by the same quality in European countries.[45] Like all enemies of the American people, the Indians are accused of cruel treatment of their prisoners of war. But Indian mistreatment is described in more colorful detail and more often than is that of other enemies and other wars. Their treatment of captive women, children, and old people is always graphically portrayed: they "cast an infirm old man into the flames, here, they dashed against the trees children snatched away from the breasts of their dying mothers."[46] Many books present pictures showing an Indian about to tomahawk a woman with a child in her arms.[47] It is safe to say that Indian cruelty is more profusely and minutely described than the cruelty assigned to other nations at war with the United States.

Injustices of the whites toward the Indians are sometimes noted, but in the child's mind the savagery of the Indians would surely justify any hypocrisy or cruelty on the part of the whites. In battles between the two, success is always attributed to the better inherent qualities of the whites rather than to superior equipment or any other material advantage. In describing Connecticut's troubles with the Pequods, the Connecticut settlers "were compelled to wage a fierce war during which they endured terrible hardships; but Indian cunning and ferocity were no match for European courage and skill, and the tribe was destroyed."[48] In actuality that war was concluded when the whites burned the tents of the Pequods, destroying men, women, and children. The terms "cunning" and "ferocity" could just as easily apply in this case to the whites, and "courage and skill" to the Indians. Certainly no massacre by Indians was more cruel than

[45] H 1873 Anderson-R, p. 40; H 1876 Doyle, pp. 19–20.
[46] R 1809 Picket, p. 181.
[47] G 1848 Mitchell, p. 51.
[48] H 1874 Anderson, p. 55; see also H 1879? Campbell, p. 38.

7. Pictures of Indian warfare are used to illustrate Indian cruelty. This example is from *An Easy Introduction to the Study of Geography* by S. Augustus Mitchell, 1848. Almost every Geography and History as well as most Readers contain such pictures.

this, yet it is passed over as a necessary measure to white settlement, whereas the Indian massacre of whites at Schenectady offered "the most shocking barbarities."[49] In another account of the Pequod massacre a boy exclaims: "But, O Mother, how they must have felt when they thought of the Indian mothers and little children that had been burned to death!" The mother reassures her son: "Yes; but their own mothers and children would have been killed, perhaps, if the Pequods hadn't been destroyed."[50] Against such an enemy any method of defense is permissible.

The mistreatment of Indians by white men is usually presented as something that happened in a remote past, when eastern America was still part of the British Empire rather than an independent nation. The burden of guilt toward the Indians falls not so much on the ancestors of present Americans as on a foreign nation. Penn's fair and pacific treatment of the Indians is usually contrasted to the unfeeling policy of Charles II rather than to the behavior of the other colonists.[51] Thus the king of England becomes the scapegoat for colonial cruelty to the Indians; he oppressed the Indians as well as his white subjects.

But the English settlement seems humane by contrast with the Black Legend of the Spanish conquest: "The atrocities exhibited by the Spaniards contrast with the settlement of the United States."[52] Many Readers contain a dialogue between Penn and Cortez, wherein each defends his Indian policy, with Penn the obvious hero and Cortez the villain.[53] The differences between the two men indicate how far Spanish cruelty exceeded the English. With the exception of two Catholic textbooks used in parochial schools, all of the schoolbooks depict the Spanish conquest in much the same way: "Although the conquerors of Mexico and Peru displayed great courage and ability, these qualities were

[49] H 1874 Anderson, p. 83. [50] H 1889 Monroe, p. 128.

[51] R 1828 Greenwood and Emerson, pp. 82–84; R 1841 Merriam, pp. 154–156; R 1843 Olney, pp. 30–32; R 1845 Goldsbury and Russell, pp. 200–202; R 1846 Swan-G, pp. 88–91; R 1849 Leavitt, pp. 117–119; R 1851 ASDUK, pp. 98–101; R 1856 Sanders-4, pp. 236–238; R 1866 McGuffey-5, pp. 225–227.

[52] R 1819 Strong, p. 46; see also G 1831 Blake, p. 15; R 1831 Hall, pp. 46, 63; G 1831 S. Worcester, p. 32; R 1860 McGuffey, p. 148; H 1866 Lossing, p. 22; H 1867 Goodrich, p. 12.

[53] R 1821 Bingham, pp. 52–55; R 1828 New York, p. 202; R 1849 Leavitt, pp. 252–255; R 1851 ASDUK, pp. 112–116.

offset by the meanest deception, the basest treachery, and the most unrelenting cruelty."[54] "The treatment of the Indians by the Spaniards forms one of the most terrible records in connection with the history of the New World. No language can do justice to the cruelty that the poor, and at first confiding natives suffered at their hands."[55] They point to the decimation of the Indian population under Spanish rule. Only one Catholic Geography observes: "The extermination of the natives was not, at any time, the policy of the conquerors of Mexico; and the native race still remain to testify by their overwhelming numbers to the general humanity of their Spanish invaders."[56] But in all non-Catholic books the Black Legend holds sway.

Although the methods used to acquire Indian lands are sometimes questioned, there is no dissent from the doctrine of the manifest destiny of the Americans to take land from the Indians. This destiny was strikingly evidenced to the first English colonists when God sent a plague to cut down the ranks of the Indians at Plymouth. "The hand of Providence is noticeable in these surprising instances of mortality among the Indians to make room for the English. Comparatively few have perished by war. They waste and moulder away; they in a manner unaccountable disappear."[57]

On the whole the decline of the Indian population remains unaccountable in the schoolbooks, but justifications for usurping their lands are frequently given. In a few instances the triumphant westward spread of Christianity sufficiently justifies the conquest of the West and thus of the Indian.[58] The most common justification, however, springs from the tremendous pride of the Americans in their own material progress. Every book contains paeans of praise to the American people for their continuing victory over the wilderness and its native inhabitants:

> Time quicken thy pace, and present a bright scene,
> In regions where none but rude men have yet been,
> Let savages cease their dark wilds to explore,
> Or roam through their desarts [*sic*]—now desarts no more.[59]

[54] H 1867 Goodrich, p. 12.
[55] H 1874 Scott, p. 29.
[56] G 1878 Catholic, p. 56.

It is always implied that this is a conquest of the wilderness, rather than a conquest of the Indian; the latter is innocent if unfortunate. "God, in his wise providence, has permitted the white man to take the Indian's land away from him. The Indian would not cut down the trees and raise grain, except here and there a little patch; but the white man, as the Bible says, has made 'the wilderness to blossom as the rose.'"[60] By the higher law of God the whites have legal and ethical right to the land: "We then ask, can the God of wisdom and nature have created that vast country in vain? Was it for nothing that he blessed it with a fertility so astonishing?"[61] And again: "It has been adopted as a principle of natural law, that Europeans had a right to take and occupy a portion of the American continent, since it was not all needed by the natives, who were comparatively few in number."[62] The superior use of the land apparently justifies its usurpation. To maintain the natives' right to the land, in the face of a superior nation, would hinder progress and contravene the law of nature's God. The expansion of North America is usually differentiated from that of any other country. It is expansion, not conquest, and it is justified by ". . . the mighty agents which were working out our greatness, our time, industry and the arts. Our augmentation is by growth, not acquisition; by internal development, not by external accession."[63] To extend the United States is praiseworthy, a necessary element in progress.

Exceptions to this attitude are rare. In a dialogue between a white and an Indian in an 1807 Reader the latter takes the position that the claim to ownership of land because of superior techniques of cultivation and need is a doctrine dangerous to the

---

[57] G 1791 Morse, p. 72; see also R 1831 Hall, p. 139; R 1831 Lowe-Second, p. 8; H 1852 E. Willard, p. 19.

[58] R 1833 Leavitt, p. 94.

[59] G 1800 Davidson, p. 56; see also R 1826 American-S, p. 247; G 1840 Olney, p. 149; S 1847 ASDUK, p. 132; G 1848 Mitchell, p. 49; H 1872 Lossing, p. 4; G 1897 Redway, pp. 44–45.

[60] H 1866 Lossing, p. 10; see also H 1881 and 1889? Steele, pp. 14–15.

[61] R 1811 Hubbard, p. 88; see also H 1870 Lossing, p. 9.

[62] R 1823 Blake, p. 218; see also R 1831 Progressive, pp. 73–74; R 1836 Cobb-N.A., pp. 441–442.

[63] Webster's speech on the Greek Revolution, 1823, quoted in R 1828 Hopkins, p. 189.

whites: it would support the claim of the poor to the land of the rich and severely limit the concept of private property.[64] But these are lonely voices. The doctrine of the destiny of the whites to possess America is axiomatic to the authors of schoolbooks. It requires no logical examination.

And what of the Indians in this process? Their civilization is depicted as inimical to progress and unlikely to change in the future. Morse in 1784 offers a most depressing view of their possibilities for usefulness in the culture of English America: "The characteristics of the Californians as well as of all other Indians, are stupidity and insensibility; want of knowledge and reflection; an excessive sloth and abhorrence of all labor and fatigue; an excessive love of pleasure and amusement of every kind however trifling or brutal; pusillanimity; and, in fine, a most wretched want of everything that constitutes the real man, and renders him rational, inventive, tractable, and useful to himself and society."[65] Eloquent, brave, and generous they may be, but having rejected the European idea of daily labor to accumulate property, they cannot be useful to American civilization.

The various programs of the government of the United States to help the Indians are generally applauded, although vaguely described. The removal of the Indians "to a fine country west of the Mississippi"[66] under Jackson is regarded as a humanitarian step. Few books express any sense of injustice about this forced migration: ". . . many of them [the Cherokees] were quite as civilized as their neighbors of the white race. They were very reluctant to leave their homes."[67] But the same book describes Indians in general as "akin to all that is rude, savage and unreclaimable . . ."[68] Two others quote from an oration by Sprague, that Providence has doomed them to perish, but we should take no step to hasten the process artificially.[69] Usually the opposition of the Indians to being removed to reservations provided by the government is seen as their refusal of progress.

[64] R 1807 Bingham-C, p. 270; see also R 1830 Emerson, pp. 174–176.

[65] G 1784 Morse, p. 107.

[66] H 1866 Lossing, p. 205.

[67] H 1872 Venable, p. 169.

[68] *Ibid.*, p. 17.

[69] R 1832 Edwards, pp. 166–170; R 1852 Town, pp. 326–328; see also R 1845 Goldsbury and Russell, pp. 160–162; R 1845 Swan, pp. 261–264; R 1849 Leavitt, pp. 296–301.

In 1868 Willard notes certain plans to introduce Indians to American culture by exposing them to mills, schools, etc.: "A grand impediment to the success of these experiments is the laziness of the men, and their contempt of labor."[70] A few books express the hope that "In the future we shall have working and thinking Indians . . . ,"[71] but this is not a common attitude. The inherent characteristics assigned to the Indians prevent them from ever becoming part of American civilization. Even practice sentences in the Spellers set the Indian apart from civilization: "He exercised his powers to humanize the nature of the Indian."[72] "It is almost impossible to civilize the American Indians."[73] It is generally assumed that these traits, hostile to civilization and even to humanity, are inherent in the Indian and not environmentally conditioned, as one can see in the tale of a white boy who grew up with the Indians, and "Although he had acquired many characteristics of the Indians, still he had some peculiarities which marked him of different origin."[74] These are delineated as follows: he neither smoked nor drank, and instead of pursuing trifles he bought things useful to himself. Thus America, proud of its ability to increase wealth and accumulate property, taught its children that since the Indian is incapable of these pursuits he is a force hostile to progress, and is best quarantined.

The extinction of the Indian is believed to be inevitable by mysterious decrees of God and nature: "The religion of nature, the light of revelation, and the pages of history, are combined in the proof, that God has ordered that nations shall become extinct, and that others shall take their places."[75] From the 1820's on every Reader contains at least one poem or essay with a title such as "Melancholy Decay of the Indians," or "Melancholy Fate of the Indians." One popular selection, from a speech by Justice Story, ascribes the gradual decline of the Indians to "a law of

[70] H 1868 Willard, p. 405; see also G 1817 Cummings, p. 7; R 1824 Lowe, p. 51; R 1825 Torrey, pp. 108–109; H 1879 Quackenbos, p. 19; G 1898 Carpenter, p. 293; R 1900 Taylor, p. 113; S 1900 Bowen, p. 90; G 1900 Tarr and McMurry-2, p. 103.

[71] H 1890 Morris, p. 234; see also G 1900 Tarbell, p. 65.

[72] S 1866 Swan, p. 68.

[73] S 1880 Webster, p. 133.

[74] R 1831 Lowe-Second, pp. 204–207.

[75] R 1813 Richardson, p. 122; see also G 1865 Mitchell, pp. 31, 91.

nature."[76] Any attempt to explain this mysterious law of nature is rare. A Speller of 1900 asserts, in the language of Parkman, "The Indian will not learn the arts of civilization, and he and his forest must perish together."[77] Several later authors, well versed in late nineteenth-century racial theories, ascribe Indian decline to racial inferiority: "With the advance of the white man, the red race is rapidly passing away in accordance with a well-established law of nature, that causes an inferior race to yield to a superior when one comes in contact with the other."[78] Now and then "'the baneful fire-water' which was the gift of civilization" is the specific agent blamed for the downfall of the Indians.[79] Another book pictures the white man as the savior of the Indian population, already in decline from natural attrition before the coming of the white man: "War, famine, and pestilence destroyed so many Indians every year, that we may doubt whether many would now be living but for the interference of the whites, whose cruelties and frauds—though they can never be remembered without shame—were mercy compared with the tortures which the barbarians inflicted on each other. Indians are more numerous now within the limits of the United States than they are supposed to have been when Englishmen first landed on our coasts. . . ."[80] The usual implication, however, is that a law of nature outside the realm of human effectiveness has doomed the Indian. It is a law operative only at the moment when two different civilizations or races meet. One cannot change it, not even ameliorate its operation, but one must "drop a tear" for the Indian.[81] "Very soon not one will be living. How sad to think of a whole nation gone forever!"[82] The reader is asked to "pay due tribute to their unhappy fate, as a people."[83] The

[76] Quoted in the following: R 1830 Emerson, pp. 68–70; R 1831 Bailey, p. 129; R 1831 Harrod, pp. 301–303; R 1832 Cobb, pp. 72–74; R 1844 Goldsbury and Russell, pp. 320–322; R 1845 Swan, pp. 66–68; R 1852 Tower and Walker, pp. 227–229; R 1856 Osgood, pp. 229, 231; R 1856 Sanders-4, pp. 144–146; R 1872 Osgood-5, p. 231; R 1873 Progressive, pp. 187–190.

[77] S 1900 Bowen, p. 90; see also H 1881 Steele, p. 15.

[78] H 1889 Chambers, pp. 82 (a Southern book); see also H 1874 Scott, p. 82.

[79] R 1898 Black, p. 54.

[80] H 1881 Thalheimer, p. 21.

[81] R 1831 S. Willard, p. 90; R 1832 Progressive, p. 107.

[82] H 1866 Lossing, p. 13.

[83] R 1867? Parker and Watson-4, pp. 330–332; R 1884 Campbell-5, p. 176.

schoolbooks abound with emotional invitations for the reader to contemplate with pleasing sadness the mysterious decline of the Indians. There are Romantic descriptions of an Indian sadly meditating at the graves of his forefathers, or dying forlornly, the last of his tribe. God has decreed the extinction of the Indian in favor of the growth of the United States. One cannot oppose such a decree; one can only meditate and weep over its inevitability just as one might contemplate architectural ruins as monuments for melancholy.

The child influenced by these books would be familiar with the Indian as the cruel enemy of his ancestors and contemporaries, in graphically detailed accounts of warfare. He would see the Indian as an obstacle to the progress of America and therefore of the world. He would be unlikely to question the justice of white behavior to the Indian, nor would he see in the decline of the Indian the moral responsibility of the white man. Attempts to ameliorate the sad condition of the Indians were to him not efforts at justice but humanitarian generosity of the whites, freely offered. The attitudes his schoolbooks encouraged are well summarized in an 1813 Reader: "His agonies at first seem to demand a tear from the eyes of humanity: but when we reflect; that the extinction of his race, and the progress of the arts which give rise to his distressing apprehensions, are for the increase of mankind, and for the promotion of the world's glory and happiness, that five hundred rational animals may enjoy life in plenty and comfort, where only one savage drags out a hungry existence, we shall be pleased with the perspective futurity."[84]

THE JEW

Throughout the century in the schoolbooks the Jews are regarded as a distinct if scattered people: "Notwithstanding the dispersion of the Jews amongst other nations, and the persecutions which have everywhere followed them, they have, to a remarkable degree, preserved their national character and religion."[85] They are a nationality "possessing no country of

[84] R 1813 Richardson, p. 123.
[85] R 1821 Bingham, p. 27, added to 1811 edition.

their own."[86] During most of the century their culture is clearly and unequivocally based on religion, but from the 1870's on they become the Semitic branch of the Caucasian race.[87] On the whole the schoolbooks depict Jewish characteristics in the same unflattering terms throughout the century, but the shift in emphasis from anti-Judaism to anti-Semitism is a significant one. A religious basis for discrimination offers the possibility for change by conversion, and eventual amalgamation into the national culture. A racial difference, by its very nature, is immutable. The Jew whose culture is assumed to come from inherited group characteristics cannot be an ingredient in the melting pot. This change mirrors an increased secularization in the schoolbooks and the culture from which they come, but it is also consonant with the spread of racial doctrine in general and anti-Semitism in particular in the late nineteenth century.

In the Geographies the Jews appear mainly as an ancient religious sect. When compared to polytheism, the Hebrew religion is approved, because it "inculcates the greatest purity of mind and of manners."[88] But when compared to Christianity it is often spoken of with contempt as "nothing but the figure of the religion, that Christ was to establish in after ages."[89] Casual references to the Jews often denigrate their religion, as in this practice sentence from Webster's Speller: "The jews [*sic*] burned sacrifices upon an altar of stone."[90] In a few books they are designated the Chosen People of God, but "when they became disobedient and wicked, He abandoned them and they have been subject to reproach and derision for nearly 1800 years."[91] In the connotation of these books, where the rewards for virtue are sure, the reader would be likely to ascribe their current difficulties to continued wickedness. In the book quoted above this is spelled out in the next sentence: "And it has always been the case that wicked people soon become unhappy, while the virtuous and good usually live in peace and happiness."[92] That Christ was a

[86] G 1866 Woodbridge, p. 313.

[87] G 1870 Cornell-P, p. 76; see also G 1870 Cornell-G, p. 97; G 1887 Quackenbos, p. 144; G 1887 Redway, p. 20.

[88] R 1813 Richardson, pp. 98–101.

[89] G 1806 Cottineau-I, p. 6.

[90] S 1842 Webster, p. 150, same in 1829 version.

[91] G 1831 Blake, p. 29. [92] *Ibid.*

Jew is very rarely mentioned, but that the Jews put him to death is usually noted. For their rejection of Christ, according to the prophecy of Scripture, they have been doomed to wander the earth. One early Reader uses the dispersion of the Jews as incontrovertible evidence for the truth of all scriptural predictions.[93]

The character assigned to this "distinct people" is usually an unpleasant one. Very rarely is a Jew favorably mentioned. The steady courage of Rebecca in *Ivanhoe* appears in one advanced Reader,[94] and in another the chariot race from *Ben Hur*, with the hero clearly identified as a Jew.[95] Several Readers include stories illustrating the patient resignation of the Jews to the will of God. McGuffey, who includes a poem of this sort, also cites a piece by Rousseau: "The Jewish authors were incapable of the diction and strangers to the morality, contained in the gospel."[96] As one would expect, the Jews are universally associated with trade, usually as crafty peddlers whose greed for money determines their business methods. This element in Jewish character is not offered to the reader as a piece of new information, but as a point of reference axiomatically accepted in the culture. The terms "old-clothes man" and "Jew" are used interchangeably in one story; the latter term is introduced midway in the story, showing that the reader would know that such a peddler could only be a Jew.[97] Such sentences as the following are typical: in describing the Greeks as untrustworthy and sly one author adds: "[They] are more barefaced in their impositions than even the Jews."[98] Another: "The woman was shrewd enough to know that a Jew would not give five shillings for anything unless it was worth a good deal more."[99] One story which shows a Jew practicing the virtues that his Christian opponent preaches, nevertheless shows the Jew's fondness for money to a ludicrous degree: he heard the word "expense" when the word "suspense" had actually been uttered.[100] The most extreme story of this variety concerns a

[93] R 1797 Alexander, p. 79.
[94] R 1898 Black, pp. 167–188.
[95] R 1896 Holmes and Hill, pp. 371–379.
[96] R 1866 McGuffey-5, pp. 280–282.
[97] R 1828 Pierpont-I, p. 59.
[98] R 1831 Lowe-Second, p. 72.
[99] G 1837 Book of Commerce, p. 66; see also R 1806 Staniford, p. 70.
[100] R 1811 Chandler, p. 119.

Jewish mother whose little boy had just been killed by falling out of a theater balcony; immediately she approached the manager of the theater:

> "Sher, I'm de moder of de poor Chew lad,
> Dat meet mishforten here so bad;
> Sher, I muss haf de shilling back, you know,
> As Moses haf not see de show." [101]

Extracts from Shakespeare's *The Merchant of Venice* frequently appear, with ambiguous effect. Many authors use Antonio's speech:

> I pray you, think, you question with a Jew.
> You may as well go stand upon the beach,
> And bid the main flood bate its usual height;
> You may as well plead pity with the wolf,
> When you behold the ewe bleat for the lamb,
> As try to melt his Jewish heart to kindness.

And one popular author prefaces this with a note: "It would convey a false moral, if it should be made to cast any reproach on a Jew, as such; for a Jew may be a good member of society; and like every other man, ought to be judged according to his acts, and not according to any prejudice which current error or bigotry has established." [102] One early Reader uses a part of the dialogue between Shylock and Tubal which nowhere identifies Shylock as a Jew. A footnote explains that Antonio was a merchant hated by Shylock.[103] But an equal number of authors who use Antonio's speech, quoted above, include Shylock's speech beginning:

> Hath not a Jew eyes?
> Hath not a Jew hands, organs, dimensions, senses? . . .

Obviously Shakespeare is not used in these cases to serve prejudice; these speeches are included in the Readers for purposes of declamation.

The initiative ascribed to the Jews in accumulating property should not exclude them from the American melting pot; indeed

[101] R 1840 Snow, pp. 216–217. This appeared in only one book.
[102] R 1839 S. Goodrich, p. 143.
[103] R 1801 Heaton-C, pp. 151–152.

such ambitions are quite consonant with the American culture depicted in these books. Getting ahead in a material sense is inculcated into every American boy. But Jewish aspirations appear with sinister overtones. All of the vices normally ascribed to the city slicker in a rural culture are attached to the Jews. They are sly, crafty, and prone to cheat in money matters. Unlike the Christians, they are singularly ungenerous: "He is as charitable as a Christian, Sir, and as rich as a Jew."[104] "The selfish Jew, in his splendor, would not give a shekel to the starving shepherd."[105] Furthermore the successful Jew is alleged to be in command of vast power. The self-made man who appears in innumerable illustrations in these books has acquired riches as a reward for the practice of virtue; this is also the case in some descriptions of the Rothschilds. But in most books, Jewish wealth is the product of greed and results in inordinate power selfishly used. Many of the most popular Geographies point out the great power of the Jews in many countries of the western world, as: "Almost all of the trade of the country [Poland] is in their hands."[106] One Geography at the end of the century suggests that the teacher should discuss the brilliance of the Jews and their contributions to intellectual progress, but at the same time she should indicate that it is "a well-authenticated fact that the European press as well as European finance are to a great extent in their power."[107] A piece by Disraeli included in an 1894 Reader asserts that the Jewish contribution to civilization is great; they have been favored by nature if not by men. But again a sinister note is injected by the observation that Jews monopolize the professional class in Germany and everywhere have great power "behind the throne."[108] The very success of the Jews, their very contributions to progress are put in terms of selfish power. Although this is far from the Jewish plot to control the world described in the spurious *Protocols of Zion*, the generation first exposed to the *Protocols* would be well disposed to an uncritical acceptance of this document and its implications.

[104] R 1813 I. Cooke, p. 279.

[105] S. 1857 Parker and Watson, p. 66.

[106] G 1824 J. Worcester, p. 106; see also G 1843 Mitchell, p. 227; G 1881 Maury, p. 112.

[107] G 1891 Morton, p. xiv.

[108] R 1894 Columbian, pp. 127–130.

In the first part of the century the characteristics assigned to the Jews as a distinct part of the population are exactly those assigned to them as a Semitic race at the end of the century. But by the end of the century these characteristics have become racial and therefore immutable. A story in an 1811 Reader depicts a Christian accusing a Jew of raising a foundling for financial speculation rather than as a humanitarian enterprise. The Jew responds: "Can you trow nothing in my face but my *religion*? . . . if Christians *profess* forgiveness of injuries, Jews can sometimes practice it."[109] In the first part of the century the Jew is always set off against the Christian; in the latter part of the century he is identified as a member of the Semitic branch of the white race. Sometimes in the earlier period, harsh Christian treatment of the Jews is used as the occasion for a lesson in Christian toleration. One Geography blames such persecution for creating the Jewish character:

It belongs to this history to state, that the Jews who followed commerce wherever it went, were everywhere dreadfully oppressed, robbed and murdered. Some of the English kings have been infamously eminent in these unjust proceedings. Such oppression had its usual effect, in making the objects of its cunning, servile, extortionate in their own defense, and to avenge the injuries they sustained.[110]

A popular Geography of 1866 takes the onus of this intolerance from the Protestants by observing that in Roman Catholic and Mohammedan countries "They are regarded with peculiar detestation, and generally suffer much from oppression and persecution.[111] A more typical precept appears in one of the Samuel Goodrich Readers: the Christian should treat the Jew kindly; he "like every other man, ought to be judged according to his acts, and not according to any prejudice which current error or bigotry has established."[112]

In the first part of the century a child might learn from these schoolbooks to be kind to Jews, but he would also learn to recognize them as a distinct and unpleasant religious and cultural

[109] R 1811 Chandler, pp. 122–123.

[110] G 1837 Book of Commerce, p. 165. This statement also incidentally added another charge against the English kings.

[111] G 1866 Woodbridge, p. 313.

[112] R 1839 S. Goodrich, p. 143.

group to be tolerated rather than accepted. By the end of the century, when Jews were migrating to America in unprecedented numbers, the schoolbooks treat them as a race whose characteristics are inherent and immutable. Unlike other alien races, they are not regarded as inferior except in morals. The alleged greed of the Jew, combined with his ambition and intelligence, might well make him an object of fear to the child. Industry and initiative in creating and collecting this world's goods should have assured Jewish amalgamation into the American population, since these were qualities of the American character much admired in nineteenth-century schoolbooks. But Jewish success was viewed as Jewish subversion, and the child who imbibed values from his schoolbooks was most likely to regard the Jew as an indigestible addition to the American melting pot.

THE NEGRO

From his description in all Geography books, the African Negro is clearly regarded as the most degraded of the races. Southerners, who by 1830 justified slavery on the grounds that the Negro was incapable of improvement, could find ample evidence for their attitudes in the schoolbooks used at the time in both North and South.[113] The generation that decreed the abolition of slavery and the disposition of the freedman after the Civil War was educated in the belief that "They [Negroes] are a brutish people, having little more of humanity but the form";[114] or, "Their mental powers, in general, participate in the imbecility of their bodies";[115] or, "Africa has justly been called the country of monsters. . . . Even man, in this quarter of the world exists in a state of lowest barbarism."[116] At best Africa is distinguished as the land where "Human nature is nowhere exhibited in a more rude and disgusting attire than in this portion of the globe."[117] Negroes are described not as destitute of education but as "destitute

[113] As mentioned above, most authors of nineteenth-century schoolbooks were from New England. Confederate books will be treated separately at the end of the chapter.

[114] G 1789 Elements, p. 30.

[115] R 1815 American, p. 139.

[116] G 1817 Cummings, p. 131; G 1830 Bazeley, p. 226.

[117] G 1816 Rudd, p. 91.

of intelligence."[118] In one story a schoolboy is indignant at being mistaken for a Negro: "Why, man, it would set our blood a boiling in December, to be mistaken for one of your West India negroes."[119] His indignation arises at being mistaken not for a slave, but for a Negro. Throughout the century a direct correlation is assumed between darkness of color and weakness of intellect. In several books, whimsical tales of the origin of man, in addition to that of Washington Irving, show God in the creative process: He first made the black man, realized He had done badly, and then created successively lighter races, improving as He went along. To the white man He gave a box of books and papers, to the black a box of tools so that he could "work for the white and red man, which he has continued to do."[120] In another, God gave the whites clothing, guns, and gunpowder, but to the Negro only cattle, rain-making, and inferior hearts.[121] The only positive characteristics assigned to them are gaiety and, in a few books published after the Civil War, loyalty.

Slavery as an institution is condemned as a moral wrong in a majority of books, although there are some which mention it without value judgments.[122] In books published before the Civil War most of the antislavery agitation is aimed not against slavery itself but against the international slave trade. Almost all of the Histories and Geographies and many of the Readers condemn the practice bitterly. Casual references frequently employ the adjectives "shameful," "unmerciful," or "abominable," particularly when describing the trade as one in which Christian nations engage. After 1807 agitation against the slave trade was no longer a demand for reform, since in that year the international slave trade was abolished for the United States. Hence the fulminations against it in American schoolbooks are essentially criticisms of other countries. Many indicate that the trade was

[118] G 1851 Smith-I, p. 157.

[119] R 1834 Angell, p. 47.

[120] R 1898 Williams G-1, p. 117.

[121] "Altered from Livingston," R 1868 Parker and Watson, p. 182.

[122] S 1822? New York, p. 73; G 1832 Olney, p. 139; G 1837 Village, p. 44; S 1838 Marshall, p. 68; G 1851 Smith-G, pp. 101–102; R 1854 Kay-3, p. 119; R 1855 Burleigh, pp. 80–82; G 1865 Mitchell, pp. 85–87. Perhaps these authors were particularly interested in selling in the South. Burleigh's Reader, according to the advertisements in the book, was used in several counties in Virginia.

foisted on English America by the Dutch before the achievement of independence, and fastened firmly by the English.[123] Throughout the century the slave trade is considered a blot on Christianity and on civilized society. By 1832 the schoolbooks acknowledge that only France, Spain, and Portugal are still slave traders, but the fulminations are just as strong.[124] The odium of the original enslavement is usually passed on to the Africans themselves by the observation that Africans enslaved each other before the Christians arrived.[125]

In pre-Civil War schoolbooks whether the slave was treated well or ill was a matter of discussion, with some difference of opinion. There are several tales of slaves who defend their masters in time of peril in return for the kind treatment they have enjoyed in the past. At times contentment with his lot is ascribed to the well-treated slave because "Many of the negroes, at the *present* day, work as easy, and live as comfortably, as any class of *labouring* people in the world."[126] It is interesting to observe that these scattered examples of good treatment are all from the period shortly before the Civil War, when the question of slavery was most strongly agitated in the society. Apparently the question was approached in an increasingly conciliatory manner as it became a more hotly contested issue. One author illustrates this caution when he says: "For the honour of humanity, I trust that the stories we hear of the cruel treatment of slaves, are *exaggerated*; but the *slave trade* is clearly founded on injustice and oppression."[127] The slave trade as a settled issue may be implacably opposed, but the institution of slavery must be approached delicately.

In books published before 1815 the condition of the slave is described as a thoroughly miserable one. In 1784 Morse gives an

[123] R 1813 Richardson, p. 28; H 1833 C. Goodrich, p. 358; G 1853 S. Goodrich, p. 71; H 1867 Goodrich, p. 69; H 1868 Willard, p. 47. In one instance the blame is put on the Spanish; see G 1900 Tarr and McMurry-2, p. 104.

[124] R 1832 Edwards, pp. 135–138.

[125] G 1800 Smith, p. 116; G 1803 Hubbard, pp. 209–210; G 1811 Workman, p. 174; G 1817 Cummings, pp. 131–132; G 1818 Mann, p. 341; G 1837 Village, p. 114; G 1848 Mitchell, p. 135; G 1897 Redway, p. 129.

[126] R 1833 Leavitt, p. 109; see also G 1835 Huntington, p. 37; G 1853 S. Goodrich, p. 68; S 1853 Vaughan-II, p. 141.

[127] R 1833 Leavitt, p. 108.

account of the punishment accorded a Negro slave for murdering an overseer: he was hung in a cage in a tree to die of starvation and exposure.[128] There are many tales of Negroes who committed suicide when faced with a life of slavery. Several of these early books include protests by slaves themselves against slavery. One includes a letter from a Negro to Lawrence Sterne pleading with him to use his pen against West Indian slavery.[129] Another presents a dialogue between a master and his captured runaway slave: the master reproaches the slave for his attempt to escape in spite of the kind treatment he has always received; the slave responds by saying that no kindness can compensate for the fact of being a slave.[130] In another case, a master and his slave are both captured and enslaved by Barbary pirates, and the slave is allowed to express his true feelings about his former master. The Negro wishes his master dead for the beatings he had received from his master in the past.[131] Thus in the early books slavery is regarded not only as an evil in itself, but as one that brings other evils in its train. The slave appears not as one who passively accepts his lot, but rather as a man in revolt to the point of his own destruction. Post-Civil War schoolbooks are not concerned with how the slave was treated. The emancipation of the slaves is accepted as an accomplished reform, and slavery is assumed to be inherently evil even by a Southern author.[132] Probably the discussion of treatment of the Negro under slavery was eliminated as a conciliatory gesture toward the defeated South.

In those books published up to the 1830's and those published after the Civil War, some attention is given to the deleterious psychological effects of slavery on the slave-owning class. In 1791 Morse sets the tone by his discussion of manners in South Carolina: "Slavery, by exempting great numbers from the necessities of labor, leads to luxury, dissipation, and extravagance. The absolute authority which is exercised over their slaves, too much favors a haughty and supercilious behaviour."[133] In his 1832

[128] G 1784 Morse, pp. 68–70; see also R 1811 I. Cooke, pp. 248–251.

[129] R 1799 New Pleasing, pp. 205–207.

[130] R 1797 Alexander, pp. 222–225; R 1801 Heaton-C, p. 39; R 1807 Bingham-C, pp. 240–242; R 1828 New York, pp. 194–197.

[131] R 1807 Bingham-C, pp. 102–118.

[132] See H 1889 Chambers, pp. 353 box, 354.

[133] G 1791 Morse, p. 217.

edition, however, he has revised this to: "The planters have large incomes, live at their ease, and possess much of the independent character of English country gentlemen." [134] His earlier attitude, however, is followed by other authors. Typical of these is the following: "They are sociable and hospitable, attached strongly to pleasure and dissipation, and highly jealous of personal independence. The holders of slaves have the same character in all countries." [135] The deleterious effect of slavery on "poor whites" is considered only in books written after the Civil War. [136] Perhaps it took this long for Helper's *Impending Crisis* (1857) to penetrate books used in the schools.

Slavery is rarely defended in any part of the century, unless the highly unfavorable descriptions of the Negro race might be regarded as justification for slavery. One early author makes this connection and draws from the assumed inherent inferiority of the Negro this rationalization for his enslavement: "Nature has formed the different degrees of genius, and the characters of nations, which are seldom known to change. Hence the negroes are slaves to other men, and are purchased on the coast of Africa like beasts for a sum of money." [137] Another seems to justify slavery because of the happy effects it produces in his eyes on the planting class: "An independent spirit, and a sort of conscious equality throughout all ranks and conditions." [138] Another uses the Bible to explain slavery: "It has been a remark of some that the wretched condition of the African negroes proves them to be descendants of Ham, on whom the curse of his father was denounced. In every portion of the earth, where their lot may have fallen they are literally the servants of servants." [139] But these justifications are isolated instances. On the whole the justification for slavery or a servile position is implied in the alleged racial traits of the Negro rather than stated. In theory at least, freedom is considered desirable by a majority of those who take any discernible stand.

[134] G 1822 Morse and Morse, p. 111.

[135] G 1796 Dwight, p. 180; see also G 1807 Parish, p. 78; R 1813 Richardson, pp. 29, 142–143; G 1819 Adams, p. 140; R 1825 Torrey, pp. 62–70; R 1828 Putnam-S, pp. 222–224, eliminated from his 1832 edition.

[136] H 1867 Goodrich, p. 232; H 1876 Doyle, p. 220; H 1900 Channing, p. 279.

[137] R 1793 Moore, p. 300.

[138] G 1818 Smith, p. 138.

[139] G 1831 Blake, p. 33.

In books published before the Civil War, it is only those from the early part of the century that advocate freedom from slavery specifically. Two of Cowper's poems are used frequently to attack the idea that differences in color indicate differences in intelligence, and therefore that they justify the servile position of the Negro. One, "The Inhumanity of Slavery," contains the lines:

> He finds his fellow guilty of a skin
> Not color'd like his own![140]

The other, "The Negro's Complaint," discusses the wrongs of the Negro snatched from peaceful domestic life into a life of slavery. The new slave complains:

> Deem our nation brutes no longer,
> Till some reason ye shall find,
> Worthier of regard, and stronger
> Than the colour of our kind.[141]

Another popular piece on the theory of equality is entitled "A Family Conversation on the Slavery of Negroes." In this dialogue the daughter asserts that she heard a man say "that negroes were not much superior to the brutes." Her father replies that Negroes "suffer from want of cultivation," but "there is no reason to suppose that they differ from us in anything but color."[142] An occasional author categorizes slavery as anti-Christian: all are equal in the sight of God.[143] But it is significant that so few relate slavery to Christianity in any way. All of these books have a profound religious bias, and they find it necessary to relate almost everything to God. Their failure to do this with slavery seems to indicate that they were treating the subject with caution.

Three books before 1830 consider slavery to be inconsistent with the American tradition. One lists the ways in which the American

[140] R 1803 Murray, pp. 204–205; R 1811 Hubbard, pp. 200–201; R 1816 Staniford, pp. 234–235; R 1823 Pierpont, pp. 181–182; R 1843 Olney, pp. 305–306.

[141] R 1819 Strong, pp. 166–167; R 1825 Blake, pp. 336–338; R 1835 Porter, pp. 120–122; R 1843 Olney, pp. 145–147; see also R 1796 Bingham, p. 87; R 1798 Enfield, pp. 178–179; G 1800 Smith, p. 117.

[142] R 1809 Picket, pp. 204–207; R 1811 Murray-I, pp. 88–93; R 1813 New York, pp. 190–199; R 1832 American-P, pp. 96–102.

[143] R 1806 Cooledge, p. 92 (Quaker); R 1834 S. Willard-P, p. 150; S 1846 Butterfield, p. 12; R 1854 Mandeville, p. 153; S 1856 Town, p. 37.

people have been blessed above others, and then pleads with them: "Why, when thus happy, thus great, thus amiable, will you suffer the national glory to be tarnished, by the inhuman avarice of a worthless few!"[144] The other two consider slavery contradictory to the principles for which America is pre-eminent: "The existence of slavery in this country is its greatest reproach. That slavery should be tolerated amongst free men, is in the most eminent degree disgraceful. . . . Genius of liberty! how long shall this detestable bondage continue to disgrace our country and remain a standing contradiction to all our professions and institutions?"[145]

Schoolbooks published after the Civil War accept without question the emancipation of the slaves, and with hindsight they condemn wholeheartedly the institution of slavery. Inherent qualities assigned to the Negro are the same unpromising ones accorded to him in the pre-Civil War period, and his future is still a matter for gloomy speculation. But slavery is universally condemned and its demise celebrated. The schoolbooks rejoice over the abolition of an institution "so repugnant to the principles of Christianity, and so fraught with danger to society, religion and the state."[146] In post-Civil War books, slavery occupies a much more prominent position in American history. Just as they view all of colonial history as leading to the American Revolution, so American historians consider that the events after the Revolution develop toward the Civil War. In a conciliatory mood toward the South, they blame both sections for the establishment of slavery; it was fastened upon America "not less by the cupidity of the north which found its profits in the slave trade, than by the cupidity of the south, which found its profits in slave labor."[147] Many authors specifically mention sentiment for the abolition of slavery in both North and South at the time of the American Revolution.[148] But the invention of the cotton gin and factory-produced cotton goods ended that possibility. Only one book puts the whole onus on the South. A homely dialogue between

[144] R 1801 Heaton-C, p. 43.

[145] R 1813 Richardson, p. 29; see also R 1828 American-R, pp. 91–93.

[146] H 1867 Goodrich, p. 152. [147] *Ibid.*, p. 69.

[148] H 1867 Goodrich, p. 152; H 1879? Campbell, p. 110; H 1890 Morris, p. 194; H 1894 Fiske, p. 301; H 1900 Channing, p. 265.

mother and child ends with the child foreseeing the defeat of the South as retribution for the sin of slavery: "So I am sure the Virginia colony would have to suffer for it sometime."[149] Most authors, far from assigning blame, would agree with Fiske, who sees the change in the sentiment to slavery as part of an evolution of the moral sense of man toward perfection:

Very few people in those days [the seventeenth century] could see anything wrong with slavery; it seemed as proper to keep slaves as to keep cattle and horses. . . . In our time nobody but a ruffian would have anything to do with such a wicked and horrible business. Changes of this sort make us believe that the world is growing to be better than it used to be. But the improvement is very slow.[150]

A post-Civil War book by a Southern author for Southern pupils takes much the same position; it observes that in the colonial period "the conscientious opposition to slavery had been stronger in the South than in the North" while the North monopolized the slave trade without scruple.[151] The only visible difference between the Southern and Northern interpretations in school-books is the greater stress in the Southern books on the constitutional right to slaves as property. The Southern book cited above also recognizes the importance of slavery to the economy of the United States: "However objectionable the system may now be generally regarded, no facts stand out clearer in American history than that the steady and directed toil of the Southern slave first placed the United States among the great commercial nations of the world. . . ."[152] It also trained the Negro to do useful work.

In books published before the Civil War the free Negro appears rarely, usually only in connection with Haiti. This self-governing Negro state is looked on with great interest and encouragement by four authors. In his 1828 edition Woodbridge sees a happy present and foresees a happy future for Haiti, because it is establishing schools and churches at a rapid rate.[153] In the 1845 edition, however, in a Nativist period, his anti-Roman Catholicism has overcome his optimism, and he notes: "They profess the Catholic

[149] H 1889 Monroe, p. 78.

[150] H 1894 Fiske, pp. 59–60, see also pp. 300–301.

[151] H 1889 Chambers, p. 353 box.

[152] *Ibid.*, p. 354.

[153] G 1828 Woodbridge, p. 89.

religion; and few are acquainted with the Bible. . . . *They are* ignorant and indolent; and the island is not well *cultivated*."[154] But in the 1866 edition, probably inspired by the Civil War, hope returns: "The Africans of Haiti give as much evidence of intelligence as any other nation so lately formed with the means of instruction."[155] Such sensitivity to current events was unusual in schoolbooks. Most authors present Negro rule in Haiti as a constant and bloody massacre: "These black or colored chiefs are now contending for the mastery, and this beautiful and fertile island is desolated by these barbarians."[156] The political instability in Haiti after achieving independence is seen to be only a natural result of Negro control; no account is taken of similar instability throughout Latin America in the same period. Certainly the existence of Haiti is here no recommendation for Negro amalgamation into American culture.

Apart from this example, the free Negro appears incidentally in very few pre-Civil War books. A Speller published in the midst of the slavery controversy uses this sentence: "The hero, though a negro, became one of the junto."[157] A Reader proudly points to the establishment of a segregated Negro orphan asylum in Philadelphia.[158] Two other books include the tale of a Negro boy who, after lending his skates to a white boy, asks that he never again be called such names as "blackamoor" and "nigger."[159]

Interestingly enough, in books published after the Civil War little more notice is taken of the free Negro than before the Civil War. Now and then he appears as a soldier fighting with the Union for his own freedom, and fighting effectively.[160] Higginson, himself an abolitionist and leader of Negro troops in the war, takes a more realistic view of the Negro soldier: "In all these states the colored population took sides unanimously with the Union; but, being composed almost wholly of unarmed and

[154] G 1845 Woodbridge, p. 221. [155] G 1866 Woodbridge, p. 354.

[156] G 1811 Workman, pp. 126–127; see also G 1806 Cottineau-II, p. 902; G 1814 Adams, p. 201; G 1818 Morse, p. 245; G 1845 S. Morse, p. 39; G 1830 Fowle, p. 54.

[157] S 1857 Parker and Watson, p. 76.

[158] R 1842 Palmer, p. 225.

[159] S 1847 ASDUK, p. 125; R 1850 Mandeville, p. 104.

[160] H 1866 Lossing, p. 230; R 1869 Wilson, p. 102; H 1870 Lossing, pp. 286–287; H 1881 Thalheimer, p. 295.

ignorant slaves, they counted at first for little."[161] In a Reader of 1867 a poem by E. L. Beers shows a dying slaveowner bestowing freedom on his faithful slave as Union armies approach. The freedman responds as did the freedman in the songs of Stephen Foster:

> Massa's berry kind to Pompey;
> But old darkey's happy here,
> Where he's tended corn and cotton
> For dese many a long gone year.[162]

He is also happy in the knowledge, imparted to him by his mistress, that if he serves God his soul will be white. In a Reader at the end of the century Booker T. Washington appears as a self-made man.[163] The moral drawn from this biography is that the progress of the Negro race is inevitable if the whites will offer guidance. Apart from these few mentions of individual free Negroes, one is struck by the lack of consciousness of the Negro after his emancipation, either as an individual or as a component part of the American population. In the treatment of Reconstruction, he appears as a mere pawn in arguments between the President and Congress, an incidental figure of contention. The real problems of Reconstruction were constitutional ones. This seems to be a valid reflection of the way the Negro was treated by political parties at the time; certainly it reflects with some accuracy the role assigned the Negro in the historiography of Reconstruction. The Negro, having been granted freedom, disappears from the schoolbooks.

In a few books published after the Civil War the future of the Negro becomes a matter for brief speculation. Some of these apply their generalized expectation of progress to the Negro: "Many of the former slaves have become landowners, and are beginning to realize the duties and responsibilities of citizens."[164] In a speech by the Goddess of Liberty another book supports Negro suffrage: "Shall color prevent an honest heart from the right of suffrage? God created all men free and equal. The black and the white man are subjects of his creation."[165] And a Speller illustrating use of the words "concur" and "demur" would accept

[161] H 1875 Higginson, p. 291.

[162] R 1867 Edwards-5, p. 257.

[163] R 1898 Black, p. 337-343.

[164] G 1872 Hall, p. 61.

[165] R 1869 Wilson, p. 102.

the Negro into American politics more readily than the Indian: "When the Judge says that the law gives the right to vote to negroes, I *concur;* but when he extends the provision to wild Indians, I *demur.*"[166] But most of the books, when they mention the subject at all, offer hope for the future of the Negro as an equal component in American civilization only if he has direct and careful guidance from the white. Unaided, he is now uncivilized and will remain so. This is a typical statement: "The negro race have, by themselves, made only the first steps in civilization and the great mass are still in the savage state. Where they have been brought up under the influence of cultured nations, however, they have shown themselves capable of a high degree of progress."[167] Another view is less optimistic but more moralistic: "The negroes are doubtless happier now than when slaves, but in spite of the efforts to educate them on the part of the whites and of some members of their own race, many still remain densely ignorant. What shall be done for their elevation is one of the greatest problems of the present time. It should be remembered, however, that their ancestors were brought here against their will, and it is now our duty to help and improve the negro."[168] This author also observes that whites are used in a cotton mill in Alabama in spite of the numbers of available Negroes, because the latter are generally believed to lack the intelligence for even such simple work.[169] Interestingly enough a post-Civil War History written by a Southerner for Southern schools sees no need to quarrel with Northern predictions of the future of the Negro: "The systematic training bestowed upon him during his period of servitude, and his contact with higher intelligence have given to the negro an impulse to civilization that neither his inherent inclinations nor his native environment would of themselves bestow."[170] Thus it is only through serious humanitarian efforts of the white race that improvement of the Negro race is possible, for the Negroes do not contain within themselves the seeds of cultural advance. And even with such help, most schoolbooks are dubious about

[166] S 1888 Shoup, p. 37.

[167] G 1866 Guyot, p. 118; see also G 1888 Redway, p. 29; G 1897 Redway, pp. 13, 127; G 1898 Payne, p. 132.

[168] G 1900 Tarr and McMurry-2, p. 106.

[169] *Ibid.*, pp. 106, 221. [170] H 1889 Chambers, p. 354.

their achieving equality with the whites.

The child influenced by these books would be unlikely to see the Negro as a participant in and a contributor to American culture. He would judge the abolition of slavery a righteous act that erased a serious blot on his civilization, a blot made by foreign nations before America had charge of its own destiny. Emancipation absolved the whites from any debt to the Negro as an equal. But the child would assume that some responsibility for the care of the Negro would necessarily devolve on the white, because the Negro was incapable of self-control and self-direction. The generations that made decisions about the Civil War, slavery, and Reconstruction, whatever they were taught about slavery, were thoroughly indoctrinated with the idea of Negro racial inferiority. It is interesting to observe that this inferiority consists in a lack of the very qualities—responsibility, industriousness, initiative—considered particularly valuable to an America "on the make." Their conspicuous absence makes the Negro a poor candidate for equality in American civilization.

It should also be noted that the image of the Negro is of the same gay, foolish, childlike creature who appeared in the writings of George Fitzhugh and Thomas Nelson Page, as well as in the consciousness of the old Southern aristocracy, and finally in the minstrel show. It is not the bestial Negro in the writings of Thomas Dixon at the end of the century, nor in the thinking of the Ku Klux Klan and the Southerners who fixed a rigid and all-pervasive segregation of the race. The Negro of the schoolbooks must be cared for by the whites as one would care for a child; he is not vicious, nor is it necessary to quarantine him. His place in America's future is clear: he will assist the whites from his menial but useful position.

THE NEGRO IN CONFEDERATE SCHOOLBOOKS

That the South was aware that it was educating its children on Northern schoolbooks has been discussed elsewhere.[171] With the institution during the Civil War of a new government based on principles different from those of the North, new schoolbooks reflecting Southern attitudes seemed imperative. And in spite of

[171] See below pp. 7–8.

the difficulties, they were written. It should be said, however, that some Confederate textbooks were written simply to supply the lack of books after the usual trade channels to the North were shut off by war, and they reflect no particular changes in attitude.[172]

Many do reflect those changes that parts of the South considered necessary. Confederate Arithmetics, for example, include many problems involving "servants" or "slaves," as: "If 5 white men can do as much work as 7 negroes, how many days of 10 hours each will be required for 25 negroes to do a piece of work which 30 white men can do in 10 days of 9 hours each?"[173] Moore's *Dixie Reader*, published in 1863, is full of comparisons between the life of the Negro slave laborer in the South and the white wage laborer in the North. In describing the production of sugar cane on a Southern plantation, the food given to slaves is appraised so: "Many poor white people would be glad of what they [the slaves] leave for the hogs."[174] The same book contains a description of "Old Aunt Ann":

> When she was young she did good work, but now she cannot work much. But she is not like a poor white woman.
>
> Aunt Ann knows that her young Miss, as she calls her, will take care of her as long as she lives.
>
> Many poor white folks would be glad to live in her house and eat what Miss Kate sends her out for her dinner.[175]

Another piece in the same book seems to be addressed to Negroes. Old Ned, a slave, had been lured to the lines of the Yankee army by their promises of freedom, and that he will "live like white folks." Soon, however, thoroughly disillusioned, he returns to his master, saying: "Ah massa, dem Yankee no be good to poor nigger, can't stay wid um. Ned lib wid you all his life." And the moral of the tale is made quite specific: "Ned says, 'he wants ebry nigger to stay at home and mind his work, and let dem Yankees do der own work.'"[176] From this kind of material the Southern child could rest assured that the slave was happier under slavery than he would be as a free man in a free society.

[172] For example, see R 1864 Campbell and Dunn.

[173] A 1863 Lander-S, p. 228; see also pp. 15, 196, 198, 209; A 1865 Browne, pp. 26, 27.

[174] R 1864 Moore, p. 50. [175] *Ibid.*, p. 22. [176] *Ibid.*, pp. 38–40.

Confederate books were few and physically poor in quality. Interestingly enough they differ little from Northern books except on the subject of the slave. With some exceptions, Northern, Southern, and Confederate books are identical in their discussions of the Negro and his racial characteristics. After the Civil War the South continued to use Northern books for the most part. A classroom technique was instituted to protect the children from interpretations offensive to the South. The teacher would hand out pins to pin together designated pages—usually those on the Civil War and Reconstruction; she would then supply a "correct" interpretation of that period. That this solution was satisfactory was indeed unlikely, for the lure of the forbidden was probably stronger then the prestige of the teacher. It would be a singularly incurious child who did not at least read the pinned pages.

Chapter 5

NATIONS AND NATIONALITY

Although, like the concept of race, nationality in nineteenth-century schoolbooks unites individuals into groups, it is a major divisive force for humanity in general. Like race, it is believed to be biologically determined, but unlike race, nationality has peculiar importance because it demands paramount loyalty from each individual. It supersedes his loyalty to family, friends, and sometimes even religion. It enlarges his field of action to the nationality group, yet it limits his development to the potentialities of his nationality. Throughout the century nationality is regarded in schoolbooks as a subdivision of race, a subgrouping with more subtly defined inherent characteristics. National traits operate within racial traits: "The character of a nation is marked in some measure, with the peculiarities of the race to which they belong." [1] Every nation can be recognized by its own peculiar and inherited traits of personality and intellect, its own national soul. One author, discussing the loss of the French empire in America to Britain, maintains that "something intrinsic in the genius of the respective nations must exist in order to produce similar effects under very divergent circumstances." [2] The word "nationality" appears for the first time in American schoolbooks in an 1828 Reader, where its introduction is explained: "Nationality is used by some writers in America, but is a new word and not to be found in the dictionaries." [3] But the idea had long preceded the word; it was represented before by the word "nation," commonly defined as "a distinct people." Ordinarily the distinct people making up a nation live under one government, but even without this form of unity they retain a national identity. This is

[1] G 1833 Willard and Woodbridge, p. 215; G 1866 Woodbridge, p. 355; see also G 1872 Hall, p. 16.

[2] G 1820 Darby, p. 28; see also R 1870 Sanders, p. 370.

[3] R 1828 Putnam-S, p. 290.

evident frequently in discussions of Poland: "Although Poland has ceased to constitute an independent single state, still the country is distinctly separated from those which surround it by national character, language and manners."[4] Essentially innate national character rather than acquired culture distinguishes one nation from another.

It is to this definition of each nation that the Geographies most assiduously apply themselves. Influenced by Romantic nationalism, they often devote more space to the definition of national character than to the description of natural features and economic development. In surveying each country they assume that an intrinsic personality inheres in each member of a particular nationality group. Readers, Histories, Spellers, and even at times Arithmetics are imbued with this spirit, but it is central to the Geographies. The pedagogical method of memorization common to schools at the time probably endowed these national qualities in the child's mind with connotations of eternal validity comparable to the physical features of the country.

In spite of the sometimes unpleasant characteristics assigned to each foreign nation, the reader of American schoolbooks is often cautioned against prejudice. In an early Webster Reader this advice appears: "Never reflect upon bodies of men, either clergymen, lawyers, physicians, or soldiers; nor upon nations and societies. There are good as well as bad in all orders of men in all countries."[5] Another warns that the part must not be substituted for the whole: "An illiberal prejudice has, in too many instances, fixed upon nations the odium which the crimes of individuals have merited. The Spaniards are said to be cruel, because a set of wretches, whose vices had rendered their fortunes desperate in Europe, were banished upon a kind of forlorn expedition, to make discoveries upon a new continent.[6] But the same book is also full of colorful tales of cruel Spaniards, calculated to catch the attention of the young reader much more than the author's warning against generalizing the behavior of individuals to their

[4] G 1840 Olney, p. 192 footnote.

[5] R 1789 Webster, p. 62; see also R 1797 Alexander, pp. 163–169; R 1802 Columbian, p. 112; R 1815 American, p. 59; R 1830 Bartlett, p. 218; R 1856 Hillard, pp. 250–256; G 1875 Swinton, p. 103.

[6] R 1809 Picket, p. 127.

8-9. This picture, and the one facing page 103, typify some of the major differences schoolbook authors observe between American and European civilization. One heads the section on the United States and the other that on Europe in Colton's *Common School Geography,* 1878. America is symbolized by simple, honest citizens engaged in useful occupations; Europe is represented by an aristocratic court, an avalanche, and remains of a past civilization.

nations. Another author, also guilty of his own charge, regrets that the French have been unfairly portrayed by the worst acts of their revolution.[7] Still another counters prejudice in a touching but naïve way by voiding meaning: "Much evil is done in China and everywhere else"; "Many vices prevail in Spain and everywhere else."[8] Later books are likely to invert this caution by describing "A Queer People" who keep members of the tiger family in the house, cover themselves with animal skins, drink water tinged with dry leaves, etc. Finally the child is told that he is reading of the manners of the Americans as they might be described by someone from another culture.[9] But such statements of tolerance are opposed both to the spirit and to the letter of the books in which they appear. The child, ingesting a heavy diet of unpleasant national characters not his own, was unlikely to be made tolerant by these bits of advice. And the prejudiced material is concrete and colorful in contrast to the often heavy moral tone of warnings against intolerance.

Attitudes toward foreign nations are particularly important in these books designed to school a democracy. The majority of voters in the United States met here their first and only formal presentation of most other nations, and they memorized what they read. From such estimates of national character and behavior they probably formed latent opinions easily called into consciousness by current international events. Furthermore the United States was and continued to be a nation of immigrants; attitudes toward nationals of other countries were likely to effect the assimilation of new groups into the nation. A direct personal relationship with a member of another nationality would obviously serve to cancel out the schoolbook image of his nation. But without such direct contradiction the stereotype of a nation in the schoolbooks was likely to greet each immigrant on his arrival here; his individual personality could be obscured by schoolbook stereotypes. Foreign nations were also useful foils for the American; by contrast their behavior could be conveniently used to point up the virtues of the American.

[7] G 1818 Mann, p. 288; see also R 1839 S. Goodrich, pp. 151–154.

[8] R 1840 Williams, pp. 92, 110.

[9] R 1884 Barnes, pp. 109–115; R 1900 Judson and Bender, pp. 19–23; see also G 1900 Dodge, pp. 2–3.

The ensuing section concerns only those nations important to the American image of itself and the world at the time: those whose governments had a significant relationship with that of the United States; those whose members migrated in some numbers to the United States; and those whose national character, defined in these books, had some relationship to the national character of the Americans.

SCOTLAND AND SWITZERLAND

The textbooks discuss only two foreign nations in wholly complimentary terms: Scotland and Switzerland. This circumstance is clearly related to the almost universal bias in favor of New England. New England's society is the ideal, and that of the Scottish and Swiss are its mirror images. Their common Calvinism may explain such unexpected admiration by New England textbook writers, and the universality of this praise may come from the wholesale copying among schoolbook authors. The specific religious sect of these countries is rarely named, but alone among European nations, both are heartily praised for their staunch Protestantism and sober religious demeanor in a tone recalling that used for New England.

The virtues imputed to the people of both countries are the same as those stressed in the people of New England. This relationship is sometimes made specific: "Like the inhabitants of New England, the Scotch are religious, moral and industrious."[10] The same adjectives are applied to the Scottish and Swiss throughout the period of investigation: both are industrious, temperate, frugal, moral, and well educated. They and Prussia are praised for opening common school education to all, an achievement usually ascribed solely to New England. These virtues and achievements are accomplishments not only of Puritan New England; they are finally generalized in the schoolbooks to America as a whole.

The Swiss have a unique distinction: although Switzerland is a small country contributing a negligible number of immigrants to America, and although it was not then important in international affairs, nevertheless one of its citizens, William Tell, appears in

[10] G 1848 Mitchell, p. 101.

almost every Reader, Geography, and Speller. As the national hero of Switzerland he has become a hero symbolic of nationalism in general, and his heroism is dressed to have obvious appeal to the young.[11] He is the brave leader of a small, poor, but liberty-loving nation, boldly defying the representative of a rich and powerful tyranny; he is the European George Washington, and the heir to the biblical David. He achieves importance as the symbol of nationalism for his spectacular feat in shooting an apple from his son's head in defiance of despotism. One might observe, incidentally, in this tale that parental love and care are subsidiary to service to one's country.

In their formal presentations of Switzerland the Geographies transfer the virtues of Tell to the whole Swiss nation. Their outstanding national characteristic is love of country. One might assume that habitual Swiss service in foreign armies would break down this concept. But, on the contrary, the overwhelming desire of the Swiss mercenary to return to his native land supersedes the fact of his leaving it. "The absent soldier weeps when he thinks on the lakes and vallies [*sic*], the brooks and the mountains, among which he passed the happiest season of his life."[12] In the first half of the century the Swiss are also distinguished as "the only nation of the Old World who govern themselves." They have therefore particular meaning for America, and like the Americans they are characterized by "great simplicity of manners."[13] In schoolbooks that admire the simple agrarian mode of life, Switzerland is seen as a pastoral paradise.

Thus the Swiss and Scottish, although not of major importance internationally, are important in American schoolbooks as prototypes for American character and civilization.

ENGLAND

On the picture of an Englishman in one of the textbooks examined in this study, a young reader had drawn horns.[14]

[11] The tale of William Tell and Gesler is usually given in the Knowles version.

[12] G 1822 S. Morse, p. 208; see also G 1807 Parish, pp. 143–144; G 1818 Mann, p. 289; G 1820 Darby, p. 173, et al.

[13] First quotation: R 1854 Kay-3, p. 131; second quotation: G 1806 Webster, p. 99.

[14] R 1828 Robbins-A, II, 4.

This illustrates the attitude toward the English one might expect to be engendered by American schoolbooks. In the course of this investigation, however, such a preconception had to be radically revised. It remains quite true that England appears as a villain when in opposition to America (as in the American Revolution or the War of 1812), and anything English is contrasted unfavorably with anything American. Yet England, next to the United States, Scotland, and Switzerland, is more favorably portrayed than any other nation. As it ranks next to the United States in the amount of space accorded it in the textbooks, so it ranks near the United States in merit.

There are many reasons for this relatively favorable attitude. One important factor was probably the continued publication in the United States, after independence, of English schoolbooks embodying English attitudes. Such editions, frequently pirated, could be cheaply published by almost any printer. Even when Americans began to write their own schoolbooks with a nationalistic purpose, it was easiest to rely on the English books for information about other countries and things unknown to the American author. We have already seen how the constant copying of one text by another often perpetuated older ideas. But the pro-British attitude of American texts did not become gradually diluted, as one would expect from mere copying. On the contrary, in consciously American schoolbooks of the mid-nineteenth century the friendship of America and Britain is stronger than ever, and it is necessary to find other explanations.

Most of the textbook writers were of British ancestry, like American culture as a whole. To impugn the British character when it conflicted with the American would cast aspersions on American ancestry; to exalt the British above other nations would compliment America. Careful distinctions are drawn between the Americans and the British on every issue; only British virtues migrated to America, and these were purified in the American atmosphere. Yet a typical statement that becomes more frequent as the century progresses appears in an 1807 Geography: "The English are our brethren. To speak ill of them would not only be false, but indecent." And in later books, Britain is ranked so: "The intelligence, enterprise and industry of its inhabitants are nowhere equalled, except in the United States."[15]

Morse's 1784 characterization of the British is followed throughout the century: "They are in general brave, and good soldiers and seamen. They are lovers of liberty and learning, generous, sincere, hospitable, industrious, of a solid judgment, a ready genious [*sic*] for mechanical arts, and improvers of whatever they undertake. Melancholy, which often leads to suicide, is a very distinguishing characteristic of an Englishman." Dwight adds that they are also humane, "and oftener perform more than they promise than fall short of it." Parish agrees almost word for word with Dwight, but adds an explanation for English melancholy: "[It] may be considered as the tax of genius and sensibility." O'Neill in 1814 ascribes this trait to the vaporous atmosphere of the island.[16] It is noteworthy that love of liberty appears as an English national characteristic in a popular book written by a nationalistic American the year after the end of the American Revolution. All of the traits found in the English in 1784 are still considered theirs in 1900. But by the end of the century the idea that they still "represent the highest type of civilization, education and culture" is sometimes specifically ascribed to race; they are Teutons or Aryans.[17] Undoubtedly increasing consciousness of race led American schoolbook authors to reclaim their British heritage. Whatever temporary aberrations, whatever cruelty the English might indulge in now and then, these are historical accidents; essentially, racially, they are good people who carry and pass on to their American heirs the germ of freedom.

In all economic activities the British are said to be pre-eminent. Several authors note that the soil is poor: "But the industry of the English has effected what nature could not do."[18] This provides an interesting contrast to the discussion of the agricultural methods of Spain, Portugal, and Italy, where although the soil is

[15] The first quotation in this paragraph is from G 1807 Parish, p. 128; the second is from G 1843 Mitchell, p. 233.

[16] Quotations in this paragraph are from these sources in this order: G 1784 Morse, p. 184; G 1796 Dwight, p. 31; G 1807 Parish, p. 128; G 1814 O'Neill, p. 230. I have not been able to trace the origin of alleged British melancholy. Madame de Staël believed it to be a British trait, but Morse's 1784 characterization antedates her use of it.

[17] G 1887 Redway, p. 98.

[18] G 1806 Cottineau-II, p. 634; see also G 1817 Cummings, p. 69; G 1878 Steinwehr and Brinton, p. 70.

fertile, agriculture languishes. Webster expresses the universal opinion: "In no country is agriculture carried to a greater degree of perfection than in England."[19] This agricultural efficiency is further complemented by an inherent love for natural beauty and the simple life in nature. "Rural Life in England" by Washington Irving points out that the English are "strongly gifted with the rural feeling"; this sensibility to the beauties of nature cannot be repressed even by slum living, where it appears in a profusion of window boxes full of flowers.[20] As a corollary to this appreciation of the simple life, England is often shown as the cradle of domestic happiness. Mrs. Heman's poem "The Homes of England" suffuses this subject with a Romantic glow.[21] And England is sometimes referred to as the "native country of female beauty" as well as of "female chastity, faithfulness and prudence."[22]

England is, of course, renowned for being the greatest commercial and manufacturing nation in the world, and for having the largest navy. Even in the Spellers Britain's industrial prowess appears in model sentences, as: "These pretty breeches were made by women in England."[23] Morse seeks the reason and decides: "For this superiority they are nearly equally indebted to national character, to the situation of the country and to their excellent constitution."[24] Others ascribe it to their energy, their stout-heartedness, or their superior natural resources.

British imperial activities, especially in India and Ireland, seem to be regarded with increasing tolerance as the American Revolution recedes in time. Perhaps America, itself becoming more interested in imperialism, developed a more lenient attitude toward such adventures. In the earlier books an extract from Sheridan's invective against Hastings is used several times to show that if one visited India one might wonder what dreadful disaster had accomplished such ruin; one would soon discover

[19] G 1806 Webster, p. 22.

[20] R 1875 Sheldon, pp. 281–285.

[21] R 1830 Emerson, pp. 73–74; R 1852 Robbins, pp. 58–60; R 1856 Osgood, pp. 166–167; R 1881 Willson, p. 319; see also S 1896 Dutton, p. 69.

[22] G 1784 Morse, p. 184; G 1818 Mann, p. 257; see also G 1812 Dwight, p. 31.

[23] S 1857 Parker and Watson, p. 74.

[24] G 1791 Morse, p. 297; G 1818 Morse, p. 279.

that it was not civil war or natural violence, but rather the lamentable results of British friendship.[25] Several instances of individual Britons who plundered India are brought up, and that the British took Gibraltar "by artifice" is mentioned.[26] On the whole, in the first half of the century Britain's relations with weaker nations often appear in a most unpleasant light, and Roman Catholic books continue to criticize England's Irish policies throughout the century.[27] In the earlier period Britain's treatment of India and Ireland is used to underscore its cruel treatment of America. An oration by Richard Rush in 1812 shows that although Britain has freedom at home, "It has been her uniform characteristic to let fall upon the remote subjects of her own empire, an iron hand of harsh and vindictive power."[28] Later in the century, British imperialism is more often a matter of pride: "And the reason why England is so famous is because the English have always been a stout-hearted people, and have loved to sail forth in ships to distant lands. Sometimes they have planted colonies of their own folk in unoccupied regions; still oftener, with strong hand, they have seized on countries belonging to other people.[29]

The British government is much admired. Morse has a Hamiltonian fondness for it, and no criticism. Britain is usually shown as the birthplace of liberty in the modern world. Murray uses a piece by Addison:

> 'Tis liberty that crowns Britannia's isle,
> And make her barren rocks, and her bleak mountains smile.[30]

Its constitution and its laws provide justice and equity, although this rarely becomes specific; Magna Carta, for example, is seldom mentioned. Apart from the issues involved in the American

[25] R 1811 I. Cooke, pp. 213–215; R 1826 American-S, p. 99; R 1830 MacLeod, pp. 101–104; see also R 1827 Pierpont, p. 201; R 1830 Bartlett, p. 252; R 1844 Goldsbury and Russell, p. 42.

[26] G 1806 Cottineau-I, p. 185; see also R 1809 Picket, p. 78; R 1815 Dickinson, pp. 138–140; R 1828 Robbins-A, p. 43; S 1829 Webster, p. 152; R 1834 S. Willard-P, pp. 280–285.

[27] G 1876 Comprehensive, pp. 84, 86; G 1878 Catholic, p. 68.

[28] R 1831 Harrod, pp. 297–298.

[29] G 1875 Swinton, p. 101; see also G 1898 Redway and Hinman, p. 93.

[30] R 1803 Murray, pp. 208–209; see also R 1803 Biglow, p. 155; R 1815 Dickinson, p. 153.

Revolution, there is relatively little criticism of the form of the British government, but corruption in administration is much criticized. Webster, in the introduction to his 1783 Speller, notes that America now looks at British political practices with different eyes: "She now sees a mixture of profound wisdom and consummate folly in the British Constitution, a ridiculous compound of freedom and tyranny in her laws; and a few struggles of patriotism, overpowered by the corruptions of a wicked administration."[31] Only one book, and that near the end of the century, observes English domestic reforms: "Many reforms have been instituted, and the rights and privileges of the common people have been greatly extended. The House of Commons no longer represents the owner of land and the rich alone, but the entire people of the kingdom."[32] By this time, when the genetic explanation had become the standard in analyzing institutions as well as individuals, the British government is generally exalted as the obvious ancestor of American political institutions. In a piece on the American flag, H. W. Beecher is reminded of the British flag, in which he sees "The noble aspect of that monarchy which more than any other on the globe has advanced its banner for liberty, law and national prosperity."[33] In general, schoolbooks assume that the British government, with a sound tradition behind it, is headed in the right direction, but it will have to go farther yet to meet American standards.

Although the British economy is prosperous and the British government sound, the British social system is severely criticized and frequently contrasted to that of the United States. In this respect Britain becomes an object lesson to America as "a nation sinking under the weight of riches and poverty."[34] Maldistribution of wealth and the great disparity between the lives of the rich and the poor are graphically illustrated: "The noble and the rich have splendid houses, elegant coaches, and many servants; while the poor live meanly and often suffer much

[31] S 1783 Webster, intro.; see also R 1813 Richardson, p. 78; G 1814 O'Neill, p. 224; G 1820 Darby, p. 141.

[32] S 1896 Dutton, p. 68.

[33] R 1898 Arnold and Gilbert, p. 227.

[34] R 1824 D. Adams, p. 216; see also G 1830 Hale, p. 175; R 1831 Cheever, p. 417.

distress."[35] This attitude is modified, however, when England is compared to the rest of Europe: "London exhibits less of the contrast between the ostentatious display of exorbitant wealth, and the squalid wretchedness of extreme poverty, than any other capital of Europe; its distinguishing characteristic is the comfortable existence and decent appearance of the middle and lower classes of the people, the happy effects of an excellent constitution and a flourishing commerce."[36] The Spellers often indicate desperate poverty in London by practice sentences and stories of poor and begging children. Readers include many tales of the miserable poor begging from door to door. One author implies that the result is much crime; the people of London bolt their houses day and night, "and generally have no handles to the doors."[37] A horrifying "Moral Picture of London" is given in one book by the following list: there are thousands who live by begging, 30,000 common thieves, 100,000 children learning crime, 4000 houses of stolen goods, 10,000 gamblers, and an infidel paper that sells 150,000 copies per week.[38]

The early textbooks, both English and their American copies, assume that England has produced the greatest literature: "With respect to learning and literary characters England stands conspicuous and unrivaled among surrounding nations."[39] Even when England is not accorded first place, its literature is always mentioned as being of "distinguished rank." And the selections in the Readers themselves are mostly extracts from English authors, which remains true of many of the more advanced Readers throughout the century.

English higher education is attacked in one very nationalistic Reader by a tale, entitled "The Dissipated Oxford Student,"[40]

[35] G 1853 Mitchell, p. 100; see also G 1837 Village, p. 70; G 1853 S. Goodrich, p. 189; G 1866 Guyot-C, p. 84; G 1875 McNally, p. 73; R 1881 Willson, p. 322, G 1898 Redway and Hinman, p. 93.

[36] G 1826 Blake, p. 114; see also G 1866 Woodbridge, p. 433.

[37] R 1831 Child, p. 43; see also S 1854 Angell, pp. 40–41; R 1868 Parker and Watson, pp. 61, 71, 88; R 1871 Monroe, p. 95.

[38] R 1850 Mandeville, pp. 156–157.

[39] G 1814 Adams, p. 232; see also G 1796 Dwight, p. 31; G 1817 Cummings, p. 69; G 1818 Mann, p. 253; G 1822 J. Worcester, p. 119; G 1825 Butler, p. 223; G 1892 Mitchell, p. 14.

[40] R 1807 Bingham-C, pp. 219–230; see also R 1814 Alden, p. 154.

that seems like a case history of the corruption inevitably learned by students in the course of a European university education according to Jefferson. And in England, as in most of the rest of Europe, "No public provision is made for the education of all the peasantry."[41] In all books the educational system of the United States is shown in direct contrast. But in England the absence of public schools is slightly mitigated by the institution of Sunday Schools. Only in the case of England is this limitation of education to children of the middle and upper classes sometimes admired: "The middle and higher ranks of England spare no expense in the education of their children."[42] In other European countries where this is true, it is regarded only as a misfortune for the lower classes rather than a positive gain for the middle and upper classes.

BRITAIN AND AMERICA

Britain is mentioned most frequently in these books in relation to America: it is fostering parent, neglectful parent, and cruel parent. However unjust the parental rules, however strained the filial relationship, the authors of American schoolbooks never forget that England was the progenitor of the United States. As the century goes on, and it was a century increasingly fond of genetic explanations, England's parental role becomes more prominent than its incidental neglect or cruelty. Only those aspects of American history that help to define British nationality and its identification with or differentiation from American nationality will be discussed here.

The American Revolution occupies more space in these texts than does any other single event. It is of primary importance not only to the United States, but to Britain: "The most remarkable epoch in the British annals is the war with her then 13 colonies in North America."[43] The Readers are full of orations from the Revolutionary period and commemorative occasions of that event. The Geographies refer to it constantly, noting the contribution of the citizens of each state to the war. Therefore

[41] G 1806 Webster, p. 27. This complaint is universal.

[42] G 1818 Morse, p. 279; G 1820 Darby, p. 142; G 1845 S. Morse, p. 46; see also G 1833 Clute, p. 232; G 1845 Woodbridge, p. 263.

[43] G 1818 Mann, p. 221.

the role of the British in this connection may condition the reader more than anything else said about the British. The material is more dramatic, it is constantly reiterated, and it is made to affect the present happiness of the reader.

The first colonists were Englishmen, but these are carefully and consistently distinguished from the English nation. Before they left England their religion had already made them different from the English as a whole; their migration to America is always pictured rather as a result of English oppression than of English interest in America. English rejection rather than English care settled America; settlers were rather pushed out of England than pulled to America. In all general discussions of settlement it is interesting that the motives of the Pilgrims are generalized into the motives of all migrants to English America. The reader is to be persuaded that Americans were created out of Europeans by devotion to a true religion, high moral principles, and a love of liberty that made life in Europe impossible. One of the most popular of the reading selections is an extract from Edward Everett's 1824 Plymouth oration, wherein he makes this point with great oratorical flourish. Although Everett thinks that all Americans should be proud to be descended from Englishmen:

It is a principle amply borne out by the history of the great and powerful nations of the earth, and by that of none more than the nation of which we speak [the United States] that the best fruits and choicest actions of the commendable qualities of the national character, are to be found on the side of the oppressed few, and not of the triumphant many. . . .

[Their trials] purified the ranks of the settlers. . . . It was these that put far away from their fathers' cause all patrician softness, all hereditary claims to preeminence.[44]

Britain's American policy to 1763 has the approval of a few of the early texts, those still British or dependent upon British texts; they talk of its fostering care.[45] Most of the others, however, define

[44] R 1826 Frost, pp. 18–20; R 1826 Greenwood and Emerson, pp. 98–102; R 1826 American-S, pp. 223–227; R 1827 Pierpont, pp. 200–205; R 1828 Hopkins, pp. 86–115; R 1828 American-R, pp. 263–265; R 1831 Harrod, pp. 176–177; R 1841 Merriam, pp. 221–223; R 1845 Swan, pp. 268–270; R 1854 Mandeville, pp. 201–202; see also H 1839 Frost, pp. 174–177; G 1887 Redway, p. 39.

[45] G 1800 Smith, p. 134; R 1806 Peirce, p. 78; G 1820 Darby, p. 72.

England's attitude toward its American colonies as neglectful or self-seeking. In the midst of their hardships "the colonists received no assistance from England; and they asked none."[46] Her neglect coupled with the self-reliance of the colonists produced immediately "the dawn of that NOBLE SPIRIT OF INDEPENDENCE which has since characterized the country."[47] All of the schoolbooks perceive the root of the Revolution in Britain's earliest policies. All are agreed that "the conduct of the British king and parliament was marked with selfishness from the first settlement of the country."[48] American colonial history is envisioned only as a struggle between England and the colonists, with the latter showing a "jealous guardianship of their rights and that determined adherence to a principle of freedom, once adopted, which runs through the whole of their history."[49] In several cases the American Revolution is called the "unnatural war";[50] this nomenclature is often used where the authors have made it seem the most natural result of the seed planted by the Pilgrims. Some of the later books use the term racially; it is "unnatural and degrading that men of English race should destroy each other."[51] Following an almost Hegelian view of history, schoolbook authors believe that the American Revolution was inevitable from the first planting of the colonies. Like Bancroft, they begin the Revolution with the first settlement. Traditional British liberty, seeded in the hearts of the settlers, would inevitably flower in opposition to the parent plant.

In the treatment of the American Revolution, England is depicted as a corrupt monster with enormous financial resources, fighting to maintain its tyranny. "America was young, and, compared with other countries, was virtuous. None but a Herod of uncommon malice would have made war upon infancy and innocence."[52] This image of young and pure America opposing old, powerful, and corrupt Britain accords with the earlier

[46] H 1852 E. Willard, p. 108. [47] H 1843 Hall and Baker, p. 92.

[48] H 1831 S. Goodrich, p. 40. [49] H 1839 Frost, p. 106.

[50] G 1784 Morse, p. 185; G 1791 Morse, p. 104; G 1800 Smith, p. 148; R 1806 Peirce, p. 80; G 1833 Clute, p. 52.

[51] H 1881 Thalheimer, p. 277.

[52] Extract from *The Crisis* by Thomas Paine, in R 1797 Thomas, p. 180; R 1844 Smith, p. 204; see also R 1810 Thomson, p. 74; R 1827 Pierpont, p. 225; R 1830 Hughs, pp. 173–174; R 1874 Hillard, p. 214.

differentiation between the British population and the first American settlers. Several later books put the struggle in more specifically class terms: "We have not England, not Great Britain, pitted against America, but the ruling class in the mother country opposed to the better class in the colonies. The distinction is important. Nothing else could explain the amount of blundering on one side, or the amount of wisdom, comparatively speaking, on the other; nor could anything else so clearly indicate the difference between the principles at stake—the principles of an old aristocracy on the one hand, and on the other, those of a young commonalty, all fervent with vigor and with hope."[53] Frequently the British "looked upon the colonists as an inferior class and had but little true sympathy with them."[54] Always, whether both sides are identified with a particular class or not, America is the poor, sturdy, right-principled champion, fighting against domination by rich and powerful Britain.

A few books, but very few, blame the outbreak of the Revolution entirely on the king. One Reader uses an amusing anecdote of Benjamin West, who invited John Adams to London to see the cause of the American Revolution. West showed him the site for a new royal palace whose construction was to be paid for by American taxes. Another Reader states that the new taxes were to be used to "make Americans pay the cost of the royal court."[55] Most schoolbooks attribute the outbreak of the Revolution to a body of parliamentary acts for control of the colonies; all of these are lumped together as "Navigation Acts." Usually they are simply defined as unjust and oppressive, but now and then they are vividly if inaccurately detailed: a farmer "couldn't cut down a single tree without the king's consent," and "The British colonists of North America had NO RIGHT to manufacture even a nail for a horse-shoe," or colonists could send goods only to England.[56] Britain's policy after 1763 is universally condemned as "the greatest act of folly on record," "rash and cruel measures,"

[53] H 1881 Eliot, p. 165; see also H 1889 Monroe, p. 192.

[54] H 1879? Campbell, p. 75; see also H 1899 Morris, pp. 137–141.

[55] For the West anecdote see R 1828 Pierpont-I, pp. 74–75; for the statement on Americans paying the cost of the royal court see R 1840 Snow, p. 234.

[56] These statements are from the following in that order: H 1885 Donnelly, p. 87; Pitt quoted in H 1874 Scott, p. 149; R 1898 Black, p. 135.

"palpable attempt to enslave the Americans."[57] At the time of the Stamp Act liberty disappeared from the English government, but it was reincarnated in America.[58] The Revolution was produced by parliamentary acts that violated British concepts of liberty. Indeed British liberties were kept inviolate by the Americans and were purified by the American Revolution.

Especially in the second half of the century, the American Revolution is shown as a continuation of the struggle for British liberties. Although the colonists loved England, "they had the spirit of those who in other days had secured and maintained the liberties of England, and they were not willing to surrender their liberty, although it should cost them their lives to preserve it."[59] Willard believes that the British "forgot that the American people were children of the same forefathers with themselves, and heirs of the same political rights." She speculates that had the British government applied the same laws in England, there would have been rebellion there too. Therefore how much more likely was revolution by Britons transported to America, where "toil and danger had made them strong and brave."[60] While British oppression produced the eruption, British nurture directed it: "Although hard things must be said of the British government as it was then administered, we ought never to forget that our fathers had the spirit and ability to repel English injustices precisely because they had been trained to the rights and duties of Englishmen."[61] Thus the rebellion of child against parent was directed by principles instilled by the parent in the child. And after the war, because they "were rocked in the cradle and nurtured in the principles of British liberty . . . the transition from those institutions to our own was extremely easy."[62]

But the Revolution appears in these books mainly as a recital

[57] These quotations are from the following in that order: G 1820 Darby, p. 72; R 1789 Webster, p. 112; H 1870 Lossing, p. 120.

[58] R 1831 Cheever, pp. 185–189; R 1839 S. Goodrich, p. 306; R 1853 Mandeville, pp. 82–85; R 1856 Sargent-4, p. 141.

[59] R 1873 Hillard, p. 147; see also H 1867 Willson, p. 194.

[60] H 1868 Willard, pp. 179–180.

[61] H 1881 Thalheimer, p. 124; see also R 1883 Swinton-5, p. 383; H 1889 Chambers, pp. 212–213.

[62] R 1831 Harrod, p. 154; see also G 1833 Clute, p. 175; R 1835 Porter, p. 284; R 1836 Cobb-N.A., p. 86.

of battles. In the geographical surveys of the United States, battlesites feature prominently in each state. Even in those books that never mention the issues involved, the battles of the war itself are carefully detailed. One constant theme is that although Britain was enormously powerful in men, money, and arms, and we were weak in all of these, yet America consistently won the battles. It is usually not mentioned that Britain was fighting other nations at the same time. That Britain had greater resources and yet lost the war implies that it had neither courage nor a just cause protected by God. All discussions of the war contrast the personnel of the two armies: the American army was one of patriots in the service of liberty; the British army was one of hirelings in the service of gold. The Hessians are discussed as though mercenary troops were not universally employed in wars of the time. Their use is a blot on the honor of the English, and proof that the British cause was so unjust that not even the British would fight for it. The degrees of courage are also disparate. Weems' "Battle of Lexington" portrays the advancing Americans as "sturdy peasants, with *flushed cheeks and flaming eyes*, eager for battle!" At the sight of them "The enemy fell back appalled!" Finally Gage arrived to rescue "the poor fellows faint with fear and fatigue."[63]

In the course of the war the British are universally charged with deliberate atrocities, "Gothic ravages."[64] They are accused of the wanton burning of towns, the profanation of churches, violating women, murdering civilians, allowing their Indian allies free rein for butchery, and mistreating prisoners of war. One enthusiast notes that in their prison ships: "It is said that *poison* was employed"; he finally rejects this rumor because it shows more mercy than the British generally showed![65] Such actions are further impressed on the reader's mind by such questions as the following: "What act of wanton barbarity was performed by the British during the action?"[66] Such attitudes are, of course, contrasted to those of the Americans. "The conduct of the Americans to their prisoners was, in general, humane

[63] R 1843 Olney, pp. 40–41.
[64] R 1789 Webster, p. 142.
[65] R 1810 Alden, pp. 120–121.
[66] R 1831 Child, p. 33.

and tender."[67] Americans not only refrained from cruelty to their prisoners, but they were shocked by the idea: "In Europe . . . events of this nature have received a dreadful kind of justification from immemorial custom. . . . But America was in her youth; and the scene here was a novelty."[68] Thus humane feelings mark another difference between Americans and their British relatives. All of the Histories are careful to point out that "While the Americans were suffering in their winter quarters at Valley Forge, the British were rioting in the luxuries of the capital of the country."[69] An 1810 oration, used in one schoolbook, says that we should not cherish recollections of the Revolution to incite children to national antipathy, but it goes on to celebrate the cruelty of the British by listing the causes of the American Revolution as: "The venal and profligate Parliament," "the haughty and unfeeling monarch," and "the illustrious crimes, which pollute while they swell the hated annals of a tyrant."[70]

British opinion opposing Britain's American policy is well represented in the Readers by speeches made in Parliament at the time. Some express admiration of American military and naval prowess as well as of the American spirit of independence, and they conclude by urging caution on the British government for fear that a war with America would be unsuccessful.[71] Some look upon America as: "The only great nursery of freedom now left on the face of the earth."[72] Thus the British people, in opposition to their government, seem to point to America as the protector of British liberties. The most popular of these speeches is one made by Pitt in Parliament on November 18, 1777, in which he opposed the use of Indians against the Americans; if this is done: "Spain can no longer boast pre-eminence in bar-

[67] R 1830 Practical-R, p. 69; see also G 1833 Clute, p. 189; H 1843 Hall and Baker, p. 231.

[68] R 1823 Blake, pp. 235–236.

[69] H 1843 Hall and Baker, p. 244.

[70] R 1811 Chandler, p. 155.

[71] R 1792 Dana, pp. 204–206; R 1807 Bingham-C, pp. 263–265; R 1830 Emerson, pp. 104–105.

[72] R 1794 Dana, pp. 184–189; see also R 1796 Bingham, pp. 185–187; R 1807 Bingham-C, pp. 58–60, 172–175, 214, 252–253; R 1810 Alden, pp. 111–112, 112–114; R 1826 American-S, pp. 36–38; R 1830 Emerson, pp. 81–82, 189–190, 310–312; R 1850 Hall, pp. 191–194; R 1854 Sargent, pp. 267–268; R 1856 Sanders-4, pp. 234–236, etc.

barity."[73] This material could have softened national antipathy by showing that not all Englishmen were unfeeling toward America. But in conjunction with the rest of the material on British behavior during the Revolution, it becomes unimpeachable evidence of British cruelty, from the British themselves. It is here used like Las Casas' opposition to the Indian policy of Spain, as unquestionable documentation of the extraordinary cruelty of his countrymen.

Interestingly enough, the War of 1812 is not prominent in these books. After their exhaustive treatment of the American Revolution, it comes as an anticlimax. A typical treatment in the Geographies is this single sentence: "In 1812, another war occurred between the British and Americans, in which the latter gained many battles on land and at sea."[74] In most books it appears only to note an atrocity perpetrated by the British. The burning of the Capitol looms large as an example. Sometimes it is used by practice sentences in the Spellers: "The British barbarously burned the capitol at Washington."[75] As in any war engaging the United States, the disparity of forces is remarked; God must have given Americans the strength to win against such odds. Again it is rarely mentioned that Britain was fighting a world war at the same time, as it was during the American Revolution. In all of the Histories the impressment of American seamen was the issue that forced the United States to declare war. The unrest of the western Indians, whenever mentioned, is shown to be the result of a deliberate plot by the British, who "resorted to every artifice to stir up the minds of the Indians against us."[76] Several later Histories call it the "second war for independence," and treat it

[73] R 1803 Murray-S, pp. 183–186; R 1810 Alden, pp. 114–117; R 1810 Picket, pp. 148–150; R 1830 MacLeod, pp. 98–101; R 1831 Harrod, pp. 202–204; R 1849 Leavitt, pp. 301–304; R 1852 Gilder, pp. 68–71; R 1852 Sweet, pp. 139–141; R 1853 Tower and Walker, pp. 392–395; see also H 1875 Higginson, p. 161; R 1883 Swinton-5, pp. 363–365; H 1881 Thalheimer, pp. 133–134; H 1889 Monroe, p. 192.

[74] G 1851 Smith-G, p. 80.

[75] S 1843 Fowle, p. 100; see also G 1818 Mann, p. 123; G 1831 Blake, p. 63; G 1833 Clute, p. 99; G 1840 Olney, p. 111; H 1852 E. Willard, p. 296; G 1853 S. Goodrich, p. 63; H 1867 Goodrich, p. 185; H 1868 Willard, p. 302; H 1879 Quackenbos, p. 227.

[76] H 1836 Olney, p. 204.

as an annex to the first.[77] Although the War of 1812 heightened American nationalism, it was no threat to the American Revolution as a symbol of nationalism; it simply added evidence that although power was on the side of the British, God was on the side of the Americans. According to these books it would be hard for the reader to discover exactly what issues were in dispute during the war. But it is both implied and stated throughout that the American cause was a just one.

From the late 1820's to the end of the century, British-American ties increase. These books do not relax their hostility to England when dealing with the American Revolution, and the general treatment of England changes little; they do, however, add friendly material to the unfriendly. Probably the need to copy previous material prevented any drastic shift in their treatment of the British. Thus, although Britain is better liked after 1825, it is not any better liked on the subject of the American Revolution. But as the Revolution became more remote, and as Britain itself began to institute political reform in the direction of democracy, it became more acceptable to Americans. Increased democracy in England was probably regarded as a compliment to America, the originator of the doctrine of democracy according to these books. Another factor probably operating in this shift in opinion was the increased immigration from non-English sources. Americans of English descent, including most of the textbook authors, now preferred to stress their English descent as a mark of differentiation from the newer immigrants. Also, as the concept of Romantic nationalism developed, it became the fashion to glorify the nation's remote past. And America's past was British. To glorify Britain in the American Revolution would trespass upon American nationalism, but glorifying Britain in the present, and ranking her next to America among major powers, would redound to American prestige. Romantic nationalism had added the inheritance of the national soul to the doctrine of nationalism, and the American soul inevitably stemmed from the English. Racial origins also increasingly became important to the late nineteenth century, with the same result.

The first instance of a statement of a community of interests between Britain and the United States is in a book published in

[77] H 1866 Lossing, pp. 183–184; H 1872 Venable, p. 147; H 1900 Channing, p. 202.

1812: "Our interests are inseparable, and nothing but extreme folly or wickedness will destroy the harmony of the two countries."[78] This indicates only a New Englander's opposition to the specific issue of the impending war with England. Later instances cannot be so interpreted. A speech by Edward Everett expresses quite well the relationship between Britain and American nationalism by the late 1820's:

What reflecting American does not acknowledge the incalculable advantages derived in this land out of the deep foundation of civil, moral and intellectual truth from which we have drawn in England? What American does not feel proud that his fathers were the countrymen of Bacon, of Newton, and of Locke? Who does not know that every pulse of civil liberty in the heart of our ancestors, the sobriety, the firmness and the dignity with which the cause of free principles came into existence here, constantly found encouragement from the friends of liberty there? For myself, I can truly say that, after my native land, I feel a strong reverence for that of my fathers.[79]

Another oration, by Powell Mason in Boston on the Fourth of July, 1827, emphasizes American improvements to the basically sound British heritage. We started well, "Inheriting the language, the laws, and the literature of the most civilized and improved nation of the world, and assisted by the energy, activity, industry and spirit of improvement, which institutions such as ours are calculated to infuse."[80] The most complete expression of this fusion of American nationalism with Britain is a poem, "America and Britons," by the American artist Washington Allston:

Though ages long have past,
Since our fathers left their home,
Their pilot in the blast,
O'er trackless seas to roam,
Yet runs the blood of Britons in our veins;
And shall we not proclaim
That blood of honest fame
Which no tyranny can tame
By its chains?

. . . .

[78] G 1812 Parish, p. 191.

[79] S 1896 Dutton, p. 129. The last sentence of this quotation appears with insignificant changes in R 1826 American-S p. 227.

[80] R 1830 Emerson, p. 32.

While the manners, while the arts,
That mould a nation's soul,
Still cling around our hearts,
Between, let oceans roll,
Our joint communion breaking with the sun;
Yet still from either beach,
The voice of blood shall reach,
More audibly than speech,
WE ARE ONE.[81]

The British themselves are seen, in an article from the *Edinburgh Review*, to acknowledge maternal pride in America and the expectation of sharing in its glory. This article, reprinted in an 1832 Reader, also chides America for its blatant boastfulness. Another article, from the *North British Review*, in an 1856 Reader, admires and reclaims the errant child: it is "too late to disparage America. . . . It breathes in accents which are our own. It is instinct with British life."[82]

This recognition of a new British-American relationship even finds expression in the practice sentences in the Spellers: "Many ties ally England and the United States."[83] Another speech by Edward Everett defines the relationship more specifically by analyzing their common heritage. America claims Milton and Shakespeare too, but more important than this are the same inherent traits in both nations: "ardent love of self-government, tempered by a proud submission to lawful sway which flowed in the veins of Englishmen for centuries before America began to be."[84] The inheritance of common traits is also clearly stated in J. K. Paulding's allegory of the American Revolution. Even while they quarrel, "everybody that had seen John Bull saw a great likeness between them, and swore he was John's own boy,

[81] R 1830 Bartlett, p. 83; R 1832 Edwards, pp. 149–150; R 1843 Griswold, pp. 40–41; R 1844 Goldsbury and Russell, pp. 131–132; R 1852 Gilder, pp. 223–224; see also S 1874 Worcester, p. 39; G 1875 Swinton, p. 102; H 1890 Morris, p. 141; S 1896 Dutton, pp. 44–45; R 1898 Arnold and Gilbert, pp. 201, 227.

[82] *Edinburgh Review* used in R 1832 Edwards, pp. 283–286; see also R 1843 Olney, p. 41. *North British Review* used in R 1856 Sargent-4, pp. 166–167.

[83] S 1857 J. Worcester, p. 39.

[84] R 1844 Goldsbury and Russell, pp. 399–402; see also G 1848 Mitchell, p. 99; G 1853 Mitchell, p. 30.

a true chip off the old block."[85] This tie is stronger than the influence of any specific event: "Man shall not be able to sever what the immutable laws of Providence have joined together. . . . The peaceful and profitable interchange of commerce, the same language, a common literature, similar laws, and kindred institutions shall bind you together with cords which neither cold-blooded policy, nor grasping selfishness, nor fratricidal war shall be able to snap."[86] This extract ends by saying that Americans will in the future go to England as Musselmen go to Mecca. Pride in the English racial heritage is also evident in a poem, "The Chimes of England," by Arthur Cleveland Coxe in an 1888 McGuffey Reader:

I love ye, Chimes of Motherland,
With all this soul of mine
And bless the Lord that I am sprung
Of good old English line.[87]

Whatever temporary misunderstandings may mar the parental relationship, the schoolbooks recognize that the inheritance and nurture have been beneficial.

Thus by the end of the century American textbooks had fully reclaimed their British heritage. The English relationship had been fused into American nationalism, giving it a glorious past and an inherited soul of virtue and prestige, but purified in the American environment. And it gives a standard against which to measure the inevitably splendid American future: "Who shall say then, contemplating the past, that England, proud and powerful as she appears, may not one day be what Athens *is*, and the young America soar to be what Athens *was*?"[88]

IRELAND

The great Irish migration to the United States in the nineteenth century gives special interest to the treatment of Ireland in these

[85] R 1850 Hall, pp. 283–285; R 1852 Tower and Walker, pp. 176–179; see also R 1871 Monroe, pp. 174–177.

[86] R 1856 Hillard, pp. 375–376.

[87] R 1888 McGuffey, pp. 287–288.

[88] R 1821 Bingham, pp. 77–78; R 1826 American-S, pp. 124–126; R 1827 Pierpont, pp. 257–260; R 1828 Putnam-S, pp. 126–130; R 1835 Porter, pp. 284–286; R 1852 Gilder, pp. 127–129; R 1858 McGuffey, pp. 116–117.

textbooks. The immigrants were greeted with great hostility, for those who came were usually too poor to move to the West, and they became labor competition in a society that was just meeting the challenge of the industrial revolution, with its consequent loss to labor of the bargaining power of the individual. The very size of the migration, especially in the 1840's, was seen to threaten American wages. Much of this hostility to the immigrant became hostility to the Irish as a national group and much of the hostility to the Irish made overt the strong anti-Catholic feeling latent in American Protestants.

The first description of the Irish is largely unfavorable: "The Irish are represented as an ignorant, uncivilized, blundering sort of people; impatient of abuse and injury; implacable, and violent in their affections; quick of apprehension, courteous to strangers and patient of hardships."[89] Later editions of Geographies by the same author are no less unfavorable, but they are somewhat mitigated by mentioning that England's economic and political restrictions have hampered Ireland.[90] Except for Catholic books used in parochial schools, the unpleasant traits assigned to the Irish remain constant until the end of the century. One very popular Reader of 1839 reviews the charges against the Irish and decides that these come from hostile English writers. He notes that similar characterizations have been made of all nationalities at various times, but that now and then such characteristics get permanently attached to one; he urges tolerance. The same author, however, later uses two extracts describing the Irish as having two inherent traits: wit and fondness for superstition.[91] Two authors, near the end of the century, using the same characteristics presented unfavorably before, now put them in a pleasant light: "The Irish are a warm-hearted and impulsive race, and are noted for their hospitality to strangers and for their domestic morality."[92]

About half of the texts note British oppression. Had the authors been so minded they might have drawn parallels between their

[89] G 1784 Morse, p. 186. The author of this work, interestingly enough, was the father of one of the leaders of the anti-Roman Catholic, anti-immigrant Nativist party, S. F. B. Morse, the painter and inventor of the telegraph.

[90] G 1791 Morse, p. 297; G 1845 S. Morse, p. 49.

[91] R 1839 S. Goodrich, pp. 151–154, 176–179.

[92] G 1892 Mitchell, p. 77; see also G 1891 Morton, p. 120.

favorite subject—English oppression of America—and English oppression of Ireland, but only one does so.[93] The Irish are not brought into the favorable orbit of American nationalism. Indeed, where Irish attempts to overthrow British rule are mentioned, the conclusion is that they simply aggravate their own difficulties, or that they perpetrate shocking cruelties in their revolts.[94] These insurrections could have been used to indicate an independent spirit, hatred of oppression, or love of liberty, but instead they are ascribed to the impulsiveness, quick temper, violence, and pugnacity of the Irish character. Religious oppression, which excites so much horror in these books when it is Catholic versus Protestant, excites no interest when it is Protestant oppression of Catholics.[95]

The poverty of the Irish peasantry is always mentioned, but frequently with unsavory connotations: "Many of the people are very poor, ignorant and wicked."[96] This poverty is usually blamed on Irish landlords, but sometimes it is ascribed to a laziness that allows a soil better than England's to remain unproductive. The Irish famine is treated in heart-rending terms in the books published after the 1840's. The tone can best be heard in the poem describing an Irish child dying of starvation:

> Give me three grains of corn, mother,
> Only three grains of corn;
> It will help the little life I have,
> Till the coming of the morn,
>
> . . . .
>
> What has poor Ireland done?
> Do the men of England care not, mother,
> The great men and the high,
> For the suffering sons of Erin's isle,
> Whether they live or die.
> There is many a brave heart here, mother
> Dying of want and cold,
> While only across the channel, mother,
> Are many that roll in gold,

[93] R 1836 Cobb-N.A., pp. 353–354.
[94] G 1806 Webster, pp. 40–41, G 1814 O'Neill, pp. 233–234; G 1830 Hale, p. 185.
[95] For example: G 1806 Cottineau-II, p. 689; G 1818 Smith, p. 79; G 1819 Willetts, p. 81; G 1827 C. Goodrich, p. 123.
[96] G 1837 Village, p. 73.

> There are rich and proud men there, mother,
> With wondrous wealth to view,
> And the bread they fling to their dogs tonight,
> Would give life to me and you.[97]

In spite of such tear-jerkers, however, the reader is often given the impression that much Irish poverty is the fault of the people themselves. They are never characterized as hard-working, and the fondness of the lower classes for alcoholic beverages becomes proverbial.

The readers of these books would have no basis for believing that Ireland had ever produced any distinguished men.[98] In stories of individuals identified only as Irishmen the tone is always derogatory, stressing idleness, fondness for drink, and fighting.[99] An anecdote of Robert Bruce refers to the Irish as "barbarians." One Speller sees fit to define: "Teague—an Irishman used by way of contempt." Another uses as a practice sentence: "The rogue has a droll brogue."[100] These casual references are always contemptuous.

On the subject of the Irish there is a dramatic difference between books used in the public schools and those written for Catholic parochial schools. In the latter the Irish are described typically as follows: "They are generous, warm-hearted, brave almost to rashness, and noted for their courtesy and hospitality to strangers. Ireland is celebrated for the production of men of superior intellect."[101] Their characteristics are very similar to those in other books, but now seen in a favorable light. Poverty and oppression are viewed most sympathetically: "For centuries the Irish people had groaned under the weight of oppression and tyranny, which

[97] R 1849 Leavitt, p. 121; R 1860 McGuffey, pp. 192–193; R 1867 Edwards-5, pp. 55–57; R 1867 Parker and Watson-4, pp. 279-281; see also R 1853 Sanders, pp. 62–64; R 1856 Denman, pp. 138–146; R 1860 McGuffey, pp. 191–192; R 1861 Sanders, pp. 201–204; G 1869 Warren-E, p. 77.

[98] Such exceptions are found in the following: G 1816 Rudd, p. 61; G 1817 Cummings, p. 74; G 1818 Morse, p. 285; G 1828 J. Worcester, p. 88; R 1867? Parker and Watson-4, pp. 279–280.

[99] For example, R 1834 S. Willard-P, pp. 86–87; S 1853 Vaughan-II, p. 78.

[100] For these three quotations references are in this order: R 1830 Practical-R, p. 78; S 1820 Kneeland, p. 57; S 1857 Parker and Watson, p. 48.

[101] G 1876 Comprehensive, p. 88; see also R 1873 Progressive, pp. 296–300; G 1878 Catholic, p. 71; R 1852 Brothers, p. 391.

a despotic government exercised over them. Often was the father's heart ready to break within his bosom, as he looked upon the son of his affection, and reflected on the wretchedness to which that son was born; often has the tear of sorrow dimmed the mother's eye, as she looked abroad upon the misery that rested on her native land, and taught her child for the first time to lisp the name of Ireland." Far from being pugnacious and quick-tempered, they always hoped "to obtain a redress of grievances by the power of reason and moral influence."[102] It is noted with pride that Ireland contributed a hero—Montgomery—to the American Revolution.[103] His heroic death also appears in many other schoolbooks, but without reference to his national origin.

A few authors mention that Irish poverty had led to migration to America. Two even assert that these immigrants make excellent citizens.[104] Fiske in 1894 notes the organization of the Know Nothing party to oppose Irish immigration, which had become "so great as to alarm many people."[105] The only specific reference to the Irish in discussing immigration in general is in Willard's popular history: she observed that foreign immigration has diminished because of disorders incident to slavery in the United States, and because Ireland has become more prosperous. She concludes: "As about three-quarters of all the crimes committed in the country have been by foreigners, we hope our state-prisons may hereafter have fewer inmates."[106]

In general, it seems obvious that except among Catholics, the Irish immigrant to the United States was bound to live among a hostile people. His economic, political, and religious sufferings were known but were viewed sympathetically only at the time of the potato famine. Although he could have been, he was not considered a fellow-sufferer with Americans of British oppression. The traits assigned to him did not come from oppression, but included an inherent impatience and violence likely to bring trouble upon himself no matter what British policies operated in Ireland. Obviously his Catholicism interfered with the sympathy

[102] H 1868 Kerney, p. 285; see also R 1873 Progressive, pp. 160–167.

[103] H 1868 Kerney, p. 143.

[104] G 1845 Woodbridge, p. 266; G 1848 Mitchell, pp. 102–103.

[105] H 1894 Fiske, p. 344.

[106] H 1868 Willard, p. 447.

usually extended to the unfortunate. The schoolbooks viewed the Irish as dubious additions to the American population.

FRANCE

Although the American Revolution is regarded as the event next in importance to the birth of Christ, the country we fought is regarded more favorably than the country that aided us in that war. Apart from its formal presentation in the Geographies, France and the French appear most often as assisting the establishment of American independence. Participation in an action unqualifiedly praised in the texts should give France a high rank among nations. But the credit for this enterprise is most often given neither to the French government nor to the French nation, but to an individual, Lafayette.

When official French aid is mentioned, the case is rather coolly treated, as: "The French, who have almost always been the enemies of the English, sent some assistance to the Americans."[107] In their accounts of the American Revolution, the Histories always note French participation in the war against England, but without enthusiasm and usually with criticism. Their aid was reluctantly and ineffectively given: they neglected to supply sufficient money; d'Estaing took his fleet into Boston for repairs at the very moment when the fleet was most needed by the Americans; the fleet was unsuccessful; foreign soldiers were given higher rank than the Americans.[108] Only one author states flatly that America would not have won the war without French aid.[109] The only evident gratitude to the French government falls on Louis XVI in the time of his trials. The execution of this "friend of America" becomes another black mark against the French and their revolution. Schoolbook evaluations of France as an ally clearly depend on the author's opinions on the course of the

[107] R 1831 Hall, p. 168; see also H 1804 Webster, p. 40; H 1833 C. Goodrich, p. 268; H 1851 Guernsey, p. 271.

[108] These instances of ineffective aid are from the following books in that order: R 1830 Practical-R, p. 168; H 1874 Scott, pp. 194, and see 197; H 1875 Higginson, p. 207; H 1874 Scott, p. 181.

[109] H 1874 Scott, p. 224, although he is critical of French aid.

10. Torrey's 1825 Speller shows Lafayette, the only foreigner ever to join the ranks of Ámerican immortals.

French Revolution. In 1791 and 1794 Morse calls France "a powerful and generous ally"; in 1818 this becomes "a powerful ally."[110] Perhaps the major factor in minimizing official French aid to the American Revolution, however, rests in the development of American nationalism: the success of the American Revolution must be shown as an American achievement. The help of an individual French hero would bolster recognition of the justice of the American cause; but to owe independence to a country whose domestic development is not regarded with favor would denigrate American achievement.

Not only is French aid seen primarily through the person of Lafayette, but Lafayette is rather carefully distinguished from the French government and nation. As the missionary of American liberty to his native land, he was cruelly rejected and forced to flee after characterizing the course of his country as anarchy.[111] In the context of these books Lafayette's separation from France and the French is also a serious indictment of the French Revolution. It is interesting to observe that while the hero Lafayette is differentiated from the French, the inglorious Voltaire and the notorious Napoleon are not.

Lafayette appears more frequently in American schoolbooks than any other non-American, and he ranks near Washington in heroic stature. "There was never half so much felt for anyone before save Washington."[112] The oft-told tale of his weeping before the tomb of Washington is added to the repertory of American nationalist literature.[113] He is mentioned several times in most of the Readers, Geographies, and Histories, always as a friend to Washington and as a hero of American nationalism. The frontispiece of Torrey's Speller in 1825 displays a portrait of Lafayette with those of Franklin and Washington. Morse in 1791 includes the date of Lafayette's arrest during the French Revolution in his brief chronological table, covering all major events since the world was created in 4004 B.C. In some books he is more

[110] G 1791 Morse, p. 60; G 1794 Morse, p. 104; G 1818 Morse, p. 109.

[111] For example, see R 1792 Dana, pp. 210–212; G 1794 Morse, p. 431; R 1825 Blake, pp. 303–310; etc.

[112] R 1829 Selection, p. 211; see also H 1872 Noque, p. 168.

[113] R 1840 Snow, pp. 169–170; H 1869 Quackenbos, p. 176; R 1870 Sanders, p. 339; H 1873 Anderson-R, pp. 308–309.

than mortal: "O Matchless chief! of glory's immortal tablets, there is one for him, for him alone."[114]

All Readers after his visit in 1824 to the United States copy speeches made on that occasion, using the material as focus for a great memorial celebration of the American Revolution and Washington. The general tenor of the extracts emphasizes Lafayette's spontaneous aid to the cause of American liberty: "He tore himself away from his country and his home, to fight the battles of freedom in a foreign land, and to make common cause with a people to whom he owed no duty."[115] Always the stress is on his action as an individual. Lafayette is to be added to the ritual of American nationalism taught to children: "Washington and Lafayette should be among the first names, which American children learn to pronounce."[116] He is personally related to the reader when a little boy instructs his sister to pray for Lafayette as her savior:

> He fought for Pa and fought for Ma
> And fought for you and me
> And helped us gain all we enjoy!
> Said Josephine, did he?[117]

American difficulties with France in the 1790's are rarely mentioned except in the Histories. The Genêt affair is treated as a piece of high-handed French impudence in which the American people were "dreading war much, but the sacrifice of honor more."[118] The XYZ affair is represented in every History by the ringing phrase, "Millions for defence, but not one cent for tribute."

In evaluating France as a country the schoolbooks always measure it against England, and the measure exceeds the measured. Physically France is described in most of the Geographies

[114] R 1826 American-S, p. 251; R 1831 Harrod, p. 73.

[115] R 1831 Harrod, p. 197, from speech of Hayne in the Senate, 1824; see also H 1833 C. Goodrich, p. 186; H 1868 Kerney, p. 148; H 1869 Quackenbos, p. 119; H 1873 Anderson-R, pp. 309–311; R 1873 Progressive, pp. 276–277.

[116] R 1838 Angell, p. 24.

[117] R 1832 American-P, p. 54.

[118] H 1826 Hale, p. 366.

as "the finest country in Europe; perhaps in the world."[119] In specific cases and in essential respects, however, it compares unfavorably with England: "Paris undoubtedly excels London in magnificence and splendor, but falls far short of it in cleanliness."[120] In books published in the late nineteenth century, Paris is usually called the most beautiful city in the world as well as the metropolis of art and fashion. In the context of these books this is not a recommendation. Paris "is the world's center of modern art, fashion, and pleasure, as London is of commerce."[121] The frivolity of Paris becomes a foil for a sober, constructive London. French agriculture is also inferior to that of England: ". . . the French people are not so good farmers as the English, and do not so well know how to make their farms rich and beautiful."[122]

As in the treatment of all nations except the United States, Scotland, and Germany, France is always accused of failing to educate its lower classes. Its literary and intellectual endeavors are recognized to be major, but ranking below those of Britain and often of Germany: "Except Great Britain, France has perhaps produced the greatest number of learned men of any kingdom in the known world. In the eloquence of the pulpit and of the bar, the French are acknowledged by the English themselves to be far their superiors, but in most other branches the English have equalled if not exceeded the French."[123] Higher education in France is believed to lead to loose morals, as in the story of an American farmer who is horrified at the sexual mores his sons have brought back from a Parisian education.[124] The universal use of the French language is acknowledged; however, "it wants force and dignity, and yet more, sublimity."[125] This judgment should be compared with the "sober majesty" and "delicacy of discrimination" of the English language.[126] The government of France is also generally inferior to that of England, although

[119] G 1789 Elements, p. 19; G 1793 Workman, p. 129; G 1812 Parish, p. 202; G 1832 Olney, p. 176; G 1840 Olney, p. 202; G 1837 Village, p. 75.

[120] G 1826 Blake, p. 114; see also G 1784 Morse, p. 150; G 1796 Dwight, p. 43; G 1806 Webster, pp. 57, 61; G 1814 Adams, p. 272.

[121] G 1880 Swinton, p. 79.

[122] G 1866 Guyot-P, p. 73.

[123] G 1784 Morse, p. 151.

[124] R 1801 Heaton-P, p. 37.

[125] G 1794 Morse, p. 290; G 1796 Dwight, p. 43; G 1806 Webster, p. 58; G 1820 Darby, p. 161.

[126] R 1831 Harrod, pp. 71–72; see also G 1796 Dwight, p. 32.

neither the governments nor the differences are specifically described. The usual attitude is: "But with all my abhorrence of the British government, I should not hesitate between Westminster Hall and a Middlesex Jury, on the one hand, and the wood of Vincennes and a file of grenadiers on the other."[127]

When they compete in colonial activities, the French are unfavorably contrasted with the English. The French settlement in Quebec began to prosper only after the British conquest.[128] And by contrast to the United States, in Missouri and Louisiana, "This settlement, like all the other French settlements, progressed very slowly. Since the country has fallen under the jurisdiction of the United States, the settlements progress rapidly."[129] The French government is not only inferior to the English and American in colonization techniques, but the French settlers "are superstitious and ignorant. The British and American . . . have better characters and more information."[130] This inferiority, one cannot help but observe, is stressed not only because they are French, but because they are Catholic. The religion of the French colonists is always mentioned, and the unfavorable comparison is made with these two Protestant nations only, never with Spain or Portugal. Several books contrast the religion of the English and American settlers in Louisiana with those of French descent; the latter are said to be "sunk in ignorance and superstition, and blindly devoted to their priests."[131]

But religion brings a still greater odium to France than accrues to other Catholic countries: France is the home of infidelity. In a discussion of the French Revolution in one of the Readers, the question is asked: "Weren't they all papists before the revolution?" The answer: "Why true enough, they had but a poor sort of religion; but bad is better than none."[132] In many Readers there are stories of "a French gentlemen, one of those wicked

[127] R 1826 American-S, p. 163.

[128] G 1830 Hale, p. 118; G 1843 Mitchell, p. 92.

[129] G 1825 Butler, p. 155; see also G 1818 Mann, p. 157; G 1822 S. Morse, p. 125; G 1825 Butler, p. 153.

[130] G 1828 Woodbridge, pp. 62–63; see also G 1812 Morse, p. 217; G 1827 C. Goodrich, p. 85; R 1830 Bartlett, p. 292; G 1833 Clute, p. 162; G 1835 Huntington, p. 106; G 1853 S. Goodrich, p. 144.

[131] G 1814 Adams, p. 188; see also G 1818 Mann, p. 168; G 1818 Morse, p. 81; G 1820 Darby, p. 51; H 1852 E. Willard, p. 116.

[132] R 1844 Smith, p. 17.

persons that did not love or fear God."[133] Some Readers include a dialogue by Lord Lyttleton between the English Locke and the French Bayle wherein Locke insists that Bayle denied God simply to make a sensation.[134] Apparently French frivolity sometimes serves infidelity. The great villain of atheism, however, is Voltaire. In one case he is pictured on his deathbed, so enraged at his own past infidelity that the physicians retire, "declaring that the death of this impious man was too terrible for them to witness!"[135] The accepted judgment on Voltaire comes from the philosopher's scale which magically weighs true worth: here the prayers of a penitent thief outbalance all of Voltaire's wit.[136] In the Geographies this state of religious affairs is assumed to be a French characteristic and one that has produced loose morals in that country. It is also a qualification for French pre-eminence in learning: "Their Encyclopedia, or dictionary of arts and sciences, while it is a monument of industry and science, proves the depravity of the writers, and tends to spread impiety and infidelity."[137] The association of atheism with the French Revolution is persistently maintained, implying not only that it was a major phase of the Revolution but that it was the state religion for many years. A book used in parochial schools describes the distress of French mothers when their husbands read from the almanac the names of vegetables instead of saints as possible names for their newborn children.[138] Furthermore, the religious infidelity of the French carries with it the danger of subversion of religion in other countries. During the American Revolution, "The atheistical philosophy, which had spread over France, was thickly sown in the American army by the French, and tended to produce a serious declension in the tone of religious feelings among the American people."[139]

[133] R 1830 Putnam-I, p. 125; see also R 1789 Webster, pp. 33 ff.; R 1806 Staniford, pp. 65–67; R 1853 Mandeville, p. 199.

[134] R 1803 Murray, pp. 101–106; R 1806 Peirce, pp. 192–197; R 1813 I. Cooke, pp. 225–231.

[135] G 1831 Blake, pp. 60–61; see also R 1853 Mandeville, p. 199; R 1823 Morrill, p. 220.

[136] R 1828 Putnam, p. 48; R 1841 Merriam, p. 213; R 1843 Olney, p. 206; R 1844 Smith, p. 164; R 1851 ASDUK-2, p. 117; R 1851 Tower, p. 140.

[137] G 1807 Parish, p. 150.

[138] H 1868 Kerney, p. 222.

[139] H 1867 Goodrich, p. 152.

The personality characteristics used to define the French soul invariably include politeness, especially to strangers. Frequently, however, this is more accusation than tribute; it becomes "their effeminate and artful corruptions."[140] Their fondness for dress is a sign of superficiality. In one tale a French cook applying for a job is so sumptuously dressed that his potential employer assumes he wants to recommend a cook rather than be one. The latter comments: "No wonder the poor are starved and the butcher unpaid."[141]

Another invariable characteristic assigned to the French is gaiety. But when it appears in incongruous situations, what might have been described as an innocent joy in life is transmuted into a thoughtless or even cruel levity. A poor soldier is shown singing "with that air of gaiety and ease which, under the most indigent circumstances, is peculiar to his thoughtless countrymen."[142] Poverty is not to be taken lightly. The most extreme example occurs during the French Revolution: "Even during the horrors of the Revolution, Paris continued to be the center of dissipation; and while in one part of the city, the revolutionary axe was immolating its numerous victims, in another, the theatres were crowded and everything wore the aspect of joyous festivity."[143] According to these textbooks gaiety in France, and especially in Paris, usually deteriorates into dissipation and corruption of morals. Barlowe's poem "Hasty Pudding," quoted several times, includes the phrase "Paris, that corrupted town."[144] A common characteristic of the city is: "Paris has long been the seat of voluptuousness and dissipation."[145] And this is frequently generalized to include all of France: "Many of the French manners and customs cannot be reconciled to ideas of physical purity;

[140] G 1807 Parish, p. 149; see also R 1799 New Pleasing, p. 82; G 1853 S. Goodrich, p. 200; H 1879 Quackenbos, p. 110.

[141] R 1803 Biglow, p. 149; see also G 1819 Adams, p. 246; R 1828 Robbins-A, p. 41.

[142] R 1811 Hubbard, p. 19; see also G 1806 Cottineau-I, p. 196; G 1807 Parish, p. 149; G 1814 O'Neill, p. 276.

[143] G 1814 Adams, p. 272; G 1818 Mann, p. 281; G 1819 Adams, p. 246.

[144] R 1797 Thomas, p. 187; R 1850 Hall, pp. 274–277.

[145] G 1814 Adams, p. 271; see also R 1796 Bingham, pp. 126–128; R 1801 Heaton-P, p. 193; G 1816 Dwight, p. 54; G 1826 Blake, p. 114; G 1828 Woodbridge, p. 127b.

and the looseness of their morals has become proverbial."[146] In the context of these books this is a serious charge. Sobriety and strict adherence to a rigid moral code had become virtues hallowed by association with the American Founding Fathers and intimately linked with the development of American civilization.

The French are also consistently portrayed as fickle, inconstant and mercurial. These characteristics may be ascribed directly to the frequent changes in the course of the French Revolution. The 1784 edition of Morse contains no such description, but the 1822 edition adds these characteristics to those already mentioned in the earlier work. Only one writer, S. Goodrich, describing the French as lively and impetuous, warns his readers not to adopt attitudes expressed by British writers, that they are also vain, frivolous, and fickle. An 1872 Reader has a Frenchman ask a Swiss why the Swiss fight for money whereas the French fight only for honor. The Swiss answers: "I suppose that each fights for what he most lacks."[147]

Although cruelty is never assigned as a general characteristic of the French, it is illustrated as such many times in the schoolbook treatment of the French–English wars of the seventeenth and eighteenth centuries, and in the French Revolution. The charge of using Indians in warfare is made against the British only when they are fighting Americans; in the French–English wars, when America is identified with Britain, the charge is made only and emphatically against the French: "They [the French] even proceeded as far as to employ Indians to come down and harass the frontiers of the colonists, by ravaging and burning whole towns, and murdering whole families of the inhabitants in the most cruel and shocking manner."[148] Indian tortures are described in minute detail. One story in two of the Readers tells of a "degenerate Frenchman" who takes over the torture of

[146] G 1820 Darby, p. 160; G 1866 Woodbridge, p. 444; S 1875 Monroe, p. 144.

[147] R 1872 Willson, p. 61.

[148] G 1784 Morse, p. 92; see also R 1811 Hubbard, pp. 95–96; R 1824 Lowe, p. 150; R 1826 Frost, p. 28; H 1826 Hale, p. 83; R 1829 Selection, p. 25; H 1831 S. Goodrich, p. 39; H 1839 Frost, p. 122; H 1843 Hall and Baker, p. 149; G 1853 S. Goodrich, p. 30–55; H 1867 Goodrich, p. 82; H 1867 Willson, p. 103; H 1869 Quackenbos, pp. 70–71; H 1885 Donnelly, p. 74.

General Putnam after the Indians have finished with him.[149] It is interesting to observe that the same bravado assigned to the Americans when fighting any enemy is allowed to the British soldiers at war with France: "Though we had no arms, one Englishman is able to beat five Frenchmen at any time."[150]

The French Revolution

With few exceptions the treatment of the French Revolution is decidedly unfavorable, endorsing the point of view of American conservatives of the 1790's. Three of the exceptions are Readers containing extracts from Republican orations which assume the French Revolution to be a continuation of the American.[151] Morse, in 1791, apparently reacting to the early, more conservative phases of the Revolution, says: "A most important and glorious revolution in favor of civil and religious liberty is now accomplished in France."[152] Since his next paragraph notes the large number of Catholic clergy in France before the Revolution (and he is strongly anti-Catholic throughout) he must be primarily concerned with the disestablishment of the Roman Catholic Church. Significantly he eliminates this favorable statement from the 1798 and all subsequent editions, after the revolution had taken a more radical turn. Very few books make any attempt to explain the causes of the revolution or the issues involved. One attributes it mainly to the "boundless demands of a rapacious clergy."[153] Thomas in 1797 quotes a speech by Joseph Allen given at Worcester two years before, attributing the Revolution to "the despotism of the court, united with bigotry, of the priests."[154] Evidently when the French Revolution in its early stages could be seen as a religious reformation for the disestablishment of the Catholic Church it could be viewed with approval.

The rest of the texts limit the descriptions of the French Revolution largely to the Reign of Terror. So Goldsmith in 1807 introduces his section on France: "This country, rendered conspicuous by the bloody progress and disgraceful termination

[149] R 1804 Webster, pp. 47–48; R 1815 R. Adams, pp. 47–60.

[150] R 1853 Tower and Walker, p. 149.

[151] R 1797 Thomas, pp. 175–176, 209–210; R 1807 Bingham-C, pp. 85–86; R 1831 Harrod, pp. 153–156.

[152] G 1791 Morse, p. 270. [153] R 1826 American-S, p. 125.

[154] R 1797 Thomas, p. 173.

of its recent revolution. . . ." Typical is the following: ". . . and perhaps more bloody havoc and greater enormity of crimes among its own citizens, during its first stages never stained the historic page."[155] Other sample phrases are: "cruelty, ferocity, and impiety, before unknown in civilized society"; "Horrible enormities"; "vast amphitheatre of carnage, a bloody arena"; "great massacre"; "a scene of blood and slaughter . . . such as was never before witnessed in any age or country"; "crimes and horrors were continually perpetrated"; "human tigers"; "torrents of innocent blood."[156] Merriam in 1835 implies that such carnage was the purpose of the revolution: "The people had been oppressed by their rulers; but instead of trying to have such a revolution as would give them better laws and better rulers, they proceeded to commit the most horrible crimes."[157] Even the Spellers in their definitions and phrases for exercise use "Reign of Terror," "guillotine—a machine for beheading persons," as examples necessary for the child's general vocabulary equipment. Books used in parochial schools even more vehemently, if that were possible, condemn the French Revolution. One sounds rather like the Marquis de Bonald condemning the modern world: "Society in Europe, threatened both with anarchy and despotism, by the Protestant Reformation in the sixteenth century, and by the French Revolution in the eighteenth century was saved finally by the church."[158] The revolution "destroyed with insane fury, all that was best and purest in France," according to books used in the parochial schools.[159]

Only a few books attempt any explanation of this violence: "But it is not temporary delirium to be expected, when twenty-four millions of people emerge from the midnight gloom of slavery, and meet the noon-tide beam of liberty?"[160] Another quotes

[155] G 1818 Mann, p. 235; see also H 1867 Goodrich, p. 161.

[156] The quoted phrases are from the following in that order: G 1807 Parish, p. 149; G 1826 Blake, p. 193; R 1830 Emerson, p. 236; S 1836 Brandreth, p. 94; G 1836 Smith, p. 206; R 1852 Town, pp. 34–35; R 1856 Sargent-4, p. 308; H 1881 Thalheimer, p. 192.

[157] R 1835 Merriam, p. 143.

[158] G 1876 Comprehensive, p. 13.

[159] G 1876 Comprehensive, p. 91; see also H 1868 Kerney, p. 221.

[160] R 1797 Thomas, p. 173; from speech of Joseph Allen at Worcester, July 4, 1795.

William Ellery Channing: "The French Revolution is perpetually sounding in our ears, as a warning against the lawlessness of the people. But when I hear that revolution quoted to frighten us from reform, to show us the danger of lifting up the depressed and ignorant mass, I must ask whence it came."[161] Here the violence of the revolution is a reaction to the violence of the Old Regime. Another book ascribes it to a lack of self-control in the impulsive nature of the French: ". . . The French people had become wild with excitement, and had done many things that were wrong and dangerous. They put a great number of people to death and made many bad and foolish laws."[162]

It seems incongruous that in the schoolbooks of a new republic the other bit of information on the French Revolution that is invariably stressed, and with horror, is the execution of the king. Morse in 1794 presents him with a martyr's crown: "the friend of America, and of the rights of mankind." Blake notes: "the meek and steady virtues of the patriot king . . . glowing with affection for his people."[163] Edmund Burke's Romantic moralizing on the fate of Marie Antoinette also seems somewhat odd in this context. Her fall proves "That the age of chivalry is gone—that of the sophister, economists and calculators has succeeded; and the glory of Europe is extinguished forever. Never, never more shall we behold that generous loyalty to rank and sex. . . ."[164]

Inevitably the French Revolution is compared with the American, and never favorably. The American Revolution is assumed to be the inspiration for the French, but liberty became perverted in transit. One author allegorically pictures the torch of liberty as a steady flame passed from Britain to America, but when passed to France it becomes a "wild Bacchante."[165] Lacking the sober spirit of the Americans, the French "did not know how to manage such affairs, and a bloody time they had."[166] Everett, in an 1856 speech, turns with relief to American history:

[161] R 1852 Gilder, pp. 153–155.

[162] H 1885 Donnelly, p. 112.

[163] G 1794 Morse, p. 354; R 1825 Blake, p. 314.

[164] R 1811 I. Cooke, pp. 211–212; R 1826 American-S, pp. 104–105; R 1830 MacLeod, pp. 64–65; R 1836 Cobb-N.A., pp. 247–248; R 1845 Swan, pp. 464–465.

[165] R 1828 Greenwood and Emerson, p. 199.

[166] H 1866 Lossing, p. 174.

"After sickening over the horrors of that dreadful period,—the butchery, I do not say of kings and queens, but of gray-haired men, of women, of priests—the atrocities of the human tigers who preyed on the life-blood of France, and dared to invoke the sacred name of republican liberty as the cover of their abominations."[167] One book points out that after their original enthusiasm the Americans soon realized that the French Revolution was on a vastly different path from their own: "With their ideas of law and order, the Americans could not go along with the French, rioters from the first, and soon destroyers and murderers, rather than freemen."[168] The two revolutions differed also in their effects on mankind. A Catholic book compares the American with the French Revolution: "The former giving birth to a new people and proving a blessing to mankind; the latter convulsing the Old World, steeping the French people in blood, and bequeathing to Europe a spirit of disorder and discontent."[169] The same contrast is evident in a piece by Jonathan Maxcy depicting a Frenchman's entrance into the hall where the first American Congress is meeting: "The ferocious Gaul would have dropped his sword at the hall door, and have fled, thunderstruck, as from an assembly of Gods!"[170]

In comparison with the American Revolution, which is always assumed to be a conservative one, the French Revolution represents two opposite trends: too much rationalism, leading to atheism; and too much violence, leading to carnage. The first is illustrated in a discussion of the American adoption of the decimal system as an outgrowth of our rational republicanism: "Here too the tree of liberty first put forth its blossoms after having been eaten for ages by the cankerworm of feudal Gothicism. France has followed our glorious example—she has declared herself free, and reduced her weights, measures *etc.* to decimal simplicity. But, as that enthusiastic nation have carried their republicanism too far, so they have stretched decimal simplicity beyond its proper limits even into decedary infidelity."[171] The second is illustrated by the oft-quoted Webster address at the laying of the corner stone for the Bunker Hill monument: "The

[167] R 1856 Sargent-4, p. 308.
[168] H 1881 Eliot, p. 294.
[169] H 1868 Kerney, p. 15.
[170] R 1875 Sheldon, p. 199.
[171] A 1795 Root, pref.

great wheel of political revolution began to move in America. Here its rotation was guarded, regular and safe. Transferred to the other continent, from unfortunate but natural causes, it received an irregular and violent impulse; it whirled along with a fearful celerity; till at length, like the chariot wheels in the races of antiquity, it took fire from the rapidity of its own motion, and blazed onward, spreading conflagration and terror around."[172] Thus the French Revolution is an unfortunate accident resulting from the American. The descriptions of the French Revolution are of a bloody debauch; there is almost no indication of injustices before the Revolution, nor of desirable social change during the Revolution. There is no intellectual background to the movement, nor is there any indication of the importance of French eighteenth-century political thought, nor of its influence in America. By contrast, this portrayal of the French Revolution supports the idea that the American Revolution was bloodless, conservative, and unique among revolutions. Only the Americans know how to make a sound revolution. The following poem indicates how lasting the infamy of the French Revolution is to be:

> Oh, shame to thee, land of the Gaul!
> Oh, shame to thy children and thee!
> Unwise in thy glory and base in thy fall!
> How wretched thy portion shall be!
>
> . . . .
>
> The savage all wild in his glen
> Is nobler and better than thou;
> Thou standest a wonder, a marvel to men,
> Such perfidy blackens thy brow!
> If thou wert the place of my birth
> At once from thy arms would I sever;
> I'd fly to the uttermost parts of the earth,
> And quit thee for ever and ever;
> And thinking of thee in my long after years,
> Should but kindle my blushes, and waken my tears.[173]

The attitude toward Napoleon is ambivalent. Curiously enough, in the schoolbooks of a republic, he is more often elevated

[172] R 1828 Hopkins, p. 130; R 1898 Williams G-2, pp. 273–274.
[173] R 1844 Smith, pp. 74–75.

to heroism than condemned as a villain, and he is almost as much discussed as Lafayette. As a villain he has the guise of a military despot and subverter of republics: "And shall republics become the instrument of him who has effaced the title of Attila to the 'scourge of God!'"[174] This quotation is, however, misleading in its violence, and unusual in its wholehearted disapproval. Most unfavorable accounts are cooler in tone: "This famous conqueror and despot, by his arms and intrigues subjugated all the nations of Europe except Great Britain."[175] But he often appears as a liberator rather than conqueror. His address to the people of Italy is used in some Readers: "People of Italy, the French army comes to break your chains . . . !"[176] In two cases, his fall is blamed on the tyrannical wish of other countries to prevent France from exercising the right to choose her own monarch.[177] But whether liberator or conqueror, his greatness is unquestioned. His was a "wonderful military genius, with great executive capacity."[178] He is always shown as the greatest general of modern times, surrounded by the pageantry of military glory. In pictures he reviews his troops while impressively seated on horseback, after the prototypes illustrating the Napoleonic legend in contemporary France.[179] A poem by one of the textbook authors, Pierpont, on the subject of Napoleon's grave is quoted in six books in the middle of the century. It typifies the legendary aura growing around his name—a legend apparently developing in America as well as in France. It is the grave of an exile mourned by the dirge of the sea.[180] Another poem on Napoleon remarks that only the ocean is large enough and worthy to hold his remains.[181]

[174] R 1826 American-S, p. 176; see also R 1811 Hubbard, p. 102; R 1830 Emerson, pp. 159–160; R 1854 Mandeville, p. 182.

[175] G 1817 Cummings, p. 85.

[176] R 1807 Bingham-C, pp. 154–155; R 1826 Greenwood and Emerson, p. 62; R 1830 Emerson, pp. 84–85; R 1831 Harrod, pp. 127–129.

[177] R 1828 Robbins-A, p. 104; R 1852 Gilder, pp. 144–145.

[178] G 1876 Comprehensive, p. 91. This book and G 1878 Catholic, p. 74, another Roman Catholic schoolbook, after expressing admiration for Napoleon, ascribe his downfall to his mistreatment of the pope.

[179] R 1843 McGuffey, p. 152; G 1853 Mitchell, p. 115.

[180] R 1831 Bailey, pp. 174–175; R 1843 Griswold, p. 141; R 1846 Swan-G, pp. 201–202; R 1852 Cobb, p. 241; R 1856 Sanders-4, pp. 230–231.

[181] R 1834 Emerson, pp. 155–156.

Why Napoleon should receive so much attention in books professedly opposed to tyranny and war presents something of a problem. Part of the answer is undoubtedly in the preoccupation with military exploits common to most of these books, in spite of the antiwar sentiments they express. Nor is militaristic nationalism despised. But, even more important, Napoleon is an outstanding example of the self-made man: "With no friend but his sword, and no fortune but his talents, he rushed into the lists where rank and wealth, and genius had arrayed themselves, and competition fled from him as from the glances of destiny."[182] His Alpine expedition not only shows his military genius but implies that anyone can accomplish anything if he really wants to. Napoleon is quoted as saying, "Impossible is the adage of fools."[183] And the Hundred Days indicate "It was difficult to confine Napoleon except in the confines of the tomb."[184] For his perseverance in the face of difficulties, an 1856 Speller places him in sober company: "Newton, Franklin, Washington and Napoleon—different as they were in many respects,—were all renowned as hard workers."[185]

But another lesson is drawn from Napoleon, especially in later books. He typifies the European hero who is interested in his own and his country's aggrandizement, but who is innocent of the moral grandeur characterizing the American hero. Many books contrast him to Lafayette, whose ambition was selfless and patriotic. Others compare his "guilty glory" with the pure fame of Washington. In thus distinguishing among heroes, the later books drew on the writings of Chateaubriand, Lamartine, W. E. Channing, and Emerson. It should be noted that Lafayette, a hero with the same moral purposes as George Washington, is Americanized in these books and rejected by his countrymen. But Napoleon's love of military exploits adds that ingredient to the French national character.[186] He represents France as Lafayette is

[182] R 1830 Emerson, pp. 162–163; see also R 1826 Greenwood and Emerson, p. 61; G 1830 Bazeley, p. 151; G 1837 Village, pp. 76–77; R 1852 Brothers, pp. 387–391; R 1854 Sargent, pp. 396–397.

[183] R 1873 American, pp. 71–73.

[184] S 1888 Shoup, p. 59.

[185] S 1856 Sargent, p. 157.

[186] G 1869 Warren-C, p. 73; G 1875 McNally, p. 73; G 1875 Swinton, p. 106; G 1878 Catholic, p. 73; G 1887 Warren, p. 87.

not allowed to do. His defeat came from a European coalition rather than from his countrymen. Thus America inherits the moral heroism of a Lafayette, and France the selfish heroism of a Napoleon.

On the whole the French appear in no very favorable light. Where sobriety is admired, the French are gay; where stability is admired, the French are fickle; where Protestantism is admired, the French are Catholic; where religion is a prime virtue, the French are infidels. Their accomplishments in the arts, the intellectual life, and in military exploits are great, but devoid of moral meaning.

GERMANY

Although not given nearly as much space as England and France, Germany occupies a small but choice position in nineteenth-century American schoolbooks. Until its unification Germany was important to nineteenth-century America mainly as a source for immigrants. Few immigrant groups are mentioned favorably in the textbooks throughout the century, but when those of German origin are described, they are considered worthy additions to the American population. When they come to the American West "... on account of their thrift and industry, they are always welcome settlers."[187] After the unification of Germany, its national economic and military progress offer a further source for American admiration.

On the whole, Germany and the Germans appear in a most favorable light. Nothing seriously derogatory is said of them, and their contributions to world culture are assessed as positive and constructive ones. Perhaps because of a lack of knowledge on the part of textbook authors, distinctions are rarely made among the various German states before or after unification. Throughout the nineteenth century they are discussed collectively as the "Germans" without reference to regionalism. And, as with other nations, the definition of their national character is the important thing for the child to learn about them. Major historical events or movements in Germany, such as unification, are rarely mentioned.

[187] G 1875 Swinton, p. 108; see also G 1791 Morse, p. 149; G 1848 Mitchell, p. 105; G 1881 Maury, p. 43.

What stands out most is that their character closely resembles the American in important respects. Germans are universally agreed to be an industrious, honest, and thrifty people. Furthermore, they alone among European nations have the same kind of mechanical ingenuity that characterizes the Americans. The Germans "can boast of a greater number of useful discoveries in arts and sciences than any other European nation." [188]

Germany is also pre-eminent in the field of learning. Among American intellectuals some knowledge of the German university and of German philosophy was widespread by 1840. The American Transcendental philosophers in the circle of Emerson were much concerned with the philosophies of Kant, Fichte, and Hegel; transported here largely through the works of Carlyle and Coleridge, they were more admired than understood. The schoolbooks reflect this recognition of German scholarship in some such terms as the following: "The schools and universities are the finest in the world and German literature is rich and varied." [189] They are also agreed that "In no other country is authorship so extensively made a business for life." Webster, in 1806, finds German concentration on the production of books overdone: "Printing and book-making are even carried to excess; but the multiplication of books, though excessive, never fails to produce many valuable works." [190]

But more important than their sponsorship of higher education and advanced scholarship is their support for common school education. The Germans are specifically noted as one of the few nationalities in the world, outside of the United States, who believe in common school education for all. This is usually stated in somewhat the following terms: "It [the Prussian state] is noted for its great and efficient armies, and the general intelligence of its people, and the most complete and comprehensive system of public schools in the world." [191] American schoolbook authors believe that the German public school system, like the American,

[188] G 1791 Morse, p. 280; see also G 1814 Adams, p. 276; G 1828 Woodbridge, p. 118; G 1845 S. Morse, p. 53; G 1875 McNally, p. 74.

[189] G 1872 Hall, p. 114.

[190] The last two quotations are from G 1824 J. Worcester, 119, and G 1806 Webster, p. 113 in that order; see also G 1848 Mitchell, p. 105; G 1866 Guyot-C, p. 81; G 1898 Redway and Hinman, p. 124.

[191] G 1894 Harper, p. 98.

was instituted "for the purpose of giving a general diffusion of useful knowledge."[192] This is much more important than eminence in the field of scholarship. A public school system, to American schoolbook authors, provides equality of opportunity for all men and is one of the primary contributions of American culture to the world. That Prussia (and no particular distinction is drawn between Prussia and Germany) also evolved such a system implies a social and political system in some measure like that of the United States.

One other major characteristic associated with the Germans could be disturbing: "The national character is of a military cast, and its influence of the first order."[193] In the context of the many selections from antiwar literature used in the Readers, one would expect this to be regarded as a most undesirable trait; but such is not the case. It is stated rather as a neutral fact or as one that indicates an admirable national strength. The same books that contain selections on the humanitarian necessity of abandoning the practice of war are also full of stories about war, or of actual battles described in splendid colors. One cannot escape the conclusion that the glorification of war and of military heroes has major value in these books. As a means of engendering nationalism, the American military past is presented *in extenso*; military descriptions occupy more space in most of the Histories than any other subject. The descriptions of battles are full of the dramatic excitement that would inevitably catch the imagination of the child, whereas the antiwar sermons are, on the whole, tiresome preachments. By the 1890's, every Geography takes note of German military interests, but in tones of admiration: "The German soldiers are the finest in Europe," or, "The Germans are remarkable for their attainments in science, literature, and art, and for their military skill."[194] Secure in their oceans, American schoolbooks could present this quality as an admirable example of efficiency in the German character rather than as a threatening militarism.

[192] G 1803 Hubbard, p. 154; see also G 1836 Smith, p. 215; G 1862 Mitchell, p. 256.

[193] R 1830 Bartlett, p. 269.

[194] These two quotations are from the following books in that order: G 1894 Harper, p. 98; G 1898 Redway and Hinman, p. 124.

Individual Germans appear infrequently. Frederick the Great is seen as a hero-king who worked hard in the service of his people. In a number of books the story is told of his benevolence to a servant who sends all his wages home to his mother. Morse alone sees in him "one of the infidel band of Philosophists; and contributed with Voltaire and others to corrupt the literature and religion of Europe."[195] In stories where the central character is identified only by nationality rather than by name, the Germans come out very well. For example, there is the story of a pious German nobleman who built schools for poor children. He is sharply contrasted to a visiting French infidel.[196] Oddly enough, in this favorable atmosphere, those Germans who helped the United States in its war for independence are rarely mentioned. The Hessians employed by the British army are always remarked in accounts of the Revolution, but the onus is put on the British rather than on the Hessians for earning money in such a way.

In the latter part of the century the Germans are identified racially as Teutons: "The inhabitants are mainly of Teutonic origin. They are remarkable for their ingenuity, enterprise and intelligence."[197] In one case Tacitus' description of the ancient Germans is concluded with this statement: "As a general rule, these same characteristics mark their descendants, the modern Germans."[198] The racial designation adds little but a verbal label to what was essentially the description of a nationality in terms of race as understood by the late nineteenth century. In any case their racial label has approval.

If schoolbook attitudes toward their nationality played any part in the formation of adult attitudes toward nationality groups, the German immigrant would be welcomed in the United States as would be few other immigrant groups. From the picture of Germany and the Germans in these schoolbooks, the Germans already possessed most of the characteristics Americans associated with themselves. This ranked them high as a nation and also meant that they could become assimilated into the American nationality with a minimum of effort or change.

[195] G 1818 Morse, p. 261.
[196] R 1830 Putnam-I, p. 125; see also R 1839 Sigourney, pp. 208–220.
[197] G 1875 McNally, p. 74.
[198] G 1870 Cornell-P, p. 76.

SOUTHERN EUROPE

The characteristics assigned to the nations of southern Europe are so alike throughout the century that the reader would assume them to be characteristics of a race. In describing this section of Europe, Woodbridge specifies from his 1828 edition on that: "The people are generally indolent, and are less virtuous and less distinguished for learning and improvements, than other nations of Europe."[199] In these books it is the inherent trait of indolence, rather than environmental factors, that has produced such a spectacular decline in Italy, Portugal, and Spain.

Catholicism, most unfavorably presented, is another common denominator closely related to their deterioration. The charges against the Roman Catholic Church made by the Nativist movement in America between 1830 and 1850 are all to be found in these books from 1784 through the Civil War. An American adult in 1830 had already as a youth been fully indoctrinated in anti-Catholicism. Criticisms of the Catholic Church made in connection with the discussion of southern Europe are used to show the dangers of the church to the body politic, a major issue in Nativist propaganda. The later books, while maintaining the bigotry and superstition of the people of Catholic countries, are somewhat more temperate on the subject.

ITALY

For the United States of this period, Italy's major importance comes from the facts that the pope resides there, that American artists went there for training, and, particularly at the end of the century, that it was the home of many future immigrants to the United States. The Italians are depicted throughout as an artistic but degenerate nation. Italy, like Greece, is regarded as the home of the arts. But in all books there is more stress on their decline than on their pre-eminence: "Italy, the garden of Europe, the parent of the arts and of civilization, and once the mistress of the world, is still a fine, populous and interesting country, but inhabited by a race of people who are become degenerated by

[199] G 1828 Woodbridge, p. 122.

superstition and political slavery."[200] Willets, in changing the term "political slavery" in the above quotation to "popish slavery," states a major reason for the decline that is implied in all texts.[201] The papacy is always referred to in derogatory terms: "that astonishing universal usurpation, the spiritual dominion of the Pope"; "Papal monster, this pretended vice regent of the *Messiah*." Morse, in describing Rome, notes: "the splendor of its public festivals (the fruits of a mistaken bigotry)."[202] This parenthetical phrase is obviously unnecessary to an objective description of festivals, but it must qualify the preceding complimentary phrase to satisfy the author's hostility to the Catholic Church. The temporal powers of the pope are often judged by innuendo: "The city of Rome was once the capital of a mighty empire, and of the civilized world, but it is verging to decay; under the dominion of Augustus its population was 2,000,000 and its circumference 50 miles, but under the Pope it is reduced to 130,000 souls."[203]

Italy's poverty is always described and usually charged to "the feudal and pontifical systems combined."[204] Naples had 30,000 beggars "while monks, priests, lawyers, nobility, fidlers and footmen are in unusual proportion."[205] Blame is usually in some degree attached to the church, and occasionally the church is made the sole agent: "The wealth of the country is amassed by the convents and rich clergy, while the streets are crowded with beggars."[206] This charge remains general when made against the state, but it is specifically illustrated as above when attached to the church. Thus the church is graphically portrayed as a positive danger to the economic and social well-being of the state.

[200] G 1804 Goldsmith, p. 21; see also G 1816 Workman, p. 79–80; G 1817 Cummings, p. 91; G 1830 Bazeley, p. 157; G 1832 Olney, p. 211; G 1840 Olney, p. 186–187; G 1866 Guyot-C, p. 86; G 1866 Woodbridge, p. 337.

[201] G 1815 Willetts, p. 62.

[202] The three quotations are from the following in that order: G 1818 Morse, p. 302; G 1818 Mann, p. 230; G 1818 Morse, p. 304.

[203] G 1830 Bazeley, p. 157; see also G 1807 Parish, pp. 156–160; G 1816 Workman, pp. 80–81; G 1835 Huntington, p. 173.

[204] R 1826 Frost, p. 195; see also G 1793 Workman, p. 136; G 1800 Smith, p. 51.

[205] G 1816 Workman, p. 80; see also G 1818 Morse, p. 305; G 1820 Darby, p. 179; S 1839 Cramer, pp. 101–102; R 1840 Angell-3, pp. 47–48; G 1853 Mitchell, p. 108.

[206] G 1806 Webster, p. 88.

The later books are more careful to distinguish between northern and southern Italy. The North is productive and the people industrious, but "The agricultural products of the rest of Italy are insufficient, and poverty is widespread, so that the people are forced to emigrate in large numbers."[207] Some imply that the poverty of the South must be a natural result of the laziness of the people, because the climate is mild and the country should be productive."[208]

The adjectives used to describe the Italian character always include: affable, superstitious, revengeful, effeminate, immoral. Modern Italians are carefully and unfavorably distinguished from their ancestors: "Italy was the country of the Romans, the conquerors of the world: but the modern Italians bear no resemblance to the Romans. They are effeminate, superstitious and slavish."[209] The general attitude is well expressed in poetry:

> Where the old Romans deathless acts displayed,
> Their base degenerate progeny upbraid.[210]

Apparently Italy was not important enough to America to appear often in the practice sentences in the Spellers, but when it is mentioned, it is as a nation in decline: "The Romans have greatly degenerated since the Augustan age."[211] A Catholic Reader, in 1852, realizing the connection between attacks on the Italians and on the Catholic Church, offers the lone dissenting voice. It states that the building of a new church in Italy "is alone sufficient to prove, that the spirit and magnificence of the ancient Romans still animate the modern Italians."[212]

From these textbooks the reader would assume that immorality and criminal propensities are national characteristics of the Italians. "Many customs which in other countries are deemed criminal, are tolerated in Italy."[213] Crime often assumes the

[207] G 1899 Tarbell, p. 95. [208] G 1866 Guyot-C, p. 86.

[209] G 1822 S. Morse, p. 223; see also G 1816 Workman, p. 81; G 1818 Mann, p. 269; G 1827 C. Goodrich, p. 133; R 1828 Robbins-P, p. 134; G 1837 Village, p. 80.

[210] R 1834 S. Willard-P, p. 101.

[211] S 1844 Clagett, p. 150.

[212] R 1852 Brothers, pp. 48–49.

[213] G 1796 Dwight, p. 82; see also G 1831 Woodbridge, p. 124; G 1831 S. Worcester, p. 48; G 1835 Huntington, p. 171; G 1845 Woodbridge, p. 290.

form of assassination, growing out of a national trait of vindictiveness.[214] One Geography devotes half a page to the love of the Italian population for their brigands. Without this popular protection, the robbers would soon be captured.[215] A McGuffey Reader uses the brigands of Italy as the only group comparable in viciousness to the prisoners in a Massachusetts jail whose rebellion he describes.[216] Immorality, in the usage of these books, apparently refers to sensuality which produces loose behavior: "The women are very amorous: so that the marriage ties, even among the higher ranks are little regarded. Hence, lascivious manners and vindictiveness—the great floodgates of all the evils of life, and its miserable end."[217] Here an alien sexual code is identified with immorality. One author relates this directly to Catholicism: "Their religion, which is the Roman Catholic, relaxes their morals, and renders them indifferent to female chastity."[218]

Only one author expects national unification to produce a brighter future: "They cannot be ranked as a very progressive people; but since they have obtained their national liberty and unity important changes have been taking place, and they now have free schools and a free press. The people are generally industrious, frugal and temperate, but excitable and passionate."[219] (The word "temperate" here probably applies only to consumption of alcoholic beverages.) In most books unification is unnoticed.

On the whole Italy is described as a vast ruin, both in architecture and people. In their morals, superstitions, and lack of interest in improvement they would seem to be the very antithesis of the Americans. Italian immigrants could not expect to find a welcome in the United States.

SPAIN AND PORTUGAL

In nineteenth-century schoolbooks Spain and Portugal can hardly be distinguished from one another; they are often spoken of together, and they are assigned the same characteristics when

[214] G 1818 Smith, p. 53; G 1830 Hale, p. 24.

[215] G 1866 Guyot-P, p. 81.

[216] R 1866 McGuffey-5, p. 301.

[217] G 1818 Mann, p. 270; see also G 1784 Morse, p. 153; R 1831 Lowe-Second, pp. 152–153; R 1847 Rickard and Orcutt-P, p. 60.

[218] G 1807 Parish, p. 157.

[219] G 1878 Swinton, p. 106.

discussed separately. The descriptions of the two countries are most striking for their delineation of Roman Catholicism and for their accounts of colonial activities in America. Both civilizations are assumed to be in a state of decline often directly attributed, in the books published in the first half of the century, to the Catholic Church, and to degeneration in those of the second half of the century. Interestingly enough, the baleful influence of the church is just as graphically portrayed in the beginning of the century as in the period of Nativism. Evidently the nativism of the New England conservative at the end of the eighteenth century had not faded from the schoolbooks before the Nativist movement of the pre-Civil War period replenished it.

While Italy is disliked as the seat of the Roman Catholic Church, Portugal is considered the home of "The most superstitious and intolerant Catholics in Europe."[220] As in the case of Italy, the clergy are pictured as numerous and parasitic: "Portugal is, at present, little less than a kingdom of priests, monks and nuns, who entirely devour the substance of the country."[221] And in Spain, Morse and others estimate 200,000 clergy.[222] Their enormous revenues in the midst of a poverty-stricken population are noted, and in Spain their presence is sometimes assumed to contribute to sexual immorality: "The national character is now stamped with the common practice of illicit commerce and adultery, under the mask of religion."[223] Spain is also distinguished for the Inquisition, described here in lurid detail. Morse's characterization, "a tribunal disgraceful to human nature," is quite generally copied.[224] Although the methods and powers of the inquisitorial courts are clearly those of the Spanish Inquisition, with its effective state support, no attempt is made to dissociate the Spanish Inquisition from that of the Roman Catholic Church. The odium attached to the Inquisition in Spain

[220] G 1822 J. Worcester, p. 149.

[221] G 1784 Morse, p. 145; see also G 1800 Smith, p. 61; G 1814 Adams, p. 292; G 1830 Hale, p. 254.

[222] G 1791 Morse, p. 268; see also G 1806 Webster, p. 66; G 1807 Parish, p. 153; G 1816 Workman, p. 78; G 1820 Darby, p. 165; G 1835 Huntington, p. 168.

[223] G 1818 Mann, p. 293; see also G 1806 Webster, p. 73; G 1820 Darby, p. 166.

[224] G 1784 Morse, p. 148.

is allowed to accrue to the church in Rome. Spain's decline in literature, prominently featured, is attributed to domination by the church. After mentioning a number of universities, Morse states: "but there is so much bigotry in the management of them that they are comparatively of little value."[225] Needless to say, it is generally believed that the clergy have contributed to popular ignorance by deliberately keeping the Bible from the people. Certainly the discussion of Spain and Portugal reflects no credit on the church.

Among the characteristics assigned to both Portuguese and Spanish, superstition and bigotry loom large. Next to religious rigidity, the quality most frequently associated with the Portuguese is indolence. There is some question whether the Spanish or the Portuguese are pre-eminent in this quality. Indolence is both a symptom and a cause of Portugal's decline from its former enterprising spirit. Luxury, consequent on the produce of their foreign possessions, evidently caused the enervation of Portuguese character.[226] All are agreed that "Agriculture, manufacturing, the arts, education and improvements of every kind are in a backward state." And "In literary excellence Portugal is among the last of the European nations."[227]

Perhaps because the period of Spain's greatness was more recent than that of the Italians, and better known in the United States than that of the Portuguese, the Spanish are described with somewhat greater respect than the people of these other two nations. Morse's description in 1784 is not seriously modified during the next century: "The Spaniards are grave in discourse, majestic in deportment, patient in adversity, temperate in eating and drinking, delicate in point of honor, faithful to their monarch; but much addicted to laziness and pride; politic, cunning, mistrustful, revengeful, and tyrants over a vanquished enemy."[228] Most of these qualities have also been applied to the people of Portugal and Italy; here, however, Spanish dignity, delicate sense of honor, bravery, and cruelty are stressed. As in the case

[225] G 1822 S. Morse, p. 218; see also G 1803 Hubbard, p. 172; G 1807 Parish, p. 154; G 1835 Huntington, p. 167; G 1866 Woodbridge, p. 346.

[226] G 1804 Goldsmith, p. 24; G 1815 Willetts, p. 64; G 1818 Mann, p. 294.

[227] These two quotations are from the following: G 1845 S. Morse, p. 51; G 1814 O'Neill, p. 294.

[228] G 1784 Morse, p. 147.

of the Italians, revengefulness is assumed to lead to frequent assassination. In the later part of the century, there is somewhat more emphasis on the indolence of both Spanish and Portuguese: "The people of Madrid work very little. In the morning the men walk idly about."[229] The after-dinner siesta is noted with equal astonishment. Besides neglecting the solid virtues, they love amusements, fancy dress, music, and "are extravagantly fond of dancing." Bereft of the virtues of Poor Richard, so admired in these schoolbooks, "They failed to catch the spirit of progress and improvement . . . which mark the age."[230] Cruelty is abundantly illustrated by their actions in Latin America, in the Inquisition, and by the frequent descriptions of bull-fighting often accompanied by pictures in the texts. The attendance of women at spectacles of "the wanton cruelty of bull-fighting" is mentioned with particular horror.[231] Such cruelty in action is presumed to be inherent in the Spanish character.

Most of the information about Spain in all textbooks centers around its conquest and administration of Latin America, and there is an enormous amount of such material in all books. The colonial activities of Spain are so prominent because America is of first importance in these books, and also because the Spanish conquest can serve as a foil for the English settlement. The English policy of taking away the land of the Indian becomes almost altruistic when compared to the Spanish policy of taking their gold, silver, and labor. That both policies were cruel and disastrous to the Indian is obscured by highlighting the Black Legend. Differences are specifically noted: "The atrocities exhibited by the Spaniards contrast with the settlement of the United States."[232] By contrast we are blessed in our ancestry: "It is fortunate for our country that the Spaniards . . . first landed at the South—leaving the Atlantic coast of North America to be settled by the English. The Spaniards were cruel and avaricious: they did not come to America to till the soil, and follow

[229] G 1866 Guyot-P, p. 79; see also G 1869 Warren-C, p. 73; G 1878 Colton, p. 71; G 1881 Maury, p. 114.

[230] The first quotation is from G 1872 Hall, p. 109; see also G 1881 Maury, p. 115; G 1887 Redway, p. 95. The second is from G 1881 Maury, p. 115.

[231] G 1833 Clute, p. 215; see also G 1845 S. Morse, p. 51.

[232] R 1819 Strong, p. 46; see also G 1831 Blake, p. 15; G 1831 S. Worcester, p. 32.

honest labor, but with extravagant hopes of becoming suddenly rich from mines of gold and silver. . . . But the English were an industrious people, who loved liberty and humanity, and earned success by energetic toil in the fields and on the sea."[233] Morse states in 1794 that the Spanish, unlike other colonizing powers, "flocked to America, for the purpose of carnage and plunder." And in 1900 the same motive is ascribed to them: "They [the Spanish] flocked in great numbers to South America, a reckless, adventurous, unprincipled horde, ready to commit any crime in order to secure gold."[234]

Admiration for their bravery, perseverance, and military prowess is counterbalanced by revulsion at their cruelty: "Although the conquerors of Mexico and Peru displayed great courage and ability, these qualities were offset by the meanest deception, the basest treachery, and the most unrelenting cruelty."[235] Good qualities made the satisfaction of greed the easier. The degree of Spanish brutality shown in these books is equalled only by descriptions of the Reign of Terror during the French Revolution. The Conquest is studded with scenes "shocking to humanity."[236] This is detailed in bizarre and colorful examples: the Spaniards stretched the Mexicans on beds of hot coals to make them reveal the hiding place of their treasure; they cut off the hands of prisoners, or burned them at the stake; they worked them to death or tore them to bits with bloodhounds.[237] In the early books Pizarro frequently appears in extracts from plays by Sheridan and Kotzebue; both picture the Peruvians as poor but self-sacrificing patriots (much like the Swiss or the Americans), defending themselves from the ruthless and avaricious Spaniards.[238] Cortez is often juxtaposed with William Penn as they debate the virtues of their Indian policies. Cortez, contemptuous of his companion, yet falls before the other's righteousness. Penn

[233] G 1869 Warren-C, p. 27. [234] G 1794 Morse, p. 292; H 1900 Shaw, p. 83.

[235] H 1867 Goodrich, p. 12; see also H 1874 Scott, p. 29; H 1874 Anderson-G, p. 24.

[236] G 1800 Smith, p. 174.

[237] These examples will be found in the following: H 1869 Quackenbos, p. 20; R 1883 Swinton-4, p. 87; G 1897 Redway, p. 70; H 1900 Shaw, p. 89.

[238] R 1806 Staniford, pp. 60, 185; R 1826 American-S, pp. 307–311; R 1831 Smiley, pp. 79–87; R 1835 Porter, pp. 293–297; R 1851 Mandeville, pp. 44–46; R 1852 Cobb, pp. 256–257; R 1856 Osgood, pp. 101–102, 242–247.

emerges as the Christian hero worthy of greater glory than the hero of the battlefield.[239] The Spanish reputation for cruelty is revealed in a popular speech by the Earl of Chatham during the American Revolution: he opposes the proposed use of Indians in that war for if they are allowed to join the British in battle, "Spain can no longer boast pre-eminence in barbarity."[240] Thus in the description of the Spanish conquest, cruelty as a primary trait of the Spanish is abundantly and graphically presented to the child in his schoolbooks.

Rarely are the selflessness and humanity of the Spanish missionaries portrayed, except in books written for Roman Catholic schools. One unusual American History, adapted from an English author, points out the kindness of Spanish missionaries to the natives of Latin America as evidence that Spaniards are not inherently cruel; this exception is unnoticed in other schoolbook accounts.[241] And only one book, a Catholic text, defends the Spaniards against the charge of greater cruelty to the Indians than that used by other colonial powers: ". . . the native race still remains to testify by their overwhelming numbers, to the general humanity of their Spanish invaders."[242]

While the contemporary Spaniard is assumed to inherit the characteristics of those ancestors who participated in the conquest, contemporary Spain has lost all of the glory of that period, largely because of the conquest. American gold has solidified Spanish indolence. This is brought to the level of the young child: "Some people believe if they have money that it makes them of more importance than if they had it not; they believe that they need not try to make themselves agreeable: that they need not do any work; that they need not improve their minds, or learn anything. Just so the people of Spain thought, when they had a great quantity of gold from South America."[243] Their present poverty

[239] R 1796 Bingham, pp. 53–54; R 1828 New York, p. 202; R 1849 Leavitt-4, pp. 252–255; R 1851 ASDUK, pp. 112–116.

[240] R 1803 Murray-S, pp. 183–186; R 1810 Alden, pp. 115–117 (here ascribed to Patrick Henry); R 1830 MacLeod, p. 101.

[241] H 1876 Doyle, p. 30. [242] G 1878 Catholic, p. 56.

[243] R 1828 Robbins-A, p. 205; see also G 1804 Goldsmith, p. 23; G 1814 O'Neill, p. 290; G 1815 Willetts, p. 63; G 1817 Cummings, p. 88; R 1830 Putnam-I, p. 103; R 1831 Hall, p. 93; G 1835 Huntington, p. 167; R 1841 Merriam, p. 79; G 1891 Morton, p. 127; G 1899 Tarbell, p. 98.

has a human rather than an economic cause. All agree that "Their manufactures are inconsiderable owing to the laziness and inactivity of the natives."[244] And this decline is the more notable because the soil is exceptionally fertile.

Thus the nineteenth-century American raised on these schoolbooks could find in his ideas of the Spanish character easy arguments for the manifest destiny of the United States toward Spanish possessions. Spanish degeneracy could not match American progress in colonial activity. Furthermore, during the Cuban revolt against Spain in the 1890's, it would take little more than new examples to convince Americans of the barbarity displayed by the Spanish in Cuba and their other colonies. The Americans were surely already convinced that cruelty was inherent in the Spanish character.

LATIN AMERICA

The people of the United States who considered the Latin American revolutions for independence from Spain, the promulgation of the Monroe Doctrine, and their own wars with Mexico and Spain were hardly prepared by their schoolbooks to accept their southern neighbors as equals. There is a certain smugness as they rejoice that the people of the United States are descended from the English rather than from the Spanish: "The people of the Spanish colonies became idle, ignorant and corrupt; and their descendants retain that character to this day. But the English were an industrious people, who loved liberty, and humanity, and earned success by energetic toil in the fields and on the sea."[245] Few distinctions are drawn between the various nations of Central and South America; the countries are distinguished from each other by geographical location, but the cultures do not vary.

In 1784 Morse sets the tone maintained throughout the nineteenth century: "The creoles have all the bad qualities of the Spaniards from whom they are descended, without that courage, firmness and patience which makes the praiseworthy part of the Spanish character. Naturally weak and effeminate, they dedicate

[244] G 1784 Morse, p. 147. [245] G 1869 Warren-C, p. 27.

the greatest part of their lives to loitering and inactive pleasures."[246] Unlike the English migrants, who were purified and strengthened in the North American environment, Spanish character declined in the enervating climate of South America: "The habits of indulgence and of repose which ensued were anything but favorable to character or to prosperity."[247] One early author, writing during the period of the revolutions for independence, assigns greater natural endowments to the American descendants of the Spanish and Portuguese but reaches a melancholy conclusion nevertheless: "The mental powers of the Creole children are very superior to those of the Europeans, in point of quick perception and rapid acquirements but their subsequent improvements do not keep pace with this early progress. . . . They are . . . naturally indolent, and altogether averse to serious thought and deep reflection."[248] In marked contrast to descriptions of North Americans, South Americans are always described as both gay and indolent, a feckless people who spend most of their time in fiestas and siestas. This image of their Southern neighbors is still unfortunately familiar in the North American mind.

South American universities are dismissed lightly: "The bigotry of those who conduct them renders them of little value."[249] And the ignorance of the lower classes is constantly stressed. Economically, "Agriculture is almost wholly neglected, and the mines are imperfectly worked. The rearing of livestock better suits the idle habits of the people."[250] The latter statement is never hinted at in describing the cattle country of the United States. Pre-Columbian civilizations, though non-Christian, are usually spoken of glowingly, but degeneration sets in immediately upon the Spanish conquest.

The revolutions for independence from Europe create surprisingly little joy in these textbooks. One of the most enthusiastic statements reflects the wish for hemispheric isolation expressed some twelve years later in the Monroe Doctrine: "The revolutions

[246] G 1784 Morse, p. 102. [247] H 1881 Eliot, p. 8.

[248] G 1818 Smith, p. 138.

[249] G 1822 S. Morse, p. 152; see also G 1818 Mann, p. 179; G 1866 Woodbridge, p. 346.

[250] G 1887 Warren, p. 66.

that have lately occurred in Europe, by enfeebling the parent countries will give these colonies an opportunity of becoming independent. Being freed from the restrictive laws of the parent state, the people will be at liberty to pursue their true interest; and the continent of America remain no longer subject to European masters." The same author also hopes that if Mexico becomes self-governing, it will "invite the industrious of all nations and religions to her friendly shores."[251] Another author, in 1818, hopes for changes throughout the whole society once the political revolutions have been accomplished: "But the revolutionary war now raging here [Mexico], as well as in South America, against their mother-country, which in principles and features much resembles that of the United States, forms a new and interesting epoch in their history. It will give a new spring to industry, arts and refinements; and probably, will terminate in their emancipation from the Spanish yoke, from their priesthood hierarchy, and in the freedom and independence of these rich and extensive parts of the globe."[252] Later in the same book he becomes less sure of the resemblance between these revolutions and that of the United States: "But whether Spain and Portugal in their exertions, have given to their colonies here, equal occasion to revolt, by taking up arms, is also not yet fully developed."[253] Sometimes, in books written during the revolutions, there is some wishful thinking that these may be religious revolts against the Roman Catholic Church.

But most authors note unemotionally: "This country has declared itself independent of Spain," or, "The government of this country is in an unsettled state." With the exceptions noted above, the Latin American revolutions are universally viewed through the eyes of conservative New England at the time of the revolts. There is here none of the enthusiasm of a Clay. When they show any interest, it is combined with the assurance that the people of Latin America are incapable of such a revolution, such a government, and such a state of society as North America has produced. And this incapacity is probably

[251] G 1811 Workman, pp. 123, 122.

[252] G 1818 Mann, p. 181; see also G 1822 S. Morse, p. 170; G 1830 Bazeley, p. 113.

[253] G 1818 Mann, p. 217.

based on the authors' estimates of the natural endowments of the people.

After 1830, the lack of approval often becomes disapproval. The authors are not disillusioned by events in Latin America, for they had never given evidence of illusion. But events following the independence movements confirm their old prejudices. In mentioning these revolutions, a Reader of 1830 notes of the Latin Americans: "But it is apprehended that the people want knowledge, virtue, and patriotism to sustain them."[254] A Geography of 1831 estimates: "At present their institutions are in a low condition. The true principles of liberty are but imperfectly understood; and Christianity has acquired but a limited and imperfect influence."[255] Increasingly, as the period goes on, Latin American republicanism is distinguished from that of the United States. In 1843 Mitchell notes that the government of Guatemala is modeled on that of the United States: "But instead of acquiring the order and prosperity of that republic, it is the seat of anarchy and civil war."[256] The same author in 1848 compares Bolivar to Washington: "This distinguished individual has been called the *Washington of South America*, and seems for a time to have almost merited that title; but his attempts afterwards, to obtain arbitrary power, and to destroy the constitution of his country place him, in character, far below the pure and virtuous patriot of North America."[257] A speech by Daniel Webster in several Readers distinguishes the American Revolution from those of Latin America. Although the former inspired the latter, yet we were never subjected to that kind of political despotism and religious intolerance: "We sprung from another stock. We belong to another race."[258] And at the end of the period, Morse's early judgment is still confirmed: "The people of South America are not remarkable for enterprise or intelligence."[259]

[254] R 1830 Bartlett, p. 297.

[255] G 1831 Blake, p. 23; see also G 1835 Huntington, pp. 114, 123, 130; G 1845 Woodbridge, p. 165.

[256] G 1843 Mitchell, p. 184.

[257] G 1848 Mitchell, p. 89; G 1853 Mitchell, p. 89; see also H 1879 Quackenbos, p. 234.

[258] R 1832 Edwards, pp. 156–158; R 1844 Goldsbury and Russell, pp. 368–369.

[259] G 1851 Smith-G, p. 129.

As shown in these books, the United States deals with its southern neighbors like a benevolent godmother rather than a sibling. Since the Latin Americans are not equal to the United States in character, productivity, or industry, they are not equals in sovereignty. Our great act of benevolence was the protective cloak of the Monroe Doctrine, to guarantee the hemisphere from European aggression; both its promulgation and its applications are spoken of with pride. It was, for example, our use of the doctrine rather than internal problems in France or Mexico that ended Maximilian's adventure in the latter country. Such actions, as well as the doctrine itself, should excite Latin American gratitude.

American expansion at the expense of Latin America is criticized only when it meant the expansion of slavery. The Ostend Manifesto "was highly discreditable to the American character, for it was a plea for the abominable doctrine that 'might makes right.'"[260] This "abominable doctrine" is never applied to our later aggressions in Latin America at the end of the century. The annexation of Texas is often opposed as an extension of slave territory, yet the Mexican War is pictured as a glorious expedition in which the American troops, though greatly outnumbered, performed magnificently.[261] The causes of the war are passed over lightly, but not the battles and victories. A typical conclusion is the following: "Such was the conclusion of the Mexican War,—a war opposed as impolitic and unjust by one portion of the American people, and as cordially approved by the other, but admitted by all to have established for our nation, by the unbroken series of brilliant victories won by our army, a character for martial heroism which knows no superior in the annals of history, and which fears no rival in the pathway of military glory."[262]

Our war with Spain in 1898 is visualized largely as a humanitarian crusade to save the suffering Cubans from Spanish cruelty. The "savage sort of warfare" the Spanish employed to accomplish "total extermination of the Cubans"[263] would be no surprise to

[260] H 1870 Lossing, p. 259; see also H 1894 Fiske, p. 340.

[261] For example, see H 1868 Willard, p. 356; H 1881 Armstrong, pp. 81–83; H 1896 Murphy, p. 110.

[262] H 1867 Willson, p. 361.

[263] G 1900 Kellogg, p. 193.

the readers of these books. This theme is familiar from tales of the conquest. Several books observe our loss of trade and investments in Cuba through Spanish devastation of the island and the destruction of the *Maine* by unquestionably Spanish hands.[264] One book suggests that there was much sentiment in the United States for taking Cuba away from Spain as punishment for the destruction of the battleship.[265] But insult to the United States is to be expected from a country so dulled to the feelings of humanity as Spain. After the war, the establishment of the American protectorate over Cuba is not a subject for question or dissent. The natives are "very poor and densely ignorant; but they are capable of advancement under proper guidance, and this, it is hoped, they will receive from the United States."[266]

Thus the Latin Americans, inheriting a degenerate character in an enervating climate, have little hope for progress unless carefully guided by the United States.

ASIA

Asia is always reported to be a principal quarter of the globe because it was the scene of the creation of man and of other events described in the Bible. It is, however, in a state of decline: "Human nature languishes and degenerates into its worst stages, amidst the bounty of Heaven and in the very region of its highest and holiest manifestations."[267] This decline is attributed to the flight of the Christian religion from the continent. A typical description of the people of Asia is the following: "The Asiatics are in general luxurious, indolent, effeminate and servile."[268]

In the nineteenth century, two parts of Asia were particularly important to the United States: China, because of the vigorous trade that flourished throughout the period but especially during

[264] H 1898 Steele and Steele, pp. 304, and supplement 1–2. Only McMaster states that the cause of the explosion is unknown, but many people felt Spain to be responsible.

[265] H 1899 Morris, p. 239.

[266] G 1900 Tarr and McMurry-2, p. 334.

[267] G 1822 Drury, p. 35; see also G 1784 Morse, p. 110; G 1853 Mitchell, p. 121.

[268] G 1815 Willets, p. 73.

the 1850's, in the heyday of the clippership; Japan, because of the dramatic diplomatic stroke of Commodore Perry in 1854 that opened Japan to trade with the United States. And both countries became sources of extensive immigration to the United States after the Civil War. Only these two sections of Asia will be considered here.

CHINA

The most popular Geographies describe the Chinese as deceitful and cunning. Morse in 1784 evaluates Chinese character in the following terms: "By the latest accounts, the Chinese are the most dishonest, low, thieving people in the world; it is a maxim that none but a Chinese can cheat a Chinese."[269] Furthermore, a mild and affable manner is usually associated with their dishonesty.[270] This combination describes a rather sinister character, one not far removed from the prototype of the Chinese common in popular fiction in early twentieth-century America, for example, Fu Manchu in the novels of Sax Rohmer. The earlier books ascribe an extreme indolence to the Chinese, whereas later ones credit them with great, indeed excessive, industriousness. Perhaps a greater knowledge of the productions of the Chinese was seeping into America. A few books make China into a land of opportunity, stating that advancement in society is a result of industriousness and virtue rather than of birth, and that every Chinese might aspire to the "highest employments."[271] The great age of Chinese civilization is mentioned in some books, but it is angrily refuted in one Reader, where it is said that Voltaire espoused this idea just to confound Scripture.[272] Late nineteenth-century schoolbooks agree that China's civilization is ancient but antiquated: ". . . we cannot say that the Chinese are a civilized people accord-

[269] G 1784 Morse, p. 193; see also G 1816 Dwight, p. 91; G 1826 Blake, p. 103; G 1827 C. Goodrich, p. 187; G 1828 Woodbridge, p. 146; R 1831 Lowe-Second, pp. 91–92; G 1840 Olney, p. 239; G 1853 S. Goodrich, p. 263; G 1869 Warren-C, p. 81; G 1887 Quakenbos, p. 109.

[270] G 1806 Webster, p. 199; G 1806 Cottineau-I, pp. 45–46; G 1816 Dwight, p. 91; G 1816 Workman, p. 86; G 1827 C. Goodrich, p. 187; G 1830 Hale, p. 288; G 1840 Olney, p. 239; G 1853 S. Goodrich, p. 263; etc.

[271] G 1830 Hale, p. 288; G 1806 Cottineau-I, p. 46; R 1823 Blake, p. 207.

[272] R 1823 Blake, p. 105; see also G 1836 Smith, p. 235.

ing to our standard, for they are not progressive . . .; their way of doing things and thinking about things is to-day just as we find it described in their books to have been 2,500 years ago."[273] An American History, reporting a delegation from China to the United States in 1868, sees some hope for a more progressive policy in the future; China "is laying aside its exclusive policy and opening its doors to a higher civilization."[274] Evidently a civilization is "higher" if it resembles that of the United States. The Chinese had a reputation for learning, but several authors characterize this as a rare pretension, without further explanation. Although they were the first to print books, they refuse to learn from other nations, and others have advanced beyond them.[275] The early books are fond of describing the Chinese habit of discarding unwanted babies, often with a colorful depiction of the cart that daily collected the bodies.

Immediately after the Civil War, waves of Chinese immigration into the United States and other countries are mentioned in almost every book. For the first time, in an 1887 Geography, apprehension is added to the statement of this fact: ". . . but the habits of the coolies (laborers) are such, that in all civilized communities their existence in large numbers has been found socially undesirable and injurious. In Oriental countries the industry and steadiness of the Chinese, united to his thrift, make him an invaluable agent in developing their resources."[276] The reader is not further enlightened about these objectionable habits. Another Geography, at the end of the century, observes that there are about 100,000 Chinese in America employed in servile positions; then it states, with no explanation: "Laws have been passed to prevent further immigration of Chinese to the United States."[277] In books which explain American hostility to Chinese migration, the simple magnitude of numbers is sometimes central. A few complain that the Chinese can live on so little that they can work more cheaply than white men, thereby depressing the

[273] G 1875 Swinton, p. 114; see also G 1880 Swinton, p. 92; G 1887 Quackenbos, p. 109; G 1897 Redway, p. 115.

[274] H 1879 Quackenbos, p. 295.

[275] G 1866 Guyot-P, p. 100; see also G 1891 Morton, p. 142.

[276] G 1887 Quackenbos, p. 109.

[277] G 1899 Tarbell, p. 33; see also G 1900 Tarr and McMurry-2, pp. 106–107.

latter's wages. In San Francisco they live "huddled together in hovels, almost like rats."[278] These explanations are usually accompanied by others more vague, with mysterious and sinister overtones: "They did not make good citizens," "They do not seem to adopt our ways," "It is not safe to visit Chinatown at night without a guide."[279] Some fear "lest the habits of heathenism which the immigrants have brought with them, may prove injurious to the morals of the community."[280] One, after describing the Chinese settlement in San Francisco: "Here may be seen opium dens, idol temples, theatres, dirt, squalor and wickedness," adds, "A few of the Chinese in California are wealthy and respected."[281] The same book, in a prefatory address to the teacher, suggests that Chinese vice may save the world from Chinese migration: "Note that the people have been made sluggish by the use of opium, and that but for this evil they might overrun the world." One book, expressing quite as much fear of the Chinese immigrant as the others, chides the methods used by some opponents of their migration to the United States: "It cannot be said, however, that the noisiest opponents of the Chinese are the most orderly or most Christian part of the population; while the heathens very often set a worthy example of quiet industry and obedience to law."[282] This lone voice of temperance cites as an example the attack of roughs on a group of five hundred Chinese miners in Wyoming territory in 1885, in which fifty of the Chinese were killed.[283]

Thus the Chinese in their own country are presented as interesting and quaint, if a bit unscrupulous. But transplanted to another country they acquire a threatening aspect. Their capacity for hard labor, ordinarily viewed in these books as a virtue, becomes sinister when combined with mysterious, heathenish habits and a large migration. Not only is their assimilation

[278] G 1900 Tarr and McMurry-2, p. 315; see also G 1898 Carpenter, pp. 277–278.

[279] The three quotations in this sentence are from the following in that order: H 1890 Morris, p. 233; G 1898 Carpenter, p. 278; G 1891 Morton, p. xxvii.

[280] H 1881 Thalheimer, p. 341; see also G 1891 Morton, p. 42.

[281] G 1891 Morton, p. 87.

[282] H 1881 Thalheimer, p. 341.

[283] H 1881 Thalheimer, p. 351.

regarded as a remote possibility, but they are a present danger to the morals, safety, and living standards of the American population.

JAPAN

The religion of the Japanese, like that of all non-Christians, is depicted most unfavorably; otherwise they are regarded as a useful nation. By the end of the nineteenth century they did not yet seem a threat either as a people or as industrial competition. Like the Chinese they are courteous, but unlike the Chinese they are also brave, frank, and just in their dealings.[284] They are agreeable and intelligent, and "the most civilized and refined nation of Asia."[285]

Their chief claim to merit seems to lie in their industrious cultivation of the "useful arts."[286] They are famous for the very quality that helps to distinguish Americans—ingenuity applied to practical purposes. Because their path follows that of the United States, they are approved as "the most progressive people of the Mongol race."[287] The introduction of railroads and the telegraph are used for evidence of this spirit. It is the Japanese, rather than the Chinese, who are portrayed in these schoolbooks as learned and refined. Because their learning, in contrast to that of the Chinese, can be applied to a useful purpose, it is worthy of praise. They combine the virtues of several civilizations: "The Japanese have been called the 'Frenchmen of Asia' because they are so polite; they have also been called the 'Yankees of the East' because they are so energetic."[288] Their suspicion of foreigners is happily a thing of the past, and their future will be prosperous, in imitation of the United States. They pose no threat to the

[284] For example, see G 1818 Morse, p. 337; G 1816 Workman, p. 94; G 1827 C. Goodrich, p. 191; G 1830 Hale, p. 296; G 1870 Cornell-P, p. 77.

[285] G 1836 Smith, p. 239; see also G 1806 Webster, p. 213; G 1816 Dwight, p. 95; G 1827 C. Goodrich, p. 191; G 1828 Woodbridge, p. 140; G 1828 J. Worcester, p. 125; G 1830 Hale, p. 296; R 1832 Progressive, p. 134.

[286] G 1806 Webster, p. 213; see also G 1818 Morse, p. 337; G 1827 C. Goodrich, p. 191; G 1828 Woodbridge, p. 140; R 1830 Bartlett, p. 249; R 1832 Progressive, p. 134; G 1866 Guyot-C, p. 62.

[287] G 1880 Swinton, p. 92; see also G 1878 Steinwehr and Brinton, p. 77; G 1888 Redway, p. 110.

[288] G 1897 Redway, p. 117.

West and are to be commended as an island of progressive civilization in a retarded East. Clearly peril from the East is Chinese, not Japanese, in origin.

AMERICA

It need hardly be said that in nineteenth-century American schoolbooks American life illustrates the best of all possible worlds; that American institutions and character are the hope of all mankind. Indeed one of the most useful keys to the social ideals of these books is to discover what institutions and ways of behavior are considered typically American. In a sense, of course, this whole study is concerned with a definition of what the schoolbooks consider "American." But it is necessary here to note the specific evaluations that schoolbook authors make of the United States and its inhabitants. These estimates appear strikingly in the capsule evaluations of each nation offered for the student to memorize. Do the Americans, made up of immigrants from other nationalities and inhabiting a country uneasily composed of diverse sections, have a style of their own distinctive enough to make them a single nationality?

There is no ambiguity in any book on the standing of the United States among nations: ". . . she is, no one seeing her doubts, the queen, the conqueror, the mistress, the teacher of the coming age." Every book offers a like estimate. In an era enamored of material progress, "*the* event of the world's history during the nineteenth century is the growth of the United States. Nothing like it has ever before taken place." "The great mass of the people are happier . . . [as well as more prosperous] than those of any other country." They are "the freest, the most enlightened, and the most prosperous in the world. The independence of man is here asserted, and the Christian religion has full sway." [289] The United States is not only the most prosperous nation and becoming a most powerful one, but, as distinct from any other country, its happy status is shared by the masses of the people.

[289] These quotations are from the following books in that order: S 1896 Dutton, p. 122 (quoting Bishop Ireland); H 1897 McMaster, pref., p. 6; G 1887 Warren, p. 31; G 1892 Mitchell, p. 19.

The earliest books deny that there is yet an American nationality. The Americans will inevitably become a nationality, but "They have not yet existed as a nation long enough for us to form an idea of what will be in its maturity, its prominent features."[290] By the time of the War of 1812, however, American characteristics had apparently become prominent enough to delineate, for they are defined in most of the Geographies after that time in the short sentences which customarily precede a discussion of the United States. The usual description, followed throughout the century, portrays Americans as "generally industrious, intelligent, and enterprising."[291] The last adjective seems to comprise "untiring energy," great business initiative, and an inventiveness that has made "the word Yankee a synonym for ingenuity."[292] "No American need be told that his fellow-countrymen are the most ingenious people the world has ever known."[293] Other characteristics of personality invariably assigned to the Americans are ardent love of liberty, courage, and strict morality. Their moral character is superior to that of any other nationality, with the possible exception of the Scottish and Swiss. Like these two they are exceptionally intelligent, and, as is noted in every book, the masses of the people are educated. They are sober, honest, and hard-working. They have retained the virtues developed in a rural life in the midst of industrial and commercial prosperity. A clear causal relationship between the inherent nature of a people and its material prosperity appears in such examples as this one used in an 1890 History in discussing the rich soil of California: "The Mexicans made nothing of it in three hundred years, but the Americans have made it a rich and populous state in forty years."[294] Material progress inevitably attends such a character, but American moral progress keeps pace with material advance. A light-hearted poem in an 1883 Reader lists some of the great saints of the past:

[290] G 1794 Morse, p. 97; see also G 1806 Cottineau-II, p. 725; G 1807 Parish, p. 17.

[291] G 1817 Cummings, p. 42.

[292] The two quoted phrases are from the following in that order: H 1879 Quackenbos, p. 70; H 1889? Steele, p. 306.

[293] H 1897 McMaster, p. 370; see also H 1874 Anderson, p. 235; G 1898 Carpenter, p. 43.

[294] H 1890 Morris, p. 183.

But Jonathan, youngest of all,
Is the mightiest saint of the lot.

. . . .

He wears a most serious face.
Well worth a martyr's possessing;
But it isn't all owing to grace,
But partly to thinking and guessing.
In sooth our American saint
Has rather a secular bias,
And I never heard a complaint
Of his being excessively pious.

. . . .

He's fond of financial improvement,
And is always extremely inclined
To be starting some practical movement
For mending the morals and mind.[295]

American morality, energy, and enterprise have produced both material and moral growth. One undesirable trait, materialism, is allowed to obtrude, but rarely, and always with extenuating circumstances: "A desire for gain is the ruling passion of the people of the United States. The avidity of becoming rich, however, does not render them avaricious. Without being profuse, or forgetting the interests of their families, they know how, at proper times to be liberal, and are ever ready to assist the unfortunate."[296] These, then, are the qualities universally assigned to Americans, but it should be remembered that Americans are also assumed to be superior in all desirable ways. For example a Geography, using the catechism method, includes the following: "Q. What is the national character of the United States? A. More elevated and refined than that of any nation on earth."[297]

Some schoolbooks offer theories to explain how the American nationality has come to be what it is. As one might expect of authors predominantly from New England, most of them ascribe the American character to our Puritan ancestry; their "intense love of liberty, and an untiring energy . . . have impressed themselves on our national character." "The descendants of these

[295] R 1883 Swinton-5, pp. 411–413, poem "St. Jonathan" by Saxe.
[296] G 1814 Adams, p. 113; see also G 1824 J. Worcester, p. 34.
[297] G 1825 Butler, p. 32.

people have displayed a strength of character and an inventive genius the like of which has been seen nowhere else in the world."[298] This superior natural endowment was purified by the life of the pioneer in a wilderness which "has given to the national character the traits of quick-wittedness, humor, self-reliance, love of liberty, and democratic feeling. These traits in combination distinguish us from other peoples."[299] An oration by Joseph Story, given at the Salem commemoration in 1828, is used many times to show the origins of the American character: "Our constitutions have never been enfeebled by the vices or luxuries of the Old World. Such as we are, we have been since the beginning—simple, hardy, intelligent, accustomed to self-government and self-respect."[300]

Sectionalism

With the exception of the Civil War period, sectionalism is almost invisible in Readers, Spellers, and some Histories. In the Geographies, which survey each state and section of the United States as well as the country as a whole, however, the case is far different. Here distinct sectional limitations on the unity of the American nation are apparent. New England and the South have separate personalities; each has its own common customs, manners and history finally gathered together by schoolbooks written at the end of the century. Although one might assume the American character to be an amalgam of the character of the different sections, the true ancestor is, in these books, New England. Traits assigned to the people of New England are clearly those considered most characteristic of America as a whole: "It is in New England that you find Jonathan at home. In the other states, there is a mixture, greater or less, of foreign populations, but in New England the population is homogeneous and native,—the emigrant does not settle there,—the country is too full of people."[301]

[298] These two quotations are from the following in that order: H 1879 Quackenbos, p. 70; G 1887 Redway, p. 39.

[299] H 1895 Eggleston, pref. pp. 5–6; see also R 1888 McGuffey, pp. 233–236; G 1887 Redway, p. 39; H 1890 Morris, p. 5.

[300] R 1869 Wilson, p. 110; H 1873 Anderson-R, p. 379; R 1872 Osgood-5, p. 267–268; R 1875 Sheldon, pp. 371–373.

[301] R 1844 Goldsbury and Russell, pp. 184–185; R 1852 Cobb, pp. 267–268.

Although schoolbook authors exhibit pride in all parts of the Union, in none is it so marked as in New England. Its society is presented as a model for social behavior. Morse's Geographies, for example, include page after page of praise for New England. Dwight in 1796 says of the section: "On the whole, they form perhaps the most pleasing and happy society in the world."[302] Every Geography uses some such description as the following for the people of New England: "The people of these states are intelligent, moral, industrious, and enterprising."[303] Through a poem by Whittier an 1888 McGuffey Reader pictures New England as "a nursery of giant men."[304] They are celebrated in almost every book for their purity of morals. It affects their manners: "Their conversation tends rather to useful than to light or gay subjects."[305] And it is often a major point of distinction between New England and the southern states: "They are for the most part well informed and regular in their habits; in the southern states they are more addicted to gaming and dissipation."[306] Another author notes that in New England, "Gambling and horse jockeying are practiced by none but worthless people who are despised by all persons of respectability, and considered as nuisances in society."[307] These very occupations are the delights of Southern society as described by books published before the Civil War. This contrast between North and South is present in every Geography even when not expressed so pointedly. Its firm support of religion is another New England virtue invariably stressed. The only characteristic assigned its inhabitants that could have unpleasant implications is "if not a love of gain, at least a disposition to traffic."[308] But as in the case of Americans as a whole this criticism is tempered: "The people are accused, indeed, of too great haste in money-making which exhausts their lives without leaving time for social pleasures; but, if they are

[302] G 1796 Dwight, p. 145.

[303] G 1840 Olney, p. 78; see also G 1866 Guyot-C, p. 109; G 1869 Warren-C, p. 30.

[304] R 1888 McGuffey, pp. 77–79.

[305] R 1835 Merriam, p. 86; see also G 1869 Warren-C, p. 30; G 1887 Warren, p. 34.

[306] G 1817 Cummings, p. 42.

[307] G 1796 Dwight, pp. 145–146.

[308] R 1835 Merriam, p. 88; see also G 1814 Adams, p. 116; G 1822 J. Worcester, p. 32; G 1827 C. Goodrich, p. 32; G 1831 Blake, p. 17.

eager in business, they carry out with the same vigorous activity, many philanthropic plans for the establishment of charitable institutions for the extension of knowledge, and for the advancement of science."[309] In the 1870's one Geography, used in Catholic parochial schools, still finds "some traces of the intolerant spirit which in matters of religious faith and opinion, was so characteristic of the early English settlers of New England."[310] But this is the only instance in which intolerance is not safely buried in New England's past.

New England is the land of equality. Morse sees it as a place "where every man thinks himself at least as good as his neighbor, and believes that all mankind ought to possess equal rights."[311] By the abolition of primogeniture "is preserved that happy mediocrity among the people, which by inducing economy and industry, removes from them temptation to luxury, and forms them to habits of sobriety and temperance. At the same time, their industry and frugality exempt them from want, and from the necessity of submitting to any encroachment on their liberties."[312] Their manners are those of a simple pastoral people: "It may in truth be said that in no part of the world are the people happier, better furnished with the necessaries and conveniences of life, or more independent than the farmers in New England. As the great body of the people are hardy, independent freeholders, their manners are as they ought to be, congenial to their employment, plain, and simple, and unpolished."[313] In a Geography which particularly praises New England's industrial development the illustrations are pastoral ones: children gathering pumpkins on a farm, and a peaceful ocean view near Newport, Rhode Island.[314]

[309] G 1872 Hall, p. 49. [310] G 1876 Comprehensive, p. 29.

[311] G 1791 Morse, p. 65; G 1798 Morse, p. 111.

[312] G 1791 Morse, p. 64; see also R 1803 Bigelow, p. 17; G 1807 Parish, pp. 31–32; G 1814 Adams, p. 116; R 1823 Blake, pp. 242–243; R 1835 Merriam, pp. 82–83; R 1845 Goldsbury and Russell, pp. 226–227; R 1845 Swan, pp. 175–177; H 1876 Doyle, pp. 63–64.

[313] G 1791 Morse, p. 67; see also G 1796 Dwight, p. 145; G 1815 Willetts, p. 20; G 1816 Picket, p. 25; G 1818 Mann, pp. 67, 89; G 1819 Adams, p. 111; G 1828 Woodbridge, p. 67; R 1831 Lowe-Second, p. 7; G 1844 Edmands, p. 45.

[314] G 1878 Steinwehr and Brinton, p. 26.

The culture of New England is noted for producing the common school. In books where the value of a whole civilization is assessed by the amount of schooling available to the masses, this is a very great distinction indeed, and it is mentioned in every book. A typical evaluation is the following: "The state of education is the most free and respectable in the world. The first settlers of New England commenced a system of education *in their primary schools*, which has extended throughout the Union, and formed a permanent basis of education that is equally enjoyed by all classes of the community. This system of education may well be denominated the *Bulwark of National Liberty*, as well as of *National Character*."[315] Several schoolbooks dub Boston the "Athens of America," a title indicating its leadership in higher education, but in the value system of these books not nearly so impressive as the title given Connecticut, "the land of schoolmasters for the nation."[316]

New England has two other distinctions; it is the "nursery of men, whence are annually transplanted, into other parts of the United States, thousands of its natives." "The hardy sons of New England have been foremost among the bold pioneers of western emigration."[317] And it provided the first stage for the drama of the American Revolution. In the geographical surveys of every state in the union the sites of important battles are always noted. But it is a matter for universal comment that it was in New England "where American liberty raised its first voice."[318]

As New England is the model for the nation, so Connecticut is often the model for New England. Its society is described as ideal and its morals as the purest in the world. Several books refer to Connecticut as the "Land of Steady Habits."[319] Rhode Island is the one part of New England sometimes portrayed in unflattering colors. The most serious criticism centers on its lack of provision for public schools until long after they were estab-

[315] G 1825 Butler, p. 32.

[316] The first phrase is quoted from G 1866 Guyot-C, p. 110 and G 1894 Harper, p. 39; the second is from R 1830 Bartlett, p. 285.

[317] The first quotation is from G 1791 Morse, p. 63; the second from H 1867 Willson, pp. 76–77.

[318] For example, see R 1853 Mandeville, p. 168.

[319] G 1869 Warren-C, p. 31; G 1887 Warren, p. 35; G 1891 Morton, p. 53.

lished in the rest of New England: "The consequence is, that the mass of the people, except in the most populous towns, are generally ignorant, many of them not being able to read and write." [320] In 1833 it is observed that although it is still behind the rest of New England, it is improving in this respect; but not until 1853 are its schools recognized as equal to those of the rest of New England.[321] This criticism was perhaps just, yet in the light of the thoroughly uncritical approach to everything else in New England, it is noticeable. One might expect Rhode Island to have its own distinction as the home of religious liberty, but until the latter part of the century this fact is not often mentioned. Indeed New England as a whole is sometimes described as the birthplace of religious freedom without any mention of Rhode Island, on the assumption that Pilgrims and Puritans came here to establish religious freedom. Probably this singling out of Rhode Island for criticism is a remnant of the prejudice against it in colonial New England, and praise of Rhode Island's past might imply criticism of the past of the rest of New England.

In general it is clear that New England is identified with the United States as a whole. What is distinctive of the former is also distinctive of the latter. New England's virtues are those of the United States; its character is the American character; its school system is the foundation of the school system of the United States. Of all sections, New England, with the exception of Rhode Island in the earlier books, is looked at uncritically. Its society and mode of life are ideal. New England is the measuring rod for all other cultures, including that of the American South.

Although the bases of criticism shift during the century, and the criticism is mitigated as the Civil War approaches, the South is the one section of the United States subject to sustained criticism in nineteenth-century schoolbooks. Post-Civil War books confine their critical remarks to the South in the colonial period, and, as has already been seen, to an already abolished slavery; only by implication when observing improvements in Southern civilization are they critical of the South in the present. But clearly,

[320] G 1814 Adams, p. 131; G 1814 O'Neill, p. 96; G 1815 Willetts, p. 19; G 1816 Dwight, p. 166; G 1818 Mann, p. 85; G 1825 Butler, p. 61; G 1828 J. Worcester, p. 25.

[321] G 1833 Clute, p. 55; G 1835 Huntington, p. 57; G 1853 S. Goodrich, p. 47.

in these Northern-oriented schoolbooks, the roots of American civilization are not Southern.

Frequently the South is held up in unfavorable contrast to that paragon of virtue—New England. Typical of the earlier books is Morse's description of Southern characteristics: "They possess a natural quickness and vivacity of genius, superior to the inhabitants of the north; but too generally want that enterprise and perseverance, which are necessary to the highest attainments in the arts and sciences."[322] In the context of these books this is a serious criticism, since quickness and vivacity are not in themselves virtues nor need they lead necessarily to virtuous behavior. In specific contrast to New England, great disparity between the lives of the rich and the poor are often noted: "We now proceed to examine another section of our country. A new shade of character commences. We shall no longer describe a hardy race of industrious farmers, living together on terms of equality. . . . We shall discover thinly scattered farmhouses. Some of them miserable hovels, and a few miles distant, a lofty mansion surrounded by 100 negro huts."[323] The myth of a two-class South with a caste of slaves was well established in American schoolbooks by the early nineteenth century. Many also accuse the South of having political power similarly concentrated in a few hands; there government is controlled "by a few eminent men who have taken the lead in all their publick transactions, and who, in short, govern Virginia; for the great body of the people do not concern themselves with politicks—so that their government, though nominally republican, is, in fact, oligarchical or aristocratical."[324]

Late eighteenth- and early nineteenth-century books with a deep commitment to sectarian religion accuse the South of insufficient support of religion. Morse devotes many pages to this charge, a most serious one in the context of these books. "There are but few religious people in these southern states; those who make any pretensions to religion are remarkable for their piety." And

[322] G 1791 Morse, p. 217; see also G 1784 Morse, pp. 67–68.

[323] G 1812 Parish, p. 105; see also R 1830 Bartlett, p. 289; G 1840 Mitchell, p. 109; G 1840 Olney, p. 107.

[324] G 1791 Morse, pp. 188–189; see *ibid.*, p. 81 for the same accusation against South Carolina; see also G 1807 Parish, p. 83.

he believes the religious education provided the youth of the South to be worse than that "given to the youth of the poorest class in Europe."[325] Southerners go to church just to show off their fine clothes; and when they do go they choose the nearest church for convenience, without any regard for denominational principles. Furthermore: "Besides the denominations already mentioned, there is a very numerous body of people, in this [North Carolina] and in all southern states, who cannot properly be classed with any sect of Christians, having never made any profession of Christianity, and are literally as to religion NOTHINGARIANS."[326] By the 1820's hostility to Southern religious institutions or lack of them seems to disappear from the schoolbooks.

Another charge prominent in books published before the Civil War, and an equally serious one, is that wealthy Southerners are immoral. Pride and ostentation replace simplicity of manners.[327] In books that deplore anything but the strictest sobriety it is said of the city of Charleston, which is considered the typical Southern town: "The inhabitants are the gayest in America." Their vices are carefully delineated; wealthy Southerners are "much addicted to gaming, swearing, horse-racing, cock-fighting, and most kinds of dissipation. . . . A spirit of literary inquiries . . . is among the body of the people, evidently subordinate to a spirit of gaming and barbarous sports."[328] They have been led into a dissipated and gay life by slavery, by a climate that is too hot, and a soil so fertile that enterprise is almost unnecessary. These factors help to explain but are not offered as an excuse for a lack of enterprise by books that consider idleness sinful as well as wasteful. Several authors consider the methods of cultivation so poor in the South that they have produced a serious decline in soil productivity.[329] In 1822 Morse notes the South's increasing absorption in cotton culture: "Since the invention by Mr. Whitney of the machine to cleanse upland cotton from its seeds, the cultivation of cotton has become so profitable, that almost everything else is

[325] G 1784 Morse, pp. 76, 77, and see also p. 85.

[326] G 1791 Morse, p. 204; see also G 1803 Hubbard, p. 102; G 1807 Parish, pp. 83, 85, 87, 90, 92; G 1819 Adams, p. 141.

[327] G 1784 Morse, pp. 67–69.

[328] The first quotation is from G 1784 Morse, p. 80; the second from G 1791 Morse, p. 189. These are typical evaluations of Southern character.

[329] R 1839 S. Goodrich, pp. 149–150; G 1845 Woodbridge, p. 181.

neglected."[330] But another author believes that the Virginians, with great natural resources and an abundant supply of cheap labor, neglect manufactures simply because they are lazy.[331]

Books published shortly before the Civil War modulate their criticisms of the South and its inhabitants by pointing out good qualities as well as bad ones. In these books a typical description of the Southern personality and character is the following: "In the higher classes they are liberal and hospitable, independent in their feelings, and irascible; the lower classes are ignorant and vicious."[332] Politeness and hospitality are assumed to be their best characteristics. One rather amusing question in an 1860 Speller asks: "Are southern people surly?"[333] In this period, criticism of the South shifts from attacking its moral and religious feelings to pointing out its inattention to public education. The lack of common schools is criticized throughout the nineteenth century, but by the 1830's, when public schools were increasing at a rapid rate in the North, it becomes a major fault, and, in some cases, the only criticism. As the South became increasingly sensitive to Northern attacks on its culture, Northern textbook writers who hoped to find Southern markets doubtless thought it wise to mitigate their more serious moral and religious charges. Throughout the period before the Civil War it is noted that "the poor are ignorant and abject"; or, "The great distinctions kept up between the wealthy planters and the labouring part of society, are very unfavourable to the general diffusion of knowledge, we consequently find common schools very much neglected, and the common people very deficient in learning."[334] With one exception, all of the books before the Civil War, however critical they may be on other issues, agree that the wealthy planters are distinguished for their refinement and education. The exception is Morse, who says: "They appear to have little taste for the sciences. . . . While each has been endeavoring to increase his fortune, the human mind, like an unweeded garden,

[330] G 1822 S. Morse, p. 112. [331] G 1853 S. Goodrich, p. 71.

[332] G 1827 C. Goodrich, p. 53; G 1853 Mitchell, p. 49.

[333] S 1860 Tully, p. 36.

[334] The first quotation is from G 1798 Morse, p. 224; the second from G 1803 Hubbard, p. 81. These sentiments are universal throughout the pre-Civil War schoolbooks.

has been suffered to shoot up in wild disorder."[335] But the fact that the upper class may be highly educated is not much of a compliment in these books, because this is true even in Europe. With regard to education the South is outside the trend of American life.

Books published after the Civil War do not usually attempt characterization of contemporary Southerners. But their view of the colonial South is in sharp contrast to their flattering portrayal of colonial New England. A typical comparison is the following:

> Life in the South was not like life in the North. In the first place, the people were different. They did not come to the New World to work or pray, as the Puritans did, and did not expect to get rich by trading with the Indians for furs, like the Dutch. Many of them had been gentlemen in England, with more pride than money. These did not know how to work, and they hoped to get rich by finding mines of gold and silver, or in some such easy way. Others of them were poor men who were sold for a time to the planters, and were little better than slaves.[336]

The hospitality, taste, and refinement of the colonial plantation aristocracy are prominent, but their indolence and enjoyment of an easy life are also matters for comment. A Southern author, describing the settlers at Jamestown, recognizes the charges against them but defends Southern ancestry: "Those who founded this settlement have been described as vagabond adventurers, turbulent, law-breaking and indolent, but we know that some of them undoubtedly were possessed of noble motives in coming to America and all paid sedulous attention to the worship of God. They were drawn from every walk in life. Forty-eight called themselves gentlemen—a term that has been quoted to their reproach." Furthermore, he goes on to say, those who were not adapted to frontier life showed themselves particularly brave by migrating in the first place.[337] The myth that the South from the seventeenth century to the Civil War was made up almost entirely of large plantations permeates all

[335] G 1798 Morse, p. 235.

[336] H 1899 Morris, p. 117; see also H 1870 Lossing, p. 93; H 1873 Anderson-R, p. 131; H 1890 Morris, p. 80; H 1893 Creery, pp. 22, 23; H 1881 Steele, p. 46; H 1900 Channing, p. 23.

[337] H 1889 Chambers, p. 112.

nineteenth-century schoolbooks, those published before as well as after the conflict. The Northern child reading these books would be unaware of a middle class in the South. He would visualize a Southern social system in form much like that of Europe as described in his schoolbooks, made up of the very rich and the very poor with the addition of slaves, clearly a very different vision from the hard-working, simple, rigidly moral, and independent society identified as American in these same books.

The South of the Revolutionary period also suffers the onus in schoolbooks of producing more Tories than any other section. Channing's History specifically contrasts the North and South in this respect: "The opponents of the Revolution were strongest in the Carolinas, and were weakest in New England."[338] In most books where the contrast is not made specific, Tories are mentioned only in the South, as: "Many of the people in Georgia and the two Carolinas were Tories."[339] Chambers, a Southern historian, notes the abundance of Tories in the Carolinas, but "The Tories of the Carolinas had the courage of conviction, and, unlike those of other colonies, were ready to do more for the English cause than extend aid, comfort and encouragement to British troops."[340] To the schoolchild, intensity of conviction would hardly excuse being on the wrong side of what his books designated as the most righteous war in history.

In post-Civil War books, as in those of the period before the war, failure to provide public schools in the pre-Civil War South is still a serious indictment of the culture. Only one book mentions that the geographically scattered nature of the population made the establishment of common schools a peculiarly difficult problem. In the other books it appears a matter of Southern disregard for what is an important American contribution to social progress.

The period after the Civil War offers hope for a South now pictured in the process of correcting its pre-Civil War deficiencies. Most schoolbooks commend the recent establishment of public schools and observe that the South has found free labor more

[338] H 1900 Channing, p. 99.

[339] H 1889 Monroe, p. 241; see also H 1868 Willard, p. 241; H 1881 Steele, p. 133.

[340] H 1889 Chambers, p. 250.

profitable than slave labor. By the end of the century the schoolbooks envision a New South. The elements they hail in this new civilization—development of manufacturing, cities, a spirit of material progress[341]—will eventually make it a copy of the North. Two books quote with particular pleasure a speech to the New England Society by the Georgia journalist Henry W. Grady, in which he discussed the recovery of the South: "We have planted the school house on the hilltop, and made it free to white and black. We have sowed towns and cities in the place of theories, and put business above politics."[342] Only the Southern historian Chambers sees the old civilization moderating the new: "But the old civilization can never be forgotten. As long as the sons of the South bear its earlier traditions, its later memories, to heart, just so long will there be a source—undefiled and pure—of patriotism, once local, now national, supplying inspiration to maintain a restored union."[343] In the other schoolbooks the institutions of the old civilization were not those that have distinguished America, and they are best forgotten. The New South, imitating the North, has now become part of American civilization as it had not been under the old regime.

The American nationality shown in Confederate schoolbooks differs very little from the general view. On the whole these books adopt the same social concepts and heroes with few significant changes. The most marked difference, as we have seen, is in attitudes toward slavery. They stress those parts of the history of the United States that had Southern features. For example, an 1863 Confederate Arithmetic includes the following problem: "The Mecklenburg Declaration of Independence was made May 20, 1775; North Carolina unanimously seceded from the United States May 20, 1861; how many days elapsed between these two great events?"[344] Confederate books do not add Southern heroes, but in discussing the heroes of the Revolution they omit such Northerners as Joseph Warren and John Adams and rest entirely on the laurels of Washington. Their military

[341] H 1897 McMaster, p. 454; G 1897 Redway, p. 57; G 1898 Redway and Hinman, p. 79.

[342] R 1900 Aldrich and Forbes-II, pp. 207–210; see also H 1896 Murphy, pp. 159–161.

[343] H 1889 Chambers, p. 414.

[344] A 1863 Lander-S, p. 219.

problems present an opportunity to glorify Southern manhood at the expense of the North: "A Confederate soldier captured 8 Yankees each day for 9 successive days; how many did he capture in all?" And again: "If one Confederate soldier can whip 7 Yankees, how many soldiers can whip 49 Yankees?"[345] But Confederate books give one no reason to believe that Union and Confederate soldiers were made of different stuff; they assign the same characteristics to Southerners that have been assigned to all Americans, with the exception of the "desire for gain."

Unlike North and South, the West in American nineteenth-century schoolbooks has no stable, distinctive character of its own. In this century it was in actuality a moving frontier, and this circumstance is reflected in the vagueness with which its geographical boundaries are discussed. In schoolbooks its function is that of a vast expanse of nature offering almost unlimited possibilities for the expansion of American civilization. Sometimes it seems to be rather an idea than a place, and it is more often seen in the future than the present. Rather than modifying national character, it provides the means by which the illimitable potentialities of the American national character will be realized.

In the Readers and Spellers, consciousness of the movement to the West becomes prominent about 1830. The word "homestead" occurs in an 1826 Speller for the first time.[346] Pictures of emigrants traveling in covered wagons or building log cabins also become prominent at this time, and descriptive poems and essays on the process of settlement appear in great numbers. The Spellers begin to include such practice sentences as the following: "His friends think he ought to go to California"; "Her beau had gone to the West."[347] Economic opportunities of the West are presented in the many success stories of the poor boy who goes West and in time becomes a man of economic and political power. Only one of the later books sees the West specifically as a safety valve for factory labor: in discussing increased immigration from Europe

[345] A 1864 Johnson, pp. 34, 44. For a general discussion of Confederate schoolbooks, see Stephen B. Weeks, "Confederate Text Books, 1861–1865," in Report of U.S. Commissioner of Education for 1898–1899. Washington, D.C.: U.S. Government Printing Office, 1900.

[346] S 1826 Alden, p. 47.

[347] These two quotations are from the following in that order: S 1851 Northend, p. 11; and S 1859 Town and Holbrook, p. 41.

to factory centers in the East in the late 1840's, an 1889 History imagines the displaced native operatives migrating to the West.[348] The West is the land of opportunity for the Easterner.

A few authors, at the beginning and end of the century, exhibit some fear of the Westerner. In 1784 Morse sounds the alarm:

Their new manners being grafted on the old stock, produce a strange sort of lawless profligacy, the impressions of which are indelible. The manners of the Indian natives are respectable compared with this European medley. . . . The New England States, however, have been an exception. No such degeneracy of manner has ever tarnished their annals; their back settlers have been kept within the bounds of decency and government, by means of wise laws, and by the influence of religion.[349]

The people of Kentucky are described by another early author in the same uncomplimentary terms: "A large portion of the people are poor, and in a low state of society, idleness and dissipation having been prevalent."[350] The word "lynch" appears in two Spellers of the 1850's, but with no value judgments. In the one case where it is explained it is simply defined as the "act of punishing done by unauthorized persons."[351] In a 1900 Reader, Parkman is quoted to the effect that not all of the migrants from Illinois were sober and serious: "Among them are some of the vilest outcasts in the country."[352] Most of those who mention lawlessness in the West, however, view it as a temporary thing, as in this note to the teacher in an 1891 Geography: "Speculation, gambling, and want of settled habits are qualities prominent among the earlier classes of people on the Pacific coast, though happily much of this spirit has since disappeared. Contrast these influences with those that formed the character of the descendants of the Puritans, fostering domestic attachments."[353]

In most books the frontiersman is described as follows: "What is the character of the people? They are hardy, brave and

[348] H 1889? Steele, p. 211.
[349] G 1784 Morse, p. 74; see also p. 73.
[350] G 1807 Parish, p. 86.
[351] S 1852 Smith, p. 49; see also S 1858 Denman, p. 46.
[352] R 1900 Aldrich and Forbes-II, p. 169.
[353] G 1891 Morton, p. xxvi.

industrious; but the lower classes are uneducated and unrefined."[354] The restlessness of the frontiersman who barely sets up a homestead when he moves on again is depicted in an essay by Washington Irving.[355] Only one schoolbook author decides that the frontier experience has developed a greater feeling of equality and self-reliance.[356] Two books aver that Westerners have as yet (1833 and 1853) no fixed character.[357] But much oratory is expended on the idea that the West will in the future be more American in spirit than any other part of the country. McGuffey includes such an oration, by Dr. Daniel Drake, called "The Patriotism of Western Literature": "Our literature cannot fail to be patriotic, and its patriotism will be American; composed of a love of country, mingled with an admiration for our political institutions . . . because the foreign influences, which dilute and vitiate this virtue in the extremities, can not reach the heart of the continent, where all that lives and moves is American. . . . Hence a native of the West can be confided in as his country's hope."[358] In this case simple geographical distance will make the Westerner the essence of the American. Post-Civil War books in general assign to the Western territories the same characteristics that they found in New England: "Their mixed population has, from the first, been remarkable for energy, intelligence, and interest in all public enterprises."[359] American character had been formed long before by a sound heritage purified in the environment of the colonial frontier. The frontier of the nineteenth century offers to the American not modification but expansion.

In several cases early textbook writers go ahead of official action in claiming land for the United States. Their claims to land are based not just on manifest destiny but on the widest possible interpretation of our treaties. For example, an 1814 Geography asserts: "By the cession of Louisiana to the United

[354] G 1827 C. Goodrich, p. 67; see also G 1828 Woodbridge, pp. 79–80; R 1835 Merriam, p. 202; G 1837 Village, p. 49; G 1853 S. Goodrich, pp. 97–98, 105.

[355] R 1823 Pierpont, pp. 244–245.

[356] R 1835 Merriam, pp. 198–203.

[357] G 1833 Clute, p. 150; G 1853 S. Goodrich, p. 96.

[358] R 1853 McGuffey E-4, pp. 313–314.

[359] G 1872 Hall, p. 72; see also R 1867 Parker and Watson-5, pp. 174–176; G 1878 Colton, p. 42; G 1894 Harper, p. 50.

States, East and West Florida have been detached from the other Spanish possessions in North America." Dwight, in 1816, takes "the Pacific . . . as the western boundary of the United States" some three years before the Adams–Onis Treaty. Another Geography in 1825 includes a section on Texas in his treatment of the United States, explaining: "The author has thought proper to consider the geography of the Spanish province Texas in this place, because the river Del Norte, which forms its western boundary, is the most natural boundary of the United States, on the west; and because the natural connection of Texas is more immediately with the United States than with Mexico, although it is under the jurisdiction of the latter." [360] Morse, as early as 1784, squints at New Mexico and California, whose resources of fish and salt are so valuable that they "might render it an invaluable acquisition to an industrious nation." And in 1791, while discussing a new settlement beyond the Mississippi, he says that although such a settlement might seem to be lost to the United States, it is not so; besides providing a buffer state between the United States and Spain: "It is well known that empire has been travelling from East to West . . . we cannot but anticipate the period, as not far distant when the AMERICAN EMPIRE will comprehend millions of souls west of the Mississippi. Judging upon probable grounds, the Mississippi was never designed as the western boundary of the American empire. The God of nature never intended, that some of the best parts of his earth should be inhabited by the subjects of a monarch four thousand miles from them." [361] And Bishop Berkeley's phrase "Westward the course of empire takes its way" appears frequently.

American conquest of the continent is carefully differentiated from the process used by European countries in their conquests. The movement of individual farmers to the west is "Like the Israelites of old led by God to the land of promise." [362] Part of an oration by Edward Everett points up the differences: "How different is the picture of the diffusion of the arts and improvements

[360] The three preceding quotations are from the following in that order: G 1814 Adams, p. 191, see also G 1818 Morse, p. 218; G 1816 Dwight, p. 156, see also R 1818 R. Adams, p. 34; G 1825 Butler, p. 163, see also G 1840 Mitchell, p. 175.

[361] G 1784 Morse, p. 166; G 1791 Morse, pp. 232–233.

[362] R 1845 Goldsbury and Russell, p. 37.

of civilization, from the coast to the interior of America! . . . It is not the irruption of wild barbarians, sent to inflict the wrath of God on a degenerate empire; it is not the inroad of disciplined banditti, put in motion by reasons of state or court intrigue. It is the human family, led on by Providence to possess its broad patrimony."[363] The political, economic, and cultural benefits to any area under the wing of the United States are those of "safety, liberty, and truth," and are themselves justification for the movement.[364] In the case of every territory taken over by the United States the great and beneficial changes that inevitably occur within a few years after annexation and settlement are always proudly noted.

Perhaps the greatest use of the West in these books, however, is as an illustration of the tremendous material progress unique to American development. This progress is one of the most frequently reiterated points of national pride in every book. Every western territory is discussed in these terms: "Thus is the period already arrived, when this state so lately a wilderness, "blossoms like the rose." . . . Wilds where but a few years since, the note of the owl and the howl of the wolf were heard, have given way to cultivated fields." or, "The marvelous development of the West is without parallel in history. It is like a tale of magic."[365] And the West assures America's future: "If we glance an eye over this immense region, connected by navigable rivers—if we regard the fertility of the soil, the variety of its productions, and if we combine those advantages offered by nature, with the moral energy of the free and active people who are spreading their increasing millions over its surface—what a brilliant prospect opens upon us through the darkness of future time!"[366] Such hopes could be duplicated in any book. Thus the West offers the golden opportunity to spread America's economic, political, and social systems into an environment which will nurture this already established ideal society.

[363] R 1831 Bailey, pp. 315–316; R 1840 Snow, pp. 85–86; R 1856 Hillard, pp. 354–356.

[364] R 1844 Goldsbury and Russell, p. 120; see also G 1818 Mann, p. 157; G 1822 Morse and Morse, p. 125; H 1852 E. Willard, p. 385.

[365] These two quotations are from the following in that order: G 1818 Mann, p. 120; H 1872 Venable, p. 164. These are typical sentiments.

[366] G 1840 Olney, p. 128.

Thus the nineteenth-century American child was taught that there is an American nationality which provides a basic unity to differentiate the nation from Europe, although it has been limited by sectionalism. Before the Civil War, North and South are shown in the schoolbooks as distinctive enough to make up separate nationalities. But by the end of the century, as the Southern historian Chambers points out at the end of his book: "In thought, and in feeling the sections are drawing closer together."[367] The South is becoming increasingly like the North, and the West provides a God-given and beneficent nature which will preserve the American character while allowing it to expand geographically. There is an American style, nurtured originally in New England, but now inherent in all sections of the country. And the American is the New Englander writ large.

[367] H 1889 Chambers, p. 436.

Chapter 6

THE INDIVIDUAL: HEROES, GREAT MEN, AND CITIZENS

To present to the child "striking instances of virtue, enterprise, courage, generosity, patriotism, and, by a natural principle of emulation, incite us to copy such noble examples" [1] was a cardinal educational canon of the nineteenth century, richly illustrated in the writing of all of the textbooks. Romanticism used its great men for inspiration, and the schoolbooks offered them for emulation and imitation. The latter abound with great men, great in virtue and achievement. But with the criterion established by the Romantics, the authors of schoolbooks allow true heroism only to the man who performs some action or series of actions which requires superhuman faculties, virtue, or aid. Franklin is the apotheosis of the great man; Washington of the hero. Their biographies are regarded as guides to action for the youth of America, and they reveal what the society considered desirable in individual and social behavior.

Needless to say, the authors of American schoolbooks reserve their accolade of greatness primarily for Americans. In selecting from the American past those who deserve the special crown of the hero they are little concerned with objective research. One is tempted to conclude that they chose the hero less because he was one in reality than because he was an illustration of what to them was ideal behavior. Once granted the status of hero, the individual then becomes a convenient peg on which to hang a cluster of virtues often irrelevant to the act for which heroism was accorded, and often unrelated to reality. Such ancillary virtues then acquire the prestige of the hero to whom they are attached. The most familiar example of this technique for teaching virtue is the cherry tree myth constructed for Washington by Parson Weems; but every great man as well as every hero is subjected to this process.

[1] H 1833 C. Goodrich, intro., p. xi.

In this chapter we shall be concerned with what makes a man a hero or a great man in the schoolbooks, and with the virtues that then accrue to his glory.

All agree that America is particularly distinguished for its great men. It "has already produced some of the greatest and best men who have ever lived. . . . Let the young strive to imitate these worthies, pressing forward in the career of wisdom and excellence till they reach the same proud eminence."[2] And its past pre-eminence in the production of great men will certainly continue in the future:

> But why may not Columbia's soil
> Rear men as great as Britain's isle;
> Exceed what Greece and Rome have done,
> Or any land beneath the sun?[3]

Another Reader includes a "Forensic Dispute, on the Question, are the Anglo-Americans endowed with the capacity and genius equal to the Europeans."[4] The winning side in this debate is obvious. American heroes are distinguished for virtue; European heroes are remembered for their vices as soldiers or as "great scholars who were the pensioned flatterers of power, and poets, who profaned the high gift of genius, to pamper the vices of a corrupted court."[5] American annals are filled only with the virtuous: "Within, no idle ornament encumbers its bold simplicity."[6] Even President Harrison, not one of our great statesmen, is used as a foil for Europe: "He is the center of a Pageant, not perhaps the most dazzling in outward show, but more sublime, in the inner idea and meaning, than all the empires of the elder world can exhibit."[7] America's prominent, great, or heroic men always radiate an inner virtue not to be found in the great men of other countries.

There are many lesser historical figures who exhibit virtue and signal achievements. Among the most important are John Smith, Roger Williams, and Daniel Boone. Smith, "the bravest, the

[2] G 1831 Blake, pp. 16–17; see also R 1831 Cheever, pp. 256–259; R 1852 Sweet, p. 267.

[3] R 1807 Bingham-C, p. 58. [4] *Ibid.*, p. 295.

[5] R 1844 Goldsbury and Russell, pp. 94–95.

[6] *Ibid.*, p. 95; see also R 1884 Monroe, pp. 135–136.

[7] R 1845 Swan, p. 288.

most intelligent and the most humane," is shown as the savior of Virginia; later in the century he is most memorable for forcing the Protestant ethic on Jamestown: "He made the idle work."[8] In the early books Roger Williams is given only occasional credit for his ideas on religious liberty, but after 1870 his independent spirit elicits more admiration, usually qualified in some way: "[He has] sometimes been blamed for so frequently changing his religious views, still he will always be held in respect for the religious toleration he established in New England."[9] In a few of the later books he even achieves greatness: George Bancroft, in a piece used by an 1873 Reader, ranks Williams above Copernicus, Kepler, and Newton as a liberator of the mind of man. "He was the first person in modern Christendom to assert in its plenitude the doctrine of liberty of conscience, the equality of opinions before the law."[10] Daniel Boone, on the other hand, typifies the frontiersman by his "romantic adventure, chivalric daring, and patient endurance, not surpassed in the history of modern times."[11] He "led the march of civilization westward."[12] It is almost always mentioned that he accomplished this end through practical rather than book knowledge.

But the most important men of America, in terms of the quality of praise bestowed upon them and the amount of space accorded to them, are in order of ascending eminence: William Penn, Columbus, Benjamin Franklin, the heroes of the American Revolution, and George Washington. After the Civil War, Abraham Lincoln is elevated to their ranks. In the ensuing section the treatment of these primary heroes will first be analyzed, then the image of their opposite, the villain Arnold, and the schoolbook evaluation of American statesmen. Finally, the heroic or villainous behavior of ordinary citizens who appear in countless anecdotes of anonymous individuals will be discussed.

[8] R 1801 Heaton-C, p. 128; H 1869 Quackenbos, pp. 30–34.

[9] H 1872 Noque, pp. 61–65; see also H 1875 Higginson, p. 69.

[10] H 1873 Anderson-R, pp. 67–70; see also H 1889 Monroe, pp. 97–106; H 1894 Fiske, p. 98.

[11] R 1852 Gilder, pp. 142–143; see also G 1820 Darby, p. 79; G 1837 Village, p. 49; G 1853 S. Goodrich, p. 105; G 1853 Mitchell, p. 49; R 1856 Sargent-4, pp. 152–155.

[12] G 1891 Morton, p. 78.

William Penn is an exemplary case of the distinction between the great men of Europe and those of America, for he was "a good man as well as a great man."[13] The simple, peace-loving American is frequently compared with the pompous and bloodthirsty European; specifically he is contrasted to Cortez and Charles the Second. He is, of course, important as the founder of a successful American colony, but his greatest distinction lies in maintaining friendly relations with the Indians. "But see our William Penn, with weaponless hands, sitting down peaceably with his followers in the midst of savage nations, whose only occupation was shedding the blood of their fellowmen, disarming them by his justice, and teaching them, for the first time, to view a stranger without distrust."[14] One popular selection from a eulogy on Penn by Duponceau stresses this point and concludes: "The character of William Penn alone sheds a never fading lustre upon our history."[15] Penn is also great for his use of the principle of religious toleration in America. Unlike the case of Roger Williams, he is wholeheartedly praised even in the early part of the nineteenth century. Perhaps the bias of schoolbook authors toward Massachusetts and Connecticut, which would not allow them to praise the founder of dissident Rhode Island, left them free to bestow responsibility for acts of religious toleration upon William Penn. Penn becomes a symbol of American nationalism both for his contributions to a religious toleration considered unique to America, and for his pacifism, which is taught as a distinctive American ideal in spite of the battles glorified in almost all of the schoolbooks.

In almost every book Columbus is a legendary hero. He even appears in arithmetic problems: "America was discovered in the year 1492; how many years is it since?"[16] Spellers use his discovery to explain how to express the year and the day: "Thus

[13] R 1789 Webster, p. 86.

[14] R 1828 Putnam, p. 76; see also G 1816 Picket, p. 26; G 1819 Willetts, p. 28; R 1825 Blake, pp. 245–257; R 1829 Selection, pp. 205, 209; G 1832 Olney, p. 87; R 1835 Pierpont-Y, p. 47; R 1836 Cobb-N.A., p. 121; G 1845 S. Morse, p. 25; G 1853 Mitchell, p. 74; H 1873 Anderson-R, p. 111.

[15] R 1823 N. Worcester, pp. 140–141; R 1830 Emerson, pp. 95–96; R 1831 Cheever, pp. 439–440; R 1831 Harrod, pp. 131–132; R 1834 S. Willard-P, pp. 264–265; R 1860 McGuffey, p. 58; see also H 1879? Campbell, pp. 50–51.

[16] A 1795 Root, p. 45; see also A 1808 Temple, p. 107.

we say, America was discovered by Columbus in the year of our Lord fourteen hundred and ninety-two."[17] Although a European, Columbus, like Lafayette, is exempt from the national characteristics of his native land. He is also carefully dissociated from the avarice and cruelty of the Spanish in the New World; these qualities entered the New World with the Spaniards coming after Columbus.[18] His motives were purely scientific; they came from a knowledge of the figure of the earth "much superior to the general notions of the age in which he lived."[19] Furthermore Columbus knew before he sailed that there was a western continent "as a necessary balance to the seas and lands then already known."[20] That God guided Columbus is made clear in the account of a storm on his first voyage, subdued when "Providence at length interposed to save a life of so much importance."[21] His landing in America is sometimes pictured with a heavenly shaft of light centered on his upturned face.[22] His abuse at the hands of the cruel Spaniards is carefully detailed in most books. The naming of America for anyone but Columbus is universally regarded as manifest injustice. His voyages are assessed as: "the most interesting to the world of any ever undertaken by man"; "the most essential services perhaps that were ever rendered by any character to an ungrateful world"; "the most important voyage ever undertaken since the history of man"; "the most important event of modern times."[23]

[17] S 1844 Russell, pp. 71–72.

[18] R 1828 Robbins-A, p. 208; R 1830 MacLeod, pp. 26–29; R 1832 Progressive, p. 159.

[19] G 1784 Morse, p. 17; R 1819 Strong, p. 44; G 1826 Blake, p. 26; see also R 1830 Bartlett, p. 223; R 1823 Blake, pp. 170–174; H 1866 Lossing, pp. 17–18; R 1866? Sargent-2, pp. 97–98; H 1868 Willard, p. 22; R 1871 Monroe, pp. 123–124; R 1899 Holmes and Hill, pp. 62–68; R 1900 Judson and Bender-3, p. 25.

[20] G 1818 Mann, p. 43; see also R 1796 Bingham, p. 40; G 1803 Hubbard, p. 26; G 1814 O'Neill, p. 45; R 1818 R. Adams, pp. 252–254; G 1822 Morse and Morse, p. 30; G 1826 Blake, p. 26; R 1845 Russell, p. 131.

[21] G 1818 Mann, p. 47; see also R 1819 Strong, p. 45; R 1852 Sweet, p. 302.

[22] G 1830 Smiley, p. 136.

[23] These quotations are from the following in that order: G 1818 Morse, p. 59; R 1789 Webster, p. 80; G 1803 Hubbard, p. 27 (see also H 1867 Willson, p. 13); G 1828 J. Worcester, p. 12.

Columbus is an unquestioned hero because of a single act, divinely guided; he becomes a figure on which all desirable qualities may be hung—and in a spate of creative writing they are: "In the life of this remarkable man there was no deficiency of any qualification, which can constitute a great character. He was grave, though courteous in his deportment, circumspect in his words and actions, irreproachable in his morals, and exemplary in all the duties of religion."[24] He "possessed a perfect knowledge of mankind, and an insinuating address; a patient perseverance, in executing any plan; the full and entire government of his own passions, and the art of acquiring the ascendancy over others."[25] Morse describes his death: "He died with a composure of mind suited to the magnanimity which distinguished his character, and with the sentiments of piety, becoming that respect for religion, which he manifested in every occurrence of his life. He was grave, though courteous, in his deportment, circumspect in words and actions, irreproachable in morals, and exemplary in all the duties of religion."[26] It should be remarked that the similarity in words and ideas in these appraisals of the character of Columbus comes rather from incessant copying among schoolbook authors than from their use of the same authorities on the life of Columbus, and that the religious feelings of so great a hero command respect even from anti-Catholic writers who show none to other members of his religion.

Next to Washington, the greatest individual depicted here is Benjamin Franklin: "What other two men, whose lives belong to the eighteenth century of Christendom, have left a deeper impression of themselves upon the age in which they lived, and upon all after time."[27] Franklin and Washington appear in these books more often than anyone else. Even in the Arithmetics they are coupled: "How much older was Franklin than Washington?"[28]

[24] R 1796 Bingham, pp. 39–43.

[25] G 1814 O'Neill, p. 47; R 1827 Pierpont, p. 10; see also H 1866 Lossing, pp. 17–18.

[26] G 1818 Morse, p. 61; see also R 1789 Webster, p. 71.

[27] Excerpt from speech by John Quincy Adams in R 1844 Goldsbury and Russell, pp. 419–420; R 1883 Swinton-5, p. 318; R 1888 McGuffey, p. 299; see also S 1825 Torrey, frontispiece; S 1856 Sargent, p. 157.

[28] A 1864 Johnson (Confederate), p. 148.

Franklin's eminence is founded not on heroic behavior in a specific incident but on the agglomeration of virtues hovering around his name. He is the greatest of men, without being a hero. In only one instance is his cosmopolitanism used as an important contribution, and in that instance probably because it appeared in the middle of a eulogy by Abbé Fauchet quoted in two Readers.[29] It is not Benjamin Franklin the cosmopolitan, nor Benjamin Franklin the democrat who appears here; it is rather Franklin, the apotheosis of the self-made man. On the eve of the industrial revolution in America his temperance, economy, thrift, and industry are praised without stint. They have become ends in themselves rather than the conveniences they were to Franklin. These virtues appear not only in his ever present biography, but every Speller and most of the Readers contain several pages of his adages, often without acknowledgement. Almost every book has some of his writings, and all breathe the spirit of his *Autobiography*. His role as a philosopher in the school-books is aptly characterized in a piece by Melville included in a McGuffey Reader of 1888: "the homely sage and household Plato."[30]

Franklin's life is proof that in America, alone of all the world, the individual who works hard can become wealthy and respected. He appears in every book as the perfect example of the man who achieves success by his own industry in spite of obstacles. Few people "even in this happy land, where the path to honourable distinction is ever open to talent, industry, and integrity, have experienced a greater reverse of fortune."[31] It is frequently pointed out that he represents another American ideal: he was devoted to the useful rather than to the speculative or ornamental.[32] Thus the same virtues that are used to characterize the Puritans and that are considered inherent in all Americans find their perfect representative in Franklin. Washington is the hero of great actions, Benjamin Franklin is the typical American writ

[29] R 1807 Bingham-C, pp. 64–68; R 1831 Harrod, pp. 188–192.

[30] R 1888 McGuffey, p. 204.

[31] R 1828 American-R, pp. 219–224; R 1831 Hall, p. 188; see also R 1832 Cobb, p. 100.

[32] R 1828 American-R, pp. 219–222; R 1831 Hall, p. 188; R 1832 Cobb, pp. 99–100; R 1839 Sigourney, pp. 67–68; R 1854 Sargent, pp. 331–333.

large. In one instance, in a piece by Greeley on self-made men, Franklin is ranked even above Washington as the "consummate type and flowering of human nature under the skies of colonial America."[33] Finally, Franklin's achievements brought to him something much desired for the America of his time—recognition from Europe.

Franklin is the outstanding example of the self-made man, but hundreds of others are mentioned, many described in some detail. The painter Benjamin West frequently appears under this guise. His importance comes not only from the fact of his being self-made, but also because he too achieved European recognition. The most popular story about West tells of him as a child, so poor that he had to pluck hairs from a cat for his paint brushes and to shoot down pretty birds for subjects to paint.[34] This story is of particular interest for violating the canon of kindness to animals firmly established throughout these books. Clearly kindness to animals is less important than the ingenious use of whatever is handy in one's environment to achieve a successful career. It is interesting to observe that talent as a factor in success in the arts seems to be ignored in considering West's importance as a painter: "Thus we see, that, by industry, ingenuity, and perseverance, a little American boy became the most distinguished painter of his day in England."[35]

As Benjamin Franklin symbolizes the American in ordinary circumstances, so American war heroes symbolize the American in extraordinary circumstances. The heroes of the American Revolution not only created the foundations of the American state but they brought the ideal of "freedom for the grateful world."[36] For both achievements they have no peers in heroism. They are more important than a man like Franklin: they are the "distinguished beings to whom heaven has given capacity to lead a nation's arms to freedom."[37] The textbooks contain too many of

[33] H 1873 Anderson-R, p. 237.

[34] R 1830 Frost, pp. 135–139; R 1831 Hall, pp. 227–230; R 1834 S. Worcester, pp. 110–112; R 1844 Bumstead, pp. 137–142; see also R 1857 Hillard-3, pp. 61–68.

[35] R 1844 Bumstead, pp. 137–142; see also R 1832 Edwards, p. 297; R 1845 D. Adams, p. 213. For the same attitude but toward J. S. Copley see R 1853 Sanders, pp. 228–230.

[36] R 1813 Richardson, p. 111.

[37] R 1815 Dickinson, p. 121.

them to mention them individually; several appear in every book. They are elevated to such transcendent heroism that their individuality is lost; all fade into one amorphous mass. But no subject is more frequently and thoroughly discussed. A few types will suffice here. Spiritual leaders of the Revolution such as Patrick Henry are assigned the virtues of "instructive sagacity," "moral courage," "naturally noble and generous heart"; it is also noted of Henry, and most of the others as well, that he was a self-made man. The treatment of a soldier who died in the Revolution is typified by the following comment on Joseph Warren: "The contemplation of such a character is the noblest spectacle which the moral world affords."[38] The town where Oliver Perry, hero of the War of 1812, died is commemorated: "This town is rendered forever remarkable in the history of the United States. It was here that the hero of Erie, the beloved and immortal Oliver H. Perry, breathed his generous and magnanimous spirit into the bosom of Him who gave it."[39] One popular Revolutionary hero, Sargeant Jasper, deserves special mention as a symbol of American nationalism. During a battle of the American Revolution he was killed in an attempt to replace the fallen flag. However meaningless to the course of battle such action may be, the exaltation of nationalist symbols seems to demand at least one such hero in every American war. In awarding heroism the authors of schoolbooks allow support of the American Revolution to take precedence over everything but religion. A hero of the Revolution could be forgiven for any other action, but the deists Ethan Allen and Thomas Paine are both severely criticized as atheists.[40] Even their service to the Revolutionary cause could not excuse this lapse.

Without doubt the greatest hero in the nineteenth-century schoolbook is the military leader of the Revolution. In all of these books, George Washington bears more resemblance to Jesus Christ than to any human being. As Christ came from heaven to bring divine salvation to human souls, so Washington was sent by the Deity to bring liberty to man. His character as a man is swallowed up in his messianic function. He is constantly

[38] R 1839 S. Goodrich, p. 141.
[39] G 1820 Darby, p. 58.
[40] See chapter 3, "God and Man."

SERGEANT JASPER AND THE FLAG.

11. In Murphy's 1896 History, Sergeant Jasper loses his life attempting to replace the fallen flag in a battle of the American Revolution.

referred to in such phrases as: "Father of his country," "Father and deliverer of his country," "The hero and father," "The savior of his country." All of these phrases, in the context of these books, take on a strong religious tinge. A 1797 Reader describes an imaginary biography of Washington in cosmic terms:

> As Alps immortal, spotless as its snows,
> The stars should be its types, its press the age;
> The earth its binding, and the sky its page.
> In language set, not Babel could o'erturn;
> On leaves impress'd, which Omar could not burn;
> The sacred work in Heav'n's high dome should stand,
> Shine with its suns, and with its arch expand;
> Till Nature's self the Vandal torch should raise,
> And the vast alcove of creation blaze![41]

The same book describes the subject of such a biography as: "The most unexceptionally, the most finished, the most Godlike human character that ever acted a part on the theatre of the world"[42]—and this is a typical attitude. Another refers to "my God-like WASHINGTON."[43] Another: "We forget for a moment that he was a man. We regard him as some propitious divinity, sent from a better world, than this, to take America by the hand, and lead her to independence, freedom and happiness."[44] He is constantly spoken of as immortal, and his name usually appears entirely in capital letters. It is generally assumed that he has been sent directly from heaven on a mission to earth:

> "Thanks to the Almighty Heaven,
> For Washington to fair Columbia given."[45]

His divine origin and dedication are indicated when the concise catechism method of teaching is used: "Who was in command in the revolution?—George Washington, Esq., whom God raised up and fitted for these times of trial and made him instrumental

[41] R 1797 Thomas, p. 174.

[42] *Ibid.*, p. 213.

[43] R 1810 Alden, p. 216; see also R 1897 Arnold and Gilbert-6, p. 90.

[44] R 1811 Hubbard, p. 92.

[45] R 1806 Staniford, p. 231; S 1824 Bentley, p. 170; see also R 1871 Sargent and May-5, pp. 65–66; H 1873 Anderson-R, p. 247; H 1881 Steele, p. 126; S 1896 Dutton, p. 86.

of delivering our country from foreign domination."[46] There are many specific instances of the hand of God extracting Washington from a dangerous position in battle.[47] In delivering the Americans from the English he is often likened to Moses delivering the Hebrews from Egypt; it is observed, however, that Washington was more favored by Providence in being allowed to reach the Promised Land himself.[48] His character is paralleled only by the chosen of God in the Bible: "The character of Washington, in its glorious beauty, in the august sublimity of its splendid combinations, looms up before my imagination, my feelings, and my judgement, as the grandest to be found in the authentic records of our race, save those records, short and simple, that contain the glorious gospel of the Son of God." In raising him up, God had a "benignant purpose . . . in regard to the interests of liberty and humanity in this land."[49]

In several cases Washington himself is assumed to be the possessor of magical powers: "*Insurrection* was so struck at his countenance, that it fled from the *shock of his aim*."[50] The effect of Washington on Napoleon would have been devastating had they met: "A single flash of justice from the countenance of Washington is sufficient to strike dead every laurel on his brow."[51] His reputation alone has now, and will have in the future, extraordinary powers. As an early Reader expresses it: "The holy influence which Washington's name and character will exert upon the world, is doubtless incalculable; while human society

[46] S 1815 Bradley, p. 146; see also G 1794 Morse, p. 106; R 1797 Thomas, p. 204; G 1800 Davidson, p. 56; R 1801 Heaton-C, p. 149; R 1803 D. Adams, p. 132; R 1810 Alden, p. 123; R 1824 Lowe, p. 242; R 1829 Selection, p. 94; R 1831 Hall, p. 167; R 1835 Porter, p. 285; R 1845 Swan, p. 420–421; R 1852 Brothers, p. 374; R 1853 Webb, p. 184–185.

[47] R 1813 Richardson, p. 117; R 1824 Lowe, p. 13; R 1845 Swan, p. 421; R 1852 Brothers, p. 374; H 1855 Berard, p. 92; H 1866 Lossing, pp. 96–97; H 1868 Kerney (Catholic), p. 126; H 1869 Quackenbos, pp. 78, 79; R 1873 American, pp. 180–184; H 1874 Anderson, p. 90; H 1879 Quackenbos, p. 78; H 1890 Morris, p. 106; H 1893 Creery, p. 49; H 1899 Morris, p. 140.

[48] R 1806 Staniford, p. 85; R 1807 Bingham-C, pp. 281–284; R 1809 Picket, pp. 188–189; R 1810 Alden, pp. 215–216; R 1810 Thomson, p. 70; R 1811 Chandler, p. 145; R 1826 American-S, pp. 121–122.

[49] R 1871 Hillard, pp. 342–343.

[50] R 1806 Staniford, p. 86.

[51] R 1811 Hubbard, p. 93.

lasts, they will never cease to shed their blessings on mankind."[52] And in later Readers: "He was the FIRST man of the time in which he grew. . . . Till the last drop of blood shall freeze in the last American heart, his name shall be a spell of power and of might."[53]

The fame of Washington is the fame of America, and it is eternal. Webster's Bunker Hill oration in 1843 makes Washington the greatest of American productions, its primary contribution to a waiting world: "America has furnished to the world the character of Washington! And if our American institutions had done nothing else, that alone would have entitled them to the respect of mankind."[54] His fame is "bounded only by the limits of the earth, and by the extent of the human mind. . . . When all is ended, when present nations are gone, when even our young and far-spreading empire shall have perished, still will our WASHINGTON's glory unfaded shine, and die not, until love of virtue cease on earth, or earth itself sink into chaos."[55] Even "the Tartar and the Arab converse about him in their tents."[56] A very popular speech by an Irishman, who claims impartiality by that fact, denationalizes Washington for the world: "No people can claim, no country can appropriate him. The boon of Providence to the human race, his fame is eternity, and his residence creation."[57] He cannot be confined to one country. He belongs to the world and the ages.

That he is unique in the ancient or modern world is universally accepted in the schoolbooks: "Neither the annals of ancient or modern times afford a parallel of the character we are con-

[52] R 1831 S. Willard, p. 119.

[53] R 1880 Harris, Rickoff, Bailey, p. 183; R 1898 Arnold and Gilbert, p. 127.

[54] R 1844 Smith, pp. 19–23; R 1844 Goldsbury and Russell, pp. 386–388; R 1852 Town, pp. 351–353; R 1859 Sargent, pp. 81–82; see also R 1801 Heaton-C, p. 156.

[55] R 1806 Staniford, p. 771; R 1810 Alden, p. 131; R 1810 Thomson, p. 68; see also R 1801 Heaton-C, p. 153; R 1815 Dickinson, p. 110; R 1819 Strong, p. 47.

[56] R 1810 Alden, p. 135; R 1823 Morrill, p. 232.

[57] R 1821 Bingham, p. 79; R 1843 Cobb, pp. 158–159; R 1853 Tower and Walker, pp. 416–417; R 1858 McGuffey, p. 204; H 1881 Steele, p. 150; R 1883 Swinton-5, p. 371; see also R 1867 Parker and Watson-5, p. 348; H 1867 Willson, p. 295; H 1890 Morris, p. 150.

templating."[58] He is greater because he is purer: "Greatness and guilt have too often been allied, but his fame is whiter than it is brilliant."[59] Washington is the culmination of all past heroism: "In the production of Washington, it does really appear as if nature was endeavoring to improve upon herself, and that all the virtues of the ancient world were but so many studies preparatory to the patriot of the new."[60] They are convinced that his period will be called the "age of Washington."[61] That this greatest of all heroes appeared in America indicates its distinction and importance in the eyes of God:

At the grand and soothing idea that this greatest instance of human perfectibility, this conspicuous phenomenon of human elevation and grandeur, should have been permitted to rise first on the horizon of America, every citizen of these states must feel his bosom beat with rapturous and honest pride, tempered with reverential gratitude to the great author and source of all perfection. . . . He will be penetrated with astonishment, and kindled into thanksgiving when he reflects that our globe had existed 6000 years before a Washington appeared on the theatre of the world; and that he was then destined to appear in America—to be the ornament, the deliverer, the protector, the delight![62]

But apparently it is not enough to glorify the man; his memorials must also be exalted. Every Geography celebrates Virginia by noting, as an outstanding fact, that Washington's home was there. Quite often half of the space allotted to the state of Virginia is devoted to this native son and his residence at Mount Vernon.[63]

[58] R 1811 Hubbard, p. 92; see also R 1806 Staniford, pp. 74–75; R 1811 Lyman, p. 65; R 1811 I. Cooke, p. 338; R 1834 S. Worcester, p. 96; R 1852 Gilder, p. 79; R 1852 Sweet, p. 288; R 1869 Wilson, pp. 151–152; H 1873 Anderson-R, p. 224; R 1884 Monroe, pp. 168–170; R 1888 McGuffey, p. 244; R 1898 Arnold and Gilbert, p. 125.

[59] R 1810 Thomson, p. 69; see also R 1831 Harrod, pp. 109–110; R 1861 Sanders, p. xii; R 1866 Sargent-4, pp. 313–316; H 1872 Venable, p. 143; H 1873 Anderson-R, pp. 244, 246.

[60] R 1821 Bingham, p. 79; R 1843 Cobb, pp. 158–159; R 1843 Olney, p. 271; R 1853 Tower and Walker, pp. 416–417; R 1858 McGuffey, p. 204; R 1883 Swinton-5, p. 372.

[61] R 1831 Smiley, pp. 260–261; R 1853 Mandeville, p. 103; R 1856 Hillard, p. 381.

[62] R 1810 Thomson, p. 70; see also R 1853 Mandeville, p. 104.

[63] For example, see G 1844 Edmands, p. 51.

By the 1830's it is a shrine: "Mount Vernon is sacred in the eyes of Americans; it is the spot to which many a Pilgrim wends his way, anxious to drop a tear at the tomb of the Father of his country."[64] The Geographies also devote much space to the statues of George Washington in Richmond, Raleigh, and Baltimore. Clute, in 1833, catalogues all three of these statues, even though the Canova statue at Raleigh had been destroyed two years earlier when the State House burned. Indeed it is still apparently extant in Geographies as late as 1835.[65] The amount of copying and the conservatism of the texts are well illustrated by the fact that the destruction of the statue is not mentioned in any text until 1840.[66] Washington memorials even appear in arithmetic problems: "A miniature statue of General Washington, the forefinger of which measures half an inch, weighed 12 pounds; what would be the weight of a similar statue cut out of the same material the forefinger of which would be $4\frac{1}{2}$ inches long?"[67]

Thus Washington's image in the schoolbooks is far more than life size. From the preceding discussion Washington emerges as the liberator of America and the world through the American Revolution; it is this Washington who is made into a hero, not Washington the administrator. His policies as President of the United States are seldom discussed, but the fact that he became the first President is an occasion for the contemplation of his glory. When comment is made on his administration, specific policies are rarely mentioned. The following is typical: "All his measures were right in intent. . . . The object of his regard was the whole country. No part of it was enough to fill his enlarged patriotism."[68] The soundness of his policies is axiomatically accepted, following naturally from his heroic stature: "But his intellect was as extraordinary as his moral nature; its essential

[64] R 1840 Snow, p. 100; see also R 1836 Cobb-N.A., p. 87; R 1851 ASDUK, pp. 251–260; R 1835 Porter, pp. 159–162; H 1867 Willson, p. 282 footnote; R 1867? Parker and Watson-4, p. 264; R 1870 Sanders, pp. 335–339.

[65] G 1833 Clute, pp. 95, 105, 112; see also G 1835 Huntington, p. 78; G 1835 J. Worcester, p. 54.

[66] G 1840 Mitchell, p. 119.

[67] A 1846 Mix, p. 290.

[68] R 1844 Smith, pp. 227–228; see also R 1801 Heaton-C, pp. 155–156; R 1856 Hillard, pp. 375–379.

quality was pure wisdom, profound, unerring, almost superhuman."[69] The quality of his mind was characterized rather by the instinctive wisdom of the Romantic hero than by reason operating on knowledge. Only the unusual schoolbook author, such as the professional historian Channing or the reformer Higginson, suggests that Washington's administrations embodied "aristocratic ideas."[70] In most books he is a symbol of national unity, necessarily above politics.

The core of his heroism in these books is his status as head of the patriot army of the Revolution, and so he is praised *ad infinitum.* His military campaigns are fully detailed in almost every book. He delivered America from its oppressors, created the American nation, and acted as midwife for the birth of freedom to the world:

> He burst the fetters of the land,
> He taught us to be free;
> He rais'd the dignity of man.
> He bade a nation be.[71]

As a soldier at the call of liberty he is a dauntless champion; in one Reader the Washington elm at Cambridge meditates:

> But lo! a mighty chieftain, neath my shades,
> Drew his bright sword, and reared his dauntless head.
> And Liberty sprung forth from rock and glade,
> And donned her helmet for the hour of dread.[72]

His bravery is, of course, prodigious, but he is carefully distinguished from all other soldier heroes. Several books contain antiwar discussions between a boy who wants to be a soldier and his parents. The latter inform their son that Washington was no professional soldier: "He is an *exception* to all soldiers [because of his virtue]. . . . Besides you know, that Washington fought for the liberties of a whole people, against what they deemed oppression and tyranny."[73] Several schoolbooks quote the reaction of a Quaker on seeing Washington praying at Valley Forge: "Thee knows that I always thought the sword and the Gospel inconsistent;

[69] R 1826 Frost, p. 159. [70] H 1900 Channing, p. 166.

[71] Chorus from anonymous ode performed at Boston, February 22, 1800, before the Mechanics Institute, in R 1806 Staniford, p. 239.

[72] R 1849 Leavitt, p. 65.

[73] R 1833 Leavitt, p. 74; see also R 1852 Town, pp. 79–82.

and that no man can be a soldier and a Christian at the same time; but George Washington has this day convinced me of my mistake."[74] The only dissent from this attitude occurs in a book written by a Quaker: "I would rather be Anthony Benezet in that coffin than the great Washington, with all his honours."[75] Needless to say, this is a single voice, alone in criticizing Washington on any grounds. Other great soldiers, such as Napoleon and Alexander, become foils for the virtues of Washington:

> Their hands were dyed with guiltless blood,
> Their aim ambition's topmost round,
> The conqueror's fame their only God,
> Their throne a vanquished world around.
> Enfranchised millions hailed HIS course—
> *His* path was dewed with tears of joy—
> *His* bosom was compassion's source.
> *His* motto, "Raise and not destroy."[76]

His rejection of proffered kingship, and his resignation from the army when the war was over, also set him apart from others: "Thus presenting to the world the rare example of a great military chief, descending voluntarily to the rank of a private citizen."[77]

Throughout the century, emphasis is put on the idea that Washington was a good man as well as a great one; he was a paragon of virtue. A sentence given for practice and correction in one of the Spellers is the following: "Who has not felt the moral *Granjeur* of Washington?"[78] Every book discusses his virtue in such tones: "To the historian few characters appear so little to have shared the common frailties and imperfections of human nature, as that of Washington."[79] One author, explaining why so many details of Washington's life are recorded in his text, says that his smallest acts are of interest because "His greatness

[74] R 1851 Mandeville, pp. 129–130; R 1853 Webb, p. 185.

[75] R 1806 Cooledge, p. 112.

[76] R 1849 Leavitt, p. 245; see also S 1797 Barry, p. 54; R 1806 Staniford, p. 82; R 1809 Picket, p. 184; R 1810 Alden, p. 214; R 1811 Chandler, p. 165; R 1811 Hubbard, p. 93.

[77] G 1843 Mitchell, pp. 104–105; see also R 1806 Staniford, p. 83; R 1810 Alden, pp. 213–214; R 1811 Chandler, p. 165; R 1828 Pierpont-I, p. 165; R 1856 Sargent-4, p. 229; G 1859 Mitchell, p. 81; H 1896 Murphy, p. 87.

[78] S 1843 Fowle, p. 96.

[79] R 1844 Goldsbury and Russell, pp. 93–94.

dignifies all his acts."[80] Needless to say it was impossible for the child to glean from these books an actual knowledge of Washington's personality; his prestige-laden figure becomes a monumental framework on which to hang all the heroic virtues to be indoctrinated. All individuality is lost. The virtues assigned specifically to him are usually filial obedience, prudence, modesty, courtesy, charitableness. He is always described as profoundly religious. One author, however, remarks that he once introduced the name of the "Supreme Being in a manner, which in common conversation is deemed irreverent," and his language was once somewhat unguarded when talking to another general in the midst of a retreat at the Battle of Monmouth. But this can be excused because it occurred at a moment of extreme emergency in the cause of liberty, and to a man who was fundamentally devoted to religion.[81] In the later books the virtues of the self-made man are generally associated with Washington. He was punctual, industrious, rose early, and his mother did not "enervate him by luxury, or weak indulgence."[82] Sometimes he is pictured not only as the possessor of the virtues of the self-made man, but as one himself.[83]

Certain stock legends appear in profusion about Washington's name. The most popular one is, of course, the cherry tree tale of Parson Weems' invention: Washington confesses to his father that he cut down a favorite cherry tree; his father, delighted with such honesty, forgets the transgression for the virtue and says to George: "Come to my arms my dearest boy."[84] In a more dismal

[80] R 1899 Holmes and Hill, p. 274.

[81] R 1811 Lyman, pp. 62–63.

[82] R 1829 Selection, p. 213; R 1834 S. Worcester, pp. 97–100.

[83] R 1845 D. Adams, p. 210; S 1847 ASDUK, p. 120; R 1855 Burleigh, pp. 41–43; R 1854 Sargent, pp. 249–251; R 1864 Sanders, pp. 233–234.

[84] S 1825 Alger, pp. 107–108; R 1828 Putnam, pp. 8–12; R 1832 American-P, pp. 110–112; R 1833 Emerson, pp. 104–106; R 1836 Abbott, pp. 176–178; R 1836 Parsons, p. 45; S 1838 Marshall, pp. 91–92; S 1841 Cobb, p. 151; S 1842 Sanders, p. 45; S 1845 Bentley, pp. 93–94; S 1847 ASDUK, pp. 119–120; S 1853 Easy Lessons, back cover; R 1853 McGuffey E-2, pp. 122–124; R 1853 Webb, pp. 39–43; S 1854 Emerson, pp. 94–96; R 1855 Burleigh, pp. 41–43; S 1865 Confederate, pp. 72–73; H 1868 Kerney, p. 123; H 1869 Quackenbos, p. 76; R 1877 Metropolitan, p. 85–86; R 1895 Hazen, pp. 217–220; R 1896 Baldwin, pp. 59–61; R 1900 Judson and Bender-3, p. 170; H 1889 Monroe, p. 181.

12. The Young Washington chops down the cherry tree, from Mandeville's 1857 Reader. The Washington of Parson Weems' legend is still indelibly imprinted on the minds of American youth.

version Washington's father comments: "Gladly would I assist to haul you in your little coffin, and follow you to your grave than that you should tell a lie."[85] Another book, which uses all of the other stock tales of Washington, tells this tale without identifying the little boy as George Washington.[86] Others present variations on the same theme: little George has killed a favorite colt by riding it hard when expressly forbidden to ride it at all.[87] The dénouement and the moral are the same. Washington's honesty is always stressed, even when the cherry tree myth and its variants do not appear. Such stress probably results partly from the myth as well as from the process of attaching desirable virtues to the proved hero. A Geography, for example, done in catechism style, includes the following passage: "Q. For what was Washington early distinguished? A. For always telling the truth."[88] Another Weems invention shows Washington on his deathbed talking to God in solitude about the future of America; this conversation is reported in direct quotations.[89] An amusing instance of attaching virtues and legends to the name of Washington is the case of the burned-cakes story of the British King Alfred, told in dialogue about Washington. The piece is entitled "The Battle of Trenton."[90]

Thus Washington, the founder of the American nation, is the pre-eminent hero of America and the personification of the American mission. In every book suggestions are made that he be both praised and imitated by all Americans, often with the engaging but impractical advice:

> Begin with the infant in his cradle
> Let the first word he lisps be WASHINGTON.[91]

Every American must worship at the shrine of Washington: he is both the saint and the symbol of American nationalism.

While Abraham Lincoln does not displace either Washington or Franklin from their august positions in nineteenth-century

[85] R 1853 Webb, pp. 39–41. [86] S 1843 Bumstead, p. 86.

[87] R 1835 Merriam, pp. 44–46; R 1851 ASDUK pp. 275–278; R 1899 Judson and Bender, pp. 170–171.

[88] G 1851 Smith-G, p. 51. [89] R 1811 Chandler, pp. 143–147.

[90] R 1803 Biglow, pp. 55–62.

[91] R 1789 Webster, title page; R 1809 Picket, pp. 180–181; S 1824 Bentley, p. 198; R 1843 Totten, pp. 53–54; etc.

schoolbooks, he becomes a curious amalgam of the two. The self-reliant greatness of Franklin, combined with the God-given heroism of Washington, produces an ideal nineteenth-century American, valid proof of the institutions established by Washington and Franklin. Whatever his character, the circumstances of his death, like that of Garfield, have guaranteed his eminence in books searching for dramatic illustrations of virtue. But Lincoln's assassination sanctified with martyrdom what was already regarded as an ideal American life: "So ended in darkness, but not in shame, the career of Abraham Lincoln. He was one of the most remarkable men of any age or country—a man in whom the qualities of genius and common sense were strangely mingled. He was prudent, far-sighted, resolute; thoughtful, calm, and just; patient, tender-hearted and great. The manner of his death consecrated his memory."[92]

Although the treatment accorded Lincoln is not as extensive as that given Washington, the quality of attention is equivalent and there are explicit comparisons. Like Washington, Lincoln was divinely appointed to his task. As Washington established the Union, so Lincoln preserved it at the time of its greatest crisis. Phrases identical to those used for Washington describe his divine appointment: "God raised him up for a great and glorious mission."[93] His appearance in America becomes a sign of divine favor: "That such a man as Abraham Lincoln represented the Union, and stood ready to live or die for it, was one of the greatest blessings which God has bestowed upon the nation."[94] He and Washington successfully faced the most crucial issues: "No president since Washington has been put to so severe a test; and no president, unless it were Washington, had so thoroughly won the confidence of the people. His simplicity, honesty and fidelity, his fearless purpose, sympathetic heart, and quaint humor, had never failed in the darkest hours of the war."[95] And America is as grateful to Lincoln as to Washington: "Probably no man since the days of Washington was ever so deeply enshrined in the hearts of the American people as Abraham Lincoln."[96] It was

[92] H 1885 Ridpath, p. 458.
[93] R 1869 Wilson, p. 135.
[94] H 1881 Eliot, p. 418.
[95] H 1875 Higginson, pp. 322–323; see also H 1881 Steele, p. 216.
[96] R 1869 Wilson, pp. 134–136; see also H 1894 Fiske, p. 349.

entirely fitting that the American flag, "mute avenger of the nation's chief," tripped and broke the leg of his assassin as he tried to escape.[97] Although this happy accident did not save Lincoln's life, it implies the same kind of magic that followed Washington in his military career. Like Washington, "The Union, free, prosperous and great is his true and appropriate monument."[98]

Lincoln's stature is secure as a true hero in the tradition of Washington, but at the same time he is also the ideal American in the tradition of Franklin. Almost every book after the Civil War represents his life as an outline of how a poor boy with persistence can achieve success in America. His success embodies a moral lesson on the virtues of the man and his country. A typical presentation of this idea is the following: "The history of Abraham Lincoln, the new president, furnishes a striking proof of the fact that in the United States, poverty prevents no citizen from rising to the highest position in the gift of the people."[99] To Channing "He was indeed the greatest because the most typical of Americans."[100] Lincoln is not only proof of the efficacy of American institutions for creating superior men; he is also, in a mystical sense, the creation of uniquely unspoiled nature in America, the fruit of the American garden. A 1900 Reader quotes from James Russell Lowell's *Commemorative Ode*:

> For him her [Nature's] Old World moulds aside she threw,
> And choosing sweet clay from the breast of the unexhausted West,
> With stuff untainted shaped a hero new,
> Wise, steadfast in the strength of God, and true.[101]

The same theme is evident in the last line of a poem under Lincoln's portrait that appears as the frontispiece to Channing's school history: "New birth of our new soil, the first American."[102] It is interesting that it is Lincoln and not Andrew Jackson who fills this role in the schoolbooks. The latter does not come up to the status of hero. It is also interesting that this picture of Lincoln, the new man produced from the American West, is presented only

[97] H 1881 Steele, p. 276. [98] S 1896 Dutton, p. 120.
[99] H 1874 Scott, p. 321.
[100] H 1900 Channing, p. 352. On page 176, in a footnote, Channing notes that Lincoln's birthday is beginning to be observed as well as Washington's.
[101] R 1900 Lane, p. 88. [102] R 1894 Columbian, p. 77.

in books published at the turn of the century, after the announcement of the official disappearance of the frontier had been made to a highly industrialized society. Perhaps nostalgia for a simpler past accounts for this Romanticized view of Lincoln, the child of nature as well as the self-made man.

As a hero, the qualities assigned to Lincoln are of some importance. His kindness appears in innumerable homely stories, as well as in his attitude to the defeated South. Like Washington, his honesty is legendary, and the sobriquet "Honest Abe" appears a number of times.[103] His simplicity and homely wit are frequently stressed, but his eloquence calls only once for favorable comment, when Fiske characterizes the Gettysburg Address "one of the masterpieces of English prose."[104] One history, written by an Englishman, contrasts Lincoln's prose unfavorably to that of Patrick Henry: "But Lincoln had none of that brilliancy of imagination and vivid strength of speech which made Henry the foremost orator among the statesmen of the Revolution."[105] In his political life he is invariably the preserver of the Union rather than the opponent of slavery. Rarely is his hostility to slavery discussed, perhaps because it might offend potential customers in the South. Primarily, the virtues of the self-made man are those of Lincoln: thrift, industry, perseverance, and practicality.

Finally it should be noted that Lincoln's position among American heroes is no different in a popular Southern History of 1889 than in books produced in the North. Again he is the self-made man who develops heroism under the force of circumstances and great crises: ". . . called to the helm of government when all was turmoil and uncertainty, the ambition of a politician gave place to the strong, earnest devotion of a patriot . . . and now that these prejudices and passions have passed away, we contemplate in all their simplicity, the elements of greatness that make his life and character heroic. His death was a calamity to the South."[106]

[103] H 1867 Willson, p. 378; H 1874 Anderson, p. 194; H 1881 Steele, p. 216; H 1894 Fiske, p. 349.

[104] H 1894 Fiske, pp. 376–377. The speech itself is included in this book as well as in R 1898 Williams G-1, p. 167; R 1898 Black, pp. 160–161.

[105] H 1876 Doyle, p. 338.

[106] H 1889 Chambers, pp. 419–420.

Villains are, of course, quite as good teaching devices as heroes, and they are used here in counterpoint to the heroes. More villains appear abroad than in the United States, and they have been discussed with their nations. But America, in spite of its excellent institutions and free soil, has produced a few villains, perhaps more culpable than those of Europe because they have had better opportunities for the life of virtue. Because he attacked Christianity, Thomas Paine often appears as a major American villain.[107] But by far the greatest blackguard is the man used as a foil for Washington, the man who betrayed the American cause to the British—Benedict Arnold. In the schoolbooks he is as well known as Washington, but after this fashion: "His conduct has stamped him with infamy and like all traitors, he is despised of all mankind."[108] In the Spellers he appears in practice sentences, as: "Benedict Arnold is the name of an American traitor."[109] In the Geographies he is mentioned in connection with the places where he lived, fought, or negotiated with the British. The descriptions of West Point usually include such a sentence as the following: "This is the post that General Arnold intended to betray to General Clinton."[110]

Arnold appears almost as often as Washington; his case is to be used as an object lesson for the worst of all possible crimes: "The study of American history not only unites us more closely, and with stronger love to our free institutions, but it ennobles the mind by the lessons of virtue and patriotism which are given in the teachings and examples of our fathers. The whole course of the American Revolution shows but one *traitor*. The infamy which is forever attached to the name of Arnold is a sufficient warning to youth not to follow in his footsteps."[111] The reader is warned that evil behavior in childhood may flower into such adult behavior as Arnold's: "The inhumanity of the boy who had played cruel tricks on his companions, robbed birds' nests and maimed the fledglings that he might enjoy the distress of the parent-birds, was fully developed in the barbarity of the baffled traitor."[112]

[107] Attitudes toward Thomas Paine are discussed in the general analysis of religious ideas.

[108] R 1789 Webster, p. 120.

[109] S 1864 Ormsby, p. 61.

[110] G 1814 Adams, p. 136.

[111] H 1851 Guernsey, pref. p. v.

[112] H 1879 Quackenbos, pp. 183–184.

Books published after the Civil War are particularly fond of pointing out how he was despised after his treachery by the very people it had served: "Thus, you see, he wandered over the earth another Cain, with the wanderer's mark upon his brow. . . . True to your country, what might you have been, O ARNOLD, THE TRAITOR."[113]

Thus the greatest villain is one who attempted to interfere in the establishment of the American nation. Not even those who reject religion merit the same disgrace. In the horror expressed at Arnold's betrayal there is something of the attitude of the true believer toward the heretic. His defection was all the more shameful and dangerous in that he too had once been a true believer. If Washington was Jesus Christ, Arnold was Judas: "His name is fixed in language, like that of Judas, as the synonym of treachery."[114]

AMERICAN STATESMEN

Any American who achieved public office is by that fact exalted in these books, however undistinguished his service might be. But it is interesting to observe which statesmen are most admired, and for what qualities. Are men of opposing political principles accorded the same amount of space and the same kind of treatment?

The presentations of Hamilton and of Jefferson provide a useful comparison. Hamilton is usually given the more extensive treatment. This undoubtedly indicates in part a true sympathy for his policies among the authors of these schoolbooks. It is necessary to note, however, that the spectacular mode of his death may also have something to do with it, since death by the duel offers a golden opportunity for a moral lesson. There are many eulogies on Hamilton, most of them including strong anti-duelling sentiments.[115] He is highly praised, but for no specific virtue. That his greatness lay in his statesmanship under Washing-

[113] R 1870 Sanders, p. 211. [114] H 1872 Venable, p. 124.

[115] R 1809 Picket, pp. 192–195; R 1811 I. Cooke, pp. 174–178; R 1815 Dickinson, pp. 110–114; R 1826 American-S, pp. 157–160; R 1836 Cobb, pp. 245–247; R 1844 Goldsbury and Russell, pp. 207–209; R 1852 Sweet, pp. 223–224; R 1854 Mandeville, pp. 223–224; R 1856 Sanders-4, pp. 259–269; R 1860 McGuffey, pp. 80–81; H 1881 Armstrong, p. 62; H 1896 Murphy, p. 88–89.

ton seems evident, and by this implication those policies would be approved: "May Heaven, the guardian of our liberty, grant that our country may be fruitful of Hamiltons, and faithful to their glory."[116]

Although he was President and Hamilton was not, Jefferson is neither so noticeable nor so happily presented in these texts. His admiration for the French Revolution sometimes elicits comment as a seriously misguided sentiment. An 1879 History observes that Jefferson came back from France "so thoroughly imbued with democratic principles that he wore a waistcoat and breeches of scarlet, red being the color adopted by the French Revolutionists." The party of Jefferson usually appears as a partisan group, whereas that of Hamilton is a national party. The same History goes on to say that the Republicans objected to Hamilton's financial plans and found Washington too aristocratic, but "in spite of politicians" Washington and Adams were re-elected.[117] Jefferson is often accused of instituting a spoils system after reaching office. In his 1802 edition Morse mentions the repeal of the judiciary bill under Jefferson with this comment: "The Federalists considered it as a direct infraction of the Constitution."[118] Nothing of this sort is ever said of a Federalist measure. In his 1811 edition Morse notes simply that Washington had been succeeded by "that remarkable patriot John Adams, Esq.: who on the third of March 1801 was superseded by Thomas Jefferson, Esq."[119] Another early Geography, which throughout exhibits hostility to wealth and slavery, discusses Virginia: "In Albemarle County is Monticello, the seat of President Jefferson. He is rich. More than eleven hundred acres of his plantation are cultivated; his negro boys manufacture a ton of nails every month."[120] There are no comparable strictures on Hamilton in any of the books. Since there was so much copying of ideas and phrases, it is not unlikely that the hostile attitudes in the earlier books forced Jefferson out of many of the later ones.

Toward the end of the century Jefferson is sometimes given both more space and more credit. Several Histories mention his

[116] R 1831 Cheever, p. 259; see also R 1844 Goldsbury and Russell, pp. 207–209.

[117] H 1879 Quackenbos, p. 203.

[118] G 1802 Morse, p. 432.

[119] G 1811 Morse, p. 118.

[120] G 1807 Parish, p. 84.

distinction in the arts and in intellectual life,[121] although in most books this matter is not important enough to record. His democratic principles also appear more often in the later books. Throughout the century he is best known for the day of his dying. That both Jefferson and John Adams should die on the anniversary of the Declaration of Independence in 1826 is regarded as a certain sign of divine approval of the United States. Orations commemorating this event crowd the schoolbooks.[122] But no individuality is evident in any of these; the two men fade into each other. They could be discourses on any two Revolutionary patriots, "heaven-called avengers of degraded man."[123]

Another prominent statesman is John Marshall. Unlike Jefferson and John Adams, he is praised for his specific achievements on the bench. His was an "almost supernatural faculty for getting to the heart of the discussion."[124] Other prominent men, especially Presidents of the United States, are now and then mentioned in the following form: "The president, James Monroe, is a wise man."[125] He is granted this sentence not because he was James Monroe, but because he was President. Evidently greatness inheres in the Presidency. A piece by James G. Blaine is twice used to describe Garfield: "Great in life, he was surpassingly great in death."[126]

Before the Civil War, Andrew Jackson enters the schoolbooks only in the bare statement of being a soldier or President of the United States. At most one finds such assertions as: "Andrew Jackson was famed for his prowess in battle."[127] After the Civil

[121] H 1881 Steele, p. 155; H 1894 Fiske, p. 271.

[122] R 1826 Frost, pp. 111–114; 261–262; R 1827 Pierpont, pp. 261–265; R 1826 Greenwood and Emerson, pp. 273–276; R 1828 Hopkins, pp. 137–184; R 1830 MacLeod, pp. 115–118; R 1831 Cheever, pp. 94–97; R 1831 Harrod, pp. 119–120; R 1835 Porter, pp. 219–221; R 1836 Cobb-N.A., pp. 301–304; R 1845 Goldsbury and Russell, pp. 206–207; R 1852 Gilder, pp. 260–262; R 1854 Swan, pp. 467–472; R 1859 Hillard, pp. 529–532, etc.

[123] R 1828 Hopkins, p. 140.

[124] R 1815 Dickinson, p. 118; see also R 1831 Cheever, pp. 68–71; R 1835 Porter, pp. 176–178; R 1853 Sanders, pp. 198–199; R 1855 Burleigh, pp. 73–74; R 1864 Sanders, pp. 198–199; R 1867? Parker and Watson-4, pp. 112–114.

[125] S 1824 Bentley, p. 228.

[126] R 1898 Williams G-1, p. 264; see also R 1900 Aldrich and Forbes-II, p. 205.

[127] S 1859 Ormsby, Cushing, and Farnham, p. 85.

War he becomes prominent as the archetype of what would now be called the inner-directed man: "He was an honest man with a strong mind, and he would always do what he thought was right, without caring a fig about what people might say."[128] In some instances this praise is qualified: "He was a man of great courage, honesty and energy, though somewhat narrow and violent."[129] Another book, commenting on his obstinacy, observes that it often led him to arbitrary and undemocratic decisions: "But men who act in that way are apt to make mischief, for it takes more than one to tell what is best to do when great questions arise."[130] These limitations apparently prevented him from becoming the great hero out of the West. Jackson is always portrayed as an honest, self-made "man of the people."[131] In this category, however, heroism is reserved to Lincoln and greatness to Franklin.

In post-Civil War schoolbooks Jefferson Davis, head of the Confederacy, is not often assessed. One History, published in 1866 refers to him as a "bold and wicked man," and specifies this wickedness as cowardice shown in his flight after Appomattox "disguised as a woman by his wife's clothes!", and dishonesty: "Jefferson Davis, the wicked head of the Confederate traitors, very much frightened, ran away from Richmond with a great deal of gold that he and his associates had stolen from the banks and the people, followed by a number of those associates."[132] A Southern schoolbook offers a diametrically opposed view: "While in public life no statesman stood higher in the estimation of the intelligent than he. . . . Respected by the aged and reverenced by the youth of that South whose past is linked with his, and whose future he and his generation have filled with memories undying, he was laid at rest. With his death the last link binding the South of today with the conflict of the past is severed."[133] But these two extremes are atypical. Post-Civil War books, either reflecting a general attitude of merciful oblivion for the past or hoping to sell books in the North and South as well, ignore him or simply mention succinctly that he was president of the Confederacy.

[128] H 1866 Lossing, p. 203.
[129] H 1875 Higginson, p. 262.
[130] H 1890 Morris, p. 176.
[131] H 1900 Channing, p. 229.
[132] H 1866 Lossing, pp. 223–237.
[133] H 1889 Chambers, p. 365.

THE VIRTUOUS CITIZEN

Examples of virtue in great men, however, are not enough. The selections of every sort, whether prose or poetry, description or narration, are designed as much to inculcate virtue as to impart information. The statements or implicit assumptions of moral lessons are so universal that the slightest exception is startling, as when, in an 1867 Reader, one finds skating and sleighing described as just simple fun.[134] Typical practice sentences in the Spellers are the following: "Aim to be good." "Abstain from evil." "Obey the law." "Remorse will haunt a guilty conscience." "Be on your guard against evil associates." "Abhor that which is evil." These are all found within three pages, interspersed with such other information as: "Bears lie dormant in the winter." "A sponge will absorb water." [135] It is only near the end of the century that descriptions of natural phenomena are allowed to stand on their own merits. There are many direct strictures on individual behavior, ranging from the general precepts quoted above to simple matters of etiquette: "Belching, coughing, sniffling, sniveling, spitting, etc. must be avoided as much as possible, especially in company and at table." [136] But moral lessons are implicit in all of the material of these books. They advocate specific virtues no different from those that have elevated the great to their positions. The child is to be religious, industrious, thrifty, persevering, devoted to his parents, obedient to authority, charitable, and chaste; he must also learn to subdue his passions.

What will concern us here is not a reiteration of the virtues the child is to develop but the rationalizations offered to the child of why virtue is necessary and desirable. Why should he be good? As described in these books, the main religious duty of man is to cultivate moral behavior; indeed, religion is more nearly a system of ethics than of theology. That virtue is necessary for happiness is sometimes stated, and likewise its corollary: "Misery is indeed the necessary result of all deviation from rectitude." [137] But evidently neither the teachings of the church

[134] R 1867 Edwards-4, pp. 31–33. [135] S 1874 Worcester, pp. 30–33.

[136] S 1798 Child, p. 110; see also R 1789 Webster, p. 62.

[137] R 1789 Webster, p. 65; see also S 1846 Butterfield, p. 5; R 1895 Hazen, p. 150.

nor conscience provide foundations solid enough for a sound superstructure of morality, for in addition the schoolbooks bombard the child with the idea, elaborately and richly illustrated, that virtue is rewarded and vice punished in an immediate and material sense. God does not wait for the after-life to distribute rewards and punishments; He metes them out inexorably, not simply in pangs of conscience and remorse, but in things of this world.

God's hand is obvious in many of the earlier books. He threatens dreadful plagues (such as eye-hungry ravens) for those who do not reverence their parents and teachers. This reverence for elders requires silence in their presence unless directly addressed, nor should the child contradict them even if certain he is right.[138] The future of the disobedient child is bleak indeed: "Soon she will be left an orphan; with neither friends nor home: and in ragged apparel she will be forced to beg from house to house."[139] In another instance, divine punishment comes immediately to children engaged in teasing Elisha, when: "raging bears . . . tore them limb from limb to death, with blood and groans and tears."[140]

But even when God's name is not specifically invoked, punishments for meretricious acts are His because His is the order of nature. The inevitability of earthly suffering for evil is abundantly illustrated. A story in several Spellers predicts the gallows for a boy who steals a book.[141] In this instance punishment is directed both to the culprit and to his mother, who neglected her parental duties by not sufficiently punishing him for this first offense. Nature is in league against those not in accord with moral laws, as in this practice sentence from a Speller: "A dog met a bad boy and bit him."[142] Innumerable other stories and statements have the same theme: accidents happen only to those who deserve them. Such childhood misbehavior as playing hookey from school is always attended with dire consequences: one boy loses his leg

[138] S 1819 Bingham, p. 60.

[139] S 1821 Hull, p. 25; see also S 1847 ASDUK, pp. 122–123.

[140] S 1809 Parlour, p. 28.

[141] S 1799 Fenning, p. 45; S 1802 Alexander, pp. 126–137; see also R 1796 Bingham, pp. 23–25; S 1846 McGuffey, p. 79.

[142] S 1823 Marshall, p. 21.

in an accident while on such an unauthorized venture from school; another drowns.[143] In the latter story the boy who fares worst is the only one of the group who could already swim, and was not even trying to learn a practical skill in excuse for the expedition. His guilt is thus double; he has been idle as well as defiant of authority. The consequences of disobeying authority are further illustrated in the story of a little boy stung by nettles and covered with cold mud after disobeying his parents. The moral is: "And as it was with Jarvis, so will it be with everyone who acts disobediently. . . . To disobey your parents, your teachers, or any authority over you, be sure that a punishment awaits you if you do not resist it."[144] In these incidents the penalty is related only to the fact of immoral behavior; it is not a natural consequence of the particular act. Such incidents clearly indicate the universal belief, firmly held and taught, that one cannot escape punishment on earth for evil deeds. Like modern psychiatrists, authors of nineteenth-century schoolbooks associate accidents with guilt. In the schoolbooks so-called accidents are really God's punishment exacted through nature. "The misfortunes of men [are] mostly chargeable on themselves."[145]

Sometimes punishment grows directly and naturally out of the crime. Although the punishments are equally dire, they do at least bear a direct relationship to the nature of the misdemeanor. The boy who cruelly pulls the wings from a bee, or thrusts a stick into a hive, is sure to be stung.[146] Another boy, habitually cruel to animals, is finally gored and tossed by a bull.[147] Two boys disobey their father, one by playing with a gun, and the other by throwing stones; one loses a leg and one an eye.[148] Another little boy teases a "crazyman" who finally hits him with a rock.[149] In these instances the ensuing event is still regarded as punishment, but it is the natural result of a particular action rather than a mysterious blow from the heavens.

In a schoolbook published in 1779 Anthony Benezet, a Quaker, complains that although children should be trained in tenderness,

[143] S 1799 Fenning, p. 47; see also R 1866? Sargent-2, pp. 115–116.
[144] R 1868 Parker and Watson, p. 110.
[145] R 1815 R. Adams, p. 146–152.
[146] R 1866 McGuffey-4, pp. 39–43. [147] S 1854 Angell, 67–68.
[148] R 1812 Daggett, pp. 15–17; R 1825 Torrey, pp. 12–13.
[149] R 1812 Daggett, pp. 20–23; see also R 1835 Pierpont-Y, pp. 10–11, 23–24.

affection, humility, and self-denial, yet "our modern education is not of this kind, our Sons are generally exhorted to improvement from principles of covetousness or a desire of distinction."[150] This was to be a valid criticism of schoolbooks for well over a century. The exhortation to virtue is most frequently backed by the certainty of material reward. The bad child would end up a miserable poverty-stricken adult; the good child a happy and prosperous one. Every individual can regulate his life by virtue or vice, but the choice inexorably determines his fortunes in this world as well as the next. Dire physical punishments may await the sinner; lack of success in this world always pursues him. In this sense all men are self-made. Conversely, God allows affluence only to the virtuous man. Hence affluence is not only a reward but also a sign of virtue. The Social Darwinism of the late nineteenth century, that saw morality in league with riches, was simply reaffirming a Puritan lesson taught steadily throughout the period of this study. It is rare indeed to find such a statement as: "There may be success in life without success in business."[151]

Thousands of anecdotes in the schoolbooks bear witness that the exercise of virtue produces material advantages. Aid to the less fortunate is both a moral duty and a practice assuring economic benefits to the giver. For example, in a story entitled "The Beggar and the Good Boy," a boy helps a beggar while others jeer at him. Later, when the beggar dies, he is found to be a miser, his £200,000 fortune willed to the boy who helped him years before.[152] Another typical form of this situation appears first in the eighteenth century and continues throughout the next century: a rich man who has helped the poor, becomes poor himself. His fortunes are recovered with the aid of those who themselves have made fortunes through his previous help.[153] Fortune also frequently rewards honesty, as in the story of the little boy who returns to a bookstore to pay for books he had bought but, by mistake, had not been charged for. He ends as

[150] S 1779 Benezet, pref., p. 5; see also R 1866 Sargent-3, p. 20.

[151] R 1871 Sargent and May-5, p. 257.

[152] R 1868 Parker and Watson, pp. 61–63; see also R 1823 Morrill, pp. 31–32; R 1866 McGuffey-4, pp. 34–36; 39–43; R 1866 Sargent-4, pp. 43–45; R 1872 Osgood-5, pp. 43–45; R 1899 Holmes and Hill, pp. 99–106.

[153] R 1792 Dana, pp. 86–90.

partner in the store.[154] In a fable in an 1890 Reader, kindness to animals leads to fortune when the animals repay their benefactor by helping him find hidden jewels.[155] Unselfishness too brings monetary reward to a little girl who always chose the smaller piece of bread while her brothers fought greedily for the largest; one day she finds a piece of silver in hers.[156] Even scrupulous observance of the Sabbath can bring material rewards: a barber, ruined by his decision not to work on Sunday, is the only barber in town willing to give up his Saturday night to shave a man with like principles. The barber tells his patron the story of his declining fortunes; in the course of conversation the customer discovers the barber to be the rightful heir to riches that are now claimed by an impostor, and thus the barber's fortune is made.[157] In this context the moral of a piece from Emerson pointing out that the man who steals, steals from himself, the swindler swindles himself, etc., is destroyed by the final sentence: "For the real price of labor is knowledge and virtue, whereof wealth and credit are signs."[158] Clearly the child is to be motivated toward virtue not by the satisfaction of performing his moral duty, but by the hope of material gain.

Combined with the assurances of material reward for virtue one finds an overweening admiration for the self-made man. Evidence is to be found in many sections of this study, and it reflects one of the most basic values in the nineteenth-century schoolbook. The concept and process of improving oneself economically will be discussed in connection with social classes in Chapter 9. Suffice it to say here that getting ahead is a moral duty enjoined on man by God; the Calvinist earthly calling is to be heard by all as clearly as the heavenly calling. In McGuffey's Fourth Reader in 1879, after one of the innumerable success stories, is the sentence: "And if you do not improve the advantages you enjoy, you sin against your Maker."[159] This is further emphasized by the question at the end of the lesson: "For what are we placed in this world?" Spencer, Darwin, and the Social Dar-

[154] R 1870 Sanders, pp. 66–69; see also R 1882 Gourley and Hunt, pp. 169–171; R 1896 McGuffey-2, pp. 131–135; R 1899 Holmes and Anderson, pp. 111–114.

[155] R 1890 Davis, p. 17.

[156] R 1866? Sargent-2, pp. 132–133.

[157] R 1866 McGuffey-5, pp. 105–107.

[158] R 1888 McGuffey, p. 231.

[159] R 1879 McGuffey, p. 115.

winists were not the inspiration for this sentiment, for it has a longer history in schoolbooks. In 1810 it was put so: "Existence is a sacred trust; he who misemploys and squanders it away is treacherous to its Author."[160] Since getting ahead economically by honest means is our primary moral duty, the virtues most helpful to that end are stressed *ad nauseam*: industry, thrift, frugality, perseverance, self-denial. These were, of course, Puritan values, as the end was a Puritan end. But they were also the virtues of the nineteenth-century American environment, necessary for survival on a frontier and useful to the expanding industrial economy. Geography and the economy had reaffirmed for the American those virtues already sanctified in the American tradition.

Was the child taught then to pursue economic prosperity for the sake of enjoying the material things acquired in the process? An emphatic "no" is necessary. Self-indulgence and sensuous pleasures have no place in the present or the future of the ideal man of the schoolbooks: "If our softness and indulgences, and foreign fashions, must inevitably accomplish our seduction, and lead us away from the simplicity, honesty, sobriety, purity, and manly independence of our forefathers, most readily and fervently should I exclaim, welcome back to the pure old times of the Puritans."[161] Luxurious living is always condemned, whether seen on a Southern plantation or in a European court. Gratification of the senses is to be avoided not only on the way up the economic ladder, when it might interfere with a rapid ascent, but at the top as well. Now and then a schoolbook lesson suggests a masochistic pleasure in denying sensuous gratification. Harry, in contrast to his lazy brother, arises at 6 A.M.; he does this with particular pleasure on cold winter mornings when he can say to himself: "Here is a fine opportunity for self-denial." When it rains just as he was preparing to go riding, he exults: "This is the best opportunity for self-denial that I have had today."[162]

God does not entrust wealth to the successful man for self-indulgence but for the benefit of the community. In addition, the

[160] R 1810 Alden, p. 43; see also R 1787 Miscellanies, pp. 39, 115; R 1797 Alexander, p. 145; R 1801 Chipman, p. 193; R 1803 D. Adams, p. 27; R 1804 New Introduction, p. 33; R 1810 Thomson, p. 80; R 1819 Strong, pp. 47–49, etc.

[161] R 1827 Pierpont, p. 218; see also G 1791 Morse, p. 138; R 1809 Picket, p. 181; R 1826 Greenwood and Emerson, pp. 102–103.

[162] R 1884 Campbell-4, pp. 182–184 from a piece by Jane Taylor.

pursuit of wealth is a pursuit of status in one's own eyes as well as in the eyes of the community. To acquire wealth is an outward and visible sign of inward and spiritual grace; it is itself a sign of virtue as well as virtue rewarded. The enjoyment of wealth lies in the sense of achievement and the surety of virtue. The evidence of schoolbooks seems to support Carl Becker's interpretation of American "materialism": "American idealism has necessarily a material basis, and Americans have often been mistakenly called materialists. . . . He [the American] cares less for money than for making money: a fortune is valued, not because it represents ease, but because it represents struggle, achievement, progress."[163] The child reared on these books was probably indeed receptive to the Gospel of Wealth. It was no news to him that morality was in league with riches. Spencerianism and Social Darwinism merely gave a pseudo-scientific gloss to already familiar truth.

[163] Carl Becker, "Kansas," *Every Man His Own Historian* (New York: Appleton-Century-Crofts, 1935), p. 12.

IV. Schoolbooks and "Culture"

Chapter 7

SCHOOLBOOKS AND "CULTURE"

Does America have a culture of its own? Has America contributed to that concept of culture which Noah Webster and the nineteenth century defined as "the enlightenment and refinement of taste acquired by intellectual and aesthetic training"?[1] This issue has been lightly and hotly debated across the Atlantic for a century and a half, and European criticism of our contributions to scholarship and the fine arts has made Americans painfully sensitive to any trans-Atlantic discussions in these areas. But the discussion in the United States has been continuous; it reached points of egocentric frenzy at times when Americans were particularly proud of themselves in other respects vis-à-vis Europe, as in the periods after the American Revolution, the War of 1812, and World War II. Two questions have been at the center of the controversy: Has the United States produced art and scholarship of a quality comparable to that of Europe? Has the United States a literary and aesthetic culture of its own?

After the Revolution these issues were posed by American writers and intellectuals when they called for the development of a distinctively American culture. Immediately after the achievement of American political independence, Noah Webster hoped to separate America from Britain culturally by the creation of a distinctive American system of spelling. Charles Brockden Brown called on American literary men to use the resources of the American scene, and in his novel *Wieland* he illustrated his point by transposing the Gothic novel from the ruined castle of Europe to the American forest. In 1837 Ralph Waldo Emerson issued his famous declaration of independence for American scholars in an address at Harvard. The activities of James Fenimore

[1] *Webster's New International Dictionary of the English Language* (2nd ed., Springfield, Mass.: G. and C. Merriam, 1946).

Cooper, William Cullen Bryant, and others in calling for an American art as well as in creating one are well known.

That the American intellectual in the first part of our national existence wished to encourage American creativity in the fine arts and in scholarship cannot be questioned. But was the ordinary American aware of this? Was he encouraged to consider these fields worth cultivating in America? Was the intellectual climate in which he lived favorable to the development of scholars, or were potential scholars generally turned into the more useful field of school teaching? Was the American public encouraged to consider the fine arts an important element in national development?

SCHOLARSHIP

The primary intellectual value embodied in nineteenth-century American schoolbooks is that the only important knowledge is that which is "useful." The word "knowledge" is so often preceded by the word "useful" that it is clear that only such knowledge is approved and that it is this kind of knowledge that a sound education provides. Useful knowledge is presumed to be uniquely characteristic of American education. The best definition of this "useful knowledge" as used in nineteenth-century schoolbooks comes from an 1807 Reader, and it was acceptable throughout the century: "Our government and habits are republican; they cherish equal rights and tend to an equal distribution of property. Our mode of education has the same tendency to promote an equal distribution of knowledge, and to make us emphatically a 'republic of letters.' I would not be understood adept in the fine arts, but participants of useful knowledge. . . . We are all scholars in the useful; and employed in improving the works of nature, rather than in imitating them."[2]

And because of our special training in this kind of knowledge, the useful arts have become the particular province of the American. A Reader of the 1850's notes: "In the arts which contribute to domestic culture and national aggrandizement, the American states will sustain no unfavorable comparison with Europe."[3] By

[2] R 1807 Bingham-C, p. 299.

[3] R 1856 Sargent-4, p. 167; see also R 1883 Swinton-5, pp. 411–413; H 1898 Steele and Steele, pp. 307–308.

the latter part of the century American achievements in this area have been recognized by all: "The ingenuity of the people of the United States has passed into a proverb. To them are due many of the inventions which have contributed most to the comfort and improvement of the race."[4] Thus useful knowledge is interpreted in a narrow sense; those arts that are functional to a more comfortable material life are equated to republicanism and to Americanism. Talents in these fields are inherent in the Americans and unique to them: "While many other nations are wasting the brilliant efforts of genius in monuments of ingenious folly, to perpetuate their pride, the Americans, according to the true spirit of republicanism, are employed almost entirely in works of public and private utility."[5]

In all of these books the fact that we have not produced scholars is mentioned with pride as a sign that knowledge is democratically diffused instead of being concentrated in the hands of an upper class: "In the monarchical and aristocratic governments of Europe . . . a few privileged orders monopolize not only the wealth and honors, but the knowledge of their country. They produce a few profound scholars, who make study the business of their lives; we acquire a portion of science as a necessary instrument of livelihood, and deem it absurd to devote our whole lives to the acquisition of implements, without having it in our power to make them useful to ourselves or others."[6] Our institutions of higher learning are not designed to produce scholars; they are institutions

> Where homebred freemen seize the solid prize;
> Fixt in small spheres with safer beams to shine.
> They reach the useful and refuse the fine,
> Found on its proper base, the social plan,
> The broad plain truths, the common sense of man.[7]

Another book notes happily: "There are none of those splendid establishments such as Oxford or Cambridge in which immense

[4] H 1879 Quackenbos, p. 305.
[5] G 1791 Morse, p. 87; see also R 1860 McGuffey, pp. 55–56.
[6] R 1807 Bingham-C, p. 299.
[7] R 1815 Dickinson, p. 188, quoted from Joel Barlow.

salaries maintain the professors of literature in monastic idleness. . . . The People of this country have not yet been inclined to make much literary display—They have rather aimed at works of general utility."[8] Instead of such aristocratic institutions, public schools and small libraries have been set up in towns and villages all over the United States, "which serve a more valuable purpose, in the general diffusion of knowledge."[9] Instead of an isolated group of scholars toiling away in useless labor we produce educated men whose minds are occupied with the improvement of society. "The greatest scholars of the country . . . have not deemed the latter [schoolbooks] an unworthy labor."[10] Most of our learned men "are so devoted to the instruction of youth, or the active employments of life, as to leave little opportunity for the prosecution of literary research, or scientific discovery."[11] And indeed the actual situation described here is sometimes elevated and abstracted into a principle of virtuous behavior for scholars: "It is not in literary production only, or chiefly, that the educated mind finds fit expression, and fulfills its mission in honor and beneficence. In the great theatre of the world's affairs there is a worthy and sufficient sphere."[12] Even on an elementary level scholarship is associated with Europe rather than with America. A delightful illustration of this occurs in an 1828 Reader. Under a picture entitled "The German" which shows a man carrying a book under his arm, is the sentence: "The Germans read, write, and think a great deal."[13] Such activities are evidently not to be regarded by the child as part of the ordinary life of man, but are worthy of note as functions of a particular foreign culture.

Besides reserving education for the elite and sponsoring useless knowledge, the European universities have another serious disadvantage which is corrected in American institutions of higher learning. "The colleges and universities of Europe differ materially from those of the United States. They are rather places of study

[8] G 1826 Blake, p. 165.

[9] G 1824 Woodbridge and Willard, p. 205.

[10] H 1872 Venable, p. 183.

[11] G 1866 Woodbridge, p. 339.

[12] R 1869 Wilson, p. 159, quoted from George R. Putnam.

[13] R 1828 Robbins-A, p. 22 (of the last chapter. Pagination begins again with this chapter for unknown reasons).

13. The bookish Germans: intellectual life is usually assumed to be a function of a particular culture rather than of men. This print is from Eliza Robbins' American Popular Lessons, 1828.

for such as wish to acquire knowledge. Scarcely any control or care is exercised over the character and conduct of the students, and their efforts are purely voluntary."[14] As a result, although the European university produced serious scholars it also produced men learned in the ways of drink, gambling, dissipation, and vice—activities that arouse transports of horror in the schoolbooks.[15]

The picture of the American college in these schoolbooks is one of an institution designed to inculcate moral values rather than intellectual ones; it should instill useful knowledge in the sense of principles useful to the maintenance of Christianity (Protestant, except in those books written for Catholic parochial schools), the American form of government, and American society. The colleges were firmly founded on the principle stated by Webster in a most popular 1805 Reader: "How little of our peace and security depends on REASON and how much on *religion and government.*"[16] The function of the American college was to produce men who were prepared to uphold the values already dominant in society rather than to examine those values critically. It was the formation of character and sound principles rather than the pursuit of truth that was to engage the university student. This conception of the function of higher education in America has interesting implications for the principle of academic freedom. If the college teacher is to be occupied primarily in the pursuit of truth in a given scholarly field his political and social beliefs are irrelevant to his profession. But if the primary duty of the professor is to indoctrinate the student with principles accepted as good by American society, then it is logical to contend that American society has the right to investigate the beliefs held by college teachers. Frequent public investigations of American college teachers are undoubtedly based on a continued acceptance in America of this fundamental difference between the aims of European and American universities.

It is not the university, however, that is regarded in American schoolbooks as the most effective carrier of civilization; it is rather the common school that will perpetuate what the authors

[14] G 1866 Woodbridge, p. 345.

[15] For an example of this, see R 1872 Osgood-5, pp. 170–173.

[16] R 1805 Webster, p. 147.

consider most important in American civilization. Every author points with pride to the public school system as one of the most distinctive features of American civilization. A typical statement, emphasizing spread rather than depth, is the following: "Education is more widely diffused in this than in any other country in the world." [17] And America's devotion to universal education is old: "The idea of popular education was brought to the new world by our forefathers. Even in the wilderness, while the wolf prowled about the log-house, and the cry of the wild-cat was still heard, the school and even the college, were established." [18]

But it is clear from the books used in these schools that the purpose of the common school as well as of the university is to train the heart rather than the head. Emma Willard's preface to her 1868 History is quite explicit: "We have, indeed, been desirous to cultivate the memory, the intellect and the taste. But much more anxious have we been to sow the seeds of virtue by showing the good in such amicable lights that the youthful heart shall kindle into desires of imitation." [19] That virtue is superior to knowledge or even wisdom is continually stressed, as in this admonition by Alice Cary: "Little children, you must seek Rather to be good than wise"; [20] or, on a more advanced level: "Man's intellect is not man's sole nor best adorning." [21] It has often been stated in histories of American education that the American public school system was instituted to train citizens, native and immigrant, and to equalize classes, but the evidence of the schoolbooks would seem to indicate that this was to be accomplished by training character as well as by imparting knowledge. The "useful knowledge" offered in the school was useful to success in the material world, but it was also expected to produce those qualities of character that we associate both with Puritanism and with the self-made man: thrift, hard work, and the rejection of frivolity.

In the early Readers and Spellers most of the literary excerpts are taken from *The Tatler* and *The Spectator*, from the writings of

[17] G 1875 McNally, p. 54.

[18] H 1889? Steele, p. 307.

[19] H 1868 Willard, preface.

[20] R 1882 Gourley and Hunt, p. 196.

[21] R 1867 Parker and Watson-5, p. 338; see also R 1866 McGuffey-4, pp. 79–80; R 1866? Sargent-2 (title page missing), p. 101; R 1870 Sanders, pp. 314–315; R 1879 McGuffey, pp. 151–153.

Franklin, Pope, Sterne, Dryden, and Swift, and from various religious tracts. From the 1820's on the contemporary literature of Romanticism became dominant, and remained so throughout the century, disregarding newer trends in literature. Unlike Romanticism in the earlier period, Realism and Naturalism at the end of the century are not reflected in school anthologies. William Dean Howells is represented in one Speller and a Reader in 1900 by a short nature poem showing none of the canons of Howells' realism. One could hardly expect a contemporary literature so unlikely to inculcate the kind of morality desired for the nineteenth-century child to find its way into schoolbooks. Indeed even the adult world found itself reluctant to accept the language and view of nature and human nature of contemporary literature of the end of the century. But with its passions subdued into sentimentality, Romanticism, long after it had declined as a literary movement, was believed eminently suitable to children's literature. Bryant, Longfellow, Whittier, Emerson, and watered-down versions of these continued to make up the core of the child's literary diet. Heroism, death, illness, decay, a mystical nationalism, a transcendental approach to nature, and the process of winning success against great odds remained the popular subjects. Underlying all of these was the premise that the heart is more important than the head. The nearest approach to realism in the late nineteenth century is in the very large literature of the self-made man; here, although the head is important in achieving success, yet success comes only to the pure in heart.

Characterizations in schoolbooks of the great men of America embody some of the same attitudes. The child reading these books would be quite unaware of the intellectual and scholarly adventures of the Puritans, of a John Adams, of a Thomas Jefferson. Scholarship as work is relegated to undemocratic societies; in such a society as that of the United States ideas seem to come almost unbidden into the minds of intelligent and good men. Furthermore, unless bent to a practical and moral end, intellectual endeavor is not used as a criterion of greatness for the individual. Moral and patriotic endeavor rather than intellectual stature creates American heroes.

As they did with all hero-figures, the textbook authors attach to Washington's prestige-giving figure the virtues they expect the child to emulate, whether these bear any resemblance to the hero's life or not. He is brave, charitable, industrious, religious, courteous, and a paragon of the domestic virtues. The best qualities of the self-made man are his. But in no instance are intelligence, learning, or disinterested inquiry associated with Washington. Indeed in some of the later books he is specifically shown as a practical man who rejected the intellectual life. It is said that "He was more solid than brilliant, and had more judgment than genius. He had great dread of public life, cared little for books, and possessed no library."[22] As a child Washington "was fonder of playing out of doors than study in school, for he was a strong, manly boy, who could best all his schoolmates in their sports."[23] This would seem to imply an unbridgeable abyss between the physically active boy and the student, between the successful man of affairs and the scholar. Manliness and scholarship would seem to be antithetical. Manliness is for the American, scholarship for the effete European.

The only public figure to whom scholarship is ever a sign of distinction is Thomas Jefferson, but he is a minor figure in these books, and only occasionally noted as a scholar. He is more than offset by Daniel Boone, who appears in a guise most attractive to schoolchildren and who was "ignorant of books, but versed in the forest and forest life."[24] The American hero-figure is stereotyped, then, as a practical, moral, hard-working man who needs "useful knowledge" to get ahead in the world, but who finds scholarship unnecessary and even, at times, demeaning.

Is the child specifically encouraged to read on his own? He is exhorted to apply the Franklin virtues to his schoolwork and to the acquisition of "useful knowledge" as a part of his struggle for success in the world. But doubts are frequently expressed as to both the quality and the quantity of books he should read. He must be careful not to read too much: "She is a strange child.

[22] H 1898 Steele and Steele, p. 150 (same in 1881 and 1889 editions); R 1879 Harris, Rickoff, Bailey, pp. 367–369; see also R 1888 McGuffey, pp. 242–244; H 1889 Monroe, p. 180; H 1881 Thalheimer (actually c. 1888), p. 187.

[23] H 1899 Morris (actually includes material to 1904), p. 131.

[24] R 1897 Baldwin-5, p. 102; see also R 1880 Harris, Rickoff, Bailey, pp. 165–168; G 1891 Morton, p. 78; R 1899 Holmes and Hill, p. 221; H 1899 Morris (actually includes material to 1904), p. 172.

She will take a book and read it while the boys and girls run and play near her. I fear she reads and thinks too much. The brain must have rest."[25] The frequent appearance of excerpts from the writings of Emerson and Wordsworth, shorn in this context of transcendental qualities, seems to recommend the achievement of the good life only by the rejection of the intellectual life in favor of direct experience. The following are typical examples:

> Up! up! my friend and quit your books
> Or surely you'll grow double;
> Books! 'Tis a dull and endless strife . . .[26]

> I laugh at the lore and the pride of man,
> At the sophists schools, and the learned clan;
> For what are they all in their high conceit,
> When man in the bush with God may meet.[27]

Taken out of context in this way, Wordsworth (more popular in the first half of the century) and Emerson (popular in the second half of the century) seem to stand for anti-intellectualism rather than for awareness of the insufficiency of reason. There are countless tales of the value of direct experience over the value of book experience. A typical case is the tale of a boy forced by family difficulties to go to work rather than to go on with school. A merchant about to hire him gives this advice: "Manhood is better than Greek. Self-reliance is worth more to a man than Latin."[28] Here, obviously, it is the self-reliance of self-support in a financial, not a spiritual, sense that is considered desirable. Emerson has been adapted to the market place.

Apart from the question of quantity, reading must be carefully limited in quality to those books that impart "useful knowledge" and that strengthen character. William H. McGuffey, for example, believed that only "good" books are to be used—books that will inspire the reader with "love of what is right and useful."

[25] R 1866 Soule and Wheeler, p. 41; see also R 1872 Willson, p. 163; R 1874 Hillard, p. 53; R 1900 Demarest and Van Sickle, p. 132.

[26] From Wordsworth's "Vacation Song," quoted in R 1884 Campbell-4, pp. 215–216.

[27] From Emerson's "Goodby," quoted in R 1884 Campbell-5, pp. 109–110.

[28] R 1871 Monroe, pp. 58–59.

He continued: "Next to the fear of God, implanted in the heart nothing is a better safeguard to character, than the love of good books. They are the handmaids of virtue and religion."[29] Conversely: "Bad books are the public fountains of vice."[30] The reading of novels (and few distinctions are made among them) is almost always condemned in the first half of the century, and frequently in the latter half. An 1868 Reader, seeking the cause for the complete deterioration of a character under discussion, asks: "Is it the bottle or the betting book? Is it the billiard table or the theatre? Is it smoking? Is it laziness? Is it novel-reading?"[31] The child is cautioned to read with great selectivity—a selectivity based not on training one's taste by wide reading but by canons laid down by authority. He is not only warned not to read too much, but his purpose in reading is subject to the censor. To read for pleasure is frowned upon: "A book which is torn and mutilated is abused, but one which is merely read for enjoyment is misused."[32]

It is clear from this evidence that anti-intellectualism is not only not new in American civilization, but that it is thoroughly embedded in the schoolbooks that have been read by generations of pupils since the beginning of the Republic. The rejection of the intellectual required the rejection of an intellectual past—that of the Puritans and of the founders of the Republic—as part of the American tradition. The frontier did not need scholarship, whereas "useful knowledge" was essential to survival. And the needs of the frontier were probably reinforced by the needs of expanding business. Thus an 1875 Speller records current attitudes in saying: "We do not blame a man who is proud of his success, so much as one who is vain of his learning."[33]

[29] R 1866 McGuffey-5, p. 92.

[30] S 1869 Day, p. 163; see also H 1868 Kerney (for Roman Catholic schools), p. 216; R 1898 Williams G-1, pp. 330, 334; R 1898 Williams P-1, pref., p. 3; R 1900 Aldrich and Forbes-I, pp. 18–19.

[31] R 1868 Parker and Watson, p. 118; see also R 1871 Sargent and May-5, pp. 146–149; R 1898 Williams G-2, p. 136. Actually certain "moral" novels were recommended, such as those by Scott and Cooper.

[32] S 1890 Kupfer, p. 58; see also R 1866 Sargent-3, Part II, p. 129; R 1898 Baldwin-5, pp. 7–9; R 1898 Black, pp. 7–12.

[33] S 1875 Monroe, p. 144.

THE FINE ARTS

To these schoolbook writers the concept of usefulness was perhaps even more important for the fine arts than for the intellectual elements in American culture. Historically, the arts occupied a quite different position from that of scholarship in American development. In undertaking to determine what was to be considered the American tradition it was possible to draw upon an actual scholarly heritage; but the arts had always been held in a distinctly subservient position in America. In the colonial period literary labors were made to serve theology and politics, but the visual and auditory arts were regarded with suspicion by New Englanders as being inconsistent with Puritan precautions against the seductiveness of the senses. It was also true that in a frontier environment relatively few had the leisure or the opportunity to participate, either as creator or as audience, in the fine arts and belles-lettres. Yet by the nineteenth century America had produced many creative artists whose art was not designed to serve some other cause; and the fact that their work was too important to be ignored raises questions as to how the schoolbooks evaluated their contributions. Was the American child in this period, for example, taught to regard the arts as worthy of serious attention? To what extent were they considered essential or, at least, important to national development?

Music and the fine arts appear in these schoolbooks primarily in discussions of three subjects: the self-made artist, national monuments, and evaluations of American art. Those paintings and sculptures that glorify American heroes and the American past are frequently noted. For example, the statues of Washington in Richmond, Baltimore, and Raleigh are almost always mentioned in the sections of the Geographies devoted to those cities. But discussions of the aesthetic qualities of such works are absent; they are to be observed for nationalistic rather than for aesthetic reasons.

Discussions of the fine arts appear mainly in the examples of self-made men in the field of the arts, and it is evident that in these tales their self-achieved success is more important than their art. The career of the Italian sculptor Antonio Canova, for example, is described in the same terms as those used to describe the career of a successful businessman of the nineteenth century. The story of his boyhood act of carving a lion out of butter to provide a substitute for a centerpiece which had not been delivered is frequently told. He is praised, however, not as a man of artistic achievement but as one who "was diligent and regular in his habits," and who saw an opportunity for success and used it.[34] One needs to be reminded here of a previously mentioned tale that appears even more often in the schoolbooks of the American painter, Benjamin West, too poor as a boy to buy paint brushes, made them of hairs plucked from his cat's tail and taught himself to paint. "Thus we see," runs the moral, "that, by industry, ingenuity, and perseverance, a little American boy became the most distinguished painter of his day in England."[35] Obviously these are not discussions of talented artists but of self-made men who happened to be artists. Their success was accomplished by diligence combined with the ability to recognize opportunity.

The aesthetic theories held in these books necessarily settle the fine arts into a position inferior to that of literature. The statement that "Statues and pictures are pleasing representations of nature"[36] expressed their attitude throughout the century, and Longfellow's aphorism, "Nature is a revelation of God, art is a revelation of man,"[37] was quoted to show that as imitations of nature works of art could never approach nature itself. According to this theory a landscape is of necessity more beautiful than a pleasing representation of it, and God, who is manifest through nature itself, can be discerned but dimly, if at all, through an imperfect imitation. Consequently in the schoolbooks painting and sculpture acquire importance only for extra-artistic qualities. Sculpture was useful to commemorate the dead, and the schoolbooks were not alone in the nineteenth century in recommending

[34] R 1866? Sargent-2, pp. 146–147; see also R 1867? Parker and Watson-4 (title page missing), pp. 73–77; R 1871 Monroe, pp. 156–157; R 1882 Gourley and Hunt, pp. 225–227; R 1888 McGuffey, pp. 170–174; R 1898 Black, pp. 21–25.

[35] R 1844 Bumstead, pp. 137–142; see also R 1832 Edwards, p. 297; R 1845 D. Adams, p. 213; R 1866? Sargent-2, pp. 76–78; R 1874 Hillard, p. 156; S 1874 Worcester, p. 123.

[36] S 1836 Brandreth, p. 98; see also R 1806 Peirce, p. 48; R 1879 Harris, Rickoff, Bailey, pp. 397–399; S 1890 Kupfer, p. 63.

[37] Quoted in S 1896 Dutton, p. 114.

tours of the cemeteries of Philadelphia and Boston. But more important than this, the fine arts were useful in engendering nationalism by portraying American heroes and historical events. This is made quite clear in what purports to be an aesthetic judgment of the field of painting: "Q. What are the most esteemed paintings? A. Those representing historical events." [38]

The most curious argument in favor of encouraging the fine arts in the United States, and indeed the only argument for encouraging them on any grounds, is presented by an 1826 Reader under the heading "Usefulness of the Fine Arts." [39] In this article the fine arts are recommended partly because they would produce a new class of people to be fed and, in the case of sculpture, would stimulate the marble and granite industries. Furthermore, those artists who did not succeed in the fine arts would then turn their talents to the useful arts in the clay, glass, and cotton industries. This process of failure in the fine arts had given England its lead in manufacturing. So, concluded this ingenious author, America should encourage the fine arts not for their own sakes, but that they may be transmuted into the useful arts and so stimulate American industry.

When the arts serve no useful project, however, they are often looked on with suspicion. In statement and by implication the schoolbooks fear that too much concentration on the arts is unhealthy and indeed dangerous to civilization. An excerpt from the writings of Hannah More as quoted in an 1876 text specifically warns of the possibility of such subversion: "It will be prudent to reflect, that in all polished countries an entire devotedness to the fine arts has been one grand source of the corruption of women. . . . And while corruption brought on by an excessive cultivation of the arts has contributed its full share to the decline of states, it has always furnished an infallible symptom of their impending fall." [40] Art and the decadence of the individual and society are regarded as natural companions in many of these books. In a frequently quoted poem by Bayard Taylor, "Napoleon at Gotha," for example, the following lines describe a German duke:

> A handsome prince and courtly, of light and shallow heart,
> No better than he should be, but with a taste for art.

[38] R 1806 Peirce, p. 48. [39] R 1826 Frost, pp. 43-44.
[40] R 1876 Young (for Roman Catholic schools), p. 203.

And when Napoleon invaded his country:

> But while the German people were silent in despair,
> Duke August painted pictures, and curled his yellow hair.[41]

In the Geographies, which survey the state of civilization in every country, Europe is always introduced as the seat of the arts and sciences. But the Europe that produced great art is also the Europe of rigid class distinctions, vice, and degeneracy. In particular, "The Italians are celebrated for their musical skill and perfection in the fine arts";[42] but the descriptions of Italian national character and Italian morals would hardly be a recommendation for accomplishment in the arts. Italy is generally described as a land of filth and beggars, and the Italians as a degenerate, superstitious, revengeful, effeminate, and immoral people. This unfavorable view of the Italians was undoubtedly the result of a strong anti-Catholic bias in American schoolbooks, but the conjunction of such a national character with the greatest talents in the fine arts of any country in the world would hardly persuade the Americans that the cultivation of the fine arts was necessary for national development.

On the other hand, in the view of these schoolbooks art can and should have a moral purpose. It should show that virtue inevitably leads to beauty, and that the only true beauty is that which is equated to goodness:

> Would'st behold beauty
> Near thee, all round?
> Only hath duty
> Such a sight found.[43]

It was rather to literature than to painting and sculpture that the schoolbooks turned for their discussion of the relationship between beauty and goodness. The literary man, according to one of them, "thinks beautiful thoughts, and tells them in beautiful words, and he helps to make people better by showing how beauti-

[41] R 1884 Monroe, p. 380; see also R 1867 Parker and Watson-5, p. 247; R 1869 Wilson, pp. 118–120; H 1881 Thalheimer, p. 96.

[42] G 1875 McNally, p. 75.

[43] R 1871 Monroe, p. 366; see also R 1868 Parker and Watson, p. 46; R 1874 Hillard, pp. 155–156; S 1888 Watkins, p. 24; R 1896 McGuffey-3, p. 65; R 1897 Baldwin-3, p. 208; R 1900 Judson and Bender-3, p. 127.

ful goodness is."[44] Even here it is content, not artistic form, that determines the merit of a literary production. The same piece (a comment on Henry Wadsworth Longfellow) goes on to say: "But it is not the way it is written that makes a poem, but rather the beautiful thought in it." Indeed it is clear from the literary excerpts in the Spellers and Readers (most of these, beyond the primer, are anthologies) that style was considered in the nature of a clever trick and was of very little importance to the authors and editors of these books. Wordsworth, Emerson, Dickens, and Irving are there, but they are outspaced by Alcott, Longfellow, Mrs. Hemans, Mrs. Sigourney, and Lydia Maria Child. Longfellow's poem "The Day Is Done" was taken to heart by these authors and editors, especially the passage in which the poet asks to have poetry read to him:

> Not from the grand old masters,
> Not from the bards sublime. . . .
>
> Read from some humbler poet,
> Whose songs gushed from his heart,
> As showers from the clouds of summer,
> Or tears from the eyelids start.[45]

That good literature is thought to be moral, and to engender morality in its readers, is evident in the following samples of the adjectives used in literary criticism in the schoolbooks: Bryant—"Lofty moral tone"; Alcott—"Healthy tone"; Whittier—"His verse is distinguished by vigor and a certain moral sweetness"; Scott—"Healthfulness of tone."[46] And since moral qualities should be paramount in his writings, it was considered entirely proper to inquire into the author's moral behavior in his own life. Scott comes out very well in this respect. More attention is given in several books to his labors to pay back creditors than to his writings: "The sterling integrity of the man shown forth in this dark hour."[47] This portrayal of an honest and industrious man

[44] R 1898 Arnold and Gilbert, pp. 29–30; see also R 1900 Judson and Bender-3, pp. 131–132.

[45] R 1897 Baldwin-4, pp. 65–66.

[46] Bryant—R 1874 Hillard, p. 155; Alcott—*Ibid.*, p. 294; Whittier—R 1884 Monroe, p. 314; Scott—R 1896 Holmes and Hill, p. 161.

[47] R 1898 Black, pp. 162–165; see also R 1888 McGuffey, p. 95; R 1898 Williams G-1, pp. 17–18.

is used as an introduction to and an evaluation of his writings. Byron, on the other hand, is to be read with caution. His poems are of "startling power on new and original themes. The principles inculcated in some of these shocked his countrymen, and still offend the moral sense of readers." Coleridge's use of opium and the dissipation of Burns interfered with and marred the work of these two writers.[48] And, ironically, Poe, the only American writer whose European reputation should have pleased American nationalists, falls into the same category. Although his writings showed "marked ability, [they] are marred by their morbid subjects and their absence of moral feeling."[49] And "He was intemperate, quarrelsome and without business ability.... Nothing that he has written can fairly be called of a high class. His chief fame rests on his cleverness in constructing plots, and his use of the grotesque and weird."[50] Only one book admits that although he led a dissipated life and died young in consequence, still "He left behind him some of the choicest treasures of American Literature."[51] Frequently the introduction to a literary excerpt, and its moral evaluation of the author, is more extensive than the piece of literature itself. Literature is to be interpreted according to its moral tone; should it lack moral qualities or embody the wrong ones it is not good literature.

It should be noted that the selectivity used in discarding "improper" pieces from the schoolbooks did not operate as effectively in some of the books published before 1820. Excerpts from Shakespeare and Molière used in that period did not always embody the lofty moral tone that later became standard in the textbooks. On the other hand, these pieces were often taken out of context in such peculiar ways that they made no sense, moral or otherwise. Pedagogical improvement changed the books in the latter respect, but it also eliminated some subjects that had heretofore appeared.

From the 1820's on, all gambling, drinking, and laziness are condemned. All women are virtuous, or wish they had been as

[48] Byron—R 1884 Campbell-5, p. 238 (see also R 1898 Williams G-2, pp. 289–294; R 1900 Aldrich and Forbes-II, p. 76); Coleridge—R 1888 McGuffey, p. 227; Burns—R 1898 Williams G-2, p. 315.

[49] R 1900 Aldrich and Forbes-II, p. 78.

[50] R 1898 Williams G-1, p. 223; see also R 1883 Swinton-5, p. 120.

[51] R 1898 Arnold and Gilbert, p. 193.

they sink into a miserable death; all widows are poor and honest; all married women are mothers with the virtues thereof; all self-respecting men try hard for financial success; there are no physical relations between the sexes even if hallowed by marriage. Yet this does not indicate a general denial of the material world, for the acquisition of goods by the individual and the nation is regarded as a national blessing. But just as Whitman is conspicuously absent from the anthologies, so the physical nature of man is a subject to be avoided or to be mentioned, if at all, as a part of the nature of man to be subdued.

Throughout the century all of the schoolbooks are sensitive to such European criticisms as those of the Abbé Raynal, who had taken America to task for producing no important artists. Those published before 1830 responded by a simple rejection of Raynal's evaluation and by catalogues of the artists America had produced, such as Trumbull, Copley, West, Barlowe, and others. Many of the lists of American artists culminated in the name of George Washington![52] This would seem to indicate that the textbook authors are not arguing that America had produced better artists than those of Europe, but that it had produced greater men; and one Washington would obviously outweigh any number of artists or scholars. A typical early evaluation of American arts asserted that "Printing, engraving and architecture among the fine arts, as well as the mechanic arts, exhibit as much native genius in the United States as in any part of the world. This genius has been cultivated for the last few years to such a degree as, in some instances, to rival the most splendid and useful exhibitions of art in Europe."[53] A few of the authors at the beginning of the century complained, however, that the American artist found it hard to make a living by his art. They ascribed this situation to the snobbish attitude of some Americans who believed that the only good art was European and refused to give any attention to art produced by an American.

After 1830 the textbook writers changed the grounds for their defense of American art. Abandoning their simple refusal to

[52] R 1797 Thomas, pp. 211–213; R 1803 Biglow, I, 164–165; R 1810 Alden, pp. 127–130.

[53] G 1820 Darby, p. 91; see also R 1807 Bingham-C, pp. 296–299; R 1797 Thomas, pp. 211–212.

accept the low evaluation of our arts by European critics, they admitted our inferiority in the arts with an explanation. This inferiority, they said proudly, came from the fact that we had deliberately neglected the fine arts in favor of the arts that produce a comfortable and happy life for everyone. If the founders of America produced no great music, painting, sculpture, architecture, or literature, "It was enough for them to lay the foundation of that noble fabric of civil liberty."[54] McGuffey in 1858 lists freedom, useful knowledge, and patriotism as American gifts to the world which more than make up for our lack of artistic contributions.[55] Our monuments are not Gothic cathedrals, said another commentary, but "an active, vigorous, intelligent, moral population."[56] Thus the American answer to European critics from 1830 through the Civil War held that although American artists might not be equal to those of Europe, America had been engaged in producing something of far greater significance to the world—a superior society.

After the Civil War, however, American schoolbooks aggressively placed American artists and writers on a level with those of Europe. Bolstered by a newly proved nationalism and backed by solid accomplishments in American literature, they were ready to refute European criticisms. One of them points proudly to our literary progress: "It is not long since it was asked 'Who reads an American book?' Now the question is, who does not cherish as household words the names of our charming fiction writers Irving, Cooper and Hawthorne—our historians, Bancroft, Prescott and Motley—our poets, Bryant and Longfellow, Halleck and Whittier, Lowell and Holmes?"[57] The same author, however, evidently had some slight doubt about the status of American belles-lettres, because he added: "In magazines and school-books especially, the United States has nothing to fear from a comparison with the most cultivated of the older nations." By the 1870's there was general and confident agreement that America had its own literary culture. America has produced many authors, "some of whom have acquired a reputation even in the Old World, and whose works have now become sufficiently numerous

[54] R 1831 Cheever, p. 417. [55] R 1858 McGuffey, pp. 259–260.

[56] R 1844 Goldsbury and Russell, pp. 119–120.

[57] H 1879 Quackenbos, pp. 305–306; see also H 1890 Morris, p. 192.

and important to form an American literature."[58] Two late nineteenth-century authors admit that in the past "The greatest triumphs achieved in the United States have been in the direction of mechanical ingenuity; and American literature, science, and art have not yet won the applause of the world quite so thoroughly as have American sewing machines and agricultural implements."[59] But both say that this is much less true in their day, and they are confident that it will be even less so in the future.

In rating American artists, the major criterion used in the schoolbooks is whether they compare favorably to European artists and whether they have been accepted abroad. Gilbert Stuart is proudly put into the first category: "Some critics think he is the best portrait painter of the age except for Joshua Reynolds."[60] And American historiography comes out well by comparison to that of Europe: "Bancroft, Hildreth, Prescott and Motley, stand among the best writers of history the world has ever produced."[61] The great landmark in American literature came with its first recognition abroad. The distinction of being the first to achieve this recognition is variously accorded to Irving and Cooper. The author who brought greatest acclaim to American literature in the eyes of Europe is Emerson, and he is placed even above European writers. McGuffey records Matthew Arnold's opinion that Emerson's work was "the most important work done in prose" in the nineteenth century.[62] At the end of the century this was reaffirmed: "Abroad, Emerson was recognized as a master-mind."[63]

What made American literature American in the eyes of writers of schoolbooks? Was it part of American literature because it was produced by American citizens, or did it have characteristics of its own? Most of the schoolbooks echo the opinion of Noah Webster in 1783 that America must be culturally independent of Europe:

> While the Americans stand astonished at their former delusion and enjoy the pleasure of a final separation from their insolent

[58] G 1872 Hall, p. 49; see also H 1874 Anderson, p. 236.

[59] H 1875 Higginson, p. 328; H 1890 Morris, p. 223.

[60] H 1876 Doyle (an English work adapted for American schools), p. 224; see also R 1867? Parker and Watson-4, pp. 82–84; H 1881 Eliot, p. 487.

[61] H 1874 Anderson, p. 237.

[62] R 1888 McGuffey, p. 229.

[63] R 1898 Arnold and Gilbert, p. 223.

sovereigns, it becomes their duty to attend to the *arts of peace*, and particularly to the interests of literature to see if there be not some error to be corrected, some defects to be supplied, and some improvements to be introduced into our systems of education, as well as into those of civil policy. We find Englishmen practising upon very erroneous maxims in politics and religion: and possibly we shall find, upon careful examination, that their methods of education are equally erroneous and defective. . . . Europe is grown old in folly, corruption and tyranny—in that country laws are perverted, manners are licentious, literature is declining and human nature is debased. For America in her infancy to adopt the present maxims of the Old World, would be to stamp the wrinkles of decrepid [*sic*] age upon the bloom of youth and to plant the seeds of decay in a vigorous constitution.[64]

To implement his desire for cultural reform Webster himself engaged in a famous attempt to differentiate American from English spelling. Other authors of schoolbooks suggest that the American artist should find his inspiration in American landscape rather than in the Alps or Westminster Abbey. The American literary man should use American scenes and situations to illustrate American virtues.[65] In this way he will improve on European literature by teaching self-control, initiative, honesty, industry, and other characteristics that differentiate the American from the European. Just as European literature reflects the vices and crimes of Europe, so American literature should reflect the virtues of America, and should then be supported for moral as well as nationalistic reasons.[66] Bryant is frequently used as the ideal American man of letters: "We find in his pages all the most obvious and all the most retiring graces of our native landscapes, but nothing borrowed from books—nothing transplanted from a foreign soil."[67] A lofty moral tone is regarded as characteristic of American authors; it is this that makes American literature unique. Lacking this quality, an American author is not considered to be a part of American literature. The most obvious case in point is Edgar Allan Poe. According to the major canon of literary eminence used in these books, European recognition, Poe should have replaced Emerson as our greatest writer by the

[64] S 1783 Webster, Part I, Introduction.
[65] R 1844 Goldsbury and Russell, pp. 222–224.
[66] R 1835 Porter, 218–219.
[67] R 1856 Hillard, p. 96.

end of the century. He was not only seriously read abroad, but he influenced the development of French literature. This accolade could not be transferred from the virtuous Emerson to the immoral Poe. Although Poe lived in America, he did not write American literature.

Whatever might be said of the past, American nationalism demanded that the future of American art be assured. With the establishment of our political and social foundations, our intellectual and artistic prospects were seen to be boundless and unprecedented. To achieve this end one need not sponsor or even encourage the arts; in fact, this is to be avoided. But it is our manifest destiny, when the time comes, to reach such eminence naturally. America is "ordained, we believe, to be the chosen seat of intelligence, of literature, of arts, and of science."[68] It shall be "The first in letters, as the first in arms."[69] Furthermore, American letters, freed from class limitations, will provide a larger audience for the arts than Europe can afford: "The universal diffusion of knowledge, which distinguishes the United States from the rest of the world, by exciting a literary thirst among the people in general, must also render the patrons of ingenuity and taste infinitely more numerous than they can possibly be in those nations, where the means, the pleasures, and the advantages of information are confined within the limited circles of nobility and wealth."[70] This confidence in the future of America was apparently based on nationalistic optimism, but also on the assumption that a superior political and social system will inevitably breed great art. Since America has the former she will inevitably develop the latter in time:

> Be just, Columbians, and assert your name,
> Avow your genius, and protect your fame.
> The clime which gave a WASHINGTON to you,
> May give an OTWAY and a SHAKESPEARE too.[71]

Thus, although the future of American art was to be as glorious as were all things American, yet no preparation whatever was

[68] R 1828 Pierpont-I, p. 167.

[69] R 1835 Webster, p. 246; see also R 1807 Bingham-C, pp. 30–34; G 1818 Mann, pp. ix–xii; R 1866 Sargent-4, p. 238; R 1867 Parker and Watson-5, pp. 164–165.

[70] R 1797 Thomas, pp. 211–213.

[71] R 1811 Chandler, p. 82.

made in the schoolbooks to encourage the development either of future artists or of a public for art. While nationalistic schoolbooks demanded pride in American productions of any sort, they were far from encouraging to the potential artist or scholar. The American was not expected to accept art, let alone sponsor it for its own sake. This was the attitude of an effete and declining Europe whose civilization the schoolbooks specifically and carefully reject. Only when art becomes propaganda for good morals, or nationalism, or when it is in the service of the useful arts is it worthy of serious attention. According to the schoolbooks it is this kind of art that Americans have produced and will continue to produce.

The child who accepted values offered by his schoolbooks would consider scholarship and the fine arts mere embellishments identified with a civilization that he was taught to reject as inferior to his own. He would expect men of talent in the arts to serve their nationality consciously in their art. He would think it a waste of time to engage himself in these fields; American creativity was and should be directed to the immediately practical. The concepts of American culture presented in his schoolbooks would prepare him for a life devoted to the pursuit of material success and a perfected character, but a life in which intellectual and artistic achievements should seem important only when they could be made to serve some "useful" purpose.

V. Social Experience

Chapter 8

ECONOMIC CONCEPTS

The nineteenth century was one of profound economic change, in the United States as in the western world. The North was in the process of shifting from a predominately mercantile economy to an industrial one; the South, increasingly dominated by cotton cultivation until the Civil War, began to industrialize after its defeat in that war. In vocabulary and in subject matter schoolbooks reflect these changes. Arithmetic textbooks, for example, unlike those in Europe, are of a practical and often vocational nature, containing "what is necessary to the merchant, the mechanic, the mariner, and the farmer."[1] Ordinarily they include a section on surveying, vital to a nation with an expanding frontier. Up to the Civil War most of the problems, except those on military or surveying processes, involve operations with tobacco, rum, and wheat. By the 1860's problems centering around the railroad and the factory increase markedly. A steam locomotive is pictured for the first time in the frontispiece of Blake's Geography in 1826, and pictures of cotton mills become common in the 1870's. As we have seen, however, with all the pride these schoolbooks take in industrial development, agricultùre is still, for them, the primary occupation. Statements of its fundamental importance to man in general and to the United States in particular appear frequently even at the end of the century: "Agriculture, the chief source of food, and the basis of all other industries, is by far the most important occupation of the people of the United States."[2] Fear of an industrial age and the changes it will make in society from the simple, honest, pious "Age of Homespun" are often expressed.[3]

On the other hand the wonders of the machine age are celebrated in glowing terms throughout the century. The benefits of

[1] A 1810 Carleton, title page.

[2] G 1894 Harper, p. 64.

[3] R 1875 Sheldon, pp. 203–204.

rapid transportation are brought home to the child in a popular reading lesson in which an uncle promises his nephews a wonderful pudding it took a thousand men to make. The children, imagining something enormous and exotic, are startled when their uncle reveals it to be an ordinary plum pudding whose ingredients come from near and far.[4] From the beginning of the century schoolbooks boast of American pre-eminence in this transportation revolution. As in the earlier books each new canal is measured with pride, so in the later books increasing railroad mileage is happily recorded. In 1791 Morse smarts under the contempt of European critics who distrust American transportation projects in general, and in particular one for the improvement of the Potomac: "Notwithstanding it was sneeringly said by some foreigners, at the beginning of this undertaking, that the Americans were fond of engaging in splendid projects which they could never accomplish; yet it is hoped the success of the first essay towards improving their inland navigation will, in some degree, rescue them from the reproach intended to have been fixed upon their national character, by the unmerited imputation."[5]

Fire, water power, and steam are sometimes talked of as the great giants whose power made man seem physically puny until he used his mind to harness them and make them his servants.[6] All books, in whatever category, assure the American child that his country has done more than any other in taming these giants. Several see American inventions and industrial development as "the first fruits of American liberty and industry" rather than as part of an international industrial revolution.[7] Most schoolbooks, however, ascribe the vast number of American inventions to mechanical ingenuity inherent in the Americans. Undoubtedly the child reading these books would view the whole industrial revolution as the product of American talents. He would also be likely to anticipate a perpetually glorious future in which man's

[4] R 1876 Hillard and Campbell, pp. 90–98; R 1882 Gourley and Hunt, pp. 203–205; R 1885 Monroe-3, pp. 201–203; see also R 1897 Baldwin-4, p. 86.

[5] G 1791 Morse, p. 174.

[6] R 1873 American, pp. 40–44; R 1890 Davis, pp. 85–92; R 1897 Arnold and Gilbert-5, pp. 125–128.

[7] H 1881 Steele, p. 184 footnote; see also G 1793 Workman, p. 180; G 1837 Book of Commerce, p. 171.

control over nature will be steadily extended: "The next hundred years may see us floating through the air, talking to each other without regard to distance."[8] One Reader envisions an intellectual Utopia as a product of the machine age: "Every man who invents a labor-saving machine does a great deal of good, for he enables working-people to give more time to study and the cultivation of their minds."[9] This point of view is unique; these books, as we have seen, rarely express concern with the life of the intellect. All others see its benefits in terms of greater power for the nation and a higher standard of living for all.

The growth of American manufacturing is noted with great pride throughout the century. The early books are particularly fond of pointing to ours as "useful manufactures" suitable to a simple, hardy population in contrast to the luxury products turned out by an effete Europe.[10] Where actual accomplishment is slight, a hopeful note is struck as in this 1814 comment: "The manufactures of Maryland are not, at present, extensive although a spirit of improvement is excited."[11] As the century advances descriptions of particular factories become more common, usually centering on the wonders of the machine. With rare exceptions labor conditions in the factories are idyllic: the labor force looks "healthy and happy," the factory is neat and clean, and it contains lecture rooms and a library; the hours of labor are ten, and "The workmen are allowed to shorten them if necessary."[12] Child labor in American factories is usually noted without comment, but child labor in European factories and mines is generally criticized because conditions in the latter are so much worse than those in the former: "Even little children, no larger than some of you, go early in the morning and work all day in the hot close rooms full of all sorts of unpleasant smells, where they are half deafened by the rattling of machinery. Don't you think they must get very tired?"[13] One author who graphically portrays children in English and Scottish mines

[8] R 1895 Hazen, p. 98; see also R 1899 Holmes and Hill, p. 203.

[9] R 1867 Edwards-4, p. 57.

[10] G 1800 Smith, p. 139; G 1807 Workman, p. 99.

[11] G 1814 O'Neill, p. 130.

[12] R 1842 Palmer, pp. 280–288; see also R 1845 D. Adams, pp. 55–56; G 1872 Hall, p. 50; R 1881 Willson, pp. 135 ff.

[13] G 1866 Guyot-P, p. 71.

crawling on all fours as they pull coal cars through the tunnels points out that children are rarely employed in American mines.[14] In the United States factory work is assumed to represent a financial opportunity for the children of the poor. Lack of educational opportunity for the factory child is sometimes noted as a problem, but it is solved as follows: "They did not go to work in summer till 6 o'clock; and if they got to the tree at four, they would have two hours to study."[15] Long factory hours should represent an educational challenge to the industrious poor, rather than a barrier. Three authors dissent from this approval of the effects of factory work. Two express horror at the waste of the child's mind and body. The other deplores female factory labor: "But while this industry reflects great honor on the female sex, it is thought not only to have impaired their constitutions, but disqualified them for other branches of domestic economy."[16] But these represent the opinion of only three out of about a thousand schoolbooks. Even these agree with the general opinion: ". . . in no other country are the laboring people so well paid and so independent."[17]

The organization of labor for political action or collective bargaining was an important element in nineteenth-century American economic development that was conspicuously absent from most of the schoolbooks of that century. In no book published before the 1870's is labor organization mentioned. The railroad strikes in that decade brought the question into prominence in the Histories and Geographies. With one exception, the professional historian McMaster, there is absolute unanimity among schoolbook authors on the evil results of labor unions. McMaster observes that the laborer benefits most from the new inventions and works fewer hours than ever before in the history of the world. He describes the role of labor in politics before the Civil War and the development of national labor unions after it. Changes in labor conditions in the postwar period he ascribes to a vast increase in the labor force through immigration and a change in

[14] G 1898 Carpenter, p. 217.

[15] R 1845 S. Worcester-2, p. 139; R 1847 Leavitt, pp. 82–87; see also S 1815 Bradley, p. iv; R 1881 Willson, p. 29.

[16] G 1818 Mann, p. 77; see also R 1847 Leavitt, pp. 91–93; R 1849 Leavitt, pp. 176–180; R 1873 American, p. 42.

[17] G 1888 Redway, p. 48.

the status of employers, who were now "great capitalists" sometimes guilty of corrupt management. He quotes from the declaration of principles of the Knights of Labor in 1869: "capitalists and corporations, unless checked, 'would degrade the toiling masses.'" Even in the 1880's what little had been done by law to correct working conditions "left untouched grievances which the workingmen and a great part of the people felt were unbearable," but by the end of Cleveland's first term "many of the demands of the workingmen had been granted."[18]

But only the child whose school used McMaster would have both so full and so balanced a view of labor in the nineteenth century. In all other books labor organization is equated with violence. No attempt is made to define "union," "strike," or other related terms used in the texts, let alone explain why labor organizations increased in the post-Civil War period. Very often the words "strike" and "riot" are used interchangeably to describe the railroad strikes of 1877: "In the summer of 1877 a riot broke out among the employés of some of the great railroads upon a general reduction of wages. A large amount of property was destroyed by the rioters in Pittsburgh, Baltimore, Chicago and other railroad cities."[19] Property destruction is always carefully detailed while grievances of the workmen are not: "Strike and labor disturbances greatly injured business prosperity. In many instances, railroad traffic was suspended, switches were misplaced, trains derailed, and valuable property destroyed. Dynamite plots added to the seriousness of the situation."[20] Many books illustrate these colorful accounts with pictures such as the half-page picture in Channing's History entitled "The Ruins after the Pittsburg riots."[21] Among the strikers were "the idle and vicious," the "dangerous classes."[22] One Geography, describing the coal strikers, indicates that they were mainly foreigners who "resort to violence, in this action losing much of the sympathy from the rest of the world which their unhappy

[18] H 1897 McMaster, pp. 375–376, 460–466.

[19] H 1881 Armstrong, p. 104.

[20] H 1889? Steele, p. 299; see also H 1879 Quackenbos, p. 303; H 1885 Donnelly, p. 219; H 1889 Chambers, p. 427; H 1899 Morris, pp. 235–236; H 1885 Ridpath, pp. 478–479; H 1900 Channing, pp. 375–376.

[21] H 1900 Channing, pp. 375; see also H 1889? Steele, p. 294.

[22] H 1879? Campbell, p. 217; H 1885 Ridpath, p. 478.

lot might otherwise win."[23] These are agitators, not reformers. And the consequences of their actions are shown to be subversive of government: "From opposition to the companies the movement became rebellion against the states and even the government at Washington which sent troops to put down the insurgents."[24] Several, by juxtaposition if not by direct causal relationship, link labor organization to communism or anarchism. In 1888 Thalheimer's History ascribes leadership in the Pittsburgh disorders to such groups: "The alarming fact was that the leaders in all these places were not railway hands, but restless 'communists,' who were traveling from place to place exciting workmen against their employers." Later in a paragraph headed "Labor Questions" he discusses the Haymarket Affair: workmen went through the streets of Chicago demanding an eight-hour day, "Riots followed, and the police, while trying to restore order, were attacked with dynamite." Another History in 1890 deals with labor problems only in a section headed "The Chicago Anarchists."[25] In all but McMaster's History not only is labor identified with violence, but this is the only context in which the organization of labor appears.

The only Reader that includes anything on the subject, and the only schoolbook other than McMaster's History that discusses the issues involved, brings the question down to the child's level by using as an example a labor dispute in berry-picking. Unlike McMaster, however, it explains the issues in the same antilabor terms as the other Histories. The price of berry-picking had been lowered from two cents to one cent a quart "and noisy Joe Barney, a man who spent much of his earnings for liquor, said he wouldn't stand it. He said many of the strawberry growers were rich men; and if all the pickers would just strike for higher wages, and refuse to pick for less than two cents a quart, . . . the growers would soon come to terms." So Joe persuades others to join, the strawberries rot in the fields as the strikers drive away those who are still working. "The pickers had a perfect right to refuse to work, if they chose to, and to try to persuade others to

[23] G 1900 Tarr and McMurry-2, p. 172.

[24] H 1881 Thalheimer, p. 340; see also H 1879 Quackenbos, p. 303; H 1879? Campbell, p. 217; H 1885 Ridpath, p. 478; H 1898 Steele and Steele, p. 294.

[25] H 1881 Thalheimer, pp. 340, 351–352; H 1890 Morris, p. 226.

14. "Riot at Pittsburgh"

Labor union activities of the late nineteenth century are identified only with violence and the horrors of class warfare, as shown in this print of the 1877 railroad strikes in Steele's 1889 History.

stop work; but they had no right to use threats or force to prevent others from working. And the growers had a perfect right to hire people to work for any price that could be agreed on between them." Tommy O'Brien, on whose side lies virtue, "thought it was better to work for what he could get—even for small wages—than to be idle." And the growers made so little, even when they paid the pickers only one cent a quart, that it was hardly worth their while having the crop harvested. When the season was over, the strikers, seeing Tommy O'Brien's forty dollars earned at the lower wage, were sorry they had joined Joe Barney; leaders of the strike were now "bitterly hated by many of their own people for having deceived them."[26] Here characterizations of strike leaders are quite similar to those in John Hay's novel *The Bread-winners*, a best-seller published three years later in 1884. They are idle, selfish, wasteful, unpleasant if not vicious in personal habits, and lazy—the antithesis of the schoolbook ideal of the American. There is no doubt that the nineteenth-century child who was influenced by his schoolbooks would identify labor organization with irresponsible violence and probably with doctrines subversive of American institutions. He would know nothing of the background of the growth of labor unions, and he would probably assume collective bargaining to be a device designed by unscrupulous men in search of personal gain. The laborer who accepted American labor conditions and worked hard would get ahead. To question American labor conditions was un-American.

Throughout the century the virtues most frequently praised in the individual are economic ones, industry and frugality, and these are given the sanction of religion. Idleness is not only economically unproductive, but "It is a great sin to be idle."[27] Ideal economic behavior rests on the combined precepts of Calvin and Benjamin Franklin; both the Bible and Franklin are liberally quoted. Nature itself is always busy by the ordinance of God; the bees, ants and beavers are the usual illustrations. The most popular selection on this subject is, of course, Isaac Watts' "How doth the little busy bee . . ." The Calvinistic doctrine of

[26] R 1881 Willson, pp. 177–179.

[27] R 1830 Putnam-I, p. 44; see also R 1810 Alden, p. 43; S 1836 Brandreth, p. 71; R 1867 Edwards-4, p. 180; R 1872 Willson, pp. 150–151; R 1898 Williams I-2, p. 149; R 1900 Williams, p. 49.

the stewardship of wealth is applied to life itself: "Existence is a sacred trust; and he who misemploys and squanders it away is treacherous to its author."[28] The importance of industry and frugality in the scale of virtues undoubtedly stems from the importance of these qualities on the continuing frontier as well as from Calvinism. Success and indeed life itself in a frontier environment required both hard work and careful husbanding of scarce and hard-won goods. Further, business opportunities in nineteenth-century America called forth these same virtues. The all-pervading religious emphasis in schoolbooks, then, sanctions virtues likely to lead to materialism rather than other-worldliness. "Riches are the baggage of virtue."[29] Now and then in the later books the code of behavior set up by Franklin for greatest convenience in material matters is used as an end in itself, and virtue would seem to be a by-product of riches. Throughout the century religion sanctions the process of making money; by the bestowal or withdrawal of material goods God rewards or punishes men immediately in the temporal realm. A landlord who suddenly doubled his rents for no other reason than a selfish increase in his profits, and despite protests by his tenants, is punished by a ruinous fire completely destroying his property.[30] Likewise honest industry acquires sound material rewards in every book: "He who rises early and is industrious and temperate will acquire health and riches."[31] Are riches the result of industry or of God's blessing? One reading selection solves this problem by reconciling two statements from the Bible: "The hand of the diligent maketh rich," and "The blessings of the lord maketh rich." God, the author explains, blesses the acquisition of wealth by the man who is industrious and honest.[32] Every book contains many tales of the rewards God bestows on such a man.

Frugality is almost as important as industry in assuring wealth:

> FRUGALITY is rich in Store;
> While SLOTH remains a beggar poor.[33]

An immediate reward for frugality is given homely illustration in the tale of a boy who, when his bowstring breaks, uses a

[28] R 1810 Alden, p. 43.
[29] S 1874 Worcester, p. 145.
[30] R 1807 Bingham-C, pp. 88–94.
[31] R 1814 Alden, p. 39.
[32] R 1839 S. Goodrich, pp. 54–56.
[33] S 1798 Child, p. 72.

piece of string saved some time before and wins the archery contest.[34]

The converse of this, that continued poverty is never a result of accident or unfortunate circumstances but only of one's own willful misbehavior, is just as abundantly illustrated. "Poverty is the fruit of idleness." [35] In most cases poverty is identified with immorality: "Declining prosperity is the usual attendant of degenerate morals in individuals, in families, and in larger communities." [36] Most stories of the poor are laid in Europe, where the opportunity to improve one's economic position is small. The poor of America who are not so because of sloth or wastefulness are usually widows and orphans. But these stories almost invariably end up as success stories wherein the orphan or widow works hard in spite of difficulties and soon achieves financial success.[37] To start life in poverty is a great blessing because it offers the chance to improve character. To end life in poverty in the United States is a certain sign of poor moral quality. The child well versed in these textbooks would regard continued poverty in an American family as either a divine punishment for misdeeds or the result of a basic inadequacy in the character of the family. Since America is the land of opportunity, to remain in a state of poverty is one's own fault. Again and again it is said that: "In this country the way for a poor little boy to become a great and happy man is to be honest, industrious and good." [38] Thus while in other countries there may be mitigating circumstances, to remain in poverty in America is a moral wrong and indicates a lack of virtue in the individual. There is but one dissent from this. In 1857 a Speller notes the "substitution of machinery for manual labor" as a cause of destitution among the poor.[39] But this is the only exception. Interestingly enough the concept

[34] R 1830 Putnam-I, pp. 36–40; R 1879 McGuffey, pp. 64–67.

[35] R 1812 A. Cook, p. 127; S 1810 Webster, pp. 151–154; S 1823 Lee, p. 63; R 1838 Angell, p. 72; R 1840 Williams, p. 158; S 1844 Clagett, pp. 86, 166, 182; S 1853 Bumstead, p. 32.

[36] R 1834 S. Willard-P, p. 132; see also R 1855 New York, p. 15; S 1857 Parker and Watson, p. 154.

[37] R 1885 Monroe-3, pp. 170 ff.

[38] R 1829 Selection, p. 10; R 1830 Putnam-I, p. 33; R 1832 Progressive, p. 46; see also G 1830 Hale, p. 175; R 1835 Webster, p. 36.

[39] S 1857 Parker and Watson, p. 148.

of poverty as the fault of the poor does not seem to be affected by the various depressions of the nineteenth century. In books published shortly after the serious 1837 depression there are often discussions of the effects of luck or misfortune, but within the same framework. An 1840 Reader notes: "Misfortune is mostly the result of misconduct."[40]

Luck plays no part in success. As Henry Ward Beecher put it: "I never knew an early-rising, hard-working, prudent man, careful of his earnings, and strictly honest, who complained of bad luck. A good character, good habits and honest industry, are impregnable to the assaults of all the ill luck that ever fools dreamed of."[41] Another expresses it so: "Many complain of Providence when the fault is all their own. If they would only labor and think, wealth and eminence would be their lot instead of poverty and disgrace. . . . Remember that all the ignorance, degradation and misery in the world, is the result of indolence and vice."[42] Even the discovery of gold in California came only to the industrious and frugal: "It was only men who were not afraid of getting wet or of laboring in the dirt that obtained the golden prize."[43] The good fortune by which the unemployed young man saves a rich man's daughter from a runaway horse or other accident (a situation commonly found in the stories of Horatio Alger as well as in schoolbooks) depends ultimately on his character in performing the duties of the job he gets as a reward. The job is opportunity; fulfillment comes from what he does with that opportunity. "Fortune has often been blamed for her blindness, but Fortune is not so blind as men are. Those who look at practical life will find that Fortune is almost invariably on the side of the industrious, the self-denying and the prudent, as the winds or the waves are on the side of the best navigators."[44]

Great wealth, if unearned, is considered undesirable in its effects on both individual and national character. The idle rich, wallowing in luxury, dissatisfied with life, careless of the community are to be found typically in Europe, rarely in America. Now and then the American South is said to harbor such para-

[40] R 1840 Williams, p. 101.

[41] R 1852 Tower and Walker, p. 186; R 1860 McGuffey, pp. 63–64.

[42] R 1855 Burleigh, p. 109; see also R 1845 D. Adams, p. 69.

[43] H 1896 Murphy, p. 182.

[44] R 1871 Sargent and May-5, p. 175.

sites. Morse cites the rich Southern planters who, in their gay Charleston, lose both health and morals.[45] But the rich man, usually self-made, who contributes to the national economy and busies himself in community affairs is very much accepted as a valuable member of society. Wealth is a gift of God and should be used for "God's glory and other men's good."[46] Wealth, improperly used, is a curse. The effects of luxury on national character are as greatly feared as its effects on the individual: "If our softnesses and indulgences, and foreign fashions, must inevitably accomplish our seduction, and lead us away from the simplicity, honesty, sobriety, purity, and manly independence of our forefathers, most readily and fervently would I exclaim, welcome back to the pure old times of the Puritans."[47] The decline of Spain from its sixteenth-century eminence, based on American gold and silver, to its nineteenth-century innocuous position sufficiently documents this idea.

That it was now possible to accumulate a larger fortune than ever before is reflected in an 1859 Speller which for the first time considers the word "millionaire" as a useful term for the young American.[48] With three exceptions big business and its founders are viewed as important additions to the American scene. The only pre-Civil War mention of the corporation, in an 1816 Reader, is an unfavorable one, referring obviously to monopolies of the mercantilist period, and essentially irrelevant to an independent America:

> Hence merchants unimpeachable of sin
> Against the charities of domestic life,
> Incorporated seem at once to lose
> Their natures; and, disclaiming all regard
> For mercy and the common rights of men,
> Build factories with blood, conducting trade
> At the sword's point, and dying the white robe
> Of innocent commercial justice red.[49]

Chambers, a Southern historian, in the last decade of the century, explains trusts as monopolies which "by limiting the supply,

[45] G 1784 Morse, pp. 80–81.

[46] R 1852 Cobb, pp. 260–261; see also R 1869 Wilson, pp. 106–107.

[47] R 1827 Pierpont, p. 218; see also G 1791 Morse, p. 138; R 1809 Picket, p. 181; R 1826 Greenwood and Emerson, pp. 102–103; H 1881 Eliot, p. 490.

[48] S 1859 Town and Holbrook, p. 105.

[49] R 1816 Staniford, pp. 238–239.

cause prices to rise above values, to the injury of the consumers." McMaster, again as on the subject of labor, is the only one who both explains the issues of land grants to the railroads, monopoly, labor problems, and the Interstate Commerce Act, and concludes: "That the development of the wealth and resources of our country is chiefly due to great corporations and great capitalists is strictly true. But that many of them abused the powers their wealth gave them cannot be denied."[50] Most books do not discuss the question; those that do so express only admiration for the new businessman. A typical instance is the following: "The man who has the original ability to bring a thousand workers together, and keep them steadily employed, cheaply and skillfully to produce the materials for their labor is entitled to a large reward for this difficult service."[51] Enormous disparity is evident here between the presentation of the organizers of business and the organizers of labor. The former are heroes in the American tradition; the latter destroyers of American institutions and traditions.

Depressions—often called "revulsions"—are regarded as periodic outcroppings of the desire to get rich quickly. In 1837, "The good old roads of honest industry were abandoned, while fortunes were made in an hour by speculation." In 1873 "There was wild speculation everywhere, many families lived in great luxury."[52] The disease is a kind of punishment for expecting wealth without work; it runs its course, and men finally return to the ways of honesty.

The sacredness of private property is implicit in the universally approved goal of accumulating property and in the many stories in every book illustrating the immorality of stealing. One of the more popular anecdotes directly on the subject involves the young Benjamin Franklin. He and his friends "borrow" the foundation stones for a house under construction to build a wharf for themselves. As the foundation for a house these would benefit only one man, says the ten-year-old Franklin, but as a wharf

[50] H 1889 Chambers, p. 432; H 1897 McMaster, pp. 464, 435–439, 459–460, 470.

[51] Washington Gladden quoted in S 1896 Dutton, p. 124.

[52] On 1837 depression see H 1868 Willard, p. 331; on 1873, see H 1890 Morris, p. 221; and H 1872 Lossing, p. 219.

they would benefit many. Franklin's father reprimands him by pointing out that taking anyone's property without leave is inexcusable even for public benefit.[53] Robin Hood's depredations of the rich for the poor are used to show how much moral progress has been made since his time: "He was, indeed, a rude and lawless fellow; but, at that time, people did not think of right and wrong as they do now."[54] In discussing the Boston Tea Party, nationalism overcomes sensitivity to the rights of property. An 1874 Reader, for example, faces the problem and encases it neatly in nationalism: "The Boston Tea Party was the opening scene of this great national drama, and well deserves to be held up to the study and admiration of American youth, not because of the destruction of property, not because of the resistance to law. These, when unnecessary and without the strongest justification, are not acts worthy of approval. The British tea chests symbolized oppression and the loss of liberty. No way was open for freedom but to strike at oppression through them."[55]

Government aid to the American economy is rarely mentioned. In 1791 Morse discusses a tariff on manufactured goods favorably, but the subject does not recur until 1844. A reader of that year uses a speech by Daniel Webster given the previous year in Rochester, suggesting that the South approve a tariff because it would aid the major consumer of Southern goods, the Northern mechanic. The only other reference to the tariff before the Civil War is also a favorable one: again the tariff is to protect the American worker.[56] Books published after the Civil War offer a surprisingly fair and detailed explanation of the issue. The subject of federal aid for internal improvements is also a rare one, but when it appears it is with approval. Freedom of competition is not yet identified with American nationalism, although it was a more valid description of the American economy before the Civil War than in a later period, when the phrase became common in American culture. Although the phrase does not appear, the spirit of competitive individual enterprise permeates

[53] R 1874 Hillard, pp. 45–55; H 1889 Monroe, p. 148; H 1899 Morris, pp. 122–123.

[54] R 1896 Baldwin, pp. 28–33.

[55] R 1874 Hillard, p. 216.

[56] G 1791 Morse, p. 297; R 1844 Smith, pp. 9–11; S 1857 Parker and Watson, p. 103.

these books. And negatively, the fact that an issue so much before the public in discussions of Granger laws, proposals of the Populist party, and labor groups does not appear is in itself significant. In the late nineteenth century, when these were controversial issues, the question of government control of the American economy for the public good appears only in McMaster's History and Tarr and McMurry's Geography; both imply a need for government regulation of the railroad. With the exception of the belief of the Puritans that government may control the economy for the good of the community, Puritan economic concepts dominate these books. Apparently the belief in government control disappeared from the American tradition in the face of an economy of abundance provided by the American environment.

All of these books accept as an axiom that the law of history is one of steady and inevitable progress toward greater material wealth and comfort as well as toward greater virtue and freedom. These two aims of evolution are inextricably linked and, the progress of the United States sufficiently substantiates their importance as keys to man's development. Just as the accumulation of material goods is a clue to the virtue of the individual, so national accumulation of material goods seems to indicate virtue in the nation. Several Readers contain selections ridiculing the idea of a Golden Age in the past from which mankind has declined. One observes that the idea of a decline in civilization is not only incorrect but immoral, because it discourages the efforts of men to improve.[57] Sometimes the example of American progress is evinced as conclusive evidence of the existence of the progress of man.

One of the distinctions unique to the progress of the American economy is its rate of acceleration; American prosperity is increasing at a more rapid rate than that of any nation in the history of the world. "No nation, either in ancient or modern times, has increased so steadily and so rapidly, in everything which indicates national wealth and prosperity as the people of the United States."[58] In the Geographies, the subject of the United States is generally introduced with something of these sentiments:

[57] R 1815 Dickinson, pp. 70–71; see also R 1834 S. Willard-P, pp. 294–298.
[58] G 1828 Morse and Morse, p. 260.

"They are distinguished for the freedom and excellence of their government; for the exceedingly rapid increase in population and wealth, and for a general diffusion of knowledge among the inhabitants."[59] All of the Readers, Histories, Geographies, and most of the Spellers include several selections indicating that a short time ago the United States was nothing but "a dense, dark and howling wilderness," but now "the wilderness . . . has become a fruitful field, and blossoms like the valley of Sharon."[60]

Such unexampled progress is attributed not only to the United States in general, but to all parts of it in particular throughout the century. The geographical surveys of the United States observe the progress of each town, however small, in the fashion of the following description of Carlisle, Pennsylvania, in an 1818 Geography: "A like instance of the rapid progress of the arts is scarcely recorded in the history of civilized life." And in Kentucky in 1791: "The progress in improvements and cultivation which has been made in this country almost exceeds belief. . . . An instance of the like kind, where a settlement has had so rapid a growth, can scarcely be produced in history." An 1843 Geography describes New York City: "It exhibits one of those amazing examples of growth and prosperity that are nowhere seen on the globe beyond our own borders."[61]

Now and then specific theories are advanced to explain this phenomenal advance. Many authors suggest the unique excellence of the American form of government as the stimulus to such a fabulous rate of progress. Others assign it to the inherent diligence of the American population. Still others see the cause in our inherent mechanical genius. But material progress is not simply the result of genius, nor of effort, nor of good government; it is also the reward of virtue. Material prosperity and virtue coincide, and the former may be used as a gauge for the latter. The unique prosperity of America is an indication that it is also uniquely virtuous, and the chosen of God.

[59] G 1836 Smith, p. 98.

[60] R 1830 Bartlett, p. 210; see also R 1811 Chandler, p. 171; S 1824 Bentley, p. 179; R 1826 Frost, p. 304; H 1851 Guernsey, p. 459; R 1856 Sargent-4, pp. 166–167.

[61] On Carlisle, G 1818 Mann, p. 103; on Kentucky, G 1791 Morse, p. 199; on New York City, G 1843 Mitchell, p. 124.

Unbounded confidence that the future material progress of the United States will be at least as spectacular as its past progress is expressed in every book. Edward Everett's oration at Plymouth in 1824 is typical:

> My friends, I tell you that we have but begun; we are in the very morning of our days; our numbers are but a unit; our natural resources but a pittance; our hopeful achievements in the political, the social, and the intellectual nature, are but the rudiments of what the children of the Puritans must yet attain. If there is anything clear in the deductions from past history; if there is any, the least, reliance to be placed on the conclusions of reason, in regard to the nature of man, the existing spectacle of our country's growth, magnificent as it is, does not suggest even an idea of what it must be.[62]

In comparison with nations of the past: "We shall elevate her to a pitch of prosperity, happiness, of honor and power, never yet reached by any nation beneath the sun." She will be "Mighty as Rome—more nobly free."[63] She will take the place of the mother country as well as all great nations of the past: "Who shall say, then, contemplating the past, that England, proud and potent as she appears, may not be what Athens *is*, and the young America soar to be what Athens *was*. Who shall say, when the European column shall have mouldered, and the night of barbarism obscured its very ruins, that that mighty continent may not emerge from the horizon, to rule for its time sovereign of the ascendant."[64] The schoolbooks are particularly proud that this is European testimony; they neglect to note that the author was Irish, with perhaps a special interest in seeing America triumph over England. All agree that the United States, the home of virtue as well as of freedom will inevitably be the greatest economic power in the world as well. As early as 1796 her future was seen in glory: "America will then increase in wealth, in commerce, agriculture and manufactures; will as far surpass all other nations on the globe in virtue, learning and abilities; and will as

[62] R 1826 American-S, pp. 220–221.

[63] R 1844 Goldsbury and Russell, p. 134; see also R 1835 Webster, p. 245; for quotation in previous sentence: R 1832 Edwards, p. 101.

[64] R 1821 Bingham, pp. 77–78; R 1826 American-S, pp. 124–126; R 1827 Pierpont, pp. 257–260; R 1828 Putnam-S, pp. 126–130; R 1835 Porter, pp. 284–286; R 1852 Gilder, pp. 127–129; R 1858 McGuffey, pp. 116–117.

much distinguish herself for humanity, nobleness of sentiment, attachment to government, and love of liberty, as the towering cedar upon the trees of the wood, or the sun in the presence of the stars."[65]

[65] R 1796 Bingham, pp. 158.

Chapter 9

SOCIAL VALUES

As we have seen, according to nineteenth-century American schoolbooks, one's religious and patriotic duty requires close attention to making the most of the material world. In a society whose members are all engaged with some hope of success in the same pursuit of wealth, the position of the individual is likely to be an unstable one. Tocqueville's shrewd analysis of the effects of economic mobility on American culture is not reflected in the simple approach of the textbooks. To Tocqueville economic mobility in the United States created a much more complex social situation than was evident in nineteenth-century European society with its traditional and generally recognized ranks. There the individual knew to which class he belonged, the relationship of his class to others in the society, and the duties and privileges of each class and therefore of himself. His social position was largely determined at birth. For the American, social position was still of great importance, but it had to be achieved by his own efforts. Perhaps position in society was even more important in the United States because it was a badge of intrinsic worth. Tocqueville saw here a social equality which forced each man to spend most of his life struggling to make or keep money and position, his every effort, his every action part of this struggle. And, according to Tocqueville as well as to some modern sociologists, he gave up his right to be different, to be eccentric if you will, in order to win social approval by conforming to public opinion. Tocqueville fixed the price of social status at a limitation on individuality, a distrust of independent judgment. This may be true of nineteenth-century adult social thought, but from the evidence of schoolbooks, nineteenth-century adults expected their children to base action on moral grounds rather than on social approval. One must always stand for what is right whatever the attitude of one's peers. Standards for judging what is right do not, of course, come from independent ethical judgment but from authority, and schoolbooks were one source of such judgments. The child was taught to expect social approval and status as an accompaniment to economic success: the latter comes only to the virtuous, and in the long run society recognizes virtue.

According to these schoolbooks one of the great distinctions of the United States is the equality of opportunity it offers to every man. Especially after 1830 most schoolbooks contrast rank and privilege in the Old World with social equality in the New:

> In the aristocracies of the Old World wealth and society are built up like the strata of rock which compose the crust of the earth. If a boy be born in the lowest strata of life, it is almost impossible for him to rise through this hard crust into the higher ranks; but in this country it is not so. The strata of our society resembles rather the ocean, where every drop, even the lowest, is free to mingle with the others, and may shine at last on the crest of the highest wave. This is the glory of our country, and you need not fear that there are any obstacles which will prove too great for any brave heart.[1]

We have seen, however, that equality of opportunity is not in fact offered to all in the New World. Religion, race, nationality, and sex are limiting factors. The mingling drops in the American ocean are assumed to be male, white, Protestant, and from Northern European shores. Was the American child made aware of classes within this favored group? Was he asked to accept different social mores according to the economic class one came from? Do different economic groups live differently, think differently, and have different aspirations? By what criteria was he to judge his own position in society?

In the early books New England society is credited with the abolition of social distinctions, presenting all with equal opportunity to get ahead. Morse asserts this of New England in general and Connecticut in particular: "Where every man thinks himself at least as good as his neighbor, and believes that all mankind ought to possess equal rights." In contrast to this typical description of New England society, most of the pre-Civil War Geographies describe the South in terms of "the great distinction kept up

[1] R 1900 Aldrich and Forbes-I, p. 159.

between the wealthy planters and the laboring part of society."[2] In spite of this description of the southern part of the United States, America is assumed to be the one country in the world offering an equal chance to all. The part is substituted for the whole, and New England, as so often happens in these books, is considered synonymous with the United States. This American contribution to the happiness of humanity is stressed particularly from the 1830's on, probably as a result of the popularization of social democracy in the Jacksonian period. In America "The genius of our institutions reduces all men to a natural level, where the highest offices and the most dignified stations are legitimate objects for the pursuit of all who choose to compete for them."[3]

Although our ancestry, the Pilgrims, "wore not the princely robes, or the sacred lawn," they had true nobility of spirit.[4] But late nineteenth-century schoolbooks, while recognizing the noble spirit of the Pilgrims, often remark on the rigid class ideas brought to America by the first settlers.[5] But "this was not the soil on which vain titles and empty pomp could flourish."[6] One book dates the shift away from European class ideas between Lafayette's first and second visits to this country. On his second (1824) visit he exclaimed with astonishment, "'Where are the common people?' He saw only crowds of well-dressed citizens, but no yeomen, mechanics, merchants, and servants—the four ranks below that of a gentleman that were to be distinctly observed at the time of his first visit."[7] Daniel Webster's Bunker Hill oration of June 17, 1843 is quoted several times to show that: "America has proved that it is practicable to elevate the mass of mankind—that portion which in Europe is called the laboring, or lower class—to raise them to self-respect; to make them

[2] On New England, G 1798 Morse, p. 111; see also pp. 107, 108, 118. On the South, G 1803 Hubbard, pp. 81, 86, 100.

[3] R 1843 Cobb, p. 127; see also R 1845 D. Adams, p. 88; R 1855 Burleigh, p. 121; S 1859 Ormsby, Cushing, and Farnham, p. 36.

[4] R 1831 Bailey, p. 213; see also H 1826 Hale, pp. 439–441; R 1852 Town, p. 283.

[5] H 1881 Eliot, pp. 66–67; H 1881 Steele, pp. 92–94; H 1890 Morris, p. 58.

[6] H 1881 Steele, p. 75; see also H 1890 Morris, p. 145; H 1900 Channing, pp. 154–155, 166.

[7] H 1889? Steele, p. 210.

competent to act a part in the great right and great duty of self-government."[8] This is a major part of the glory of America; it levels all by raising the lowly.

America is not a land for the rich; they would be happier in Europe. A piece by George Curtis, entitled "Our Best Society," asks who are "essentially Americans," our best society, and answers: all who are "simple and steady, and whether rich or poor, are unseduced by the sirens of extravagance and ruinous display help make up the 'best society.'" He asks rhetorically: "Who are enamored of a puerile imitation of foreign splendors? Who strenuously endeavor to graft the questionable parts of Parisian society upon our towns? Who pass a few years in Europe and return skeptikal of republicanism and human improvement, longing and sighing for more emphasized social distinctions? . . . Who regard their Americanism as a misfortune?"[9] There are then some elements in American society who would like to establish a European aristocracy here, but most of the schoolbooks agree that such a system is happily impossible in America because wealth changes hands too fast: "The poor in one generation, furnish the rich of the next. . . . The rich man who treats poverty with arrogance and contempt, tramples upon the ashes of his father or his grandfather; the poor man who nourishes feelings of unkindness and bitterness on wealth, makes war with the prospects of his children, and the order of things in which he lives."[10] With the exception of the pre-Civil War planter, the American rich are on the whole sympathetically treated on the assumption that their wealth is the result of their labors. Their philanthropy is well illustrated, and their usefulness to society described: "Rich people, my son, have to work as well as those that are not so rich" because people need books, churches, and pictures. "Many of the best things that adorn life are the work of men who are not poor."[11] But the idle rich, usually given European illustration, are despised, not because they are rich

[8] R 1844 Smith, p. 19; R 1852 Gilder, pp. 194–196; see also R 1845 Swan, p. 172.

[9] R 1871 Sargent and May-5, pp. 217–218; see also R 1813 Richardson, p. 26; R 1831 Cheever, p. 443; R 1845 D. Adams, p. 47.

[10] R 1839 Sigourney, p. 124.

[11] R 1873 Hillard and Campbell-3, pp. 30–31.

but because they are idle. One striking and singular picture of the idle rich in America appears in a poem, "A Picture of Broadway," by N. G. Shepherd. An idle and thoughtlessly cruel woman "in her elegant carriage" runs over a poor man, "a bag of bones." That night

> The bundle of bones on the hospital bed
> Moans, and tosses its restless head.
> While the haughty Madame Millionaire
> In her chamber, where the indolent air
> Is heavy with perfume from fragrant urns,
> And the waxen taper drowsily burns,
> With the sumptuous curtains closely drawn,
> Sleeps on her pillow of snowy lawn.[12]

This is a most unusual, indeed a unique picture of the idle rich in America.

True quality lives in virtue rather than in rank. There are many tales of a poor man proving more capable in a crisis than the rich or the titled who look down upon the poor. In one instance used in several books a boy is jeered by his schoolmates for driving a cow to pasture before school. The mockers are nonplussed, however, when it develops that the boy is actually well to do but is helping a poor widow.[13] An anecdote used several times shows a rich man asking his secretary, with contempt in his voice, why his father hadn't brought up his own son in his own low profession—that of a saddler. The secretary retorts: why didn't your father bring you up in his profession—a gentleman?[14] There are also many tales proving that noble blood is unimportant; virtue is the true nobility: "He who is worthy, he who is honest or wise, has no need of ancestors."[15] The man who does his work honestly

[12] R 1872 Willson, pp. 208–210.

[13] R 1870 Sanders, pp. 47–51; R 1884 Campbell-4, pp. 88–93; see also R 1875 Sheldon, pp. 26–33.

[14] R 1871 Monroe, p. 130; R 1872 Osgood-4, pp. 191–192; R 1883 Swinton-4, pp. 356–358.

[15] R 1813 New York, p. 78; S 1824 Bentley, p. 125; see also R 1803 Carey, p. 57; R 1813 I. Cooke, pp. 220–222; R 1830 Practical-R, pp. 20, 21, 89; R 1834 S. Willard-P, p. 202; R 1836 Cobb-N.A., pp. 287–288; R 1850 Hall, pp. 124–126, 161–162; R 1850 Mandeville, p. 71; R 1852 Gilder, pp. 71–72; R 1852 Sweet, p. 87; R 1853 Tower and Walker, pp. 180–183; R 1856 Hillard, pp. 344–346.

and well is of the elite: "The plowman is an aristocrat, if he excels in his vocation: he is an aristocrat if he turns a better or a straighter furrow than his neighbor. The poorest poet is an aristocrat, if he writes more feelingly, in a purer language, or with more euphoric jingle than his contemporaries . . ." The same book contains a dialogue between brother and sister in which Caroline wishes she had been born in a monarchy; she hates liberty and equality. Her brother replies that she might have been born into the lower classes. "Is it not better to be born under a government where there are no such ranks, and where *the only nobility is talent and virtue?*" Caroline thinks wealth constitutes our nobility, but her brother disagrees: "You mistake. Money may be *temporary power*, but *talent* is *power itself;* and *when united with virtue, is God-like power*, before which the mere man of millions quails."[16] Burns' "A man's a man for a' that . . ." appears may times, too.

In any case, whether equal or not, the poor are to be respected. The child is taught that he is not to despise servants (and it is astonishing how often the term "servant" appears in the schoolbooks of a society that preferred to employ "hired men," "Mother's helpers," etc.):

> Not all the fine things that fine ladies possess,
> Should teach them the poor to despise,
> For 'tis in good manners and not in good dress,
> That the truest gentility lies.[17]

The poor are necessary to society; the work they do is useful. But even more important is the fact that great men have come from their ranks. A few of the books accept an environmentalist psychology in stating that "The differences in manners and abilities of men proceed more from education than from any imperfections or advantages derived from their original formation."[18]

All then are agreed that the poor should be respected, that the poor should have a chance to get ahead as they can in America

[16] R 1870 Sanders, p. 141, 135–138; see also R 1872 Willson, p. 262.

[17] R 1825 Torrey, p. 133; see also S 1824 Guy, p. 5; R 1834 S. Willard-P, p. 110.

[18] R 1801 Chipman, p. 17; see also R 1830 Emerson, pp. 59–60.

if possessed of enough virtue, and that virtue rather than rank should be the true index of character. It would be a serious mistake, however, to conclude that nineteenth-century American schoolbooks were not class conscious, or that they opposed the idea of distinctions of rank. Pre-Civil War books especially offer an overwhelming weight of evidence indicating belief in class distinctions and sometimes active advocacy of their importance. All of these texts rejoice that the United States has abolished social classes, but what they usually mean is that the United States has secured the abolition of titles and a caste system. An 1807 Geography puts the case so: "Though there are no distinctions acknowledged by law in the United States, fortune and the nature of the professions form different classes. Merchants, lawyers, physicians and clergymen form the first class; farmers and artisans the second; workmen, *who let themselves by the day or month*, the third. In public amusements these classes do not intermix." [19] One of the most popular single statements appearing in the pre-Civil War books on the subject of social classes is the following: "Society, when formed, requires distinctions of property, diversity of conditions, subordination of ranks, and a multiplicity of occupations, in order to advance the general good." [20] Such differences are vital to social organization and progress. A Speller states the case more directly: "Before I enter upon the subject of liberty, I would premise that I am no friend to that kind of liberty which consists in levelling all distinctions of rank." [21] In the Readers a most popular piece is Edmund Burke's reaction to the execution of Marie Antoinette, wherein he romanticizes social stratification: "Never, never more, shall we behold that generous loyalty to rank and sex, that proud submission, that dignified obedience, that subordination of the heart, which kept alive, even in servitude itself, the spirit of an exalted freedom." [22]

[19] G 1807 Parish, p. 28.

[20] R 180? Murray, p. 25; R 1806 Peirce, p. 133; R 1811 Lyman, p. 18; R 1815 R. Adams, p. 16; S 1837 Hawes, p. 187; S 1846 Butterfield, p. 11; see also R 1803 Murray, p. 48; R 1839 S. Goodrich, p. 90.

[21] S 1844 Clagett, p. 62.

[22] R 1811 I. Cooke, pp. 211–212; R 1826 American-S, p. 105; R 1830 MacLeod, pp. 64–65; R 1836 Cobb-N.A., pp. 247–248; R 1845 Swan, pp. 464–465.

Throughout the century there are constant references to one's "rank" or "station in life" as a frame for daily activities as well as a mold to one's future. The concept itself is clearly defined in the Spellers by the use of these terms and their definitions: "rank of persons," "grade in life," "station in life."[23] The limitations rank imposes on habits are evident in the story of a woman who is considering the purchase of some rather expensive veiling. In judging the propriety of this purchase, it is not enough that she should decide whether she can afford it; she must also take into account whether "it is becoming her station in life."[24] In another instance a certain lady Townley goes to bed late to give herself "the air of a woman of quality" as opposed to the early retiring "of a plodding mechanic, that goes to bed betimes, that he may rise early to open his shop."[25] Such lessons in class consciousness are brought down to the level of the school child by one of the most popular stories in pre-Civil War Readers, a dialogue between a mother and her daughter Sally, entitled "On Different Stations in Life." Sally, who has just come from visiting a rich friend, asks her mother why they cannot have a coach and the accoutrements of wealth, since they seem to be as worthy as the family of her friend. The mother replies by saying that since they have no extra money, their lives must be different: "Everything ought to be suited to the station in which we live, and the wants and duties of it."[26] In another popular story, a mother explains to her complaining daughter that she must study household accounts, reading, and writing, rather than music, dancing, and drawing: "because, my dear, it is the purpose of all education, to fit persons for the station in which they are hereafter to live; and you know there are very great differences in that respect, both among men and women." The daughter objects to this analysis, saying that she had always

[23] S 1823 Marshall, p. 24; S 1837 Chichester, p. 132; S 1844 Clagett, p. 25; S 1853 Northend, p. 91; S 1853 Vaughan-I, p. 51; S 1866 Watson, p. 41; S 1872 Watson, pp. 32–33.

[24] R 1841 Merriam, pp. 86–87; see also R 1839 S. Goodrich, pp. 89–90.

[25] R 1813 I. Cooke, pp. 288.

[26] R 1799 New Pleasing, pp. 226–230; R 1801 Heaton-C, pp. 19–21; R 1813 I. Cooke, pp. 82–86; R 1828 Robbins-A, pp. 132–136; R 1832 American-P, pp. 46–52; R 1832 Progressive, pp. 141–145; R 1833 Leavitt, pp. 139–142.

thought all ladies lived alike. Her mother responds: "It is usual to call all well educated women, who have no occasion to work for their livelihood, *ladies* . . .," but actually there are very great differences among them because their husbands and fathers are of "different ranks and situations in the world." [27] The idea that there are different stations in life requiring different modes of behavior is thoroughly accepted in pre-Civil War books. The child is taught to respect these differences and to fit his life into their pattern.

After the Civil War the situation is less clear. The rich still live very differently from the poor, but there is less emphasis on "rank" or "station in life." Although the terms do appear at times, tales such as the above disappear. Perhaps Jacksonian equalitarianism had finally seeped into the schoolbooks. Several anecdotes indicate some change in feeling. A little girl, planning her birthday party, is chided by her mother for not wanting to invite Ella Brown, who, though she is a good little girl, has no fine clothes. At the party one little girl objects when Ella is given the prettiest flower, because Ella has "a common calico dress on." The other children shame her for her snobbery. [28] The poor live differently from the rich, but they have a right to be treated as equals.

Although it may illustrate nothing but the glamor surrounding nobility in the eyes of republicans, it is interesting that there are so many tales involving aristocrats in a casual way, apart from those used to teach lessons about aristocrats. The Arithmetics are full of problems involving nobles even when the books are, by their own testimony, adapted "for the improvement of American youth," or deliberately planned for the poor. [29] Several of the Readers agree with the sentiments expressed in one of them from the writings of Washington Irving: "Brought up as I have been, in republican principles, I can feel nothing of the servile reverence for titled rank, merely because it is titled. But I trust I am neither churl nor bigot in my creed. I do see and feel how

[27] R 1797 Alexander, pp. 216–222; R 1801 Heaton-C, pp. 109–112; R 1830 Frost, pp. 143–151; see also R 1834 Angell, pp. 41, 98.

[28] R 1873 Hillard and Campbell-3, pp. 193–200; see also R 1866 Sargent-3, pp. 61, 68–70; R 1869 Wilson, pp. 79–89.

[29] A 1788 Gough, title page, pp. 69–70; A 1809 Grout, pref., p. 32.

hereditary distinction, when it falls to the lot of a generous mind, may elevate that mind into true nobility."[30] It is assumed throughout that noble birth marks a man indelibly. It is visible even in lowly circumstances, and it always conquers these circumstances. One hero professes to know of a woman in very lowly circumstances, "by her air and mien that she was not of vulgar birth."[31] But courts, courtiers, and the titled nobility of Europe are often objects of contempt. In the magic philosopher's scales which weigh true worth, a lord and lady weigh less than a bee.[32]

In accordance with the doctrine of the stewardship of wealth, those who are relatively well provided with goods of this world have a clearly defined relationship to those less well off. They are to behave toward the poor as the father of the day was to behave toward his children. They are to adopt a fostering air toward them, oversee their efforts at improvement, keep patience with them, and provide charity for the most unfortunate. Since wealth comes through God, the possession of wealth is a sign of superior wisdom and virtue. In pre-Civil War books the poor are to be treated with benevolence, but not equality. One story describes the thoughts of a gentleman who plucks a rose without leave from the garden of a stranger's cottage, then enters the house and proceeds upstairs to offer payment for the rose: "Impelled by a curiosity which, considering the rank of the inhabitants, I did not feel it necessary to resist."[33] In dispensing charity it is not fitting to give a poor child your own cast-off muslin dresses; give only things suitable to her condition, lest she aspire to your situation.[34] The idea that the permanently poor are incapable of looking after themselves intelligently is well illustrated in an extract entitled "Progress of Society." The author explains that migration occurs from a country when that country is overcrowded, and "Many of the poor go thither, with some

[30] R 1823 Pierpont, pp. 295–297; see also R 1802 Alden, p. 43; R 1834 S. Willard-P, pp. 261–264.

[31] R 1802 Columbian, p. 10; see also R 1818 R. Adams, pp. 74–77; R 1830 Hughs, pp. 35–36.

[32] R 1828 Putnam, p. 50; R 1841 Merriam, p. 213; R 1843 Olney, p. 207; R 1844 Smith, p. 165; R 1851 ASDUK, p. 118; R 1851 Tower, pp. 140–141.

[33] R 1819 Strong, pp. 37–39.

[34] R 1812 Daggett, pp. 57–66; R 1845 S. Worcester-I, pp. 88–89.

wise and industrious persons, to take care of them, and to tell them what they shall do."[35] Generally charity in the pre-Civil War books is an act of distinct and conscious condescension to inferiors, as "Have patience with a man in low estate, and delay not to show him mercy," or "Condescend to men of low estate," or "Pity the sorrows and sufferings of the poor. Disdain not to enter their wretched abodes, or to listen to their moving lamentations."[36]

Much of the condescension to the poor disappears from post-Civil War books, but the charity to be dispensed is often obviously designed rather to sweeten the character of the giver than to make the life of the poor easier. The child is assured that one can bestow happiness on the poor cheaply and easily: "A poor widow and her children live in that humble dwelling: send in half a peck of sweet apples, and they will all be happy."[37] In another instance a little boy suggests to his father that they give money to a poor lame girl and her mother who live nearby in miserable circumstances. The father considers money inappropriate, but says they can be helped most by a present of fruit and "smiles."[38] McGuffey's 1866 Reader includes the story of an orphan forced to ride on the outside of the coach in the rain. One of the passengers remonstrates with the driver and brings her inside the coach. Later, when he investigates and finds that she comes of a good family, he adopts her.[39] Apparently unfortunate children can be helped out of the rain, but not permanently unless they are of your own class. "The Tea Rose" by Harriet Beecher Stowe in an 1871 Reader seems to reflect some change in the general attitude that the long-range poor are a different breed with different feelings and aspirations. In this story a girl complains when her friend, who is about to go away, bestows her rose plant on a poor girl "When one of your most intimate friends in your own class would value it so highly. What in the world can people in their circumstances want with flowers?" The friend disagrees: "There

[35] R 1828 Robbins-A, p. 124; R 1832 Progressive, p. 73.

[36] S 1825 Bolles, p. 100; S 1843 Fowle, p. 69; R 1832 Cobb, p. 25; see also R 1855 New York, p. 20.

[37] R 1872 Willson, p. 60.

[38] R 1879 McGuffey, pp. 35–38.

[39] R 1866 McGuffey-5, p. 48.

are many of the poor who have fine feelings and a keen sense of the beautiful, which rusts out and dies, because they are too hard pressed to procure it any gratification." People "in all ranks of life" yearn for the beautiful.[40]

The question of dispensing charity indiscriminately is posed by Webster: "When persons are reduced to want by their own laziness and vices, by drunkenness, gambling and the like, is it a duty to relieve them?" And he answers: "In general, it is not."[41] The only other book that asks this question directly provides a quite different answer: "The Christian woman, who sincerely loves God and her neighbor, in imitation of her heavenly Father, is kind to the evil as well as the good, to the unthankful as well as the grateful."[42] One suspects that if charity is to be given at all, it must be extended in the latter spirit, since these books assume that poverty is a result of disfavor with God if not of sin itself. In America there should be no deserving poor except widows and orphans, and in the long run they too will prosper if they try. A 1797 Reader dissents from this stand on charity: a young man sets forth the idea that the poor have a right to subsistence and need not be grateful for charity. Benevolence is simply prudence on the part of the rich: "lest the poor, driven to despair, should take all." Hanging the poor for stealing in desperation would be "a mild punishment in place of starving." And finally he urges his uncle to "speak a few words for the poor, as a senator" so that they will not need charity.[43] But such doctrine appears only once, and it is in direct contradiction to attitudes considered proper in all other books toward the poor.

In spite of the constant reminders to get ahead, throughout the century much praise is bestowed on poverty as the happier state in this world and the best preparation for the next. When faced with death the poor man awaits it happily as a deliverance from misery; the rich man, on the other hand, is filled with despair because he must leave his luxuries.[44] The poor man is more likely

[40] R 1871 Monroe, pp. 151–153. [41] S 1810 Webster, p. 163.

[42] R 1826 Greenwood and Emerson, p. 142.

[43] R 1797 Alexander, pp. 195–197.

[44] R 1787 Miscellanies, p. 14; R 1834 S. Willard-P, p. 318; R 1844 Sanders, pp. 226–227; R 1896 McGuffey-2, p. 34.

to achieve heavenly reward, because he is less tempted to sin; poverty leaves him no time for dissipation.

> Affliction is the good man's shining scene,
> Prosperity conceals his brightest rays.[45]

Poverty also produces more health and greater enjoyment of food and rest: the rich may have better meat, but the poor have better stomachs; the rich may have better doctors, but the poor do not need them.[46] With an extraordinary lack of realism, one young girl tells her friend: "I think it is beautiful to keep house with not very much money."[47] Schoolbooks generally agree that "Poverty is oftener a blessing than a curse."[48] Furthermore, the rich have troubles too, and "The discontents of the poor are much easier allayed than those of the rich." The poor can be made happy by a simple gift, "But the surfeited rich are more difficult to satisfy."[49] Wealth brings cares, responsibilities, and boredom, whereas:

> Contented poverty's no dismal thing,
> Free from the cares unwieldy riches bring.[50]

The rich are to be pitied: "If the feelings of pleasure are more numerous, and lively, in the higher departments of life, such also are those of pain."[51] There are innumerable stories of the happy poor in contrast to the care-burdened rich. A wealthy family loses its money, discovers in poverty its first true happiness, and expresses gratitude for being reduced to this state.[52] A poem by

[45] Young quoted in S 1890 Kupfer, p. 113; see also R 1873 Progressive, pp. 60–64; R 1866 Sargent-3, pp. 38–39.

[46] R 1792 Dana, p. 86; R 1803 Murray, p. 48; R 1814 Alden, p. 22; S 1819 Alden, p. 137; R 1830 Frost, pp. 154–160; R 1838 Blake, pp. 119–120; S 1839 Williams, p. 165; R 1859 Sargent, p. 161.

[47] R 1884 Monroe, p. 102. A note on page 104 on the author of this piece, A. D. Whitney, says: "Her books present a natural and delightful portraiture of 'real life' as lived by 'real people.'"

[48] R 1855 Burleigh, p. 55.

[49] R 1872 Willson, p. 178; quotation in previous sentence is from R 1787 Miscellanies, p. 93; R 1828 New York, p. 13; see also R 1896 Baldwin, pp. 96–99.

[50] R 1787 Miscellanies, p. 101.

[51] R 1801 Chipman, pp. 138–139.

[52] R 1844 Bumstead, pp. 147–148; R 1846 Swan-G, pp. 32–35.

James Russell Lowell best sums up the heritage of these two contrasting states:

> The rich man's son inherits lands,
> And piles of brick, and stone and gold;
> And he inherits soft white hands
> And tender flesh that feels the cold.
> . . . .
> The rich man's son inherits cares:
> The bank may break, the factory burn
> A breath may burst his public shares,
> . . . .
> And soft white hands could hardly earn
> A living that could serve his turn;
> The rich man's son inherits wants
> His stomach craves for dainty fare.

But the poor man's son inherits:

> Stout muscles and a sinewy heart,
> A hardy frame, a hardier spirit;
> King of two hands he does his part
> In every useful toil and art;
> . . . .
> Content that from employment springs,
> A heart that in his labor sings.[53]

In going from poverty to riches a man proves himself, but the man who inherits wealth misses this chance. Many books point out that the best things in life are free anyway, as in the essay "My Property" by Henry Ward Beecher: "The world was made for poor men, and therefore the greatest part of it was left out of doors."[54] The wealth of the poor is pointed out in reply to a lad who complains of his lack of property; he is asked for how much he would sell his eyes, ears, etc.[55] In all books the hidden blessings of poverty are heavily stressed at the same time that youth is told to work hard to get out of that state. Happiness is fairly evenly distributed, even though worldly goods are not. Almost every book

[53] R 1868 Parker and Watson, pp. 161–162; R 1898 Williams G-2, pp. 132–133.

[54] R 1867 Edwards-5, pp. 221–224; see also R 1871 Sargent and May-5, pp. 102–104; R 1884 Monroe, pp. 288–293.

[55] R 1879 McGuffey, pp. 74–77; R 1884 Campbell-4, pp. 64–70.

has at least one essay or poem called "Rank and Riches Afford No Ground for Envy," or "On the Justice of Providence in the Distribution of Riches."

One of the most curious consolations offered the poor lies in the contrast between their domestic lives and those of the rich. According to these schoolbooks, in innumerable anecdotes, only the poor enjoy a happy family life. This also seems to be the case in the writings of such prominent authors of nineteenth-century juvenile literature as Louisa May Alcott and Frances Hodgson Burnett. An anonymous poem, "Mrs. Lofty and I," is illustrated with a picture of a poor woman wheeling her baby carriage past a mansion:

> Mrs. Lofty keeps a carriage,
> So do I.
> She has dapple grays to draw it,
> None have I.
>
> . . . .
>
> I hide his face lest she should see
> The cherub boy and envy me
>
> . . . .
>
> For I have love and she has gold;
> She counts her wealth;—mine can't be told.[56]

A mansion evidently cannot harbor a healthy, happy child. The child reading these books would certainly assume the cottage to be the nursery of domestic peace, the mansion, of domestic strife; only the poor love their mates and their children and enjoy life together. Indeed from many of these tales he might get the idea that marriage among the rich is a totally different experience: they rarely have children, and if they do they find it hard to love them.

While putting great stress on the duty of the individual to escape poverty by hard work, these same books also emphasize the beauty of contentment in a poverty that one has been unable to escape. In order to foster contentment in the poor the texts not only paint poverty in attractive colors, but they state sternly and emphatically that in society, stratified by classes as it is, contentment with one's lot is a major duty to society and to God.

[56] R 1872 Osgood-5, pp. 119–120; see also R 1872 Willson, pp. 27–29.

Discontent is sinful since it is God who has allotted our social stations to us: "What better proof can we give of our wisdom than to be content in the situation in which Providence has placed us."[57] Several use the biblical phrase: "It is the Lord who maketh poor and maketh rich, who bringeth low and lifteth up."[58] Discontent with one's station is criticism of God. God may bless your industry and relieve your poverty, but should that not happen, you are to accept your station happily. Alexander Pope's "Whatever is, is right" is quoted many times. In this context the poem loses all metaphysical subtlety and becomes a simple lesson in contentment with one's economic and social status, even though one does not understand its justice. The same point is made in more concrete terms in a poem entitled "The Two Weavers." One complains that his wife is ill, prices are too high for his small wages, etc., while at the same time some people have more than they need. The other replies that this distribution must be just, because arranged by God; as finite beings we cannot see the whole scheme and are not fit to judge its wisdom. After death all will be revealed to us.[59] The one equality assured to man is equality after death. This will be consolation for inevitable inequalities on earth. Hans Christian Andersen's story of the little match girl illustrates this moral in innumerable books. Her death brings glory and true happiness far outweighing the miseries she experienced in life. And on earth everyone has the duty of fulfilling the station assigned to him in life: "In our several stations, we are all sent forth to be laborers in the vineyard of our heavenly Father. Every man has his work allotted, his talent committed to him."[60] One author warns: "We do not gain anything by going out of our station, but by conforming to it."[61] Illustrations of the principle that each station in life, however low, has a necessary and important function to perform are often drawn from nature. One tale, entitled "Class Opinions," tells of a lamb teased by the lion for her silly roar, by the deer for her

[57] S 1815 Picket, p. 133; see also R 1785 New England Primer, p. 16; R 1787 Miscellanies, pp. 62–97; R 1799 New Pleasing, p. 147; etc.

[58] R 1819 Strong, p. 66; R 1828 New York, 23.

[59] R 1844 Smith, pp. 31–32; R 1848 Tower, pp. 141–143; R 1851 Tower, pp. 41–42; R 1858 Sanders, pp. 68–70.

[60] S 1865 Mulvany, p. 74. This is a general sentiment.

[61] R 1853 Mandeville, p. 257.

foolish leap, by the tiger for not eating human meat, ends: ". . . and yet it was a good lamb nevertheless."[62] A poem by Sarah Orne Jewett allows a robin to give advice to a discontented buttercup:

> Look bravely up into the sky
> And be contented with knowing
> That God wished for a buttercup
> Just here where you are growing.[63]

In another the humble heart's-ease consoles other flowers for being so apparently insignificant:

> Sigh not for stations placed beyond our reach
> But strive to serve thy Maker where thou art:
> The gardener soweth only tiny seeds
> Where he designs to raise but simple flowers;
> . . . .
> But all he asks from each of us while here,
> Is that with calm contentment we should rest
> In our appointed and appropriate sphere,
> And there, with loving spirit, do our best.[64]

There are many stories of individuals who illustrate the duty, beauty, and benefits of contentment. Several of the early books endeavor to show the material benefits that accrue to the individual who stays within his own station rather than risking disaster in attempting a too rapid improvement of his fortune. Most of the stories with a contentment moral, however, simply describe the beautiful character that results from resignation—a character that could be plotted between Pollyana and Candide. One popular poem describes such a character:

> One honest John Tomkins, a hedger and ditcher,
> Although he was poor, did not want to be richer.
> . . . .
> If I cannot get meat, I can surely get bread.[65]

[62] R 1868 Parker and Watson, pp. 60–61; see also pp. 55–60.

[63] R 1882 Gourley and Hunt, p. 168; see also R 1884 Campbell-4, p. 166; R 1900 Williams, pp. 50–55.

[64] R 1872 Monroe, p. 175.

[65] R 1830 Putnam-I, pp. 97–98; R 1831 Hall, p. 170; R 1833 Leavitt, p. 86; R 1845 D. Adams, p. 127.

John Tomkins, with his apparent lack of ambition to get ahead, would seem to contravene the American dream that every man can and should get ahead in the United States. Actually he does not. He recognizes his own limitations, but within them he is the best hedger and ditcher he can be and earns a competency thereby, which he might not be able to do in another country. The American gets ahead not by working for riches, nor by envying them, but by working as hard as he can in the job he is fitted to do. Riches come as a reward for talent in combination with the Puritan virtues, and it is the equality of opportunity in the United States that allows such men to come to the fore. Another tale describes a Dutchman who, after a series of misfortunes, breaks a leg but rejoices that it was not his neck. In another case a poor man planning to make soup of an onion, meat, bread, salt, and pepper, loses each of these ingredients successively except the onion; he goes on his way singing, consoled by the fact that at least this meal will be better than that of the last night.[66]

In the pre-Civil War books the duty of the poor not only to acquiesce in their condition but to obey their betters is often specifically mentioned. Pierpont notes: "The poor disciplined into order, respect the rich." In another text the same author uses an essay by Greenwood who sets at rest fears that public school education will give the poor unwarranted ideas of equality: "Nor is it at all rational to suppose, that a judicious education of the poor, conducted to any attainable extent, will be liable to abuse in their hands, and lead them to forget their station and their duty. . . ."[67] In this period their station involves certain attitudes transgressed by the idea of equality. A Reader outlines their duties: "It is the duty of poor folks to labour hard, take what we can get, and thank the great and wise God, that our condition is no worse."[68] A Speller stresses obedience: "Obedience to superiors is requisite in all society; it is consistent with propriety and adds to general convenience."[69] Later books avoid specific

[66] R 1803 Murray, pp. 45–48; R 1806 Peirce, pp. 165–166; R 1833 Leavitt, pp. 137–138; R 1835 Pierpont-Y, pp. 81–82; R 1843 Swan, pp. 100–103.

[67] First quotation from R 1823 Pierpont, p. 22; second from R 1827 Pierpont, p. 161.

[68] R 1825 Torrey, p. 94.

[69] S 1836 Brandreth, p. 102; see also R 1858 McGuffey, pp. 279–280.

statements on the subservience of the poor, but it is clear that those who have made a success in this world are better morally as well as in the talents it took to achieve eminence in that field than those who have not been so successful. All would agree with Webster's 1835 statement: "Hence the poor have no right to complain, if they do not succeed in business. They all enjoy the same rights; and if they continue in poverty, it is usually for want of industry, or judgment in the management of their affairs, or for want of prudence and economy in preserving what they earn. They have no more right to invade the property of the rich, than the rich have to invade the rights of the poor."[70] It seems that in the United States permanent poverty is peculiarly one's own fault, and complaint is unjustifiable. Small comfort this must have been to those who suffered in the depression two years after this was published.

Thus even in the Jacksonian period American children were taught that all society is stratified; class distinctions not only exist but they are desirable for progress. Each rank in life is circumscribed by the duties and prospects allotted to it. Although special lessons in class consciousness diminish after the Civil War, still the child is taught that there are two classes as different as two nations; they exhibit different modes of behavior in even the most basic relationships. The behavior of one class to another is to be carefully regulated. The man who has made his own wealth is to be treated as a man of superior virtue and ability; if he were not superior in God's eyes, he would not be wealthy. He, in turn, is to provide guidance and charity as well as patience for the poor. If not able to achieve wealth themselves, the poor are to be contented with their lot, to work hard, and to respect the rich. Everyone must be industrious in hope of both material and spiritual reward, but one's ambition must be tempered with contentment with whatever station in life one can achieve.

But the child reading these books would also be thoroughly aware of the great American contribution to social structure. America does not provide equality among classes: that is both impossible and undesirable. Its contribution lies in giving class fluidity to the individual. Distinctions by wealth among men are necessary for the recognition of virtue. Classes exist in the United

[70] R 1835 Webster, p. 170.

States, but America provides the opportunity whereby a poor individual, singled out by God through his own ability, can cross class barriers and achieve affluence and standing in the community. Such chosen people were oppressed in Europe and their talents hidden. No theme appears more often: "There is no country in the world where a poor boy has the chance to become rich or great as he has in our land of liberty. There are many rich men among us to-day who began life without a penny." And its illustrations are countless. Early poverty, to test one's character, is the rule in America, but later success attends the emergence of character. Most prominent men in the United States were "with scarcely an exception, men who began in the world without a dollar."[71] One should choose honesty over riches, but usually the hard-working boy who makes the proper choice ends up with riches as well. America not only represents the doctrine of opportunity for all, but it should act as a missionary to spread its social system to the world.

One wonders what effect these ideas would have on the reader who remained poor in spite of the opportunities his country offered him, and in spite of rigid adherence to the doctrine of hard work. His failure to get ahead in Europe could be ascribed to a lack of opportunity, but his failure to get ahead in America, he is constantly told, is his own fault. If he followed the tenets of his schoolbooks, he would develop a strong feeling of his own inadequacy, not just in business but in moral character as well. He might be content with his station, but hardly with himself.

[71] First quotation in this paragraph from H 1899 Morris, pp. 215–216; second quotation from R 1873 American, p. 74.

Chapter 10

POLITICAL CONCEPTS

In producing books for use in the schools of a democracy, writers were very much aware of educating an electorate. Even in their first pages most of the Spellers include such words as "legal," "tyrant," "senator," "democracy."[1] Educating the child in the technical terms of politics was important, but clearly the first duty of schoolbook authors in their own eyes was to attach the child's loyalty to the state and nation. The sentiment of patriotism, love of country, vies with the love of God as the cornerstone of virtue: "Patriotism . . . must be considered as the noblest of the social virtues."[2] Every book contains many pieces sustaining the doctrine that one's loyalty to country must be paramount to all other loyalties. In the early Readers most of the selections on the subject of patriotism are taken from the antique world; as the century advances, many of these are kept but gradually outnumbered by illustrations from American history. Every Reader contains several selections on the theme "Let our object be, *our country, our whole country, and nothing but our country.*"[3] Walter Scott's poem

> Breathes there a man with soul so dead
> Who never to himself has said
> This is my own, my native land . . .

is ever present.

Loyalty to country always supersedes loyalty to family or friends. There are many tales similar to the one in which Brutus, a Roman official, becomes a hero when he condemns his own son

[1] For example, see S 1825 Torrey, pp. 23, 24, 48, 60.

[2] R 1811 I. Cooke, p. 338.

[3] R 1828 Hopkins, p. 136. A very popular extract from a Webster oration at Bunker Hill.

to death for betraying Rome.[4] In another case a father whose son has been killed in the same battle that ended the career of Turenne, the French general, says: "It is not for my son you must weep; but for that great man, and the irreparable loss which your country will sustain in his death!"[5] And in almost every Reader William Tell appears risking his son's life in a demonstration of national heroism. Nor must love of friends, though an admirable trait, interfere with love of country. Brutus' speech from Shakespeare's *Julius Caesar* beginning "Not that I loved Caesar less, but that I loved Rome more . . ." appears many times.

Finally patriotism requires that one should be willing to lose not only family and friends but life itself for one's country. Hume's tale of raising the siege of Calais is one popular instance given in the early books: several of the most prominent citizens of Calais offer to give themselves up to death from the enemy in return for lifting the disastrous siege of the town.[6] Most Readers and Spellers contain such general sentiments as the following in prose or poetry:

> On this foundation would I build my fame,
> And emulate the Greek and Roman name;
> Would think its peace bought cheaply with my blood;
> And die with pleasure for my country's good.[7]

Most books associate pleasure as well as heroism with such an act: "It is pleasant and glorious to die for one's country," or, at the end of the century:

> May the hearts of our people re-echo the cry,
> "'Tis sweet, oh 'tis sweet for our country to die."[8]

Most of the Readers include four or five poems, stories, or essays

[4] R 1797 Thomas, p. 138; see also R 1802 Columbian, p. 82; R 1803 Carey, p. 195; R 1810 Alden, pp. 100–101; R 1823 Morrill, pp. 233–236; R 1830 Practical-R, pp. 18–19, et al.

[5] R 1810 Alden, p. 100; R 1823 Morrill, p. 233.

[6] R 1796 Bingham, pp. 56–60; R 1797 Alexander, pp. 90–95; R 1804 Webster, pp. 57–61; R 1806 Staniford, pp. 88–92; R 1823 Blake, pp. 152–156.

[7] R 1811 Lyman, p. 267; R 1830 Practical-R, p. 172; see also the poem "How Sleep the Brave" by William Collins in R 1867 Parker and Watson-5, p. 393; R 1873 American, p. 105; R 1879 Harris, Rickoff, Bailey, p. 41; R 1896 Holmes and Hill, p. 106; R 1898 Black, p. 320.

[8] S 1851 Northend, p. 59; H 1896 Murphy, pp. 44–45.

on the glories of giving one's all to one's country. From the treatment of individuals in all countries and none more than the United States it is evident that the greatest heroes of all are these. Pages are crowded with American heroes who left their lives on various battlefields in various American wars.

Whatever the form of their government, men owe it their primary allegiance, but they will perform their obligations more willingly when the government has been instituted for the good of the governed. "Men love their country when the good of every particular man is comprehended in the public prosperity, and the success of their achievements is improved to the general advantage. They undertake hazards and labors for the government, when it is justly administered; when innocence is safe, and virtue honored. . . ."[9] Americans, then, have special reason to love their country, and the United States depends on their loyalty more particularly than would an absolute government. "We have reasons for patriotism, greater and higher, than now can, or ever could be possessed by the inhabitants of any nation on the globe."[10]

But, as we have seen, national loyalty is not just to a government but to a people—a nation; not to an aggregation of individuals living in a common territory but to a group with common, if often mystical, aspirations. "What Constitutes a State?" a popular poem by Sir William Jones used from the 1870's on, defines a state not by its territory or physical accoutrements, but by its "high-minded men" who know their right and duties.[11] In several instances the fatherland is discussed not as one's native place, but wherever freedom is.[12] George W. Curtis, quoted several times in an essay called "Patriotism," challenges the statement "My country, right or wrong" because "a man's country is not a certain area of land,—of mountains, rivers, and

[9] R 1832 Edwards, p. 189.

[10] R 1811 Chandler, p. 19; R 1813 Richardson, pp. 57–58; see also R 1844 Goldsbury and Russell, p. 148; R 1856 Osgood, pp. 258–260; R 1858 McGuffey, pp. 52–53.

[11] R 1873 Progressive, p. 132; R 1879 Harris, Rickoff, Bailey, pp. 99–100; R 1896 Holmes and Hill, p. 161–162; R 1897 Arnold and Gilbert-6, pp. 85–86; R 1898 Black, pp. 203–204; R 1898 Williams G-2, pp. 199–200; R 1900 Aldrich and Forbes-I, p. 240.

[12] S 1874 Worcester, p. 157; R 1884 Campbell-4, pp. 225–226.

15. William Tell risks his son's life for his country. The picture is from Blake's 1825 Reader, but the story is to be found in almost all Readers and Spellers.

woods,—but it is a principle; and patriotism is loyalty to that principle." True patriotism demands not blind loyalty but loyalty to truth.[13]

In nineteenth-century schoolbooks, as we have seen, a nation inherits character and personality; it also generates national ideals. In a nation as diverse as the United States, loyalty to the ideals theoretically held in common by the nationality make up nationalism. In a sense the schoolbooks are guardians of what their authors consider those national ideals to be. In defining proper attitudes and behavior for American youth they spell out the ideals seen by their authors as those of the American nationality. By the quality and quantity of pieces on this subject, the authors of schoolbooks clearly saw nationalism, not necessarily of a chauvinistic sort, but love of the American nation, as a primary value to be developed in youth. We have already examined the individual and social beliefs and behavior that schoolbook authors expected to inculcate in young America, the ideals they hope the American nation will represent. All books agree that the American nation politically expressed is the apostle of liberty, a liberty personified, apostrophized, sung to, set up in God-like glory, but rarely defined. To discover what liberty means in these books is a murky problem. The child reader could be certain that it is glorious, it is American, it is to be revered, and it deserves his primary loyalty. But for the child to find out from these books what this liberty is would be astonishing.

He can be sure that freedom does not associate with monarchy. Monarchy is often defined objectively, but it appears most often in unfavorable contexts. In the Spellers he would use such practice sentences as the following: "A crown is worn by a king. It is a toy for which much blood has, at times been shed"; or "Kings are sometimes guilty of flagrant wrongs."[14] One Reader implies that a country is governed by a king only as a punishment from God.[15] A History, using the example of the Puritans, warns: "The Bible says 'Put not your trust in Princes.' The Puritans did so, to their sorrow."[16] Others see monarchy as a source of oppression of the poor. Even the best monarchy is seeded with tyranny.

[13] R 1883 Swinton-5, pp. 320–331; R 1898 Arnold and Gilbert, pp. 249–250.
[14] S 1822? New York, p. 31; S 1865 McGuffey, p. 40.
[15] R 1846 Sanders, pp. 82–83. [16] H 1866 Lossing, p. 42.

A few of the early books, copies of English schoolbooks, treat monarchy as a normal state of affairs and with approval, but these books become a minority increasingly outnumbered as the century goes on. Monarchy is constantly contrasted to republicanism, seen in perfection in the United States. The fate of monarchy in North America in the eighteenth century is expected to be the pattern for the fate of European monarchy. Just as schoolbook authors saw the American Revolution as an inevitable result of the first planting of colonies here, so they confidently expect European monarchy to disappear in the ordinary but inevitable process of political evolution. Eventually all the world will be republican.

Liberty, then, seems to exist only in a republic: "In such a constitution we find a country deserving to be loved, and worthy to be defended."[17] Universally a republic is defined as "a country governed by a number of men chosen by the people for a limited time."[18] There is not, however, the same unanimity in describing democracy. Often it is not described at all, even though democracy as extension of the suffrage was a major issue in the first quarter of the century. The distinction usually made between a republic and a democracy is this: a republic is ruled by representatives of the people whereas a democracy is one where the people meet directly to make decisions. Since the latter is obviously impossible in a country so large as the United States, democracy is impossible here. That a republic can be more or less democratic according to how much power the people as a whole have in it is rarely mentioned. Several of the early books identify federalism with republicanism: "A *republick* is where the supreme power is entrusted by the people to councils, composed of members chosen for a limited time, and where there are several independent states united into one general government."[19] Here the definition of a republic has been tailored to fit the governmental system of the United States. Clearly freedom includes a republican form of government, though not necessarily democracy. And quite as clearly a free government is identical with that of the United States.

[17] R 1792 Dana, p. 207. [18] G 1831 Blake, p. 63.

[19] G 1817 Cummings, p. 93; see also G 1818 Mann, p. 31; G 1818 Morse, p. 44.

Definitions of types of government do not include such new doctrines as socialism or anarchism. Even in books of the late nineteenth century, when such definitions might be useful to the child, only McMaster's History mentions the Utopian communities. Many times, especially in the later books, the failure of communal ownership in the colonial period is pointed out. Steele, for example, in discussing the Pilgrims, observes: "The plan of working in common having failed, here as at Jamestown, land was assigned to each settler."[20] Socialism or communism is mentioned only once by name, in a paragraph headed "Communism" in which the railroad strikes of the 1870's are blamed on the "communists."[21] Socialism, like labor organization, is identified only with unscrupulous agitation and violence. After the Haymarket affair in 1886 anarchism, still undefined, is sensationally portrayed in action. Even practice sentences in the Spellers introduce the child to the violence of anarchism: "Some bombs and other missiles were found by the police in the anarchist's magazine."[22] The Haymarket affair itself is described as "an awful scene of murder" in which foreign agitators created tragedy and senseless destruction.[23] The child could have no idea from his schoolbooks of nonviolent forms of socialism and anarchism. The Populist party is mentioned rarely, and only in the few books written by professional American historians. Such political doctrines are without question alien to political concepts approved in schoolbooks.

Freedom of the individual from government interference in opinion, press, assembly, and religion is often pointed out as a particular contribution of the American governmental system. Without explaining these rights in detail it is generally agreed: "Respect for individual rights and opinions and a generous confidence in every man's reason and capacity for self-control, have been distinguishing features of American society almost from its beginnings, and have resulted in a degree of personal freedom unknown under older governments. . . ."[24] Liberty and

[20] H 1881 Steele, p. 55; see also H 1889 Monroe, p. 95.

[21] H 1881 Thalheimer, p. 340. [22] S 1888 Shoup, p. 45.

[23] H 1890 Morris, p. 220; see also H 1881 Thalheimer, p. 351; H 1889? Steele, p. 299; H 1899 Morris, p. 247.

[24] H 1881 Thalheimer, pref., p. iii.

license in these matters are often distinguished. An essay by Frederick William Robertson on "False Notions of Liberty" is a typical example: "The only liberty that a man should ask for is the privilege of removing all restrictions, inward and outward, that prevent his doing what he ought to do." If he obeys the law he is free, but dissidence is regarded with suspicion: "I can see nothing very noble in a man who is forever going about calling for his own rights."[25] One wonders what is meant by freedom of speech in Scott's History when he says that Anne Hutchinson and her friends "brought with them extreme notions with regard to the rights of free speech."[26] Freedom of the press is usually approved and detailed by an exposition of the Zenger case. In these discussions, however, the emphasis is less on the principle of freedom of the press than on the Zenger case as an example of colonial revolt against British tyranny.[27] And in the early books when religious liberty is defined, its definition offers something less than one expects of the term. The New England background of most of the authors is frequently revealed when they praise religious freedom in New England, and note at the same time with pride that there "The inhabitants are all taxed for the support of worship; but it is left to everyone's choice to what particular sect his payment shall be appropriated."[28] One is left with the distinct impression that religious freedom does not extend to Mormons, atheists, or deists; that freedom of the press, speech, and assembly do not extend to socialists, labor leaders, or anarchists. These individual freedoms seem to be designed in the textbooks for the great middle, those who do not disagree too much.

The Alien and Sedition Acts, sharply challenging freedom of speech, the press, and elections, are unnoticed in many Histories. When they are described, they are usually described well, but their significance is a matter for disagreement. About half of the books that discuss them indicate that they were wrong in principle, and contrary to our Constitution.[29] The others make no such

[25] R 1884 Monroe, pp. 56–57. [26] H 1874 Scott, p. 62.

[27] For example, see H 1866 Lossing, pp. 76–77; H 1881 Eliot, pp. 140–141; H 1885 Ensign, pp. 18–19.

[28] G 1807 Goldsmith, p. 11, and see Chapter 2, "The Nature of Man."

[29] H 1881 Thalheimer, p. 200; see also H 1885 Donnelly, p. 125; H 1894 Fiske, p. 269; H 1900 Channing, pp. 174–175; H 1889 Chambers, p. 288.

observations but see their importance only in their unpopularity and the resulting downfall of the Federalists. Political parties in general play a minor role in these books; they appear in any significant way only in the Federalist period.

In the overwhelming majority of these books, liberty is a desirable but undefined and almost mystical entity. The term is used constantly in an amorphous fashion, but it has one very specific quality: it came into the possession of the United States government at the time of the American Revolution and is now enshrined there. The free American government was born full grown in the American Revolution.

All are agreed that in the United States and in any free government all men must have equal natural and civil rights. All must be equal before the law. Some of the Spellers use the following statement: "We hold these truths to be self evident, that all men are created equal, that they are endowed by their Creator with certain, inalienable rights, that among these are life, liberty and the pursuit of happiness. This is the language of America, of Reason and of Truth."[30] Interestingly enough this philosophy is not often ascribed to its source in the Declaration of Independence. Some books include copies of the Declaration of Independence in an appendix, but relatively few do this. Almost all mention its promulgation as a supreme event in the history of man, but they neglect to state that it contained any political philosophy at all. It is to be revered but not examined. It represents a major step in the advance of liberty, not because of any doctrine it contains but rather because it ushered an independent United States into the world. In reading most of these books one would think that the only thing said in the Declaration of Independence was that the United States was free from English rule.[31] It is important here not for its influence on the spread of democracy but because it marks the birthdate of the American nation, and it is to be so celebrated.

Political dissidence in other countries is often viewed benignly, but in an America already freed by the American Revolution it is not so happily tolerated. Rebellion against tyrants is approved:

[30] S 1822? New York, p. 160; S 1823 Picket, p. 197; S 1824 Bentley, p. 197; S 1839 Crandall, p. 110; see also H 1885 Ridpath, p. 490.

[31] For example, see G 1789 Elements, p. 15; G 1818 Morse, p. 106; G 1820 Darby, p. 80; S 1847 ASDUK, pp. 135–136; G 1848 Mitchell, p. 46, etc.

"Tyrants are rebels against the first laws of Heaven and society; to oppose their ravages is an instinct of nature—the inspiration of God in the heart of man."[32] On these grounds the American Revolution was entirely justified. It is unique among revolutions because it was ordered and principled; it was neither organized nor carried out in a spirit of riot. It was a conservative revolution to maintain the rights denied us by the British. The men who participated in the American Revolution were not rebels, but men of law and order. Successful revolutions quickly adopt respectability and a new orthodoxy, and surely the schoolbooks helped in this process. To rebel against the American government is the greatest crime, because almost by definition the United States represents liberty and cannot be tyrannical. Rebellion against it is rebellion against liberty.

Bacon's rebellion in Virginia in 1676 is usually approved as an early act in the struggle of the Americans for freedom from British tyranny. In 1870 Lossing's History points out that Bacon was resisting attempts of the British to do away with representative government in Virginia: ". . . for a hundred years, loyalists called the leader a *traitor*. Such would have been Washington's title, had our Revolution failed."[33] Another History indicates what Bacon was fighting against by quoting Governor Berkely: ". . . I thank God there are no free-schools nor printing presses here, and I hope we shall not have them these hundred years. God keep us from both." Another describes Berkely as "The first representative of English monarchy in America to encourage armed resistance when his authority was exercised to oppress the people."[34] A few books in discussing this rebellion, however, regard it not as the first struggle against British tyranny but as a civil war between various groups within the colony; as such it is heartily disapproved. In such cases it is analyzed not in terms of the justice of the rebels' grievances but of the destruction that ensued and "was felt 30 years after."[35]

[32] Josiah Quincy, Jr., quoted in R 1831 Cheever, p. 37; see also R 1790 Webster, pp. 141–142.

[33] H 1870 Lossing, p. 54; see also H 1874 Anderson, p. 41.

[34] These two quotations are from the following in that order: H 1874 Scott, p. 44; H 1889 Chambers, p. 172.

[35] G 1833 Clute, p. 107; see also G 1825 Butler, p. 103.

American rebellions before the Revolution are part of the Revolution, and the grievances are usually explained in these terms. American rebellions after the Revolution are always the work of unscrupulous agitators arbitrarily fomenting trouble, and the grievances are rarely mentioned. Shays' Rebellion was begun by "disorderly citizens" with a "turbulent leader."[36] Although the participants were free men, "yet many had formed no just idea of freedom, for they considered any restraint or encumbrance an encroachment upon their liberty."[37] All agree that Shays' Rebellion showed the need for a stronger national government, but there is no indication that it might also show a need for help to the desperate farmers of Massachusetts. The Whiskey Rebellion is treated in much the same fashion. It was a "criminal resistance." One historian blames it on Genêt. Another sees it as the work of "artful men who wished to overthrow all laws." Its failure proved to the "lover of anarchy" that this is no place for an "unconstitutional attempt."[38] Only one History, McMaster's, explains why the grain farmers of remote western Pennsylvania felt so strongly about this tax.[39] The Civil War is regarded as unjustified rebellion, but also as unmitigated tragedy. The right of revolution in the United States is confined to the American Revolution against the British, and it is evaluated not in terms of social aims but in terms of its success in establishing the American government.

Most of the Geographies introduce their section on the United States by saying something to the effect that it is distinguished for the excellence of its government. "It is called a Republic—which is a free government, and may be considered the happiest and best in the world"; or "Here everything that is rational in political liberty is enjoyed."[40] The superiority of the American government to all others is constantly stated: "We can boast of a

[36] H 1822 Grimshaw, p. 198–199.

[37] H 1843 Hall and Baker, pp. 280–281; see also H 1855 Berard, p. 171.

[38] The quoted phrases on the Whiskey Rebellion are from the following in that order: H 1822 Grimshaw, p. 205; H 1881 Thalheimer, p. 192; H 1839 Frost, p. 323. H 1874 Scott, pp. 235–236 ascribes it to the machinations of Genêt.

[39] H 1897 McMaster, pp. 203–204.

[40] The two quotations in this sentence are from the following in that order: S 1845 Bentley, p. 166; R 1836 Cobb-N.A., p. 347.

code of laws superior to that of any nation; of institutions, blessed and blessing in their influence, and character produced by the same noble and patriotic spirit, which formed our system of government."[41] The Constitution of the United States is a unique instrument of government not only because it embodies "liberty," but also because it was not "imposed upon us by power which we dare not or could not resist."[42] When the word "Constitution" refers to the American, it is usually preceded by the epithet "our glorious."[43] It represents "the collected patriotism of ages ripened to maturity"; the convention that designed it "contained the wisest men of the country"; "Never was more important work committed to human hands."[44] Differences in the Constitutional Convention are sometimes mentioned in the Histories, but without description or explanation: "Some found fault with it."[45] Opposition to its ratification is not mentioned in the early books; it is assumed that all were naturally united behind this document of liberty from the moment it was conceived. More attention is given to the opposition by the Southern historian Chambers than by any other, although he concludes by saying, "Yet all in all, it was a wonderful achievement; and it stands to-day the greatest written instrument ever executed by man."[46] One author sinks to a nadir in accuracy by stating that the Constitution was adopted in 1783 after the close of the Revolution: "This Constitution, principally from the pen of THOMAS JEFFERSON, more happily embraces the equal rights and liberties of man, than any other system on the globe."[47] The Constitution itself appears in many Readers, but with no analysis of its provisions; and state constitutions, always from the New England states, are given now and then. Speeches favorable to the adoption of the Federal Constitution made at the time of the issue occur in some books, but with no explanation of why it was necessary to urge the adoption of what here seems to be a perfect plan of government. The child reading these books was most unlikely to have any realistic

[41] R 1852 Town, p. 283. [42] R 1813 Richardson, p. 58.

[43] H 1869 Quackenbos, p. 141.

[44] These three statements on the Constitution are from the following in that order: R 1813 Richardson, p. 58; H 1869 Quackenbos, p. 141; H 1881 Thalheimer, p. 183.

[45] H 1869 Quackenbos, p. 142. [46] H 1889 Chambers, p. 271.

[47] G 1818 Mann, p. 63.

appreciation of the difficulties of making and adopting the Federal Constitution, although—or perhaps because—it was exalted to biblical status.

The question of amending and changing the Constitution is not often broached, but when it is the Jeffersonian concept of a fluid government is usually rejected. A few authors note that the people have the right "of reforming, altering, or totally changing the same, when their protection, safety, prosperity and happiness require it."[48] Many others, however, warn seriously of the dangers of altering a constitution. The Constitution is "an old and sacred bargain" to be revered and preserved.[49] The children of those who have successfully completed a revolution and have entrenched their interests and security in a governmental system are urged, if they would be patriots, to defend that system as it stands.

The theory of federalism in the early books seems to be a theory of federation in which the states retain a great deal of independent sovereignty and the central government is simply a loose confederation. In these books the United States is always referred to as a plural rather than a singular entity. A typical description from that period is the following: "A confederation or federal republic, is a union of several independent states, for mutual aid and defence, under the direction of a congress or general assembly; as that of the United States."[50] The later books increasingly emphasize the dual sovereignty of state and federal governments: "Each state is independent, and has the exclusive control of all concerns merely local; but the defence of the country, the regulation of commerce, and the general interests of the confederation are committed to a general government."[51] Here the independence of the state is operative only in local matters. Textbook authors seem to follow the transformation in constitutional theory undergone by New England at the time.

As we have seen, Northern and Southern parts of the United States are contrasted all through the century, with New England's

[48] R 1813 Richardson, p. 37; see also R 1854 Sargent, p. 287.

[49] H 1857 Lossing, p. 170; see also H 1839 Frost, p. 51; R 1835 Webster, p. 174; R 1854 Mandeville, pp. 310–311.

[50] G 1827 C. Goodrich, p. 18; see also G 1796 Dwight, p. 194; S 1815 Bradley, p. 145.

[51] G 1845 S. Morse, p. 16; see also G 1832 Allen, p. 22; G 1835 Huntington, p. 43; G 1840 Olney, p. 61.

manners, virtues, and institutions identified with those of America as a whole. But there seemed to be no fear that the two sections would separate until the issue of the tariff presented the doctrine of nullification to American politics. Only two books published at the time New England Federalists threatened secession exhibit any fears for the union of the states. One presents Washington and the other Hamilton on the absolute necessity of union.[52]

From the 1830's to the Civil War there is much evidence of a new fear of disunion in the increased number of selections in the Readers on the importance of union. In this period every Reader contains at least one selection on the subject. The prestige of Washington is invoked in many books; to him the permanency of the Union was a vital necessity for each state and each section of the United States.[53] Fear is reflected even in the Spellers, which now use such practice sentences as: "Stand by the Union!" or "In union there is strength," or "Liberty is the ligament that binds the states together."[54] Earlier, liberty was the force that distinguished America from Europe; it is still that, but now it must also act as a binding force in America.

The dangers of disunion are now constantly pointed out. One Speller uses a parable wherein a father shows his son that he cannot break a bundle of sticks tied together, but he can easily break them singly. Another explains how two quarreling chickens were finally eaten up by a wolf who found his chance in their lack of harmony.[55] Several speeches from the period of the formation and adoption of the Constitution are now revived. A speech by Hamilton in which he shows graphically the disastrous effects a dissolution of the Union would bring in its train is used several times.[56] One rather novel argument is set forth in an essay entitled "The Union of These States Is Indispensable to our Literature." It is this union that has created conditions favorable to the development of our literature.[57] In the light of the attitude

[52] R 1810 Alden, p. 135; R 1811 I. Cooke, pp. 343–348.

[53] R 1834 Emerson, pp. 63–65; R 1844 Smith, p. 228; R 1853 Tower and Walker, p. 403; R 1856 Sargent-4, p. 180; R 1860 McGuffey, pp. 81–82.

[54] These three sentences are from the following in that order: S 1856 Sargent, p. 119; S 1860 Tully, p. 63; S 1857 Parker and Watson, p. 110.

[55] These two parables are from the following in that order: S 1854 Emerson, p. 99; R 1830 Putnam-I, pp. 17–19.

[56] R 1831 Cheever, pp. 242–245; R 1836 Cobb-N.A., pp. 401–403.

of these schoolbooks to the arts, this would seem to be a rather weak argument. Webster quotes Poinsett, a Southerner speaking in the South, to the effect that to maintain respect abroad, "we must maintain our place in the Union."[58]

Several books attempt to reconcile the sections by listing the habits, institutions, and ideas that the North and South have in common. They plead that similarities are much more important than their differences. This idea is maintained poetically in the following:

> Who would sever freedom's shrine?
> Who would draw the invidious line?
> Though by birth one spot be mine.
> Dear is all the rest.
>
> . . . .
>
> Now receive our solemn vow
> While below thy throne we bow,
> Ever to maintain as now,
> UNION, LIBERTY.[59]

That nullification is both illogical and dangerous is frequently observed. The Webster-Hayne debates are rather prominent. But in only one case is Hayne's speech one in which he presents the case for states' rights, and which expresses his fear of "*the consolidation of government.*"[60] The same book contains Webster's reply. Interestingly enough, when Hayne's and Webster's speeches appear side by side in other books, they are not discussing constitutional theory but the contributions of the various sections to the American Revolution. But Webster's speeches, especially the one that ends "Liberty and Union, now and forever, one and inseparable," appear a great many times with no counteragent.

The major general political concept of these books is that of the vague and undefined liberty mentioned above. It is extolled innumerable times in every book. The whole of history is seen as a Hegelian process for the realization of the idea of freedom. Reverses may hinder its progress, but "the cause of human nature,

---

57 R 1835 Porter, p. 218; R 1853 Mandeville, p. 119.
58 R 1835 Webster, p. 160.
59 R 1852 Sweet, pp. 162–163.
60 R 1831 Harrod, pp. 243, 251–267.

and of God must triumph."[61] Having been achieved in the American Revolution, it becomes a relatively static thing. Liberty is what the Americans institutionalized during and just after the Revolution; the United States and liberty are identified in an almost mystical way. "It is here that freedom has found an asylum, and here it will probably reside, as long as virtue shall be the ruling principle of the nation."[62] The superiority and the freedom enshrined in the American government are recognized not only by its own citizens. "The government of the United States is acknowledged by the wise and good of other nations to be the most free, impartial and righteous government of the world."[63] Liberty must be extended not by changing the American government but by spreading our influence abroad. The progress of liberty in the future is to be horizontal rather than vertical. Its nature will never change here, but it is the mission of America to extend its doctrine to the world. "The liberty of this country is a sacred depository—a vestal fire, which Providence has committed to us for the general benefit of mankind."[64]

The method to be used in fulfilling this mission is unclear except on this continent. Here our manifest destiny to spread to the West is manifest largely because it will accomplish this duty in what the Americans preferred to think of as uninhabited land. That we should conquer Europe and the rest of the world for this purpose is not expected, although the mission idea is so firmly embedded that one almost looks for the idea of conquest in the schoolbooks. Washington's Farewell Address as well as other selections are used to prove that we should stay apart from Europe in order to preserve what we have here from the dangers of overextension and contamination. In the early books liberty is not to be extended by conquest, but our example is to inspire others. Our perfect model has already produced results in the rest of the world, and it will inevitably continue to do so. America "hath established her own independence, and the flame of her liberty has spread

[61] R 1844 Goldsbury and Russell, p. 286; see also R 1811 Chandler, p. 125; R 1828 Hopkins, p. 150; H 1833 C. Goodrich, p. 35; S 1844 Clagett, p. 14; R 1845 Goldsbury and Russell, pp. 144–145, S 1851 Northend, p. 46.

[62] G 1796 Dwight, p. 142; S 1799 Fenning, p. 164; see also R 1796 Bingham, p. 158.

[63] H 1868 Willard, p. 15.

[64] R 1852 Gilder, p. 249; R 1866 Sargent-4, p. 259.

itself to the remotest parts of the earth; the effect of which great example has not yet spread its force, but must continue to operate throughout ages, and form a grand ingredient in the active fermentation in the history of nations."[65] One author rejoices that the sound of the liberty bell, proclaiming our independence, "crossed the Atlantic, pierced the dungeons of Europe, the work-shops of England, the vassal fields of France. That sound spoke to the slave, bade him look from his toil, and know himself a man."[66] Every book contains some such panegyric. Americans have a great trust; they are stewards to God for the concept of liberty. They must be thoroughly aware of this responsibility and ready to guard it at all times, because "The good and wise of every land look to your country to move, before the nations, as did the pillar of fire before the Israelites, to lead the way to liberty and happiness. It rests with you to realize, or disappoint their hopes."[67]

Only eternal vigilance against unidentified enemies will preserve freedom and allow its extension. Bryant is quoted several times to the effect that liberty is not a gentle young girl but a fierce old man, armed and battle-scarred.[68] That this duty of ours is a critical one for the rest of the world is forcefully expressed: "We stand under a fearful responsibility to our Creator and our fellow creatures. It has been His divine pleasure that we should be sent forth as the harbingers of free government on the earth, and in this attitude we are now before the world. The eyes of the world are upon us; and our example will probably be decisive of the cause of human liberty."[69]

Is America to act only as an example to the rest of the world,

[65] A 1790 Sterry and Sterry, preface; see also R 1797 Thomas, p. 173; R 1826 American-S, p. 124; R 1827 Pierpont, p. 257–260; R 1828 Greenwood and Emerson, pp. 198–200; R 1828 Putnam-S, pp. 126–130; R 1835 Porter, pp. 284–286; R 1836 Cobb-N.A., p. 83; R 1852 Gilder, pp. 127–129; R 1858 McGuffey, pp. 116–117.

[66] R 1853 Mandeville, p. 118.

[67] G 1826 E. Willard, p. 109; see also R 1790 Webster, p. 167; R 1832 Edwards, p. 99.

[68] R 1871 Sargent and May-5, p. 66; R 1884 Monroe, p. 323; R 1898 Arnold and Gilbert, pp. 27–29.

[69] R 1831 Harrod, p. 153; see also R 1844 Goldsbury and Russell, pp. 261–262, 324; R 1845 Swan, pp. 285–286.

or is it to take a more active part in the extension of liberty? Some say that Americans are "votaries of freedom, as friends to the rights of man, and bound to support them wherever invaded." But the word "support" is of limited meaning here; the same book also contains a piece in which it is clear that only moral support is intended: "On whatever part of God's creation a human form pines under chains, there Americans drop their tears."[70] Others believe the spirit of liberty goes forth from America "Like an emanation from heaven."[71] Most of the pre-Civil War books, then, expect our example to be sufficient for the extension of our political system: "May we be guided by our forefathers to make Columbia, the bright example for all the struggling sons of liberty around the Globe!"[72] The task of our citizens is to guard and preserve our system against "the vices and luxuries of the old world." "If we sink into luxury, vice, or moral apathy, our brightness will be lost, our prosperity deprived of its vital element."[73] Only one book before the Civil War mentions the possibility of active support: "May this country be found fighting in the vanguard for the liberties of men. God himself hath summoned her to the contest and she may not shrink back."[74]

The spread of American political influence by means other than its own radiance is broached late in the century by many books. National power as well as national virtue becomes an aim worthy of a moral nation. Maury's Geography in 1881, in discussing Asia, introduces this new note: "Men are respected according to their virtues, but a nation is regarded with respect by her fellows and treated with consideration, according to her physical strength and the prowess of her sons."[75] Imperialism, hitherto seen largely through the issues of the American Revolution as ruthless strength taking advantage of innocent weakness, now appears in a rather different light. As early as 1869 the white man's burden appears, in this case assigned specifically to "the Germanic Aryans"; "It is clearly their mission to bring the

[70] R 1797 Thomas, pp. 176, 205.

[71] R 1844 Smith, p. 225; see also R 1831 Bailey, pp. 210–213; R 1845 Swan, pp. 340–341; R 1856 Hillard-1, p. 504–508.

[72] R 1854 Mandeville, p. 187; see also R 1830 Emerson, pp. 130–131.

[73] The last two sentences are from the following in that order: R 1858 Hillard-1, p. 506; R 1844 Goldsbury and Russell, p. 262.

[74] R 1826 American-S, p. 259. [75] G 1881 Maury, p. 127.

blessings of their culture to the indolent or barbarian nations of the passive races . . ."[76] The racial argument for expansion has a new ring only in that it is concerned with overseas expansion; to American ears it must have had familiar overtones because it sounds so similar to American explanations of their dealings with Indian and Negro. Even Chambers, the Southern historian, now talks of colonies from the point of view of the mother country rather than the colonists.[77] It is felt generally that the extension of American power cannot help but be a liberating force. Poems and essays on the American flag seem especially prone to view it as "the luminous symbol of resistless and beneficent power."[78] Unfortunately this study stops at the time when American expansion abroad was just beginning, and the accounts of activity in the Philippines sound rather like news dispatches. Several books mention Philippine insurgence against American troops after the Spanish-American War. One observes that our country lost more soldiers in this war than in the war against Spain, but concludes that the United States then gave them so fine a government that they were finally satisfied.[79] But apart from the general change in attitude toward imperialism, this account can come to no conclusions about specific areas of American expansion.

By whatever method, the spread of American influence throughout the world is inevitable. Its ultimate results are painted in transcendent terms: "The grand political millennium is at hand; when tyranny shall be buried in ruins; when all nations shall be united in one mighty republic, when the four angels, that stand on the four corners of the globe, shall with one accord, lift up their voices to heaven, proclaiming peace on earth, and good will to men!"[80] Thus the millennium of peace and freedom is to come to the world as an emanation from the United States. America has been chosen by God as his agent in this great work. The duty of the American citizen as his part in the fulfillment of this cosmic plan is to protect liberty as it exists in the United States—to protect the *status quo*.

[76] G 1869 Warren-E, p. 93; see also G 1892 Maury, p. 16; G 1894 Frye, pp. 59–60.

[77] H 1889 Chambers, p. 164.

[78] R 1898 Arnold and Gilbert, p. 228; see also R 1871 Hillard, pp. 169–173.

[79] H 1899 Morris, p. 246.

[80] R 1797 Thomas, p. 177, et al.

Chapter 11

SOCIAL REFORM MOVEMENTS

The nineteenth century was one of great social ferment in the Western world, and not least in the United States. Old issues were reviewed in the light of new nineteenth-century conditions. Problems of the industrial revolution were challenged by theories as diverse as Transcendentalism and collective bargaining. Public schools, women's rights, the abolition of slavery, perpetual peace, temperance, labor laws, and laws to control big business were all being discussed as possible improvements in society. All were represented by organizations designed to promote legislation for the cause, and the public school was already in the process of establishment.

The treatment of reform movements in schoolbooks involves the problem of schoolbook sensitivity to contemporary social issues. Contemporary writers were well represented in the literary anthologies for schools, but with few exceptions the child was not encouraged to notice that his society was divided by social issues. Thomas Wentworth Higginson, himself a reformer, and the professional historian McMaster discuss reforms in their schoolbooks, but these two are exceptional. Venable in his 1872 History sees a tendency since the Civil War to "revolutionize and reconstruct institutions and to make the new republic, nobler, grander and purer than the old." But he concludes: "The best people in the country . . . [are] acting upon the conviction that a nation is bettered only by bettering her individual citizens, and that public welfare depends upon the wise regulation of private life."[1] Webster's 1835 Reader expresses the typical attitude toward reform when he says: "He who has so little knowledge of human nature, as to seek happiness by changing anything but his own

[1] H 1872 Venable, p. 246.

disposition, will waste his life in fruitless efforts, and multiply griefs which he purposes to remove."[2]

The process by which a book written for schools achieved wide use might well inhibit an author from describing social cleavages or expressing approval of social reform movements. To find an audience the schoolbooks had to be adopted by district boards usually made up of men successfully established in the community and unlikely to be pleased at the prospect of social upheaval. To assure wide adoption the author would do well to avoid current controversy or to take the conservative position when the issue could not be evaded. Nineteenth-century schoolbooks were designed to train the child's character rather than his powers of critical thought. As we have seen, they were not expected to be neutral. Their authors freely express fervent faith in religion, patriotism, honesty, and hard work as well as in temperance and public schools, opinions hardly disturbing to the body politic and bound to be well received in the country as a whole. But problems and reform movements that might lead to social change in their society are to be avoided if possible. As we have seen, socialism, anarchism, Populism, and the labor movement in its various nineteenth-century phases were either completely ignored or regarded as alien to the American tradition, and the abolition of slavery was discussed freely only before it became a matter of immediate action or after it was an accomplished fact. America was glorified as the missionary of political liberty and economic opportunity for the world, but it was evidently not the apostle of social change.

THE STATUS OF WOMEN

Although individual women of prominence such as Margaret Fuller and Frances Wright had been agitating for an improvement in the status of women since early in the century, and a full-fledged movement advocating equal rights for women appeared in mid-century, the idea of equality of the sexes in law or in economic and social opportunity is invisible in nineteenth-century American schoolbooks. Only one book, and that not a popular

[2] R 1835 Webster, p. 45; see also R 1806 Murray, p. 13.

one, brings up the subject of woman suffrage, and this 1890 History expects some knowledge on the part of the student in answer to such questions as: "What is meant by Woman Suffrage? Name prominent persons in favor of the movement. Name others who oppose it. State your own ideas on the subject." [3] That women worked outside the home would be evident to the child from 1875 on, because most of the Geographies include a picture of a New England cotton mill run by women operatives. But such a change in status is neither mentioned nor reflected in the texts accompanying the pictures. It should be said immediately that schoolbooks, except those few specifically designed for female education, are addressed to boys. In the minds of most schoolbook authors "the child" is male; it is he who is enjoined to work hard and follow the example of great men. This view of their audiences as male was probably characteristic of all authors of serious literature as well. By the ways in which women appear in the texts one can see how the child was expected to regard them; one can conjecture how, with this background, he might react to the demand for women's rights.

The importance of women in society is unquestioned. Woodbridge's Geography, a very popular one and one copied wholesale by others, uses the status of women as an indication of the degree of a country's civilization. Pagans treat women as domestic animals; in the next stage of civilization, the "half-civilized," women are bought and sold but are given a little domestic education; in the stage known as "civilized," "The *Christian religion* only, declared females to be immortal beings—recognizes their equality with men—and vindicates their claims to respect." [4] The equality he describes here is a statement of what he sees as the *status quo* in the United States of 1824, and has little to do with political and legal rights. In certain countries the status of women is perfectly satisfactory and nothing more remains to be done: "*England*, *Scotland* and *the United States* appear to be the only countries in which attention is generally paid to the intellectual improvement of females; and the general standard of purity in morals and manners, is more elevated than in any other

[3] H 1890 Eaton and Foster, p. 57.

[4] G 1824 Woodbridge and Willard, p. 212; see also G 1836 Smith, p. 85; G 1843 Mitchell, p. 45.

nations."[5] According to Woodbridge—and his attitude is a typical one—women are already equal to men in the United States, and no improvement is necessary.

The ideal woman of nineteenth-century American schoolbooks has no interests or ambitions of her own. Her every desire, her every action is bent to serve her husband and children. She is a model of self-abnegation; her only role in life, her only fulfillment comes in helping the male fulfill his ambition. She has no choice in determining policy, state or familial, nor does she want any. She is modest, meek, and silent. Women, like violets, are

> Born to dignify retreat,
> Unknown to flourish, and unseen be great.[6]

She spends her life in happy submission to the will of others. Absolute obedience of wife to husband is sanctified by God: "Nor does the truly feminine mind desire to exceed this limitation of Heaven."[7] In the early books this sentiment appears often from the pen of Milton in a speech Eve makes to Adam:

> My author and disposer, who though bidst
> Unargued I obey; so God ordains;
> God is thy law, thou mine, to know no more
> Is woman's happiest knowledge, and her praise.[8]

Before marriage she owes obedience to her father even if he treats her cruelly; the latter case "By no means releases me from my duty to him; had he a thousand errors, he is still my father."[9] There are many examples of girls who refuse to marry someone they love because it is their duty to care for their parents; boys never face this choice. Thus in schoolbooks throughout the century women exist only by and through others. Their wills are submerged in those of father or husband.

Chastity is, of course, an absolute necessity for unmarried women, and in books published before the Civil War it is fre-

[5] G 1824 Woodbridge and Willard, p. 212.

[6] R 1787 Miscellanies, p. 25; see also R 1831 Bailey, p. 83; R 1831 Harrod, pp. 51–52; R 1873 Progressive, p. 103; R 1876 Young, pp. 89–92.

[7] R 1831 Bailey, p. 283.

[8] R 1802 Alden, p. 140; R 1803 Murray, p. 191; R 1811 I. Cooke, p. 367; see also S 1810 Webster, p. 82.

[9] R 1799 New Pleasing, p. 125; see also R 1801 Heaton-P, pp. 33–36.

quently discussed.[10] Such lessons are directed only at girls, never at boys, although Webster notes: "Misconduct of daughters is more fatal to family peace, though perhaps not more heinous in a moral view."[11] Although women "are by nature weak and defenseless," they are also "guardians of purity."[12] In later books, perhaps for modesty's sake, chastity is not discussed as such. But fallen women, usually lured by liquor to sin, appear now and then. One piece on this subject, called "Beautiful Snow," by Watson, seems to anticipate with pleasure the coming of the cold evening when the particular Magdalen of this selection is fated to freeze to death.[13] Another writer, perhaps overcome by his fine choice of homonyms, violates all moral canons of schoolbooks by allowing this practice sentence in his Speller: "A snake chased the chaste girl,"[14] a sentence Freud would have particularly enjoyed.

Restrictions on female behavior are carefully delineated, and they begin in childhood. Because public speaking is "highly improper" for her, the girl is not to be trained in oratory, the most popular subject in her brother's curriculum. She is cautioned: "Be good, sweet maid, and let who will be clever."[15] Small girls should not engage in their brothers' activities. Even a little girl who wants to help her brother build a cart is restrained because it is not "a proper employment for a young lady."[16]

In the later nineteenth century there is some disagreement as to how much outdoor exercise a girl should have. The typical attitude is: "Kate is a good girl. She will not speak in a loud tone when her aunt is ill. Nor will she leap, and run, and act like a boy," and "A girl fell from a swing . . . A swing is not a safe thing for a little girl."[17] A Confederate Reader observes that

[10] For example: R 1801 Heaton-P, p. 209; R 1823 Blake, pp. 82–83; S 1857 Parker and Watson, pp. 76, 113, 164.

[11] R 1789 Webster, p. 66; see also R 1797 Thomas, p. 35; R 1811 Chandler, p. 59; S 1835 Cobb, pp. 164–165.

[12] R 1813 Richardson, pp. 20–23; see also S 1819 Alden, p. 140.

[13] R 1872 Osgood-5, pp. 305–307; see also R 1869 Wilson, pp. 51–53.

[14] S 1866 Watson, pp. 49–50.

[15] Kingsley poem in R 1897 Baldwin-3, p. 166. The quotation in the previous sentence is from R 1799 New Pleasing, preface.

[16] R 1803 Biglow, p. 71.

[17] The quotations in this sentence are from the following in that order: R 1866 Soule and Wheeler, p. 32; R 1871 Sargent and May-1, p. 26.

boys have most of their exercise out of doors, while "Girls have most of theirs in the house or some sort of cover." But this author suggests getting the girls out of the house for part of their play.[18] An 1883 Reader indicates what happens to boys' activities when girls infiltrate them. In a particular school the girls belong to a tatting club and the boys to a woodchuck-hunting society. At first the boys refuse when the girls ask for admission to the woodchuck club. After the girls promise to wear veils to avoid freckles and to learn woodchuck lore, the boys allow them to join, but the girls find it impossible to face killing the woodchuck at the end of the hunt. In the end the girls disband the woodchuck society and turn it into a picnic club.[19] Thus a symbolic emasculation awaits boys who admit girls into their activities. Contrasting attitudes toward athletic activities for girls appear in an unusual piece in an 1866 Reader. An aunt complains to her niece's teacher that the girl is becoming vulgarly robust because of school activities: "She was as pale and delicate a child as I would wish to see," but now she has "lost that graceful stoop," and has gotten tan. "Who wishes to see such a rude state of health as hers? It may do for a washerwoman, but not for Ruth Penway." Furthermore, she now uses a shovel and goes on skates, "moving at most unbecoming speed over the ice . . . like a boy." In reply the teacher defends such activities on grounds of health; she assures the aunt that the girl will never play football, but only because feminine dress forbids it.[20] This tale is unique in the schoolbooks because the author's sympathies are clearly with the sentiments of the teacher, and his ridicule is reserved for the foolish prejudices of the aunt. In this dialogue the aunt's strictures against athletic activities for girls are derived from class feeling, and they probably realistically reflect class differences in girls' activities. A poor girl needs to be active and healthy; only the girl backed by some means can afford to be pale and wan and grow up to be an item of conspicuous leisure desirable to a wealthy husband.

In the early books women are strictly enjoined from direct public influence. In public, female modesty demands that the woman reflect the thought of others rather than expressing her own: "She giveth not her opinion unasked, nor stoppeth her ears

[18] R 1864 Moore, p. 46. [19] R 1883 Swinton-4, pp. 33–46.
[20] R 1866 Sargent-3, pp. 60–64.

to that of another."[21] There is no encouragement here for the female reformer: "But what can be more disgusting than to see innocent, and timid females, whose excellence in part, consists in their modesty, and silence before superiours, encouraged to reverse the order of nature, by playing the orator on a public stage!"[22] In private conversation modesty and decorum "both forbid a young woman to lead the conversation." And frustration for the woman with something to say is further refined: "Girls should be taught to give up their opinions betimes, and not pertinaciously to carry on a dispute, even should they know themselves to be in the right."[23] The ideal female is most easily described in negative terms: "Her voice is gentle; her pronunciation is delicate; her passions are never suffered to be boisterous; she never talks politics; she never foams with anger; she is seldom seen in any *masculine* amusements; she does not practice archery. . . . I will venture to prophesy that she will never canvas for votes at an election."[24] Late nineteenth-century books adopt much the same attitudes, although they do not spell out the restrictions so minutely.

In spite of all this the influence of the woman is said to be vast; it radiates from her home through her influence on her husband and male children. She renders better service to her country in this position than by becoming a direct participant in political processes: "It is in the inculcation of high and pure morals . . . that in a free republic woman performs her sacred duty; and fulfils her destiny."

Her effect
Lies not in voting, warring, clerical oil,
But germinating grace, forth-putting virtue.[25]

A poem, "The Future of Women," in an 1871 Reader suggests that the lack of women's achievements in the world in the past indicate her proper future:

[21] S 1798 Child, p. 100; see also R 1799 New Pleasing, p. 26.

[22] R 1807 Bingham-C, pp. 193–194.

[23] R 1804 Peirce, p. 67. Quotation in previous sentence is from R 1787 Miscellanies, p. 189.

[24] R 1797 Alexander, pp. 25–26.

[25] R 1850 Hall, p. 352. Quotation in previous sentence is from R 1856 Hillard, p. 485; see also R 1866 Sargent-4, pp. 178–180.

What highest prize hath woman won
In science or in art?
What mightiest work by women done
Boasts city, field, or mart?
"She hath no Raphael," Painting saith;
"No Newton," Learning cries;
"Show us her steamship, her Macbeth,
Her thought-won victories!"

She has made no mark in these fields, nor has she striven for wealth or power, but instead she has been able "to make of earth a heaven."[26] "Within the circle of her own family and dependents lies her sphere of action."[27] And she can console herself by realizing that moral rectitude is greater than mental achievements. Few authors state flatly that the mind of woman is not constructed for large questions: "It has less breadth, large-mindedness, connection of ideas" than a man's, although it has more "delicacy of perception, more quickness of apprehension."[28] But the mental inferiority of women is clearly implied in most schoolbooks even when not so stated.

The ideal wife is more mother than mate to her husband. She is cautioned: "The end of thy being is to soothe him with tenderness and to recompense his care with soft endearments." Her influence will "refine, civilize, tame and humanize" the male. In misfortune she is a rock. According to Washington Irving, a woman "'who is the mere dependent and ornament of a man in his happier hours' is his stay and solace in disaster."[29]

Interestingly enough it is only in the late nineteenth century that the cult of motherhood begins. In the early books, respecting and obeying one's parents is a duty that one performs without question as part of one's obedience to the authority of God. George Washington, who gave up his desire to go to sea because his mother did not want him to, is frequently used as an example of proper behavior to a parent. In the later books fathers as such are less frequently mentioned, but mothers appear in saccharine tales *ad nauseam*.

[26] R 1871 Sargent and May-5, p. 255, poem by Elliot.

[27] R 1876 Young, p. 177. [28] R 1876 Young, p. 71.

[29] The three quotations in this paragraph are from the following in that order: S 1824 Bentley, p. 162; R 1876 Young, pp. 120–132; R 1872 Osgood-4, pp. 128–131.

Part of this is unquestionably an aspect of the general nostalgia for a simpler past so widespread in the late nineteenth century. "Mother, Home, and Heaven . . . are three of the most beautiful words in the English language."[30] There are hundreds of poems, essays, and stories in which the author revels in a tearful backward glance at his dear old mother, who loved him better than anyone else ever will. Several pieces, one by Mrs. Sigourney and another by Dr. Brownson, depict an adult standing at his mother's grave bitterly regretting that he had not helped her graciously enough when she was on her deathbed.[31] Here the injunction is to love and help one's mother not as a duty, but for one's own future happiness. A popular piece in the 1880's and 1890's entitled "Somebody's Mother" shows a boy explaining to his friends after he has assisted an old lady across the street that although she is aged, poor, and slow, she is "somebody's mother."[32] She is not helped across the street because she needs assistance but because she might be a mother. Her need is less important than her status.

Most of the texts believe that girls should have some education, but all agree that their schooling must be of a special kind suited to women's functions. Schoolbooks do not usually claim that women are the intellectual inferiors of men, although they recognize this as a popular opinion: "It is considered by many, by far too many, that woman is often of an inferior order of intellect, of minor capacity, in short, literally, the 'weaker sex,' in other senses than a physical one." But the same author insists that the political influence of women should not extend to a personal encounter with the ballot box, but should be confined to purifying the morals of those who have the suffrage.[33] Women's lives must be contained in the home, not so much because they are inadequate to the world outside but rather because they perform a social function which must be filled. This is reminiscent of one of the Southern pro-slavery arguments: Negroes may or may not be inferior, but if they were free there would be no one to

[30] R 1872 Osgood-5, p. 262.

[31] R 1866 McGuffey-4, pp. 239–241; R 1872 Osgood-4, pp. 218–222; R 1873 American, pp. 143–145; R 1873 Progressive, pp. 118–120; R 1876 Young, pp. 181–184; R 1879 McGuffey, pp. 253–255.

[32] R 1881 Willson, pp. 346–348; R 1890 Davis, p. 161; R 1899 Holmes and Hill, pp. 234–236.

[33] R 1836 Cobb-N.A., p. 103, 28.

16. "Somebody's Mother"

In Davis' 1890 Reader the old lady is helped across the street not because she is feeble but because she might be somebody's mother. Motherhood became a cult in the late nineteenth century.

fulfill the functions of their station in life. Because women inhabit a realm different from that of men, their education must also be different. They should know the rudiments of reading, writing, and ciphering, but above all they must be educated in household economy. Women of a higher station may also learn music, literature, and embroidery.[34] A poem by Hannah More refutes the idea that an educated woman is a slattern in her housekeeping or loose in her morals; on the contrary education improves her in both respects. In the past this has not always been so (as in Greece):

> But in our chaste times 'tis no offense,
> When female virtue joins with female sense.

The poem ends, however, on the note that for women virtue is more important than wit.[35] Hannah More is also quoted in several other books to the effect that management of a family should be a much more important part of a girl's education than any other subject. Religion is also the special province of women because it guards and develops "your supreme delicacy, your modesty."[36] The virtues that came to dominate nineteenth-century Christianity were those virtues stressed above as belonging peculiarly to women: gentleness, love, and mercy. The mind of the female, then, is to be filled with three subjects: home, duty to the family, and religion.

Higher learning for women is usually derided. "The modest virgin, the prudent wife, or the careful matron, are much more serviceable in life than petticoated philosophers, blustering heroines, or *virago* queens."[37] Most of the schoolbooks would agree that higher education is not proper to woman's sphere and subverts her proper fulfillment of her very necessary functions in society: "When a woman quits her own department, she offends her husband, not merely because she obtrudes herself upon *his* business, but because she departs from that sphere which is assigned to her in the order of society, because she neglects *her* duty and leaves *her own* department vacant. . . . The same rule which excludes a man from an attention to domestic business,

[34] R 1799 New Pleasing, pp. 9–22, 185; R 1796 Bingham, pp. 104–105.

[35] R 1813 I. Cooke, pp. 380–382; R 1831 Smiley, pp. 78–79; R 1851 Swan-L, pp. 97–99.

[36] R 1814 Alden, p. 52; see also S 1823 Picket, p. 193.

[37] R 1801 Heaton-P, pp. 164–170; see also R 1797 Alexander, pp. 137–139.

excludes a woman from law, mathematics and astronomy." Webster further suggests that she "leave the masculine virtues, and the profound researches of study to the province of the other sex."[38] A learned woman is threatened with being found unattractive to the other sex.[39] Peirce, quoting Hannah More, goes further than this in saying: "That the female mind, in general, does not appear capable of attaining so high a degree of perfection in science as the male. . . . Nature, propriety and custom have prescribed certain bounds to each; bounds which the prudent and the candid will never attempt to break down."[40] Tower in 1852 includes an amusing satire on a "Learned Lady" who becomes so excited about her own learning and the rights of women that she shuts herself in a garret and does nothing but meditate on those subjects while her father keeps house. When he dies and she is forced to earn her own living she attempts to do so by producing a book entitled "The Lady's Instructor, or the Whole Art of Becoming Learned Made Easy."[41] Perhaps this is a way to deal with one branch of competition in Tower's own field. One of the few exceptions to this opposition to higher learning for women occurs in a note to the teacher in an 1881 Geography written by a woman. She calls attention to the new emphasis given the higher education of women in the United States as "one of the striking evidences of the advancement of the United States" and suggests that the teacher "contrast this state of affairs with the inferior position that women occupy in some of the countries of the Old World."[42]

Some women are exalted to heroic stature. They achieve distinction either because they died for love or because they performed great deeds to help husband, parents, or children. A few are nationalist heroines. It is interesting to note that the less important Mary Stuart is treated much more sympathetically than Queen Elizabeth of England, who, though a good queen,

[38] R 1790 Webster, p. 231.

[39] R 1790 Webster, p. 231; R 1815 Dickinson, p. 84; R 1828 American-R, p. 84; R 1852 Tower and Walker, p. 143.

[40] R 1804 Peirce, pp. 10–11; see also R 1815 Dickinson, pp. 84–85; R 1831 Lowe-Second, p. 191; R 1835 Merriam, p. 127; R 1876 Young, p. 71.

[41] R 1852 Tower and Walker, pp. 137–147.

[42] G 1891 Morton, p. xviii–xix; see also H 1868 Willard, p. 303; H 1881 Thalheimer, pp. 362–363.

had none of the qualities of gentleness enjoyed by her cousin; she was less womanly.[43] Both appear frequently, and always in this relationship. There are several heroines of American nationalism. One woman aids in burning her own home to help the American cause in the Revolution; another makes spoons into bullets for the American army in that war.[44] Several are frontier women braving Indian attacks. Webster includes the story of the brave wife of a British army officer during the American Revolution, who crosses the American lines to nurse her wounded husband.[45] To grant heroic status to a citizen of an enemy country during a war with the United States is unique in these schoolbooks. But it is a primary example of the kind of heroism suitable for women.

Only a few suggest any improvement in the lot of American women. As we have seen, some applaud the institution of higher learning for women. Another, a Quaker, remarks that some Quaker women are allowed to preach in accordance with the practices of the early Christian Church. Another suggests that the widow's third may be unfair apportionment, since her labor may have been used to build up the whole estate.[46] These are the only favorable comments on improving the position of women in America.

American women are believed to have certain distinguishing characteristics: they are superior to all others in virtue. They are healthy, pure, domestically inclined, modest, and they use no artificial aids to beauty. A book of English origin would include English as well as American women in this superior rank: "Of all the women in the world, none are so remarkable for propriety of behavior as the American and English women."[47] American women exactly fulfill the ideal woman portrayed in these books. The model seems to be taken neither from an urban environment nor from the large Southern plantation as portrayed here. Washington's mother is suggested as a paragon of womanhood,

[43] For example, compare R 1854 Sargent, pp. 145–146 with pp. 244–245.

[44] R 1830 Practical-R, p. 167; R 1828 Pierpont-I, pp. 75–76; see also H 1869 Quackenbos, pp. 121, 123, 128–129; H 1896 Murphy, pp. 80–81.

[45] R 1804 Webster, pp. 43–46; R 1835 Webster, pp. 67–69.

[46] R 1806 Cooledge (Quaker), p. 178; R 1828 Willard-G, p. 105.

[47] S 1836 Brandreth, p. 157.

and she is especially praised for her industry and her devotion to her son.

Throughout the century women are regarded as inferior beings whose good lies only in complete dependence in thought, word, and deed on men. Webster, in an address to women in his 1790 Reader, summarizes the position nicely: "That it may be necessary for political purposes, to consider man as the superior in authority is to me probable—I question whether a different maxim would not destroy your own happiness."[48] To preserve the social order women are to look for guidance to men, just as the poor must look to the rich, the child to the parent, the Negro to the white. The child who used these books would assume that women were a breed apart, happy in servility, important for instinct rather than intelligence. An extension of women's rights would not seem to him a desirable part of the American future. Indeed it might be subversive of the social order and of the happiness of women as well as men. Women had already achieved all that was necessary for their contentment.

THE PUBLIC SCHOOL MOVEMENT

The public school movement in the United States is strongly supported, and indeed applauded, in all schoolbooks. The many discussions of this issue in pre-Civil War books reflect most of the arguments used by proponents of public schools at the time. In books published after the Civil War the issue as an issue is moribund because the basic reform had been achieved. The system would be refined and expanded, but the principle of public support for schools was already established. Public schools became another laurel in the American crown, pointed to with pride but not discussed in the later schoolbooks.

In the early books one of the important functions believed to be inherent in a system of universal education is the prevention of crime. Daniel Webster offers support for this contention: "We regard it as a wise and liberal system of police by which property and life and the peace of society are secured."[49] Free education

[48] R 1790 Webster, p. 232.

[49] R 1854 Sargent, pp. 184–185; see also R 1811 Lyman, p. 294; R 1826 Greenwood and Emerson, pp. 263–264; G 1826 Blake, pp. 158–159; R 1843 Cobb, pp. 142–143; R 1845 S. Worcester-2, p. 140.

for the poor will allow those of great talent—such people as Benjamin Franklin—to develop their talents constructively and add them to the national store.[50] One piece used several times assures the upper classes that education will not induce the poor to forget their station: "Nor is it at all more rational to suppose that a judicious education of the poor, conducted to any attainable extent, will be liable to abuse in their hands, and lead them to forget their station and their duty, than it will have similar effects on those who are nourished in the lap of affluence."[51] Public schools will insure rather than upset the social order.

In a republic steadily becoming more democratic, the political welfare of the public depends on an educated electorate. Tyrants use ignorance to dupe the people, and they live in fear of the diffusion of knowledge since it "ultimately terminates in their destruction."[52] "But in a government where the people fill all the branches of sovereignty, intelligence is the life of liberty. An American would resent his being denied the use of his musket; but he would deprive himself of a stronger safeguard, if he should want that *learning* which is necessary to a knowledge of his institutions."[53] Because the property qualifications for the suffrage were abolished in most states by 1825, those who could not afford private schooling were now part of the electorate, and the need for public schools was acute. To the writers of these schoolbooks, education is not a question of developing the logical and critical powers of the individual; it is a process of indoctrination in national traditions. Free education is of vital importance not only to educate an electorate to read, but to teach children the social, political, economic, and religious concepts considered desirable for national preservation and progress. Public school education was expected to help in the formation of a distinctive American nationality; in the important work of teaching national ideals, schools are outranked only by mothers.[54] A major function of the

[50] S 1815 Bradley, pp. iii–iv; R 1826 American-S, pp. 254–256; G 1826 Blake, p. 158; R 1827 Pierpont, pp. 160–162; R 1830 Emerson, p. 131; R 1836 Cobb-N.A., pp. 107–110; R 1849 Leavitt, p. 74.

[51] R 1826 American-S, pp. 254–256; R 1827 Pierpont, pp. 160–162; R 1836 Cobb-N.A., pp. 107–110.

[52] A 1817 Preston, p vi; see also R 1796 Bingham, p. 107; R 1828 American-R, pp. 14–15; R 1839 Sigourney, pp. 66–67.

[53] R 1796 Bingham, p. 107; R 1836 Cobb-N.A., pp. 126–127.

[54] R 1836 Cobb-N.A., p. 24.

teacher is to produce "an acquaintance with their country and an attachment to its interests."[55] One cannot start this process too soon: "Begin with the infant in his cradle. Let the first word he lisps be WASHINGTON."[56] The safety of the nation depends particularly on the teaching of patriotism and nationalism to all American children.

In the Geographies one of the major standards used to assess the degree of civilization of a nation is the state of learning achieved by the masses of the people. As we have seen, higher learning is for an elite and is not essential to the national welfare, whereas common literacy is vital. Many Geographies repeat almost the same phrase on the subject of education for every country other than the United States, though this leaves them with so little room that they can say almost nothing else about the country. For example, the sentence "The state of learning is very low" appears in the same book in descriptions of Spain, Portugal, and Italy; in Hungary, "The state of learning is low"; in Norway and Russia, "The state of learning and civilization is low"; in Sicily, "Learning and civilization are in a low state."[57] All conclude that although in some European countries the upper classes are well educated, "The lower classes are generally ignorant, superstitious and degraded."[58]

The United States, on the other hand, is the land of the common man in education. Almost every book throughout the century makes some such statement as the following: "In no part of the world is education more generally diffused than in the United States. . . . The enlightened policy of most of the states brings the means of knowledge to every man's door, and renders it as cheap as possible."[59] Our growing system of public schools is just another example of the wide opportunity opened to the poor man in the United States.

[55] G 1818 Morse, p. iv; see also S 1826 Principal, p. 95.

[56] R 1789 Webster, title page; R 1809 Picket, pp. 180–181; S 1824 Bentley, p. 198; R 1843 Totten, pp. 53–54.

[57] G 1813 Nichols, pp. 59, 58, 65, 68, 69, 73.

[58] G 1832 Olney, p. 156; see also G 1828 Woodbridge, p. 104; G 1831 Blake, p. 24; G 1835 Huntington, p. 145; G 1836 Smith, p. 185; G 1843 Mitchell, p. 215; G 1865 Mitchell, p. 64.

[59] G 1826 Blake, p. 164. On higher education see chapter 7, section on "Scholarship."

In contrast to Europe, then, all of the United States is in the forefront of the common school movement; there is, however, a good deal of differentiation in the pre-Civil War Geographies among the various states of the United States. In all books New England is acknowledged as the cradle of the public school movement. Every author speaks with pride of the schools of Massachusetts and Connecticut particularly. Morse sets the tone in 1791 by noting of Connecticut: "In no part of the world is the education of all ranks of people more attended to than in Connecticut."[60] Rhode Island, the pariah of New England in these books, is an exception to the general high level of New England in this respect too: "The bulk of the inhabitants . . . are involved in greater ignorance perhaps than in most other parts of New England. An impartial history of their transactions since the peace, would evince the truth of the above observations."[61] Another author describes the state of education in Rhode Island with scorn: "The body of the people are involved in ignorance, not known in any other part of New England." He further notes that they have recently repealed a public school education law: "And they now can be *legally* ignorant."[62]

Judgments of educational facilities in the Middle states seem to be quite erratic. Pennsylvania is sometimes praised for its attention to education, but with none of the fervor visible in descriptions of New England schools. Here is a typical comment on the schools of Pennsylvania: "Not in a very flourishing state, and many of the labouring people are very ignorant."[63] By mid-century some progress in education is noted in New York, but this is assumed to be the result of the large immigration from New England to that state.[64] One reason offered for the relatively backward condition of the schools in the Middle states is that they ". . . have been subject to a great influx of emigrants from

[60] G 1791 Morse, p. 112; see also G 1800 Smith, p. 150; G 1803 Hubbard, p. 57; G 1807 Parish, p. 56; G 1814 O'Neill, p. 101; G 1816 Rudd, p. 27.

[61] G 1791 Morse, p. 101; see also G 1796 Dwight, p. 155; G 1798 Morse, p. 148; G 1803 Hubbard, p. 54; G 1814 O'Neill, p. 96; G 1816 Rudd, p. 27; G 1818 Morse, p. 138.

[62] G 1807 Parish, pp. 49–50.

[63] G 1803 Hubbard, p. 70; see also G 1791 Morse, p. 82; G 1816 Rudd, p. 31.

[64] G 1843 Mitchell, p. 123.

Europe of the labouring class."[65] In states where the present condition of the schools cannot be praised, a hopeful note is struck, as in this description of the school system of New York: "It is inferior to that of New England, but the desire to acquire knowledge is evidently diffusing."[66] No such optimism mitigates descriptions of the situation in Europe; in the United States it is probably the product more of wishful thinking than of any actual survey. The flat statement of no progress in education is made only in the case of Rhode Island; in other Northern states of the United States, where authors can say nothing flattering, they hope.

In the pre-Civil War schoolbooks the lack of popular education in the South is often used as a basis for criticism of that section. "The higher classes are distinguished for hospitality, and many of them are well educated; but, among the lower classes, education is much neglected."[67] A few authors, usually those most opposed to slavery, are more critical: "The general want of schools, and the gospel ministry, exclude the common people from religious and literary information."[68] But many express the same kind of hope for the future they had for the Middle states; Morse, having commented on the low condition of education in Maryland, concludes: "But the Revolution, among other happy effects, has roused the spirit of education, which is fast spreading its salutary influence over this and the other southern states."[69] Several observe that the population is so spread out as to make the construction of an effective common school system almost impossible. Only one book is concerned with the education of the slave: "The slaves of these states are rarely taught even to read; and in many parts of the country, it is considered dangerous to give them any instruction."[70]

Thus common school education is highly valued in the schoolbooks of the period, and its spread is considered a peculiarly American contribution to world culture. Scholarly specialization

[65] G 1824 Woodbridge and Willard, p. 191.

[66] G 1814 O'Neill, pp. 108–109; see also G 1816 Rudd, p. 29; G 1818 Smith, p. 13.

[67] G 1828 J. Worcester, p. 38.

[68] G 1807 Parish, pp. 83, 95, 97.

[69] G 1791 Morse, p. 164.

[70] G 1824 Woodbridge and Willard, p. 191.

is regarded with scorn, and the lack of professional scholars in the United States is looked on almost as a virtue. The proper aim of education is a diffusion of useful knowledge throughout all ranks of society—an ideal in process of achievement in the United States.

TEMPERANCE

No reform movement is more heartily and universally endorsed than the temperance movement, from the 1820's on. Many practice sentences in each Speller reflect the evils of drink: "If you use that beverage beggary will be your destiny." "Rum will stupify and cause suicide." "Our laws should interdict the sale of rum."[71] Webster's 1880 Speller includes eighteen such sentences. The Readers are full of stories whose melodrama would catch the child's imagination, showing how the drinking habits of one member of the family (almost invariably the father) lead to poverty, ruin, and death for the rest of the family. Every Reader includes at least one such story. When the word "temperance" appears in schoolbooks it is not to be interpreted as moderation in all things; it refers only to the use of alcoholic beverages. Nor does it mean moderation even in this connection, but total abstinence. I have found only one exception to this, in a practice sentence in an 1890 Speller: "Total abstinence from anything in life is not necessary to a man who can trust himself to practice temperance."[72]

Liquor is believed to have almost magical properties: one drink will lead to ruin. A ragged old man has become so because his father gave him a drink to taste, and he became "a sot, and got drunk and beat his nice wife."[73] There are innumerable tales of the disastrous effects of a single drink taken on a social occasion. Inevitably it changes even a successful and contented man into a drunkard in an inevitable progression; he ends up in complete mental, moral, and material ruin.[74] Often fermented juices are

[71] S 1866 Watson, pp. 98, 113, 133. [72] S 1890 Kupfer, p. 128.

[73] R 1864 Moore (Confederate), p. 9; see also R 1866 Sargent-3, p. 30.

[74] R 1812 Daggett, pp. 25–28; R 1835 Porter, pp. 168–170; R 1842 Palmer, p. 59; R 1846 Swan-G, pp. 204–208; R 1843 McGuffey, pp. 204–206; R 1853 Mandeville, p. 51; R 1859 Sargent, pp. 173–174; R 1856 Denman, p. 151; R 1862 Sterling and Campbell (Confederate), p. 66; R 1881 Willson, pp. 186, 188; R 1896 McGuffey-3, pp. 111–113.

referred to as "poison."[75] In one instance this process of decline is begun by a man who "stands treat" while running for political office.[76] One deceives oneself in saying, "When I find that temperate drinking is injuring me, I will give it up!"[77] In schoolbooks there is no such thing as a temperate drinker.

Perhaps the major argument against the use of alcoholic beverages is the waste of time and money resulting in the loss of one's individual fortune and national wealth as well. This is usually delineated by heart-rending tales of the ruin of the drinker and his family. That laborers work better when plied with liquor is vociferously denied. In fact, the poor should be even more careful to shun liquor than the rich, because they have less margin between themselves and the poverty that inevitably follows drink.[78] Another argument, also profusely illustrated, holds that liquor endangers the soul by weakening the man and making him less able to resist temptations to crime. One text cautions the reader to consider "the unutterable pangs in a future state, to the soul! The sword has slain its millions, yet, awful reflection, strong drink more!"[79] Apart from the danger to the soul, the body is prepared for an early grave by drinking: "He came to his bier through too much beer."[80] Drinking is a national disaster because it is a major cause of poverty as well as crime: "Three fourths of the poverty and crime that lead to the alms-house and the penitentiary, spring from this fruitful source."[81] McGuffey contemplates a future in which total abstinence prevails: "Poverty shall pass away from the land."[82] Another proves the ruinous properties of rum by remarking that it was one of our chief weapons against the Indians.[83]

[75] S 1880 Webster, p. 77; R 1890 Davis, pp. 255–258.

[76] R 1845 D. Adams, pp. 46–54.

[77] R 1872 Willson, p. 91.

[78] R 1803 D. Adams, pp. 138–141; R 1827 Pierpont, pp. 27–29; R 1828 American-R, pp. 102–107; R 1881 Willson, pp. 25–27.

[79] S 1822? New York, p. 159; see also S 1878 Worcester, p. 51; R 1881 Willson, p. 25; R 1829 Selection, p. 188; R 1839 Sigourney, pp. 74–78; S 1880 Webster, pp. 92, 120.

[80] S 1900 Bowen, p. 29.

[81] R 1835 Merriam, pp. 84–85; G 1837 Book of Commerce, p. 37.

[82] R 1866 McGuffey-5, p. 197; see also S 1878 Worcester, p. 51; S 1880 Webster, p. 40; R 1881 Willson, p. 188; R 1884 Campbell-4, p. 266.

[83] R 1811 Hubbard, pp. 180–181.

17. "The Drunkard".

Such is the inevitable future of many who indulge in a single social drink. This print is from Osgood's fourth reader, 1872.

As He deals with other vices, so God punishes drunkenness often in the form of a seeming accident. One wine-drinker tosses his empty cup out of the window, killing his son who happened to be passing below. Another is so full of alcohol that he explodes when attempting to light his pipe.[84] And a poem by J. G. Saxe, "The Cold Water Man," tells of a drunken fisherman pulled into the water by a duck on his line:

> And he who will not "sign the pledge";
> And keep his promise fast,
> May be, in spite of fate, a stark
> Cold-water man at last![85]

In the earlier books the substitution of wine for hard liquor is sometimes suggested. But one of the Readers making this suggestion in one selection rejects it in another, and it finally identifies the effects of wine with those of liquor.[86] In later books no distinction is made between the effects of the two: "Champagne will inflame, abase and deprave the sedate man." In another case a general, drinking a toast in water, explains that he was one of a class of seventeen boys; "the other sixteen fill drunkards' graves, all through the pernicious habit of wine-drinking."[87]

Many extol the virtues of cold water as a gift of God. One such essay, by the temperance reformer J. B. Gough, contrasts with the still the sparkling brook and the fresh spring. God's liquid comes "Not in the simmering still, over smoky fires choked with poisonous gases, and surrounded with the stench of sickening odors and rank corruptions."[88] After a glowing description of birds on a crisp, sunny day, John Pierpont asks in a poem called "Temperance Song":

> Why do they twitter and sing, do you think?
> Because they've had nothing but water to drink[89]

84 The first accident is from R 1883 Swinton-5, pp. 404–408; the second is from R 1844 Smith, pp. 58–59.

85 R 1898 Black, p. 254–256; R 1900 Aldrich and Forbes-II, pp. 131–133.

86 R 1830 Bartlett; compare pp. 62–63 with p. 130.

87 S 1866 Watson, p. 55 on champagne. On the general, R 1881 Willson, p. 24.

88 R 1869 Wilson, pp. 57–58; R 1872 Osgood-5, pp. 241–242; see also R 1873 Hillard and Campbell-3, pp. 56–58.

89 R 1867 Edwards-4, p. 51; see also R 1885 Monroe-3, p. 115.

Many schoolbooks ask their small readers to take the temperance pledge.[90] Several describe little boys enlisted in the total abstinence movement as national heroes who now bend their energies enthusiastically in persuading others to join them in the pledge. One such precocious child is quoted saying: "We may be little mice, but we shall gnaw off every thread of the great net that has bound down so many in our country for so many years."[91]

The early books use the virtues of the Founding Fathers to give prestige to the temperance movement. These forefathers of ours who never touched liquor were "quite different from what we are; they were much more healthy and strong."[92] (One wonders whom this author had in mind.) Later books ignore the question of liquor in the American past. One 1890 History, however, notes a great growth of temperance societies after the Mexican War and adduces them as part of the general progress of morals through evolution: "In former times nothing was thought of seeing people drunk, and even church people would drink strong liquors." But as morals evolved "It became a disgrace to be seen drunk and it is becoming more and more a disgrace every day."[93] The evolution of morals to their present perfection is a favorite subject of late nineteenth-century schoolbooks.

Several books caution the reader on the effects of liquor in a republic where votes may be influenced; this they see as a special danger to the United States. A few at the beginning of the century hope that abstinence from ardent spirits will help to abolish the slave trade because so many slaves are used to produce the sugar and molasses for the making of rum.[94] Morse and Webster, two of the most popular schoolbook authors of the nineteenth century, both believe that "Intemperance is the grievous sin of our country."[95] Morse suggests that by turning from liquor to home-produced wine and beer we would save our

[90] For example, R 1832 Edwards, pp. 59–62.

[91] R 1853 Webb, p. 63; see also R 1852 Cobb, pp. 265–266; R 1861 Sanders, pp. 199–200.

[92] R 1828 New York, p. 135; see also R 1796 Bingham, pp. 122–123; R 1802 Alden, p. 62; R 1804 Webster, pp. 61–64; R 1831 Cheever, p. 57–59.

[93] H 1890 Morris, pp. 190–191.

[94] R 1796 Bingham, pp. 122–123; R 1802 Alden, p. 62; R 1804 Webster, pp. 61–64.

[95] S 1829 Webster, p. 75; see also G 1791 Morse, pp. 57–58.

health and morals and at the same time build up our country's economy.[96]

On the other hand the use of liquor is referred to quite casually in the early Arithmetics and many Spellers. There are, for example, many problems involving measures of rum and brandy, and the Spellers include in their practice sentences such sentences as the following: "Gin is made from berries"; "You may put the gun, the tub, the mug and the jug of rum in the hut."[97] One Reader describes in detail the process of making gin, brandy, and wine.[98] Thus the child is habituated to spirituous liquors as part of his normal environment at the same time that their use is forbidden.

In a few scattered textbooks the use of tobacco is decried as a dirty and wasteful habit: "The Indians taught them [the colonists] to smoke it, but the more filthy habit of chewing it they learned themselves." This author goes on to warn the reader not to use it in any way: smoking it is better than chewing it; but he who smokes it finds that

> It robs his pocket, soils his clothes,
> And makes a chimney of his nose.[99]

Another hopes the reader will be inspired by a little boy:

> I'll never use tobacco, no
> It is a filthy weed.
> I'll never put it in my mouth,
> Said little Robert Reid.[100]

And a Speller advises the young lady: "A lady should not choose a man who chews tobacco." In one book tea is regarded as little short of poison, and if it is to be drunk at all, one should at least dilute it with cream and sugar. On the whole, however, one should

[96] G 1791 Morse, p. 58; G 1818 Morse, p. 91.

[97] Arithmetics: A 1800 Daboll, p. 160; A 1807 Walsh, p. 67; A 1808 Thomson, p. 88; A 1808 Temple, p. 79; A 1809 Hutton, p. 38; A 1863 Fish, p. 335; A 1863 Loomis, p. 144. Spellers: S 1843 Fowle, p. 11; S 1857 Parker and Watson, p. 25.

[98] R 1830 Bartlett, pp. 129–130.

[99] H 1866 Lossing, p. 28.

[100] R 1881 Willson, p. 23; see also R 1871 Monroe, pp. 53–55.

deny oneself completely "the indulgence so fascinating, but so insidious."[101]

To favor total abstinence would seem to put one on the side of the angels. Because this movement was least likely to produce social upheaval, let alone success, there could be no serious objections to its approval by schoolbooks; and the approval is unanimous. It required no law but expected human perfection and the kind of do-it-yourself virtue so beloved by textbooks. They show no interest in encouraging self-control but hope to inculcate in their young readers a kind of absolute but mechanical abstinence and denial of sense indulgence. The schoolbooks not only heartily endorse this ineffective reform movement, but they enlist their small readers actively in the cause. One's imagination balks at the vision of the child confronting his parents with the total abstinence pledge, as his schoolbooks expected him to do. Dramatic tales illustrating the evils of self-indulgence through alcohol were hardly likely to keep young people with a healthy amount of curiosity from a first taste of the forbidden liquor with its extraordinary and mysterious powers. But consciousness of danger and possibly of sin were almost certain to accompany that first glass.

THE PEACE CRUSADE

If one examined only those stories and precepts in the Readers whose moral is antiwar, one would assume that schoolbooks were in the forefront of the peace crusade of Ladd, Burritt, and others. All but one of the schoolbooks see war as a scourge of man which they confidently and vaguely hope will end in time as evolution brings increased moral progress.[102] Every Reader and Speller contains at least one pacifist essay or story. A favorite shows Alexander the Great reproached by several convicted

[101] On tobacco, S 1879 Westlake, p. 56; on tea, G 1837 Book of Commerce, p. 28.

[102] G 1869 Warren-E, p. 93: "Thus *wars* rouse uncivilized people from their indolence and lethargy. They require a union of forces, and they are thus led to *combined action*, so important for the development of a people. One of the chief consequences of war is the establishment of *fixed relations* between neighboring peoples, which render friendly intercourse possible, and bring about an interchange of commodities and ideas." This attitude is unique.

robbers, who say that Alexander's military triumphs are actually nothing but robberies on a vast scale. He is much more guilty than they.[103] In another discussion, extraordinarily popular from the 1820's on, war is identified with murder for which a single individual is punished by death, but an army is praised. This explanation, in the form of a simple dialogue between a father and his little boy, is made on the child's level.[104] Another popular essay describes the instruments of war as of much less value than the humblest of the instruments of peace. In weighing true value on the magic philosopher's scales Alexander weighs less than Dorcas' garment; ten chariots weigh less than one plow; a sword weighs less than one ten-penny nail; a shield, helmet, buckler, and spear weigh less than one widow's tear.[105] Interestingly enough these discussions of the horrors of war, appearing just after the defeat of Napoleon, use the more remote Alexander rather than Napoleon as the personification of the evils of military conquest.

The great hero of the peace movement is, of course, an American—William Penn. In one popular dialogue he argues with Charles II of England. Penn says he wants no soldiers to protect his infant colony; his colony, based on justice, is more secure and prosperous than all the rest of Charles' well-guarded empire.[106] Penn also discusses the issue with Cortez, comparing their colonization policies. The colony of the pacifist is seen to be more

[103] R 1806 Staniford, pp. 184–185; R 1809 Picket, pp. 202–203; R 1819 Strong, pp. 201–202; R 1823 Pierpont, pp. 438–440; R 1828 New York, pp. 198–200; R 1836 Cobb-N.A., pp. 435–437; R 1831 Smiley, pp. 23–24; R 1846 Swan-G, pp. 170–172; R 1867 Edwards-5, pp. 255–256; R 1883 Swinton-4, pp. 268–271; R 1884 Campbell-4, pp. 260–263.

[104] S 1821 Perry, pp. 102–103; R 1830 Frost, pp. 112–113; R 1830 Putnam-I, pp. 86–88; R 1831 Hall, pp. 103–105; R 1833 Olney, pp. 80–81, 112–114; R 1834 Angell, pp. 260–262; R 1836 Parsons, p. 138; R 1837 Fowle, pp. 67–69; R 1843 McGuffey, pp. 66–68, 68–70; R 1867 Edwards-4, pp. 254–256; R 1866 McGuffey-4, pp. 113–117; R 1868 Parker and Watson, pp. 213–214; R 1873 Hillard and Campbell-3, pp. 100–102.

[105] R 1828 Putnam, pp. 46–51; R 1841 Merriam, pp. 212–213; R 1843 Olney, p. 206; R 1844 Smith, pp. 164–165; R 1851 ASDUK, p. 117; R 1851 Tower, pp. 140–141.

[106] R 1828 Greenwood and Emerson, pp. 82–84; R 1841 Merriam, pp. 154–156; R 1843 Olney, pp. 30–32; R 1845 Goldsbury and Russell, pp. 200–202; R 1846 Swan-G, pp. 88–91; R 1849 Leavitt, pp. 117–119; R 1851 ASDUK, pp. 98–101; R 1856 Sanders-4, pp. 236–238.

successful than that of the conqueror.[107] Penn, as hero of the peace movement, is contrasted only with the representatives of foreign powers rather than with the founders of other American settlements that eventually grew into the United States. Comparing him with the latter would violate the canons of American nationalism by depicting American ancestors in unseemly attitudes.

Most of the appeals to end war are couched in humanitarian terms. There are touching descriptions of the sad widow and unprotected orphans left in the wake of battle:

> See how the bands of war and woe
> Have rifled sweet domestic bliss;
> And tell me, if your laurels grow,
> And flourish in a soil like this?[108]

After the Civil War heart-rending tales and poems of the aftermath of battle proliferate. Almost every Reader contains a tale of mothers and sisters searching the battlefield for their dead. At this time too Southey's poem "The Battle of Blenheim" occurs frequently, contrasting the old soldier's "It was a famous victory . . ." with the actual carnage of that battle. Several books in the 1820's charge war with ruining the character of the soldier through the violence and licentiousness of army life. And some see war as contrary to God's will.[109] One author points to the social benefits that would accrue to the benefit of all men if war were perpetually ended: "Give me the money that has been spent in war, and I will purchase every foot of land on the globe. I will clothe every man, woman and child in an attire of which kings and queens would be proud. I will build a schoolhouse in every valley and a church on every hill."[110] But the major argument for perpetual peace is the waste of human life that inevitably attends war.

Sentiments against a standing army manifest themselves mainly at the beginning and at the end of the century, in both cases contrasting the United States with Europe in this respect. In the

[107] R 1821 Bingham, pp. 52–55; R 1828 New York, pp. 200–205; R 1849 Leavitt, pp. 252–255; R 1851 ASDUK, pp. 112–126; see also R 1839 Sigourney, pp. 134–142; R 1853 McGuffey E-2, pp. 160–161.

[108] R 1823 Blake, p. 192.

[109] For example, R 1823 Pierpont, pp. 124–127; R 1823 N. Worcester, pp. 22–23.

[110] S 1875 Monroe, p. 53.

early books a standing army is a symbol of British oppression at the time of the American Revolution; at the end of the century the subject recurs evidently in response to the newly conscripted armies of Europe. The later books suggest the lack of such military expenditures in the United States as one reason for greater prosperity in America than in Europe: "These enormous armaments are maintained by a grinding taxation, and, in many countries, by a merciless conscription that withdraws millions of young men for years from all productive industry."[111] Only one book mentions the need for a navy in time of peace, because there is always danger of war and "Every great nation has a navy," an argument unacceptable for an army.[112] A strong navy in peacetime apparently presents none of the dangers of despotism offered by an army; at least there are no warnings against such an establishment. Civil authorities should always be superior to the military: when General Greene assumes that his aide need not appear before a civil judge in a case of libel, the judge corrects him firmly.[113] The United States need not support a standing army because it can assemble an efficient citizen army so rapidly in case of danger: "No nation or kingdom in Europe can bring into the field an army of equal numbers, more formidable than can be raised in the United States."[114] This is based on the assumption that the American government can count on a purer and more widespread patriotism than can the less free governments of Europe.

That the great American hero, Washington, was a soldier is explained in antiwar stories in several books: by profession Washington was a farmer, not a soldier. He was a citizen-soldier who devoted himself to defending his country when attacked, but who never engaged in aggressive war. He is often contrasted to Alexander, Caesar, and Napoleon in this respect. Nevertheless his heroism in these books is the result of military exploits and his capacity as a soldier.

One cannot, however, judge the attitude of these books toward the movement for the abolition of war, and still less the effects of

[111] G 1894 Harper, p. 91; see also H 1890 Morris, p. 228; G 1898 Redway and Hinman, p. 121.

[112] G 1898 Carpenter, p. 36; compare with p. 38.

[113] R 1830 Practical-R, p. 63.

[114] G 1794 Morse, p. 102; see also G 1898 Carpenter, p. 38.

their antiwar stories on youthful readers, by looking only at these stories. After careful examination books by only four authors emerge as truly pacifist: Readers by Cooledge and N. Worcester, the McGuffey Readers, and Higginson's History. Cooledge, a Quaker, takes a unique position in saying, "I would rather be Anthony Benezet, in that coffin, than the great Washington, with all his honours."[115] This is not only unprecedented but heretical. And only one of the authors who oppose war suggests any concrete hope for peace; Higginson lauds the 1871 agreement over Civil War claims between Britain and the United States and recommends such use of peaceful arbitration in future disputes.[116] Most of the Readers include one or more selections detailing the horrors of war, but many more than that depicting colorful battles. For example, Sargent's 1866 Reader includes four antiwar pieces but nine splendid descriptions of heroism in battle.[117] Nor is quantitative measurement alone a wholly accurate gauge of how such pieces would affect a young reader. The antiwar selections, although full of sentiment and high moral tone, lack the drama, color, excitement, and immediacy of the battle descriptions. The latter would appeal to the child's own natural aggressiveness, and they would have the further advantage of being eminently suitable for play with toys or friends. Not a natural peacemaker, the child might easily daydream himself into the position of a hero winning the battle against heavy odds. Against this there could be little competition from such analogies of peace as "The Happy Family" by Elihu Burritt, in which a peaceable collection of different animals is regarded as a model for the human race.[118]

Nationalism and pacifist sentiments are often mutually exclusive, and in these books, with the few exceptions noted above, nationalism always conquers. American participation in past wars is not only approved but depicted in glorious terms. The opponents of the United States in any war are, of course, the aggressors. The general concept of fighting for one's country is exalted into

[115] R 1806 Cooledge, p. 112. [116] H 1875 Higginson, pp. 326–327.

[117] For example, Sargent's 1866 Fourth Reader (R 1866 Sargent-4) includes four anti-war pieces (pp. 34–36, 75–76, 208–210, 282–285), but the following pages are devoted to heroism in battle: 87–90, 104–105, 125–126, 127–128, 146–148, 210, 211, 213–214, 235–236.

[118] R 1872 Monroe, pp. 189–190.

94 GOING TO THE WAR. [1775

8. One mother fitted out her eldest son with a fowling-piece and slugs made out of her pewter spoons. Her younger boy was only

sixteen. For him she had nothing but an old rusty sword. Giving him this, she dashed away a tear, and bade him follow his brother. "Beg or borrow a sword, my child," she said; "or you will find one. Some coward, I dare say, will be running away. Then take his gun and march forward."

9. At Barn'-sta-ble, the only child of a farmer joined a company that was about to march to Cambridge. As they passed the father's house on leaving the village, he came forth and said: "God be with you all, my friends! and, John, if you, my son, are called into battle, take care that you behave manfully, or else let me never see your face again." This was the spirit everywhere. Twenty thousand patriots were soon in arms around Boston.

18. A typical page from the section on the American Revolution in an American history. This is from *Primary History of the United States,* 1869, by G. P. Quackenbos.

the most illustrious activity in which one can engage. "It is pleasant and glorious to die for one's country" is a sentiment found in most books. Mrs. Hemans' poem "The Hero's Death" is typical of the plethora of selections on this subject:

His was a death, whose rapturous high
Transcends all that life could yield;
His warmest prayer was so to die
On the red battlefield.

And they may feel, who love him most,
A pride so holy and so pure,—
Fate hath no power o'er those who boast
A treasure thus secure.[119]

There are hundreds of stirring speeches by generals rallying their troops; these come not only from past American battles, but from those of ancient Greece, Rome, England (when not at war with the United States), Peru, Poland, and other places. In each case the battle is in defense of nationality, but the cause is usually lost in elaborate descriptions of battle scenes. The latter, concretely and colorfully detailed, would certainly make more impression on the mind of a child than the abstract issues over which the battle began. The distinction made by authors of schoolbooks between an aggressive war and one to defend an abstract principle is less easily grasped than the glories of military action. In any case by far the greater part of each selection is devoted to descriptions of actual fighting undefiled by the issues involved.

Major evidence for the basically militaristic cast of these books is in the space given to war as opposed to other subjects. The very books that express the most solemn strictures against war devote much of their space to glamorous descriptions of it. For example, of the 432 pages of Frost's 1839 *History of the United States*, 144 are devoted exclusively to military operations in the American Revolution and the War of 1812 alone.[120] Another History offers

[119] R 1874 Hillard, p. 137.

[120] Of 177 pages in Anderson's 1877 History (H 1877 Anderson), 72 are devoted to descriptions of battles. Of the 396 pages of Scott's 1874 History (H 1874 Scott), 177 are devoted to battles. Of the 305 pages of Lossing's *Common School History of the United States*, 1870 edition (H 1870 Lossing), 122 are military. Of the 302 pages in Steele's 1881 History (H 1881 Steele), 108 are military.

eight maps of battlefields in the Revolution and suggests that the teacher draw these on the blackboard and ask the children to describe the battle from memory, using the maps to illustrate the movements of the troops involved.[121] Warfare, like a game, is governed by rules. Grimshaw contrasts the shocking cruelties of certain British officers to the humanity of others who "did not forget the laws of established warfare."[122] It is always the enemy of the United States that commits the foul.

Such concentration on military history might be expected of school Histories since the historiography of the period was decidedly military. Two authors apologize for including so much warfare: "But, alas! Too much of the story is made up of wars and disputes—of the doings of bad men and the sufferings of good men."[123] Higginson, himself deeply concerned in reform movements, disputes this: "Times of peace, the proverb says, have few historians; but this may be more the fault of historians than the times."[124] But the Readers too, with few exceptions, grant a great deal of space to battle scenes. For example Blake, who is quoted above in one of his antiwar selections, includes nineteen descriptions of battles, all displayed in glorious colors. Frost, who explained in a dialogue that war is nothing but murder on a gigantic scale, includes fourteen accounts of battles.[125] Almost every Reader contains one piece of antiwar sentiment, but the same Readers include several times as many imaginative descriptions of battles. In their surveys of the American states the Geographies note the site of every battle of even minor importance fought on American soil. Many primary Readers exhibit pictures of boys playing soldier with such captions as "What fun it is to beat a drum and march with a gun."[126]

[121] H 1843 Hall and Baker, p. 5.

[122] H 1822 Grimshaw, p. 263; see also H 1826 Hale, pp. 296, 366.

[123] H 1866 Lossing, pp. 201–202; see also H 1899 Morris, p. 136.

[124] H 1875 Higginson, pref., p. iv.

[125] R 1823 Blake, pp. 40–42, 42–47, 51–54, 60–61, 69–70, 70–75, 90–97, 176–191, 193–197, 197–205, 225–229, 229–234, 236–241, 253–261, 274–279, 279–285, 285–291, 295–298; R 1826 Frost, pp. 33–34, 40–41, 45–47, 75–80, 91–92, 121–124, 126–130, 137–138, 138–141, 147–150, 193–194, 194–195, 251–253, 264.

[126] R 1883 Barnes, p. 33; see also: R 1896 McGuffey-3, pp. 184–187; R 1899 Judson and Bender, pp. 9–10, 76–78; R 1900 Demarest and Van Sickle, pp. 51–53.

The Spellers and Arithmetics show the same delight in military glory. An 1808 Arithmetic, for example, contains fifteen military problems.[127] Typical of these are the following from a Confederate Arithmetic: "A Confederate soldier captures 8 Yankees each day for 9 successive days; how many did he capture in all?" or "If one Confederate soldier kills 90 Yankees, how many can 10 Confederate soldiers kill?"[128] The Spellers are full of military words. A ratio of seven military words on one page of 50 words to be learned is the norm. In a list of sixty collective nouns, ten are military terms.[129] An 1890 Speller includes only four non-military items in a list of 20 words called "Historical Terms."[130] The examples cited are all from Spellers produced during times of peace.

Wars in which the United States has engaged are not only approved but exalted. One book concludes an antiwar piece by saying that the American Revolution was a justifiable war, although most wars are not.[131] In evaluating the justice of wars it seems clear that schoolbook authors are motivated not by critical assessment of the causes but by nationalism. The American Revolution and its attendant events probably occupy more space in the Readers than any other single subject. Revolutionary oratory is most popular in the Readers and Spellers, descriptions of battles in the Histories and Geographies. Emerson's 1830 Reader offers ten selections from Revolutionary orators. In these books wars are the watersheds of history, and none serves this function so well as the American Revolution: "Here opened the first scene of the great drama, which in its progress exhibited the most illustrious characters and events, and closed with a revolution, equally glorious for the actors and important in its consequences to the human race."[132]

In the Geographies and Histories the treatment of the American Revolution is largely military. Morse considers the following the significant questions to ask his reader: "At what time was the

[127] A 1808 Thomson, pp. 18, 19, 36 (two problems), 45, 48, 49 (three problems), 68, 133, 134, 166, 171 (two problems).

[128] A 1864 Johnson (Confederate), pp. 34, 38.

[129] S 1809 Parlour, p. 45; S 1846 S. Worcester, pp. 35–37.

[130] S 1890 Kupfer, p. 89.

[131] R 1831 Hall, p. 105.

[132] G 1811 Morse, p. 107; G 1818 Morse, p. 103.

Battle of Bunker Hill? Who was the commander-in-chief of the American armies? When was he appointed?"[133] Of the thirteen pages allotted to the Revolution in the same book, eleven are devoted to battles. Most of the Geographies explain the part played by each state in the military history of the American Revolution. New York, for example, "had a full share of the military operations in the revolutionary war. In this state many battles were fought, and whole armies vanquished. Remains of their fortifications are visible in many places."[134] The American cause in the Revolutionary War was unique, and its battles heroic. As a war for principle rather than gain, it is to be set apart from all other wars: "This single circumstance, aside from the magnitude of the object, or the event of the contest, still stamp a peculiar glory on the American Revolution, and mark it as a distinct era in the history of mankind."[135] It is differentiated from all other revolutions (particularly the French) because it "had its origin, neither in ambition nor avarice, nor envy, nor in any gross passion; but in the nature and relation of things and in the thence resulting necessity of separation from the parent state."[136] The Americans could have paid the taxes involved, but they fought for a principle and for posterity. The principles "were not the suddenly acquired property of a few bosoms; they were abroad in the land in the ages before; they had always been taught like the truths of the Bible."[137] Furthermore, it was a conservative and orderly revolution; in contrast to that of the French it was mild in process and unshaken by passion. The Americans, forced to fight, did so for the future of mankind: "The cause of the American colonies fighting for their independence was the cause of mankind. There was no generous soul throughout the civilized world who did not give it his entire sympathy. All who prized liberty looked with intense interest upon the struggle of the weak

[133] G 1818 Morse, p. 363. [134] G 1807 Parish, p. 62.

[135] R 1790 Webster, p. 168, quoting a Barlow oration; see also R 1797 Thomas, pp. 204–211; R 1810 Alden, p. 123.

[136] R 1826 Greenwood and Emerson, p. 199; R 1830 Emerson, p. 167; see also H 1872 Venable, p. 90.

[137] R 1827 Pierpont, pp. 214–215; R 1836 Cobb-N.A., p. 181; see also H 1870 Lossing, p 115; H 1872 Venable, p. 90; R 1873 Hillard, pp. 146–147; H 1874 Anderson, p. 41; H 1889 Chambers, pp. 212–213; R 1898 Arnold and Gilbert, pp. 108–109.

against the mighty."[138] The Revolution, then, was a war reluctantly undertaken but sanctified by its goals. Obviously none of the strictures against war apply to that one. Are they applied to any other American wars?

Since most of these books were produced in a New England that opposed the War of 1812, one might expect some reflection of division among the American people to appear in the treatment of the war. Many give no hint of the causes of the war. Most suggest British depredations on our commerce and seamen as the cause. Others refer to it vaguely as a war for the defense of national honor. In the early books British incitement of the Indians on our frontiers is rarely mentioned, but after the Civil War it appears often. Many simply state that a war occurred in which we won many battles. On the whole, the War of 1812 makes its appearance in schoolbooks mainly as another example of American courage and glory on the battlefield, and of the cruelty of the enemy. Four Readers use Clay's speech "National Honor," in which he assesses the value of the war and derides those critics who say we accomplished nothing. What we achieved is national glory and prestige at home and abroad: "Every act of noble sacrifice to the country, every act of patriotic devotion to her cause has its beneficial influence. A nation's character is the sum of its splendid deeds. They constitute one common patrimony, the nation's inheritance."[139] Thus the War of 1812, though not as important a nationalist symbol as the American Revolution, becomes an annex to that war, and a primary instrument for exaltation of the concepts of national honor and military and naval glory. We had either to fight or "become slaves, as it were, to Great Britain again."[140] Since more complicated issues are skirted, it appears as a simple but magnificent embellishment to American military prestige in defense of a vague national honor.

The Mexican War is also treated as a triumphant American pageant rather than an expedition involving life and death. It too

[138] H 1874 Anderson, pp. 142–143; see also R 1871 Hillard, p. 343; R 1871 Monroe, p. 261.

[139] R 1826 American-S, pp. 215–216; R 1830 Emerson, pp. 92–93; R 1831 Harrod, pp. 293–294; R 1843 Cobb, pp. 58–59; see also H 1894 Fiske, p. 289.

[140] H 1872 Lossing, p. 192.

manifests itself only in battlescenes of splendid American victories, or it becomes a crusade to save the gallant Texans from brutal Mexicans. Throughout these discussions the American nationality of the Texans is stressed in opposition to the Spanish characteristics of the Mexicans. The disparity of forces is emphasized as in all other wars in which the United States has participated; always Americans win against great odds: "In these battles 32,000 Mexicans had been engaged and defeated by 9000 Americans."[141] One History sees this war as firmly establishing our military power "by the unbroken series of brilliant victories won by our army, a character for martial heroism which knows no superior in the annals of history, and which fears no rival in the pathway of military glory."[142] There are but two exceptions to this generally approving treatment of the Mexican War. One quotes a speech by Calhoun to the Senate in February, 1847 in which he denounces the war as useless: we already have Texas, and California is not worth taking because it will bring in millions of people of alien lineage and religion with a "concentrated and powerful priesthood." The other uses the Mexican War in a poetic dialogue between father and son as an illustration of an unjustifiable war of conquest.[143]

Unlike the other wars in which the United States has engaged, the Civil War bears an aura of tragedy in schoolbooks as it did in reality. There is none of the buoyancy and easy optimism so evident in descriptions of other American wars, nor quite the zest for portraying its battles. In this war only is it acknowledged that "Both sides thought they were in the right, and both were ready to give all they had that the right should rule."[144]

Just as the whole colonial period led to the Revolution, so American history since the Revolution led to the Civil War: "It may be said that when the United States emerged from the gloom of the Revolution, it entered the shadow of the War between the States."[145] The question of slavery occupies the

[141] H 1856 First Lessons, p. 156; see also G 1845 S. Morse, p. 37; H 1867 Goodrich, p. 211.

[142] H 1867 Willson, p. 361.

[143] R 1856 Denman, pp. 236–237; the quotation in the previous sentence is from R 1849 Leavitt, pp. 283–289.

[144] H 1899 Morris, p. 228.

[145] H 1889 Chambers (Southern), p. 352.

center of the stage in that period for all post-Civil War books except a Southern one. The latter sees the issue of the Civil War as a matter of states' rights: "the contention for this right [states' rights] was the direct cause of the war, and not slavery as has been frequently and erroneously given."[146] All see the struggle as an inevitable one in which the two sections were "urged on by some power beyond their control, rushing to a conflict the most terrible in history. This conflict was inevitable before the Americans could become one people, and from it both emerged with a heritage of noble deeds and memories of gallant heroes, with mutual respect, and a clasping of hands in friendship, all barriers to which from that time forward it is their duty to remove."[147]

A few, but very few, mention inhuman treatment of prisoners of war in the South, and one Southern text describes the "fierce avarice of the invaders [who] despoiled women and children, the aged and infirm."[148] Most of the battlefield scenes, however, are of soldiers of North and South dying together and recognizing their common humanity.[149] In death all are heroes. A popular poem on this theme, "The Blue and the Gray" by Francis Miles Finch, appears in eight Readers. All finally agree that the war has consolidated the Union: "It was natural that such a strife between North and South would leave some bitterness, and yet never in the history of the world were hostilities so amicably settled and the lines of enmity so completely eradicated."[150] This consolidation as well as the end of slavery are good results of this tragic war: "We cannot but feel that God has worked in a mysterious way to bring good out of evil."[151]

The Civil War, then, is the exception to American wars. In others in which the United States has fought, all heroes were on one side, all American soldiers were heroes, all causes just, all battles glorious. Nationalism required that American wars fought against the American Indians or foreign powers be so; it

146 *Ibid.*, p. 369.

147 *Ibid.*, p. 16; see also H 1872 Venable, p. 195; H 1881 Steele, p. 198 footnote.

148 H 1889 Chambers, p. 408, box.

149 R 1866 McGuffey-4, pp. 228–229; R 1876 Hillard and Campbell, pp. 186–191.

150 H 1896 Murphy, p. 151; see also H 1867 Goodrich, p. 310.

151 H 1867 Willson, p. 434; see also H 1866 Lossing, p. 238.

also required the Civil War to be in quite a different category with the emphasis on the reunion of all Americans immediately after the war. "The civilization of America is today a much higher one than it was thirty years ago," says an 1890 History.[152]

Thus although war is condemned in the abstract, it is presented fully and gloriously in the concrete. Obviously the latter instances would be much more appealing to the mind of the child, and much more easily grasped. And the concrete instances far outnumber the abstract precepts. War for conquest, presented as such, is condemned. But when undertaken in self-defense or in the defense of an undefined national honor it is justified. All wars of the United States are of this sort. The disgrace of aggression is always foisted on the enemy nation. The enemy not only began the war as one of conquest but resorted to inhuman behavior in its course. Conversely, the United States is the harbinger of peace in all circumstances.

It should also be noted that history throughout these books consists primarily of warfare, a reflection of much of the historiography of the period. From schoolbook descriptions one would draw the conclusion that war is a natural and normal relationship between nations; it is dreadful but inevitable. And its horror is full of interest.

[152] H 1890 Morris, p. 217.

VI. Conclusion

Chapter 12

SCHOOLBOOKS, THE CHILD, AND THE CULTURE

The world created in nineteenth-century schoolbooks is essentially a world of fantasy—a fantasy made up by adults as a guide for their children, but inhabited by no one outside the pages of schoolbooks. It is an ideal world, peopled by ideal villains as well as ideal heroes. Nature is perfectly if sometimes inscrutably planned by God for the good of man, with progress as its first and invariable law. Nothing can hinder this march toward material and moral perfection, a movement particularly visible in the United States. Nature is benign, and the life close to nature inevitably a happy and healthy one. Individuals are to be understood in terms of easily discernible, inherent characteristics of their race and nationality as much as in terms of their individual character. Virtue is always rewarded, vice punished. And one can achieve virtue and avoid vice by following a few simple rules. Assuredly the adult world did not live by this pattern but elected to believe in it as what *should* be true, as the inhabitants of Samuel Butler's *Erewhon* believed in their "musical banks." Wishfully, adults in any age would like to proffer to their children a neatly patterned model of life, however mythical, which the child can accept and, following it, live happily ever after. But inevitably the growing child soon sees that life is not so simple: that the life close to nature may not only be a hard one but unrewarding and frustrating; that virtue is not always rewarded on this earth and that not even his schoolbooks can really know whether there is compensation for this after death; that progress in one area comes at great cost in another, that Catholics may be sincere, Indians gentle, Negroes intelligent, and Jews generous. To live in the real world the child would eventually have to abandon the simple model of his schoolbooks. And, with luck, he will develop experientally, and perhaps experimentally, a more adequate world view.

Perhaps the most fundamental assumption in nineteenth-century schoolbooks is the moral character of the universe—an assumption at the base of American culture in this period. Religion itself is rather a matter of morals than theology. Furthermore, all nature as well as man is invested with morality; animal and plant life both follow moral law. In schoolbooks, when ants store up food they do so as an act of moral responsibility rather than as instinctual behavior. Conversely, the grasshopper's careless ways in not preparing for winter are his own fault, and his hunger in lean times is a richly deserved punishment. Whether a man succeeds in his business is not so much a question of the application of intelligence and energy to the problems of that business, but a result of good character. Success in business is viewed in schoolbooks largely as a by-product of virtue. It is to be sought not for material comforts it will bring, but as a sign of virtue, a status symbol if you will. Similarly, natural resources, location, availability of capital, and labor are minor factors in evaluating the decline and fall of nations; only a moral nation can achieve lasting power. The decline of Spain and the growth of the United States are illustrations of this. Everything in life is to be judged in moral terms. Nineteenth-century intellectuals might view nature as amoral, but the Puritan tradition still provided the basis of popular culture.

Unlike many modern schoolbooks, those of the nineteenth century made no pretense of neutrality. While they evade issues seriously controverted in their day, they take a firm and unanimous stand on matters of basic belief. The value judgment is their stock in trade: love of country, love of God, duty to parents, the necessity to develop habits of thrift, honesty, and hard work in order to accumulate property, the certainty of progress, the perfection of the United States. These are not to be questioned. Nor in this whole century of great external change is there any deviation from these basic values. In pedagogical arrangements the schoolbook of the 1790's is vastly different from that of the 1890's, but the continuum of values is uninterrupted. Neither the Civil War nor the 1890's provide any watershed in basic values. There is no hint here of Darwin's natural selection from chance variations, nor of the Higher Criticism, comparative religion,

William James' pluralism, nor of the neutral nature depicted by literary realists. Ethics do not evolve from particular cultural situations, nor are they to be developed by the individual from his own experience and critical thinking. Nor are they to come from his peers. They are absolute, unchanging, and they come from God. The child is to learn ethics as he learns information about his world, unquestioningly, by rote. His behavior is not to be inner-directed, nor other-directed, but dictated by authority and passively accepted.

Also in contrast to many modern texts, those of the nineteenth century, while ideologically simple, are not entirely bland. However glossed with sentiment, death and disease are a natural part of the world of the schoolbook. Reality is portrayed not so much through the postman, fireman, and things familiar in the child's environment, but through the deeper reality of hardship, tragedy, passionate devotion to a cause, the satisfactions in overcoming obstacles. To be well adjusted the nineteenth century child must be in harmony with the decrees of God and nature rather than with his peers. The life schoolbooks prepare him for is one of struggle and hardship in competition with his contemporaries. The horrors of failure as well as the glories of success are endlessly illustrated. While oversimplifying life to an extraordinary degree, his schoolbooks made the nineteenth-century child thoroughly aware that life is hard and full of natural and man-made pitfalls. It is his duty to strive for success, but he will struggle hard on the way.

Like the schoolbooks of other nations, those of the United States are bent on persuading the child that his nation is superior to all others. The development of American ideas and institutions is usually depicted without its proper world setting, and important forces in American life—such as freedom and the industrial revolution—are assumed to be creations of this hemisphere. Indeed freedom is frequently discussed as a chemical component of the very air of America. In order to be a good American, the child must reject Europe and things European. Unfortunately this results in the repudiation of scholarship and the fine arts, associated in schoolbooks with an effete and aristocratic Europe. The child is, however, expected to develop a fervent faith that the American example will inevitably and gloriously save Europe from its present state of corruption and decline. America is to be a source for Europe, not Europe for America.

Each race and its subdivisions—nationalities—are defined by inherent mental and personal characteristics which the child must memorize. Individual personality is largely submerged in race and nationality. And these traits are used to determine the rank of each race and nation. In describing typical members of such groups the part must be substituted for the whole. The American, as the ideal man, is of the white race, of Northern European background, Protestant, self-made, and if not a farmer at least retaining the virtues of his yeoman ancestors. As race becomes an increasingly significant way to think about human beings, the English are exalted to a position just below the Americans. They misbehaved at the time of the American Revolution, but this was a temporary aberration. Essentially, racially, they are superior; to impugn the English character would degrade American stock. Yet the American population is not identical with the English because the American environment sieved the English population. The weak would not come, and only the pure in heart could survive. The American is a distilled Englishman.

Although schoolbook authors consider themselves guardians of liberty, they can be more accurately described as guardians of tradition. On social questions the tenor of the books is consistently conservative. The United States is always identified with freedom, but this freedom is best defined as that established in 1783 after separation from Great Britain. The nineteenth-century child was taught to worship past achievements of America and to believe in the inevitable spread of the American system throughout the world. But contemporary problems are conspicuously absent, and reform movements which would have profound social or political effects are either ignored or derided. While Jeffersonian and Jacksonian democracy agitated the adult world, the child was taught the necessity of class distinctions. Nor are Jefferson and Jackson ever ranked as heroes; their social philosophies provided new forms of Americanism in other circles, but in the schools Hamilton and Daniel Webster governed the minds of the children. Problems of the farmer after the Civil War are not mentioned; instead, farm chores are suffused with bucolic charm, and farming is described as the ideal life close to God and nature.

The industrial revolution wonderfully increased American power, but it left no divisions in American society. The organization of labor does not appear at all until the late nineteenth century, and when it does it is identified with violence and property destruction carried out by irresponsible elements in American society. Women in the United States have already been awarded all the rational liberty suitable to their natures, and more than in other countries. Dissatisfaction with their status is both unwomanly and ungrateful. Always the child is shown an America serene and united. He must be tolerant of other religions, but he should not recognize them as equal to Protestantism on pain of subversion of both church and state. He should be moved emotionally by the inhumanity of war, but he should admire without reserve the exploits of military heroes and be happy to sacrifice his life in any war in which his country is engaged. Before the Civil War he may pity the slave, but he must stay away from the abolitionist movement. After the Civil War he can look back to the evils of slavery now safely buried in the past, but he need not concern himself with the freedman; the latter quickly fades from the pages of his schoolbooks. He must revere values already established in American society by his schoolbooks rather than attempt to institute new ones or expand the old. Ironically their very efforts to present a united society prevent these schoolbooks from mirroring America as a whole; only the social ideals of the more conservative members of the society were offered the nineteenth-century child. It is these social ideals that nineteenth-century schoolbooks admit to the American tradition and hope to preserve.

By defining what they consider American, these schoolbooks perform a function required in few other societies. To be English, French, or German is usually taken for granted, but Americans have always worried about what "Americanness" is, and whether they have it. Perhaps their immigrant background explains this, but surely their mobility and the fact that they were building a new society also contribute to this strange but pervasive American phenomenon. Unlike the European, whose life was lived within a fairly settled pattern of society, the American had to set up social patterns afresh and find his place in them. These might be the same patterns of culture already developed by older societies, but he had to make conscious and unconscious choice of what he would use. Optimism and buoyancy, but also probably insecurity, resulted from this task. The American is not clear on who he is, and he tends to wear his Americanness like a cloak he puts on rather than a skin that grows with him. Most nineteenth-century schoolbooks include specific descriptions of the American character, but in a larger sense everything they teach the American child is part of this attempt to find out what the American is and should be. Whatever is good in ideas, behavior, and institutions they identify with the United States and its citizens. By selecting what they consider most essential to preserve in America, nineteenth-century schoolbooks offered to the broadest and most impressionable American audience an image of themselves as a guide to the future.

BIBLIOGRAPHY

The essential bibliography for this study is the list of schoolbooks used in American schools from 1776 to 1900. The following have also been useful.

Allport, Floyd. "The Psychology of Nationalism." *Harper's Magazine*, CLV (August, 1927), 291–301.

Altschul, Charles. *The American Revolution in Our Schoolbooks*. New York: George H. Doran Co., 1917.

American Journal of Education, 1826–1830. Edited by William Russell and William C. Woodbridge. Boston: Wait, Green and Co., 1826–1830.

American Journal of Education. Edited by Henry Barnard. 32 volumes. 1855–1882. Hartford: F. C. Brownell, 1856–1882.

Baron, Salo W. *Modern Nationalism and Religion*. New York: Harper and Bros., 1947.

Becker, Carl. "Kansas," in *Every Man His Own Historian*. New York: Appleton-Century-Crofts, Inc., 1935.

Bethune, George Washington. "The Claims of Our Country on Its Literary Men." An oration before the Phi Beta Kappa Society of Harvard University, July 19, 1849. Cambridge: John Bartlett, 1849.

Billington, Ray. *The Protestant Crusade, 1800–1860*. New York: The Macmillan Co., 1938.

Boehm, Max Hildebert. "Nationalism, Theoretical Aspects." *Encyclopedia of the Social Sciences*, XI, 231–240.

Bolwell, Robert Whitney. "Concerning the Study of Nationalism in American Literature." *American Literature*, X (January, 1939), 405–416.

Brooks, Van Wyck. *The Flowering of New England, 1815–1865*. New York: E. P. Dutton and Co., Inc., 1937.

Brown, Ralph. "The American Geographies of Jedidiah Morse." *Annals of the Association of American Geographers*, XXXI (September, 1941), 145–267.

Burton, Warren. *The District School as It Was by One Who Went to It*. Boston: Phillips Sampson and Co., 1833.

Butts, R. Freeman. *A Cultural History of Education*. New York: McGraw-Hill Book Co., Inc., 1947.

Butts, R. Freeman and Lawrence A. Cremin. *A History of Education in American Culture*. New York: Henry Holt and Co., 1953.

Cahill, Holger. *Emblems of Unity and Freedom: The Index of American Design*. New York: Metropolitan Museum of Art, 1942(?).

Caldwell, Otis W. and Stuart A. Courtis. *Then and Now in Education, 1845–1923*. Yonkers-on-Hudson, New York: World Book Co., 1924.

Carpenter, Charles. *History of American Schoolbooks*. Philadelphia: University of Pennsylvania Press, 1963.

The Common School Journal. Edited by Horace Mann. Boston: Marsh, Capen, Lyon and Webb, 1839–1852.

The Connecticut Common School Journal. Published under the direction of the Board of Commissioners of the common schools of Connecticut. Vol. I. Hartford, 1838–1839.

Counts, George S. *The Social Foundations of Education*. New York: Charles Scribner's Sons, 1934.

Cremin, Lawrence A. *The Transformation of the School*. New York: Alfred A. Knopf, 1962.

Cubberley, Ellwood P. *Public Education in the United States*. Boston: Houghton Mifflin Co., 1934.

Curti, Merle E. *The Growth of American Thought*. New York: Harper and Bros., 1943.

———. *The Roots of American Loyalty*. New York: Columbia University Press, 1946.

———. *The Social Ideas of American Educators*. New York: Charles Scribner's Sons, 1935.

———. "Wanted: a History of American Patriotism." *Proceedings of the Middle States Association of History and Social Science Teachers*, XXXVI (October 29, 1938), 15–24.

Earle, Edward Mead (ed.). *Nationalism and Internationalism: Essays inscribed to Carlton J. H. Hayes*. New York: Columbia University Press, 1950.

Fell, Sister M. L. *Foundations of Nativism in America*. Washington, D.C.: Catholic University of America, 1941.

Flanders, Jessie Knowlton. *Legislative Control of the Elementary Curriculum*. New York: Teachers College, Columbia University, 1925.

Gabriel, Ralph H. *The Course of American Democratic Thought*. New York: The Ronald Press, 1940.

Gardener, Albert Ten Eyck. *Yankee Stone-Cutters: the First American School of Sculpture, 1800–1850*. New York: Published for the Metropolitan Museum of Art by Columbia University Press, 1945.

Grimke, Thomas. "Oration Delivered before the Western Literary Institute and College of Professional Teachers at their Fourth Annual Meeting, October, 1835." Cincinnati: Josiah Drake, 1835.

Handman, Max Sylvius. "The Sentiment of Nationalism." *Political Science Quarterly*, XXXVI (March, 1921), 104–121.

Hansen, Allen Oscar. *Liberalism and American Education in the Eighteenth Century*. New York: The Macmillan Co., 1926.

Hayes, Carlton J. H. *Essays on Nationalism*. New York: The Macmillan Co., 1928.

———. *Historical Evolution of Modern Nationalism*. New York: R. R. Smith, Inc., 1931.

———. "Nationalism, Historical Development." *Encyclopedia of the Social Sciences*, XI, 240–248.

———. "Some Reflections on Nationalism." *Proceedings of the Association of History Teachers of the Middle States and Maryland*, Number 21 (1923), pp. 24–38.

Heene, Anne Louise. "American Opinion on American Cultural Nationalism as Reflected in American Periodicals, 1790–1830." Unpublished Master's Essay, Columbia University, 1944.

Hofstadter, Richard. *Anti-Intellectualism in American Life*. New York: Alfred A. Knopf, 1963.

Hunter, Earle L. "A Sociological Analysis of Certain Types of Patriotism." New York: Columbia University Dissertation, 1932.

Intergroup Relations in Teaching Material, a Report of the Committee on the Study of Teaching Materials in Intergroup Relations. Directed by Howard E. Wilson. Washington, D.C.: American Council on Education, 1949.

Jackson, Sidney L. *America's Struggle for Free Schools: Social Tensions and Education in New England and New York, 1827–1842*. Washington, D.C.: American Council on Public Affairs, 1941.

Jefferson, Thomas. Letter from Paris to J. Bannister, October 15, 1785, in Saul K. Padover (ed.), *The Complete Jefferson*. New York: Duell, Sloan and Pearce, Inc., 1943, pp. 1055–1057.

Johnson, Clifton. *Old Time Schools and Schoolbooks*. London: Macmillan and Co., Ltd., 1917.

Judd, Charles N. *Education and Social Progress*. New York: Harcourt, Brace and Co., 1935.

Kepner, Tyler. *The Influence of Textbooks Upon Method*. Philadelphia, 1935. Pp. 143–172 in *Yearbook of National Council for the Social Studies. Fifth Yearbook*. Philadelphia, 1935.

Kiefer, Monica. *American Children Through Their Books, 1700–1835*. Philadelphia: University of Pennsylvania Press, 1948.

Knight, Edgar W. *Public Education in the South*. Boston: Ginn and Co., 1922.

Kohn, Hans. *American Nationalism*. New York: The Macmillan Co., 1957.

———. *The Idea of Nationalism*. New York: The Macmillan Co., 1948.

Koral, Bella. *George Washington*. New York: Random House, 1954.

Kraus, Michael. *A History of American History*. New York: Farrar and Rinehart, Inc., 1937.

Lowenthal, David. *George Perkins Marsh*. New York: Columbia University Press, 1958.

Luther, Seth. "Address to the Workingmen of New England on the State of Education and on the Condition of the Producing Classes in Europe and America." Philadelphia: Published for the author, 1836.

Mabee, Carleton. *The American Leonardo: A Life of Samuel F. B. Morse*. New York: Alfred A. Knopf, 1943.

Martin, Helen. *Nationalism in Children's Literature*. Chicago: University of Chicago Press, 1934.

Merriam, Charles E. *Civic Education in the United States*. New York: Charles Scribner's Sons, 1934.

Monroe, Paul. *The Founding of the American Public School System*. Vol. 1. New York: The Macmillan Co., 1940.

Morgan, J. W. "Our School Books." *De Bow's Review*. Edited by J. D. B. De Bow. Vol. XXVIII (1860).

Nietz, John A. *Our Textbooks*. Pittsburgh: University of Pittsburgh Press, 1961.

New England History Teachers' Association. "Textbooks in American History," Number 2 in History Study Pamphlets. Report of Standing Committee of the Association. Boston, October 15, 1898.

Page, David P. *Theory and Practice of Teaching*. New York: A. S. Barnes, 1885. First published in 1847.

Parrington, Vernon L. *Main Currents in American Thought*. New York: Harcourt, Brace and Co., 1930. 3 vols.

Parsons, Theophilus. "Duties of Educated Men in a Republic." Address delivered before the Phi Beta Kappa Society of Harvard University, August 27, 1835. Boston: Odiorne and Co., 1835.

Peake, Cyrus Henderson. *Nationalism and Education in Modern China*. New York: Columbia University Press, 1932.

Peers, Rev. Benjamin. *American Education: or, Strictures on the Nature, Necessity and Practicability of a System of National Education, suited to the United States*. New York: John S. Taylor, 1838.

Pierce, Bessie L. *Citizens' Organizations and the Civic Training of Youth*. New York: Charles Scribner's Sons, 1933.

———. *Civic Attitudes in American Text-Books*. Chicago: University of Chicago Press, 1930.

Pinson, Koppel. *A Bibliographical Introduction to Nationalism*. New York: Columbia University Press, 1935.

Potter, Alonzo. *The School and the School Master. A Manual for the Use of Teachers, Employers, Trustees, Inspectors, etc., etc., of Common Schools*. Boston: W. B. Fowle and N. Capen, 1843.

Potter, David M. *People of Plenty.* Chicago: University of Chicago Press, 1954.

Quaife, Milo. *The Flag of the United States.* New York: Grosset and Dunlap, 1942.

Reeder, Rudolph R. "The Historical Development of School Readers and of Method in Teaching Reading." *Columbia University Contributions to Philosophy, Psychology and Education.* Vol. VIII, Number 2, May, 1900.

Reisner, Edward M. *The Evolution of the Common School.* New York: The Macmillan Co., 1930.

———. *Nationalism and Education Since 1789.* New York: The Macmillan Co., 1922.

Roorbach, Agnew O. "The Development of the Social Studies in American Secondary Education Before 1861." Philadelphia: University of Pennsylvania Dissertation, 1937.

Rose, John Holland. *Nationality in Modern History.* New York: The Macmillan Co., 1926.

Rush, Benjamin. *The Selected Writings of Benjamin Rush.* Edited by Dagobert D. Runes. New York: The Philosophical Library, Inc., 1947.

Russell, William F. "The Entrance of History into the Curriculum of the Secondary School." *History Teachers' Magazine*, Vol. V, Number 10, December 1914.

Schlesinger, Arthur M. *Learning How to Behave: a Historical Study of American Etiquette Books.* New York: The Macmillan Co., 1946.

Shillito, Edward. *Nationalism: Man's Other Religion.* New York: Willet, Clark and Co., 1933.

Smith, Henry Nash. *Virgin Land.* Cambridge: Harvard University Press, 1950.

Snyder, Louis. *The Meaning of Nationalism.* New Brunswick, N.J.: Rutgers University Press, 1954.

Spencer, Benjamin T. "A National Literature, 1837–1855." *American Literature*, VIII (May, 1936), 125–159.

———. *The Quest for Nationality.* Syracuse: Syracuse University Press, 1957.

Spieseke, Alice Winifred. *The First Textbooks in American History, and Their Compiler, John M'Culloch.* New York: Teachers College, Columbia University, 1938.

Sumner, Charles. "The True Grandeur of Nations." An oration delivered before the authorities of the city of Boston, July 4, 1845, in *Orations and Speeches.* Boston: Ticknor, Reed and Fields, 1850.

Stephens, H. Morse. "Nationality and History." *American Historical Review*, XXI (January, 1916), 225–236.

Targ, William (ed.). *Bibliophile in the Nursery*. Cleveland: The World Publishing Co., 1957.

Tryon, Rolla. *The Social Sciences as School Subjects*. New York: Charles Scribner's Sons. Part XI of the Report of the Commission on the Social Studies in the Schools. American Historical Association, 1935.

Veblen, Thorstein. "On the Nature and Uses of Patriotism." Chapter 2 in *An Inquiry into the Nature of Peace and the Terms of its Perpetuation*. New York: The Macmillan Co., 1917.

Walworth, Arthur. *School Histories at War—Study of the Treatment of our Wars in the Secondary School History Books of the United States and in those of its Former Enemies*. Cambridge: Harvard University Press, 1938.

Webster's New International Dictionary of the English Language. Springfield, Massachusetts: G. and C. Merriam Co., 1946. 2nd ed.

Wecter, Dixon. *The Hero in America: A Chronicle of Hero Worship*. New York: Charles Scribner's Sons, 1941.

Weeks, Stephen B. *Confederate Text Books, 1861–1865*. In Report of The United States Commissioner of Education for 1898–1899. Washington, D.C.: Government Printing Office, 1900.

Willson, Marcius. *Report on American Histories*. New York: Mark H. Newman and Co., 1847.

Wirth, Louis. "Types of Nationalism." *American Journal of Sociology*, XLI (May, 1936), 723–737.

Internationales Jahrbuch für Geschichtsunterricht, Internationales Schulbuchinstitut, Braunschweig, Germany, 1953–1963.

BIBLIOGRAPHY OF TEXTBOOKS USED

READERS

Key	*Publication*
R 1785 New England Primer	*The New England Primer Improved.* Boston: E. Draper for B. Larkin, between 1785 and 1790. Reprint by Ginn and Co., New York, n.d.
R 1787 Miscellanies	*Miscellanies, Moral and Instructive, in Prose and Verse; collected from Various Authors for the use of schools, and improvement of Young Persons of both sexes.* Philadelphia: Jos. James, 1787.
R 1789 Webster	Webster, Noah. *An American Selection of Lessons in Reading and Speaking.* Hartford, Conn.: Hudson and Goodwin, 1789.
R 1790 Webster	Webster, Noah. *An American Selection of Lessons in Reading and Speaking.* Boston: Isaiah Thomas and Ebenezer T. Andrews, 1790.
R 1792 Dana	Dana, Joseph. *A New American Selection of Lessons in Reading and Speaking.* Boston: Samuel Hall, 1792.
R 1793 Moore	Moore, J. Hamilton. *The Young Gentleman and Lady's Monitor and English Teacher's Assistant.* New York: Samuel Campbell, 1793.
R 1794 Burgh	Burgh, James. *The Art of Speaking.* Boston: Thomas Hall, 1794.
R 1794 Dana	Dana, Joseph. *A New American Selection of Lessons in Reading and Speaking.* Boston: Thomas and Andrews, 1794.
R 1794 Guide	*A Guide, or Counsellor of Human Life.* Springfield, Mass.: Edward Gray, 1794.
R 1794 Webster	Webster, Noah. *An American Selection of Lessons in Reading and Writing.* 1st ed. New York: George Bruce and Co., 1794.
R 1794 Webster-2	Webster, Noah. *An American Selection of Lessons in Reading and Speaking.* Hartford, Conn.: Hudson and Goodwin, 1794. (Same as preceding book.)

R 1794 Webster-3	Webster, Noah. *An American Selection of Lessons in Reading and Speaking*. Worcester, Mass.: Thomas and Andrews, 1794. (Same as New York Edition.)
R 1795 Burgh	Burgh, James. *The Art of Speaking*. Danbury, Conn.: Edmund and Ephraim Washburn, 1795.
R 1795 Moore	Moore, J. Hamilton. *The Young Gentleman and Lady's Monitor and English Teacher's Assistant.* Hudson, N.Y.: Ashbel Stoddard, 1795.
R 1796 Bingham	Bingham, Caleb. *The American Preceptor*. Boston: Manning and Loring, 1796.
R 1797 Alexander	Alexander, Caleb. *The Young Gentlemen and Ladies' Instructor*. Boston: E. Larkin and W. P. and L. Blake, 1797.
R 1797 Bingham.	Bingham, Caleb. *The American Preceptor*, 4th ed. Boston: Manning and Loring, 1797.
R 1797 Thomas	Thomas, Alexander. *The Orator's Assistant.* Worcester, Mass.: Isaiah Thomas, Jr., October, 1797.
R 1798 Enfield	Enfield, William. *The Speaker: or, Miscellaneous Pieces, selected from the Best English Writers*. Hudson, N.Y.: Ashbel Stoddard, 1798.
R 1799 Dana	Dana, Joseph. *A New American Selection of Lessons in Reading and Speaking*. 3rd ed. Worcester, Mass.: Thomas and Andrews, 1799.
R 1799 New Pleasing	*The New Pleasing Instructor: or, Young Lady's Guide to Virtue and Happiness*. Boston: Thomas and Andrews, 1799.
R 1799 Webster	Webster, Noah. *An American Selection of Lessons in Reading and Speaking*. Boston: Thomas and Andrews, 1799.
R 180? Murray	Murray, Lindley. *The English Reader*. No publisher, no place, no date.
R 1800 Burgh	Burgh, James. *The Art of Speaking*. Philadelphia: Charles Cist, 1800.
R 1801 Bingham	Bingham, Caleb. *The American Preceptor*. Boston: Manning and Loring, 1801.
R 1801 Chipman	Chipman, George. *The American Moralist.* Wrentham, Mass.: Nathaniel Heaton, 1801.
R 1801 Heaton-C	Heaton, Nathaniel, Jun. *The Columbian Preceptor*. Wrentham, Mass.: N. Heaton, 1801.

R 1801 Heaton-P — Heaton, Nathaniel. *The Pleasing Library.* Wrentham, Mass.: N. Heaton, 1801.

R 1802 Alden — Alden, Abner. *The Reader.* Boston: Thomas and Andrews, 1802.

R 1802 Bingham — Bingham, Caleb. *The American Preceptor.* Boston: Manning and Loring, 1802.

R 1802 Columbian — *The Columbian Reading Book, or Historical Preceptor.* Philadelphia: M. Carey, 1802.

R 1802 Miscellanies — *Miscellanies, Moral and Instructive, in Prose and Verse.* Philadelphia: Henry Sweitzer, 1802.

R 1803 D. Adams — Adams, Daniel. *The Understanding Reader: or, Knowledge before Oratory.* 5th ed. Boston: Isaiah Thomas, 1803.

R 1803 D. Adams-7th — Adams, Daniel. *The Understanding Reader: or Knowledge before Oratory.* 7th ed. Boston: Isaiah Thomas, 1803.

R 1803 Biglow — Biglow, William. *The Youth's Library.* Vol. I. Salem, Mass.: Joshua Cushing, 1803.

R 1803 Carey — Carey, Mathew. *The School of Wisdom, or, American Monitor.* 2nd ed. Philadelphia: S. C. Ustick, 1803.

R 1803 Enfield — Enfield, William. *The Speaker: or Miscellaneous Pieces Selected from the Best English Writers.* Baltimore: Warner and Hanna, 1803.

R 1803 Moore — Moore, J. Hamilton. *The Young Gentleman and Lady's Monitor and English Teacher's Assistant.* Wilmington, Del.: Peter Brynberg, 1803.

R 1803 Murray — Murray, Lindley. *The English Reader: or, Pieces in Prose and Poetry.* Boston: E. Larkin, 1803.

R 1803 Murray-S — Murray, Lindley. *Sequel to the English Reader: or, Elegant Selections in Prose and Poetry.* 2nd ed. Philadelphia: Ben Johnson and Jacob Johnson, 1803.

R 1804 Adams — Adams, Daniel. *The Understanding Reader: or, Knowledge before Oratory.* 2nd ed. Leominster, Mass.: Adams, 1804.

R 1804 Alden — Alden, Abner, *The Reader.* 2nd ed. Boston: Thomas and Andrews, 1804.

R 1804 Bingham — Bingham, Caleb. *The American Preceptor.* Boston: Manning and Loring, 1804.

R 1804 New Introduction	*A New Introduction to Reading: or, a Collection of Easy Lessons.* 7th ed. with additions. Alexandria, Va.: Cottom and Stewart, 1804.
R 1804 Peirce	Peirce, Charles. *The Portsmouth Miscellany: or, Lady's Library Improved.* Portsmouth, N.H.: November 1, 1804.
R 1804 Webster	Webster, Noah. *An American Selection of Lessons in Reading and Speaking.* New York: Evert Duyckinck, 1804.
R 1805 Webster	Webster, Noah. *An American Selection of Lessons in Reading and Speaking.* Salem, Mass.: Cushing and Appleton, 1805.
R 1806 Bingham	Bingham, Caleb. *The American Preceptor.* 29th ed. Boston: Manning and Loring, 1806.
R 1806 Cooledge	Cooledge, Daniel. *The Pious Instructor.* Walpole, N.H.: Charter and Hale, 1806.
R 1806 Murray	Murray, Lindley. *Sequel to the English Reader.* 2nd ed. New York: Collins, Perkins and Company, 1806.
R 1806 Peirce	Peirce, Charles. *The Arts and Sciences Abridged with a selection of Pieces from celebrated modern authors . . .* Portsmouth, N.H.: Charles Peirce, 1806.
R 1806 Staniford	Staniford, Daniel. *The Art of Reading.* Boston: John West, 1806.
R 1807 D. Adams	Adams, Daniel. *The Understanding Reader: or Knowledge before Oratory.* Cambridge Port, Mass.: Thomas and William Parker, 1807.
R 1807 Bingham-C	Bingham, Caleb. *The Columbian Orator.* 8th ed. Boston: Manning and Loring, 1807.
R 1807 Bingham	Bingham, Caleb. *The American Preceptor.* 32nd ed. Boston: Manning and Loring, 1807.
R 1807 Moore	Moore, J. Hamilton. *The Young Gentleman and Lady's Monitor and English Teacher's Assistant.* 3rd ed. Hartford, Conn.: O. D. Cooke, 1807.
R 1807 Staniford	Staniford, Daniel. *The Art of Reading.* 6th ed. Boston: John West, 1807.
R 1808 Alden	Alden, Abner. *The Reader.* Boston: Thomas and Andrews, 1808.
R 1808 Enfield	Enfield, William. *The Speaker, or Miscellaneous Pieces.* Boston: Joseph Larkin, 1808.

R 1808 Webster	Webster, Noah. *An American Selection of Lessons in Reading and Speaking*. 3rd ed. Utica, N.Y.: Seward and Williams, 1808.
R 1809 Murray-S	Murray, Lindley. *Sequel to the English Reader*. 1st ed. Boston: Lincoln and Edmands, 1809.
R 1809 Picket	Picket, Albert. *The Juvenile Mentor*. New York: Smith and Forman, 1809.
R 1810 Alden	Alden, Abner. *The Speaker*. Boston: Thomas and Andrews, 1810.
R 1810 MacDonnel	MacDonnel, D. E. *A Dictionary of Select and Popular Quotations which are in Daily Use*. 1st American ed. from 5th London ed. Philadelphia: A. Finley, 1810.
R 1810 Picket	Picket, Albert. *The Juvenile Expositor*. New York: Smith and Forman, 1810.
R 1810 Thomson	Thomson, Ignatius. *The Patriot's Monitor, for New Hampshire*. Randolph, Vt.: Sereno Wright, 1810.
R 1811 Bingham	Bingham, Caleb. *The American Preceptor*. 42nd ed. Boston: Manning and Loring, 1811.
R 1811 Bingham-C	Bingham, Caleb. *The Columbian Orator*. 5th ed. Troy, N.Y.: Parker and Bliss, 1811.
R 1811 Chandler	Chandler, Joseph. .*The Young Gentleman and Lady's Museum*. Hallowell, Me.: N. Cheever, 1811.
R 1811 I. Cooke	Cooke, Increase. *The American Orator*. New Haven, Conn.: Increase Cooke and Company, 1811.
R 1811 Hubbard	Hubbard, John. *The American Reader*. 5th ed. Walpole, N.H.: Isaiah Thomas and Company, 1811.
R 1811 Lyman	Lyman, Asa. *The American Reader*. Portland, Me.: A. Lyman and Company, 1811.
R 1811 Murray-I	Murray, Lindley. *Introduction to the English Reader*. 6th ed. Wilmington, Del.: Matthew R. Locherman, 1811.
R 1811 Peirce	Peirce, Charles. *The Arts and Sciences Abridged*. 2nd ed. Portsmouth, N.H.: Charles Peirce, 1811.
R 1811 Staniford	Staniford, Daniel. *The Art of Reading*. 8th ed. Boston: John West and Company, 1811.

R 1812 Bingham-C — Bingham, Caleb. *The Columbian Orator.* 15th ed. Boston: Manning and Loring, 1812.

R 1812 A. Cook — Cook, Amos Jones. *The Student's Companion.* Portland, Me.: Arthur Shirley, 1812.

R 1812 Daggett — Daggett, Herman. *The American Reader.* 2nd ed. Poughkeepsie, N.Y.: Paraclete Potter, 1812.

R 1813 I. Cooke — Cooke, Increase. *Sequel to the American Orator.* New Haven, Conn.: Increase Cooke and Company, 1813.

R 1813 Moore — Moore, J. Hamilton. *The Young Gentleman and Lady's Monitor and English Teacher's Assistant.* New York: Evert Duyckinck, 1813.

R 1813 New York — *The New York Reader #2.* New York: Samuel Wood, 1813.

R 1813 Richardson — Richardson, Joseph. *The American Reader.* 2nd ed. Boston: Lincoln and Edmands, 1813.

R 1814 Alden — Alden, Abner. *The Reader.* 4th ed. Boston: Thomas and Andrews, 1814.

R 1814 Murray-I — Murray, Lindley. *Introduction to the English Reader.* 1st ed. Trenton, N.J.: Moore and Lake, 1814.

R 1814 Staniford — Staniford, Daniel. *The Art of Reading.* 10th ed. Boston: West and Richardson, 1814.

R 1815 R. Adams — Adams, Rufus. *The Young Gentleman and Lady's Explanatory Monitor.* 2nd ed., revised and corrected. Zanesville, Ohio: David Chambers, 1815.

R 1815 American — *The American Class Book.* 2nd ed., revised and corrected. Philadelphia: John Richardson, 1815.

R 1815 Bingham — Bingham, Caleb. *The American Preceptor.* Boston: B. and J. Collins, 1815.

R 1815 Bingham-C — Bingham, Caleb. *The Columbian Orator.* 6th ed. Troy, N.Y.: Parker and Bliss, 1815.

R 1815 Dickinson — Dickinson, Rodolphus. *The Columbian Reader.* 1st ed. Boston: R. P. and C. Williams, 1815.

R 1815 Murray — Murray, Lindley. *The English Reader.* Burlington, Vt.: Samuel Mills, 1815.

R 1815 Murray-I — Murray, Lindley. *Introduction to the English Reader.* Boston: Lincoln and Edmands, 1815.

R 1816 D. Adams	Adams, Daniel. *The Understanding Reader: or, Knowledge Before Oratory.* 8th ed. Boston: Isaiah Thomas, 1816.
R 1816 Murray-1	Murray, Lindley. *The English Reader.* 1st ed. Burlington, N.J.: David Allinson, 1816.
R 1816 Murray-3	Murray, Lindley. *The English Reader.* 3rd ed. Wilmington, Del.: R. Porter, 1816.
R 1816 Murray-I	Murray, Lindley. *Introduction to the English Reader.* New York: Collins and Company, 1816.
R 1816 Murray-S	Murray, Lindley. *Sequel to the English Reader.* Boston: Lincoln and Edmands, 1816.
R 1816 Staniford	Staniford, Daniel. *The Art of Reading.* 11th ed. Boston: West and Richardson, 1816.
R 1816 Webster	Webster, Noah. *An American Selection of Lessons in Reading and Speaking.* 7th ed. Philadelphia: David Hogan, 1816.
R 1817 Bingham	Bingham, Caleb. *The American Preceptor.* 10th ed. New York: Evert Duyckinck, 1817.
R 1817 Bingham-C	Bingham, Caleb. *The Columbian Orator.* Boston: Caleb Bingham and Company, 1817.
R 1817 Staniford	Staniford, Daniel. *The Art of Reading.* 12th ed. Boston: West and Richardson, 1817.
R 1818 R. Adams	Adams, Rufus. *The Young Gentleman and Lady's Explanatory Monitor.* 5th ed. Columbus, Ohio: B. Griswold, Jun., 1818.
R 1818 Bingham	Bingham, Caleb. *The American Preceptor.* Rutland, Vt.: Fay, Davison and Burt, 1818.
R 1818 I. Cooke	Cooke, Increase. *The American Orator.* New Haven, Conn.: Sidney's Press, 1818.
R 1818 Daggett	Daggett, Herman. *The American Reader.* Poughkeepsie, N.Y.: Paraclete Potter, 1818.
R 1818 Murray	Murray, Lindley. *The English Reader.* Albany, N.Y.: G. J. Loomis and Company, 1818.
R 1819 D. Adams	Adams, Daniel. *The Understanding Reader.* 9th ed. Boston: Isaiah Thomas, 1819.
R 1819 Murray	Murray, Lindley. *The English Reader.* Fredericktown, Md.: George Kolb, 1819.
R 1819 Strong	Strong, T. *The Common Reader.* 2nd ed. Greenfield, Mass.: Denio and Phelps, 1819.
R 1820 Murray	Murray, Lindley. *The English Reader.* Exeter, N.H.: John J. Williams, 1820.

R 1821 D. Adams	Adams, Daniel. *The Understanding Reader.* 10th ed. Leicester, Mass.: Hori Brown, 1821.
R 1821 Bingham	Bingham, Caleb. *The American Preceptor Improved.* 64th ed., 4th improved ed. Boston: Caleb Bingham and Company, 1821.
R 1821 Murray	Murray, Lindley. *The English Reader.* Exeter, N.H.: John J. Williams, 1821.
R 1821 Murray-S	Murray, Lindley. *Sequel to the English Reader.* Woodstock, Vt.: D. Watson, 1821.
R 1822 Alden	Alden, Abner. *The Reader.* 5th ed. Boston: James Loring, 1822.
R 1823 Blake	Blake, J. L. *The Historical Reader.* Concord, N.H.: George Hough, 1823.
R 1823 Morrill	Morrill, Isaac. *The Scholar's Companion.* Norwich, Conn.: Robinson and Dunham, 1823.
R 1823 Murray	Murray, Lindley. *The English Reader.* Exeter, N.H.: John J. Williams, 1823.
R 1823 Murray-I	Murray, Lindley. *Introduction to the English Reader.* Boston: Lincoln and Edmands, 1823.
R 1823 Pierpont	Pierpont, John. *The American First Class Book.* Boston: William B. Fowle, 1823.
R 1823 Richardson	Richardson, Joseph. *The American Reader.* 3rd ed. Boston: Lincoln and Edmands, 1823.
R 1823 N. Worcester	Worcester, Noah. *Friends of Youth.* Boston: Cummings, Hilliard and Company, 1823.
R 1824 D. Adams	Adams, Daniel. *The Agricultural Reader.* Boston: Richardson and Lord, 1824.
R 1824 Lowe	Lowe, A. T. *The Columbian Class Book.* Worcester, Mass.: Dorr and Howland, 1824.
R 1824 Murray	Murray, Lindley. *The English Reader.* Boston: Lincoln and Edmands, 1824.
R 1824 Pierpont	Pierpont, John. *The American First Class Book.* Boston: T. P. and J. S. Fowle, 1824.
R 1824 Strong	Strong, T. *The Common Reader.* 3rd ed. Greenfield, Mass.: Denio, Clark, and Tyler, 1824.
R 1825 Blake	Blake, J. L. *The Historical Reader.* Concord, N.H.: Isaac Hill, 1825.
R 1825 A. Cook	Cook, Amos J. *The Student's Companion.* 2nd ed. Concord, N.H.: Isaac Hill, 1825.
R 1825 Lowe	Lowe, A. T. *The Columbian Class Book.* 2nd ed. Worcester, Mass.: Dorr and Howland, 1825.

R 1825 Murray — Murray, Lindley. *The English Reader*. Hartford, Conn.: Oliver D. Cooke and Company, 1825.

R 1825 Pierpont — Pierpont, John. *The American First Class Book*. Boston: Cummings, Hilliard and Company, 1825.

R 1825 Torrey — Torrey, Jesse, Jr. *A Pleasing Companion for Little Girls and Boys*. 2nd revised ed. Philadelphia: John Grigg, 1825.

R 1826 American-S — *The American Speaker, or Exercises in Rhetorick*. Boston: Cummings, Hilliard and Company, 1826.

R 1826 Frost — Frost, John. *The Class Book of American Literature*. Boston: J. H. A. Frost, 1826.

R 1826 Greenwood and Emerson — Greenwood, F. W. P. and G. B. Emerson. *The Classical Reader*. Boston: Lincoln and Edmands, 1826.

R 1826 Lowe — Lowe, A. T. *Second Class Book*. Brookfield, Mass.: E. and G. Merriam, 1826.

R 1826 Murray-I — Murray, Lindley. *Introduction to the English Reader*. Raleigh, N.C.: John Gates and Sons, 1826.

R 1826 Murray — Murray, Lindley. *The English Reader*. Philadelphia: S. Probasco, 1826.

R 1826 Murray-M — Murray, Lindley. *Murray's English Reader*. Concord, Mass.: Jacob B. Moore, 1826.

R 1826 Murray-2 — Murray, Lindley. *The English Reader*. Manchester, Vt.: J. R. Shute and Company, 1826.

R 1826 Pierpont — Pierpont, John. *The American First Class Book*. Boston: Hilliard, Gray, Little and Wilkins, 1826.

R 1827 Blake — Blake, J. L. *The Historical Reader*. Concord, N.H.: Manahan, Hoag and Company, 1827.

R 1827 Lowe — Lowe, A. T. *The Columbian Class Book*. 3rd ed. Worcester, Mass.: Dorr and Howland, 1827.

R 1827 Murray — Murray, Lindley. *The English Reader*. Brattleborough, Vt.: Holbrook and Fessenden, 1827.

R 1827 Murray-2 — Murray, Lindley. *The English Reader*. Bellows Falls, Vt.: James I. Cutler and Company, 1827.

R 1827 Murray-3 — Murray, Lindley. *The English Reader*. Cooperstown, N.Y.: H. and E. Phinney, 1827.

R 1827 Murray-4 — Murray, Lindley. *The English Reader*. Utica, N.Y.: Hastings and Tracy, 1827.

R 1827 Pierpont — Pierpont, John. *The National Reader*. Boston: Hilliard, Gray, Little and Wilkins, 1827.

R 1828 American-R — *The American Reader*. Brookfield, Mass.: E. and G. Merriam, 1828.

R 1828 Blake — Blake, J. L. *The Historical Reader*. Concord, N.H.: Horatio Hill and Company, 1828.

R 1828 Greenwood and Emerson — Greenwood, F. W. P. and G. B. Emerson. *The Classical Reader*. Boston: Lincoln and Edmands, 1828.

R 1828 Hopkins — Hopkins, Jesse. *The Patriot's Manual*. Utica, N.Y.: William Williams, 1828.

R 1828 Murray — Murray, Lindley. *The English Reader*. Concord, N.H.: Horatio Hill and Company, 1828.

R 1828 New York — *The New York Reader, #3*. New York: Samuel Wood and Sons, 1828.

R 1828 Pierpont-I — Pierpont, John. *Introduction to the National Reader*. Boston: Richardson and Lord, 1828.

R 1828 Pierpont-N — Pierpont, John. *The National Reader*. Boston: Hilliard, Gray, Little and Wilkins, 1828.

R 1828 Putnam — Putnam, Samuel. *The Analytical Reader*. 4th ed. Dover, N.H.: Samuel C. Stevens, 1828.

R 1828 Putnam-S — Putnam, Samuel. *Sequel to the Analytical Reader*. Portland, Me.: Shirley and Hyde, 1828.

R 1828 Robbins-A — [Robbins, Eliza.] *American Popular Lessons*. New York: R. Lockwood, 1828.

R 1828 Robbins-P — [Robbins, Eliza.] *Poetry for Schools*. New York: White, Gallaher and White, 1828.

R 1828 Willard-G — [Willard, Samuel.] *The General Class-Book*. 1st ed. Greenfield, Mass.: A. Phelps and A. Clark, 1828.

R 1829 Bingham — Bingham, Caleb. *The American Preceptor Improved*. 68th ed., 8th improved ed. Boston: J. H. A. Frost, 1829.

R 1829 Greenwood and Emerson — Greenwood, F. W. P. and G. B. Emerson. *The Classical Reader*. Boston: Lincoln and Edmands, 1829.

R 1829 Lowe — Lowe, A. T. *The Columbian Class Book*. 4th ed. Worcester, Mass.: Dorr and Howland, 1829.

R 1829 Miscellanies — *Miscellanies, Moral and Instructive, In Prose and Verse*. 2nd Burlington ed. Philadelphia: Edmund Morris, 1829.

R 1829 Murray — Murray, Lindley. *The English Reader*. Albany, N.Y.: W. Disturnell, 1829.

R 1829 Murray-2 — Murray, Lindley. *The English Reader*. Cooperstown, N.Y.: H. and E. Phinney, 1829.

R 1829 Murray-3 — Murray, Lindley. *Murray's English Reader*. Windsor, Vt.: Simeon Ide, 1829.

R 1829 Murray-4 — Murray, Lindley. *The English Reader*. Cooperstown, N.Y.: H. and E. Phinney, 1829.

R 1829 Murray-M — Murray, Lindley. *Murray's English Reader*. Albany, N.Y.: S. Shaw, 1829.

R 1829 Pierpont — Pierpont, John. *The American First Class Book*. Boston: Hilliard, Gray, Little and Wilkins, 1829.

R 1829 Pierpont-N — Pierpont, John. *The National Reader*. Boston: Richardson, Lord and Holbrook, 1829.

R 1829 Selection — *A Selection of Reading Lessons for Common Schools*. Keene, N.H.: George Tilden, 1829.

R 1830 Bartlett — Bartlett, M. R. *A Common School Manual*. 2nd revised ed. New York: M. R. Bartlett, 1830.

R 1830 Emerson — Emerson, B. D. *The Academical Speaker*. Boston: Richardson, Lord and Holbrook, 1830.

R 1830 Frost — Frost, John. *The Easy Reader*. 2nd ed. Boston: Carter, Hendee and Babcock, 1830.

R 1830 Hughs — Hughs, Thomas. *The Universal Class Book*. Philadelphia: Uriah Hunt, 1830.

R 1830 MacLeod — MacLeod, Donald. *The Orator's Text Book*. Washington City, D.C.: Pishey Thompson, 1830.

R 1830 Murray — Murray, Lindley. *The English Reader*. Newark, N.J.: Benjamin Olds, 1830.

R 1830 Pierpont — Pierpont, John. *The American First Class Book*. Boston: Hilliard, Gray, Little and Wilkins, 1830.

R 1830 Pierpont-I — Pierpont, John. *Introduction to the National Reader*. Boston: Richardson, Lord and Holbrook, 1830.

R 1830 Pierpont-Y — Pierpont, John. *The Young Reader*. Boston: Richardson, Lord and Holbrook, 1830.

R 1830 Practical-R — *Practical Reading Lessons on the Three Great Duties which Man owes to His Maker—His Fellow Beings—and Himself*. Philadelphia: E. L. Carey and A. Hart, 1830.

R 1830 Putnam — Putnam, Samuel. *The Analytical Reader.* 6th ed., enlarged. Dover, N.H.: Samuel C. Stevens, 1830.

R 1830 Putnam-I — Putnam, Samuel. *Introduction to the Analytical Reader.* 2nd ed. Boston: Perkins and Marvin, 1830.

R 1830 S. Willard — Willard, Samuel. *Rhetoric, or the Principles of Elocution and Rhetorical Composition.* Boston: Leonard C. Bowles, 1830.

R 1831 Bailey — Bailey, Ebenezer. *The Young Ladies' Class Book.* Boston: Lincoln and Edmands, 1831.

R 1831 Daggett — Daggett, Herman. *The American Reader.* Poughkeepsie, N.Y.: Paraclete Potter, 1831.

R 1831 Cheever — Cheever, G. B. *The American Common-Place Book of Prose.* Boston: Carter and Hendee, 1831.

R 1831 Child — *The Child's Assistant in Acquiring Useful and Practical Knowledge.* 4th ed. Brookfield, Mass.: E. and G. Merriam, 1831.

R 1831 Hall — Hall, Harriet W. *The School Companion.* Cincinnati: Robinson and Fairbank, 1831.

R 1831 Harrod — Harrod, John J. *The Academical Reader.* 2nd ed. Baltimore: John J. Harrod, 1831.

R 1831 Lowe-Second — Lowe, A. T. *Second Class Book.* Worcester, Mass.: Dorr and Howland, 1831.

R 1831 Murray-S — Murray, Lindley. *Sequel to the English Reader.* Philadelphia: S. Probasco, 1831.

R 1831 Pierpont — Pierpont, John. *The American First Class Book.* Boston: Hilliard, Gray, Little and Wilkins, 1831.

R 1831 Pierpont-I — Pierpont, John. *Introduction to the National Reader.* Boston: Richardson, Lord and Holbrook, 1831.

R 1831 Pierpont-N — Pierpont, John. *The National Reader.* Boston: Richardson, Lord and Holbrook, 1831.

R 1831 Progressive — *The Progressive Reader or Juvenile Monitor.* Concord, N.H.: 1831.

R 1831 Smiley — Smiley, Thomas T. *The United States Speaker.* 23rd ed., enlarged and improved. Philadelphia: Henry Longstreth, 1831.

R 1831 Sullivan — Sullivan, William. *The Moral Class Book.* 1st ed. Boston: Richardson, Lord and Holbrook, 1831.

R 1831 S. Willard — [Willard, Samuel.] *Secondary Lessons, or the Improved Reader*. 5th ed. New Haven, Conn.: Durrie and Peck, 1831.

R 1832 American-P — *The American Primary Class Book*. Providence, R.I.: A. S. Beckwith and Hutchens and Shepard, 1832.

R 1832 Bailey — Bailey, Ebenezer. *The Young Ladies' Class Book*. Boston: Lincoln and Edmands, 1832.

R 1832 Cobb — Cobb, Lyman. *Cobb's Juvenile Reader. #3*. Oxford, N.Y.: Chapman and Flagler, 1832.

R 1832 Edwards — Edwards, B. B. *The Eclectic Reader*. Boston: Perkins and Marvin, 1832.

R 1832 Pierpont — Pierpont, John. *The American First Class Book*. Boston: Carter, Hendee and Company, 1832.

R 1832 Pierpont-N — Pierpont, John. *The National Reader*. Boston: Richardson, Lord and Holbrook, 1832.

R 1832 Progressive — *The Progressive Reader or Juvenile Monitor*. Montpelier, Vt.: George W. Hill, 1832.

R 1832 Putnam-S — Putnam, Samuel. *Sequel to the Analytical Reader*. Dover, N.H.: E. French, 1832.

R 1833 Bailey — Bailey, Ebenezer. *The Young Ladies' Class Book*. Boston: Lincoln and Edmands, 1833.

R 1833 Barnum — Barnum, H. L. *The Child's Third Book of Spelling and Reading*. Boston: Carter, Hendee and Company, 1833.

R 1833 Colburn — Colburn, Warren. *Second Lessons in Reading and Grammar*. Boston: Hilliard, Gray and Company, 1833.

R 1833 Emerson — Emerson, B. D. *The First-Class Reader*. Claremont, N.H.: Claremont Manufacturing Co., 1833.

R 1833 Leavitt — Leavitt, Joshua. *Easy Lessons in Reading*. Keene, N.H.: J. and J. W. Prentiss, 1833.

R 1833 Murray — Murray, Lindley. *The English Reader*. Philadelphia: Samuel W. Neall, 1833.

R 1833 Murray-I — Murray, Lindley. *Introduction to the English Reader*. Boston: Lincoln and Edmands, 1833.

R 1833 Olney — Olney, J. *The Easy Reader*. New Haven, Conn.: Durrie and Peck, 1833.

R 1833 Pierpont-N — Pierpont, John. *The National Reader*. Boston: Carter, Hendee and Company, 1833.

R 1833 S. Willard — [Willard, Samuel.] *The General Class Book*. 10th ed. Greenfield, Mass.: A. Phelps, 1833.

R 1834 Angell — Angell, Oliver. *The Union #5*. Philadelphia: Marshall, Clark and Company, 1834.

R 1834 Emerson — Emerson, B. D. *The First Class Reader*. Boston: Russell, Odiorne and Metcalf, 1834.

R 1834 Murray — Murray, Lindley. *The English Reader*. Elizabethtown, N.J.: T. O. Sayre, 1834.

R 1834 S. Willard-G — [Willard, Samuel.] *The General Class Book*. 12th ed. Greenfield, Mass.: A. Phelps, 1834.

R 1834 S. Willard-P — [Willard, Samuel.] *The Popular Reader, or Complete Scholar*. Greenfield, Mass.: A. Phelps, 1834.

R 1834 S. Worcester — Worcester, Samuel. *A Fourth Book of Lessons for Reading*. Boston: Carter, Hendee and Company, 1834.

R 1835 Merriam — [Merriam, Charles.] *The Intelligent Reader*. Springfield, Mass.: G. and C. Merriam, 1835.

R 1835 Murray — Murray, Lindley. *The English Reader*. Boston: Robert S. Davis, 1835.

R 1835 Pierpont — Pierpont, John. *The American First Class Book*. 30th ed. New York: George F. Cooledge, 1835.

R 1835 Pierpont-I — Pierpont, John. *Introduction to the National Reader*. 16th ed. Boston: Carter, Hendee and Company, 1835.

R 1835 Pierpont-N — Pierpont, John. *The National Reader*. 40th ed. New York: George F. Cooledge and Brother, 1835.

R 1835 Pierpont-Y — Pierpont, John. *The Young Reader*. 20th ed. New York: George F. Cooledge, 1835.

R 1835 Porter — Porter, Ebenezer. *The Rhetorical Reader*. 22nd ed. New York: Mark H. Newman, 1835.

R 1835 Webster — Webster, Noah. *Instructive and Entertaining Lessons for Youth*. New Haven, Conn.: S. Babcock and Durrie and Peck, 1835.

R 1836 Abbott — Abbott, Messrs. *The Mount Vernon Reader*. New York: Collins, Reese and Company, 1836.

R 1836 Cobb — Cobb, Lyman. *Cobb's Juvenile Reader #3*. Philadelphia: James Kay, Jr. and Brother, 1836.

R 1836 Cobb-N.A. — Cobb, Lyman. *The North American Reader*. Trenton, N.J.: B. Davenport, 1836.

R 1836 Murray	Murray, Lindley. *The English Reader.* New London, Conn.: W. and J. Bolles, 1836.
R 1836 Parsons	Parsons, Lemuel H. *The Grammatical Reader.* Philadelphia: William Marshall and Company, 1836.
R 1836 Pierpont	Pierpont, John. *The American First Class Book.* 25th ed. Boston: Charles Bowen, 1836.
R 1836 Pierpont-N	Pierpont, John. *The National Reader.* 28th ed. Boston: Charles Bowen, 1836.
R 1836 Porter	Porter, Ebenezer. *The Rhetorical Reader.* 23rd ed. New York: Leavitt, Lord and Company, 1836.
R 1837 Fowle	Fowle, William Bentley. *The Primary Reader.* Boston: published by the author, 1837.
R 1837 Progressive	*The Progressive Reader or Juvenile Monitor.* Montpelier, Vt.: George W. Hill, 1837.
R 1837 Putnam	Putnam, Samuel. *The Introduction to the Analytical Reader.* Portland, Me.: William Hyde, 1837.
R 1838 Angell	Angell, Oliver. *The Union Number Two: or, Child's Second Book.* 10th ed. Philadelphia: W. Marshall and Company, 1838.
R 1838 Blake	Blake, J. L. *The First Reader: A Class-book for Schools.* Concord, N.H.: Horatio Hill, 1838.
R 1838 Cobb	Cobb, Lyman. *Cobb's Juvenile Reader #3.* Sandy Hill, N.Y.: David Howland, 1838.
R 1838 Colburn	Colburn, Warren. *Third Lessons in Reading and Grammar.* Boston: Hilliard, Gray and Company, 1838.
R 1838 Murray	Murray, Lindley. *The English Reader.* Concord, N.H.: John F. Brown, 1838.
R 1838 Putnam	Putnam, Samuel. *Sequel to the Analytical Reader.* New York: Samuel S. and William Wood, 1838.
R 1838 S. Worcester	Worcester, Samuel. *A Third Book for Reading and Spelling.* 20th ed. Boston: Charles J. Hendee and G. W. Palmer and Company, 1838.
R 1839 S. Goodrich	Goodrich, S. G. *The Fourth Reader.* Boston: Otis, Broaders and Company, 1839.
R 1839 Greenwood and Emerson	Greenwood, F. W. P. and G. B. Emerson. *The Classical Reader.* Boston: Robert S. Davis, 1839.
R 1839 Pierpont	Pierpont, John. *The American First Class Book.* 25th ed. Boston: David H. Williams, 1839.

R 1839 Pierpont-N — Pierpont, John. *The National Reader*. 28th ed. Boston: David H. Williams, 1839.

R 1839 Pierpont-Y — Pierpont, John. *The Young Reader*. 15th ed. Boston: David H. Williams, 1839.

R 1839 Porter — Porter, Ebenezer. *The Rhetorical Reader*. 52nd ed. Andover, Mass.: Gould and Newman, 1839.

R 1839 Robbins — [Robbins, Eliza.] *American Popular Lessons*. New York: R. Lockwood, 1839.

R 1839 Sigourney — Sigourney, Mrs. L. H. *The Boy's Reading-Book*. New York: J. Orville Taylor, 1839.

R 1839 S. Willard — Willard, Samuel. *Secondary Lessons*. 35th ed. Greenfield, Mass.: Phelps and Ingersoll, 1839.

R 1839 S. Worcester — Worcester, Samuel. *A Fourth Book of Lessons for Reading*. Boston: C. J. Hendee and Jenks and Palmer, 1839.

R 1840 Abbott — Abbott, The Messrs. *The Mount Vernon Reader*. Boston: William Crosby and Company, 1840.

R 1840 Angell-2 — Angell, Oliver. *The Union #2; or, The Child's Second Book*. 11th ed. Philadelphia: Marshall, Williams and Butler, 1840.

R 1840 Angell-3 — Angell, Oliver. *The Union, or the Child's Third Book*. 11th ed. Philadelphia: Marshall, Williams and Butler, 1840.

R 1840 Pierpont — Pierpont, John. *The American First Class Book*. 25th ed. Boston: David H. Williams, 1840.

R 1840 Porter — Porter, Ebenezer. *The Rhetorical Reader*. Andover, Mass.: Gould and Newman, 1840.

R 1840 Snow — Snow, P. H. *The American Reader*. Hartford, Conn.: Spaulding and Storrs, 1840.

R 1840 Williams — Williams, Smith. *The Supplement, or Deficiency Supplied*. Concord, N.H.: I. S. Boyd, 1840.

R 1841 Merriam — Merriam, George and Charles. *The Village Reader*. Springfield, Mass.: G. and C. Merriam, 1841.

R 1841 Murray — Murray, Lindley. *The English Reader*. Newark, N.J.: Benjamin Olds, 1841.

R 1841 Pierpont — Pierpont, John. *The American First Class Book*. 26th ed. Boston: David H. Williams, 1841.

R 1841 Pierpont-I — Pierpont, John. *Introduction to the National Reader*. Boston: David H. Williams, 1841.

R 1841 Pierpont-N — Pierpont, John. *The National Reader*. 28th ed. Boston: David H. Williams, 1841.

R 1841 Porter	Porter, Ebenezer. *The Rhetorical Reader.* 100th ed. New York: Dayton and Saxton, 1841.
R 1841 Tower	Tower, David B. *The Gradual Reader.* Boston: Charles Stimpson, Jr., 1841.
R 1842 Palmer	Palmer, Thomas H. *The Moral Instructor.* Boston: William D. Ticknor and Company, 1842.
R 1842 Porter	Porter, Ebenezer. *The Rhetorical Reader.* 116th ed. New York: Dayton and Newman, 1842.
R 1843 Abbott	Abbott, The Messrs. *The Mount Vernon Reader.* Boston: T. H. Carter and Company, 1843.
R 1843 Cobb	Cobb, Lyman. *Cobb's New Sequel to the Juvenile Readers.* New York: John C. Riker, 1843.
R 1843 Emerson	Emerson, B. D. *The Third Class Reader.* Claremont, N.H.: Claremont Manufacturing Company, Mass.: 1843.
R 1843 Griswold	Griswold, Rufus W. *Readings in American Poetry.* New York: John C. Riker, 1843.
R 1843 McGuffey	McGuffey, William H. *The Eclectic Third Reader.* Cincinnati: Winthrop B. Smith, 1843.
R 1843 Olney	Olney, J. *The National Preceptor.* 6th ed. New York: Robinson, Pratt and Company, 1843.
R 1843 Pierpont	Pierpont, John. *The American First Class Book.* 26th ed. Boston: David H. Williams, 1843.
R 1843 Pierpont-Y	Pierpont, John. *The Young Reader.* 15th ed. Boston: David H. Williams, 1843.
R 1843 Pippin	Pippin, Parley. *The Orator's Ladder in Three Parts.* New York: Nafis and Cornish, 1843.
R 1843 Russell	Russell, William. *Primary Reader.* Boston: Tappan and Dennet, 1843.
R 1843 Swan	Swan, William D. *The Primary School Reader.* Boston: Charles C. Little and James Brown, 1843.
R 1843 Totten	Totten, John C. *The Child's Instructor Improved.* Newark, N.J.: Benjamin Olds, 1843.
R 1844 Bumstead	Bumstead, J. F. *Third Reading-Book in the Primary School.* Boston: William D. Ticknor and Company, 1844.
R 1844 Emerson	Emerson, B. D. *The First Class Reader.* Claremont, N.H.: Simeon Ide, 1844.
R 1844 Goldsbury and Russell	Goldsbury, John and William Russell. *The American Common-School Reader and Speaker.* Boston: Tappan and Whittemore, 1844.

R 1844 Murray — Murray, Lindley. *The English Reader.* New London, Conn.: Bolles and Williams, 1844.

R 1844 Sanders — Sanders, Charles W. *The School Reader Third Book.* 20th ed. New York: Mark H. Newman, 1844.

R 1844 Smith — Smith, Marcus. *The Boston Speaker.* 6th ed. Boston: Joseph Dowe, 1844.

R 1844 Swan-G — Swan, William D. *The Grammar School Reader.* Boston: Charles C. Little and James Brown, 1844.

R 1844 Swan 2nd — Swan, William D. *The Primary School Reader. Part Second.* Boston: Charles C. Little and James Brown, 1844.

R 1844 Swan 3rd — Swan, William D. *The Primary School Reader. Part Third.* Boston: Charles C. Little and James Brown, 1844.

R 1845 D. Adams — Adams, Daniel. *The Monitorial Reader.* Concord, N.H.: Luther Roby, 1845.

R 1845 Goldsbury and Russell — Goldsbury, John and William Russell. *Introduction to the American Common-School Reader and Speaker.* Boston: Charles Tappan, 1845. 21st thousand.

R 1845 Russell — Russell, William. *Sequel to the Primary Reader of Russell's Elementary Series.* Boston: Tappan and Whittemore, 1845. 80th thousand.

R 1845 Swan — Swan, William D. *The District School Reader, designed for the Highest Class.* Boston: Charles C. Little and James Brown, 1845.

R 1845 S. Worcester-I — Worcester, Samuel. *An Introduction to the Third Book for Reading and Spelling.* Boston: Charles J. Hendee and Jenks and Palmer, 1845.

R 1845 S. Worcester-2 — Worcester, Samuel. *A Second Book for Reading and Spelling.* Boston: Jenks and Palmer, 1845.

R 1846 Goldsbury and Russell — Goldsbury, John and William Russell. *Introduction to the American Common-School Reader and Speaker.* Boston: Charles Tappan, 1846.

R 1846 S. Goodrich — Goodrich, Samuel G. *The First School Reader.* Louisville, Ky.: Morton and Griswold, 1846.

R 1846 Murray — Murray, Lindley. *The English Reader.* Philadelphia: Uriah Hunt and Son, 1846.

R 1846 Murray-I — Murray, Lindley. *Introduction to the English Reader.* Philadelphia: Uriah Hunt and Son, 1846.

R 1846 Russell — Russell, William. *Sequel to the Primary Reader.* Boston: Charles Tappan, 1846.

R 1846 Sanders — Sanders, Charles W. *The School Reader. First Book.* New York: Newman and Ivison, 1846.

R 1846 Swan-D — Swan, William D. *The District School Reader. Designed for the Highest Class.* Boston: Charles C. Little and James Brown, 1846.

R 1846 Swan-G — Swan, William D. *The Grammar School Reader . . . Designed to Follow the Primary School Reader. Part 3rd.* Boston: Charles C. Little and James Brown, 1846.

R 1846 S. Worcester — Worcester, Samuel. *A Third Book for Reading and Spelling.* 107th ed. Boston: Charles J. Hendee, 1846.

R 1847 Emerson — Emerson, B. D. *The Third Class Reader.* Philadelphia: Hogan and Thompson, 1847.

R 1847 S. Goodrich — Goodrich, Samuel G. *The Third School Reader.* Louisville, Ky.: Morton and Griswold, 1847.

R 1847 Leavitt — Leavitt, Joshua. *Easy Lessons in Reading for the Younger Classes in Common Schools.* Boston: John P. Jewett and Company, 1847.

R 1847 Maglathlin — Maglathlin, Henry. *The Practical Elocutionist.* Boston: Robert Davis, 1847.

R 1847 New York — *The New York Reader Number 3.* New York: Samuel S. and William Wood, 1847.

R 1847 Rickard and Orcutt-C — Rickard, Truman and Hiram Orcutt. *Class Book of Prose and Poetry.* Boston: Robert S. Davis, 1847.

R 1847 Rickard and Orcutt-P — Rickard, Truman and Hiram Orcutt. *Poetical Selections from the Best of English and American Authors.* Boston: Robert S. Davis, 1847.

R 1847 Russell-H — Russell, William. *Harper's New York Class Book.* New York: Harper and Brothers, 1847.

R 1847 Russell — Russell, William. *Primary Reader.* Boston: Tappan, Whittemore and Mason, 1847.

R 1847 Sanders-2 — Sanders, Charles W. *The School Reader. 2nd Book.* New York: Ivison and Phinney, c. 1847.

R 1848 Rickard and Orcutt-C — Rickard, Truman and Hiram Orcutt. *Class Book of Prose and Poetry.* Boston: Robert S. Davis, 1848.

R 1848 Robbins-A — [Robbins, Eliza.] *American Popular Lessons.* New York: Roe Lockwood and Son, 1848.

R 1848 Robbins-I [Robbins, Eliza.] *Introduction to Popular Lessons for the Use of Small Children in Schools.* New York: Roe Lockwood and Son, 1848.

R 1848 Sanders Sanders, Charles W. *The School Reader. 3rd Book.* New York: Mark H. Newman and Company, 1848.

R 1848 Swan-I Swan, William D. *The Instructive Reader.* Philadelphia: Thomas, Cowperthwait and Company, 1848.

R 1848 Swan-D Swan, William D. *The District School Reader. Designed for the Highest Class.* Philadelphia: Thomas, Cowperthwait and Company, 1848.

R 1848 Swan Swan, William D. *The Primary School Reader.* Philadelphia: Thomas, Cowperthwait and Company, 1848.

R 1848 Tower Tower, David B. *The Gradual Reader.* New York: Cady and Burgess, 1848.

R 1849 Angell-2 Angell, Oliver. *The Child's Second Book.* Philadelphia: E. H. Butler and Company, 1849.

R 1849 Angell-3 Angell, Oliver. *The Child's Third Book.* Philadelphia: E. H. Butler and Company, 1849.

R 1849 Bumstead Bumstead, J. F. *Third Reading Book in the Primary School.* Boston: William D. Ticknor and Company, 1849.

R 1849 Cobb Cobb, Lyman. *Cobb's New Juvenile Reader, Number 2.* Ithaca, N.Y.: Mack, Andrus and Company, 1849.

R 1849 Leavitt Leavitt, Joshua. *Selections for Reading and Speaking for the Higher Classes in Common Schools.* Boston: John P. Jewett and Company, 1849.

R 1849 Mandeville Mandeville, Henry. *The Second Reader.* New York: D. Appleton and Company, 1849.

R 1849 Swan-G Swan, William D. *The Grammar School Reader.* Philadelphia: Thomas, Cowperthwait and Company, 1849.

R 1849 Swan-I Swan, William D. *The Instructive Reader.* Philadelphia: Thomas, Cowperthwait and Company, 1849.

R 1849 S. Worcester Worcester, Samuel. *A Third Book for Reading and Spelling.* Boston: Jenks, Palmer and Company, 1849.

R 1850 Cobb-3 — Cobb, Lyman. *Cobb's Old Juvenile Reader, Number 3*. New York: J. C. Riker, 1850.

R 1850 Cobb-New 3 — Cobb, Lyman. *Cobb's New Juvenile Reader, Number 3*. New York: John C. Riker, 1850.

R 1850 Hall — Hall, Miss A. *The Literary Reader, for Academies and High Schools*. Boston: John P. Jewett and Co., 1850.

R 1850 Mandeville — Mandeville, Henry. *The Third Reader*. New York: D. Appleton and Co., 1850.

R 1850 Swan — Swan, William D. *The Introduction to the Instructive Reader*. Philadelphia: Thomas, Cowperthwait and Co., 1850.

R 1850 Webb — Webb, J. Russell. *Webb's Normal Reader. Number 2*. New York: Mason Bros., 1850.

R 1851 ASDUK — Prepared by a Committee of the American Society for the Diffusion of Useful Knowledge. *The American Readers*. New York: Leavitt and Co., 1851.

R 1851 Furst — *Furst Fonetic Redur*. Boston: Otis Clapp, 1851.

R 1851 Hall — Hall, Miss A. *The Literary Reader*. Boston: John P. Jewett and Co., 1851.

R 1851 Mandeville — Mandeville, Henry. *The Third Reader*. New York: D. Appleton and Co., 1851.

R 1851 Swan-L — Swan, William D. *The Young Ladies' Reader*. Philadelphia: Thomas, Cowperthwait and Co., 1851.

R 1851 Swan-P — Swan, William D. *The Primary School Reader. Part First*. Philadelphia: Thomas, Cowperthwait and Co., 1851.

R 1851 Tower — Tower, David B. *The Gradual Reader* . . . New York: Cady and Burgess, 1851.

R 1852 Brothers — Brothers of the Christian Schools. *The Third Book of Reading Lessons*. New York: Edward Dunigan and Bros., 1852.

R 1852 Cobb — Cobb, Lyman. *Cobb's New Sequel to the Juvenile Reader, or, Fourth Reading Book*. New York: J. C. Riker, 1851.

R 1852 Gilder — Gilder, William H. *New Rhetorical Reader and Elocutionist*. New York: J. C. Riker, 1852.

R 1852 Leavitt — Leavitt, Joshua. *Selections for Reading and Speaking*. Boston: John P. Jewett and Co., 1852.

R 1852 Rickard and Orcutt — Rickard, Truman and Hiram Orcutt. *Class Book of Prose and Poetry*. Boston: Robert S. Davis, 1852.

R 1852 Robbins — [Robbins, Eliza.] *A Class Book of Poetry for the Use of Schools*. New York: D. Appleton and Co., 1852.

R 1852 Sweet — Sweet, Samuel Niles. *Practical Elocution*. Albany, N.Y.: Erastus H. Pease and Co., 1852.

R 1852 Tower and Walker — Tower, David B. and Cornelius Walker. *North American Second Class Reader; the Fourth Book of Tower's Series for Common Schools*. New York: Cady and Burgess, 1852.

R 1852 Town — Town, Salem. *The Grammar School Reader*. Portland, Me.: Sanborn and Carter, 1852.

R 1853 Lingual — By a Literary Association. *The Lingual Reader*. New York: Alexander Montgomery, 1853.

R 1853 McGuffey E-1 — McGuffey, William H. *McGuffey's Eclectic First Reader*. Cincinnati: Sargent, Wilson and Hinkle, 1853.

R 1853 McGuffey E-2 — McGuffey, William H. *McGuffey's Eclectic Second Reader*. Cincinnati: Sargent, Wilson and Hinkle, 1853.

R 1853 McGuffey E-4 — McGuffey, William H. *McGuffey's Newly Revised Eclectic Fourth Reader*. Cincinnati: Sargent, Wilson, and Hinkle, 1853.

R 1853 Mandeville — Mandeville, Henry. *The Fourth Reader*. New York: D. Appleton and Co., 1853.

R 1853 Sanders — Sanders, Charles W. *The School Reader—Third Book*. New York: Ivison and Phinney, 1853.

R 1853 Tower and Walker — Tower, David B. and Cornelius Walker. *North American First Class Reader; the Fifth Book of Tower's Series for Common Schools*. New York: Daniel Burgess and Co., 1853.

R 1853 Town — Town, Salem. *The Second Reader*. Buffalo: Phinney and Co., 1853.

R 1853 Webb — Webb, J. Russell. *Webb's Normal Reader, Number 3*. New York: Lamport, Blakeman and Law, 1853.

R 1854 Bumstead — Bumstead, J. F. *The Second Reading Book in the Primary School*. Boston: Ticknor and Fields, 1854.

R 1854 Burleigh — Burleigh, Joseph Bartlett. *The American Primary School Reader*. Philadelphia: Lippincott, Grambo and Co., 1854.

R 1854 Kay-1 — Kay, James, Jr. *Kay's Infant and Primary School Reader and Definer, Number 1*. Philadelphia: Hayes and Zell, 1854.

R 1854 Kay-3 — Kay, James, Jr. *Kay's Infant and Primary School Reader and Definer, Number 3*. Philadelphia: Hayes and Zell, 1854.

R 1854 Mandeville — Mandeville, Henry. *A Course of Reading for Common Schools and the Lower Classes of Academies*. New York: D. Appleton and Co., 1854. (Sold also in Ohio and Louisiana.)

R 1854 Pierpont-N — Pierpont, John. *The New Reader*. Philadelphia: Lippincott, Grambo and Co., 1854.

R 1854 Pycroft — Pycroft, Rev. James. *A Course of English Reading, Adapted to every taste and capacity*. New York: D. Appleton and Co., 1854.

R 1854 Sargent — Sargent, Epes. *The 1st-Class Standard Reader*. Boston: Phillips, Sampson and Co., 1854.

R 1854 Swan — Swan, William D. *The Grammar School Reader*. Philadelphia: Cowperthwait, DeSilver, and Butler, 1854.

R 1854 Town — Town, Salem. *The Grammar School Reader*. Portland, Me.: Blake and Carter, 1854.

R 1855 Burleigh — Burleigh, Joseph Bartlett. *The Thinker, a Moral Reader . . . designed to arouse the minds of youth, and to inculcate pure and noble principles. Part 1*. Philadelphia: Lippincott, Grambo and Co., 1855. (Used in Baltimore, Pennsylvania, Virginia.)

R 1855 Lovell — Lovell, J. E. *Lovell's Progressive Readers, Number 2*. New Haven: Henry H. Peck, 1855.

R 1855 New York — *The New York Reader, Number 2*. New York: Samuel S. and William Wood, 1855.

R 1855 Webb — Webb, J. Russell. *Webb's Normal Reader, Number 3*. New York: Sheldon, Lamport, and Blakeman, 1855.

R 1856 Denman — Denman, J. S. *Third Reading Book*. 16th ed. New York: Farmer, Brace and Co., 1856.

R 1856 Hillard — Hillard, G. S. *A First Class Reader*. Boston: Hickling, Swan and Brown, 1856.

R 1856 Mandeville — Mandeville, Henry. *Fourth Reader for Common Schools and Academies*. New York: D. Appleton and Co., 1856.

R 1856 Osgood — Osgood, Lucius. *Osgood's Progressive Fourth Reader*. Pittsburgh: A. H. English and Co., 1856.

R 1856 Randall — Randall, S. S. *Randall's Fourth Reader*. Albany, N.Y.: E. H. Bender, 1856.

R 1856 Sanders-4 — Sanders, Charles W. *The School Reader. Fourth Book*. New York: Ivison and Phinney, 1856.

R 1856 Sanders-New 4 — Sanders, Charles W. *The New School Reader, Fourth Book*. New York: Ivison and Phinney, 1856.

R 1856 Sargent-1 — Sargent, Epes. *The Standard First Reader for Beginners*. Boston: Phillips, Sampson and Co., 1856.

R 1856 Sargent-4 — Sargent, Epes. *The Standard Fourth Reader*. Boston: Phillips, Sampson and Co., 1856. 8th thousand.

R 1856 Hillard-1 — Hillard, G. S. *A First Class Reader*. Boston: Hickling, Swan and Brewer, 1856.

R 1857 Hillard-3 — Hillard, G. S. *A Third Class Reader*. Boston: Hickling, Swan and Brewer, 1857.

R 1857 Mandeville — Mandeville, Henry. *The Second Reader*. New York: D. Appleton and Co., 1857.

R 1858 Hillard-1 — Hillard, G. S. *A First Class Reader*. Boston: Hickling, Swan and Brewer, 1858.

R 1858 Hillard-2 — [Hillard, George S.] *The Second Primary Reader*. Boston: Hickling, Swan, Brewer and Tileston, 1858.

R 1858 Hillard-3 — [Hillard, George S.] *The Third Primary Reader*. Boston: Brewer and Tileston, 1858.

R 1858 McGuffey — McGuffey, William H. *McGuffey's New Eclectic Speaker*. Cincinnati: Winthrop B. Smith and Co., 1858.

R 1858 Sanders — Sanders, Charles W. *Sanders' Young Ladies' Reader*. Philadelphia: Sower, Barnes and Co., 1858.

R 1859 Hillard — Hillard, G. S. *A First Class Reader*. Boston: Hickling, Swan and Brewer, 1859.

R 1859 Pierpont — Pierpont, John. *The Young Reader*. Philadelphia: J. B. Lippincott and Co., 1859.

R 1859 Rickard and Orcutt	Rickard, Truman and Hiram Orcutt. *Class Book of Prose and Poetry*. Boston: Robert S. Davis, 1859.
R 1859 Sargent	Sargent, Epes. *The Standard Third Reader*. Boston: Phillips, Sampson and Co., 1859. 125th thousand.
R 1859 Webb	Webb, J. Russell. *Webb's Normal Reader, Number 3*. New York: Sheldon and Co., 1859.
R 1860 Hillard	Hillard, George S. *The Second Primary Reader*. Boston: Swan, Brewer and Tileston, 1860.
R 1860 McGuffey	McGuffey, William H. *McGuffey's New Juvenile Speaker*. Cincinnati: Wilson, Hinkle and Co., 1860.
R 1860 Sanders	Sanders, Charles W. *The New School Reader: 4th Book*. New York: Ivison, Blakeman, Taylor and Co., 1860.
R 1860 Sargent	Sargent, Epes. *The Standard Fourth Reader*. Boston: John L. Shorey, 1860.
R 1860 Willson	Willson, Marcius. *The Fourth Reader of the School and Family Series*. New York: Harper and Bros., 1860.
R 1861 Hillard	Hillard, G. S. *A First Class Reader*. Boston: Swan, Brewer and Tileston, 1861.
R 1861 Sanders	Sanders, Charles W. *Sanders' Union Reader, Number 2*. New York: American Book Co., 1861.
R 1862 Webb	Webb, J. Russell. *Webb's Normal Reader, Number 2*. New York: Sheldon and Co., 1862.
R 1863 Hillard	Hillard, G. S. *The Intermediate Reader: for the Use of Schools*. Boston: Brewer and Tileston, 1863.
R 1863 Sanders	Sanders, Charles W. *The New School Reader: Fourth Book*. New York: Phinney and Co., 1863.
R 1864 Hillard-I	Hillard, G. S. *The Intermediate Reader: for the Use of Schools*. Boston: Brewer and Tileston, 1864.
R 1864 Hillard-4	Hillard, G. S. *The Fourth Reader—New Series*. Boston: Brewer and Tileston, 1864.
R 1864 Sanders	Sanders, Charles W. *The School Reader—Third Book*. New York: Ivison, Phinney, Blakeman and Co., 1864.

R 1865 Willson — Willson, Marcius. *A Third Reader*. New York: Harper and Bros., 1865. Used in New York City schools.

Confederate Readers

R 1862 Sterling and Campbell — Sterling, Richard and J. D. Campbell. *Our Own Second Reader*. Greensboro, N.C.: Richard Sterling and J. D. Campbell, 1862.

R 1864 Campbell and Dunn — Campbell and Dunn. *The Child's First Book*. Richmond, Va.: Ayres and Wade, 1864.

R 1864 Moore — Moore, Mrs. M. B. *The First Dixie Reader*. Raleigh, N.C.: Branson and Farrar, 1864.

R 1866 Edwards and Webb — Edwards, Richard and J. Russell Webb. *Analytical First Reader*. New York: Taintor Bros. and Co., 1866.

R 1866 McGuffey-4 — McGuffey, William H. *McGuffey's New Fourth Eclectic Reader*. Cincinnati: Wilson, Hinkle and Co., 1866. (Stamp in front indicates that this copy was used in Georgia.)

R 1866 McGuffey-5 — McGuffey, William H. *McGuffey's New Fifth Eclectic Reader*. New York: Van Antwerp, Bragg and Co., 1866.

R 1866? Sargent-2 — Sargent, Epes. *Sargent's Standard Second Reader*. (Title page missing.)

R 1866 Sargent-3 — Sargent, Epes. *The Standard Third Reader*. Part II. Boston: John L. Shorey, 1866. (Note on back cover: over 2 million copies now in use.)

R 1866 Sargent-4 — Sargent, Epes. *Standard Fourth Reader*. Boston: John L. Shorey, 1866.

R 1866 Soule and Wheeler — Soule, Richard and William Wheeler. *First Lessons in Reading*. Boston: Lee and Shepard, 1866.

R 1867 Edwards-4 — Edwards, Richard. *Analytical Fourth Reader*. New York: Taintor and Co., 1867.

R 1867 Edwards-5 — Edwards, Richard. *Analytical Fifth Reader*. New York: Mason Bros., 1867.

R 1867? Parker and Watson-4 — Parker, Richard Greene, and James Madison Watson. *The National Fourth Reader*. (Title page missing.)

R 1867 Parker and Watson-5 — Parker, Richard Greene, and James Madison Watson. *The National Fifth Reader*. New York: A. S. Barnes and Co., 1867.

R 1868 Parker and Watson — Parker, Richard Greene and James Madison Watson. *The National Third Reader*. New York: A. S. Barnes and Co., 1868.

R 1869 Wilson — Wilson, Floyd B. *Wilson's Book of Recitations and Dialogues*. New York: Dick and Fitzgerald, 1869.

R 1870 Sanders — Sanders, Charles W. *Sanders' Union Fourth Reader*. New York: Ivison, Phinney, Blakeman and Co., 1870.

R 1871 Hillard — Hillard, George Stillman. *The Franklin Fifth Reader*. Boston: Brewer and Tileston, 1871.

R 1871 Monroe — Monroe, Lewis B. *The Fifth Reader*. Philadelphia: Cowperthwait and Co., 1871.

R 1871 Sargent and May-1 — Sargent, Epes and Amasa May. *The New American First Reader*. Philadelphia: J. H. Butler and Co., 1871.

R 1871 Sargent and May-5 — Sargent, Epes and Amasa May. *The New American Fifth Reader*. Philadelphia: E. H. Butler and Co., 1871.

R 1872 Monroe — Monroe, Lewis B. *The Fourth Reader*. Philadelphia: Cowperthwait and Co., 1872.

R 1872 Osgood-4 — Osgood, Lucius. *Osgood's American Fourth Reader*. Pittsburgh: A. H. English and Co., 1872.

R 1872 Osgood-5 — Osgood, Lucius. *Osgood's American Fifth Reader*. New York: Taintor Bros. and Co., 1872.

R 1872 Willson — Willson, Marcius. *The Fifth Reader*. New York: Harper and Bros., 1872.

R 1873 American — *The American Educational Readers: Fifth Reader*. New York: Ivison, Blakeman and Co., 1873. (This copy used by a boy in South Carolina; signed by him.)

R 1873 Hillard — Hillard, G. S. *The Franklin Fourth Reader*. New York: Taintor Bros., Merrill and Co., 1873.

R 1873 Hillard and Campbell-2 — Hillard, George S. and Loomis J. Campbell. *The Franklin Second Reader*. New York: Taintor and Bros., Merrill and Co., 1873.

R 1873 Hillard and Campbell-3 — Hillard, G. S. and L. J. Campbell. *The Franklin Third Reader*. New York: Taintor Bros., Merrill and Co., 1873.

R 1873 Monroe-1 — Monroe, Lewis B. *The First Reader*. Philadelphia: Cowperthwait and Co., 1873.

R 1873 Monroe-2 — Monroe, Lewis B. *The Second Reader*. Philadelphia: Cowperthwait and Co., 1873.

R 1873 Progressive — *Fourth Progressive Reader*. New York: P. O'Shea, c. 1873. (From internal evidence a Roman Catholic book.)

R 1874 Hillard — Hillard, George S. *The Franklin Advanced Fourth or Intermediate Reader*. New York: Taintor Bros., Merrill and Co., 1874.

R 1875 Sheldon — Sheldon, E. A. *The Fifth Reader*. New York: Scribner, Armstrong, and Co., 1875.

R 1876 Hillard and Campbell — Hillard, George S., and Campbell, Loomis J. *The Third Reader*. New Series. Boston: Brewer and Tileston, 1876.

R 1876 Young — *The Young Ladies' Progressive Reader*. New York: P. O'Shea, 1876. (From internal evidence, for Roman Catholic readers.)

R 1877 Metropolitan — By a member of the Holy Cross. *The Metropolitan First Reader*. Toronto: W. Warwick, 1877. (Roman Catholic book, perhaps intended for United States use; includes stories about citizens of the U.S.)

R 1878 Harris, Rickoff, Bailey-1 — Harris, William T., Andrew J. Rickoff, and Mark Bailey. *The First Reader*. New York: D. Appleton and Co., 1878.

R 1878 Harris, Rickoff, Bailey-2 — Harris, William T., Andrew J. Rickoff, and Mark Bailey. *The Second Reader*. New York: D. Appleton and Co., 1878.

R 1879 Campbell — Campbell, Loomis J. *The Franklin Advanced Second Reader*. New York: Taintor Bros., Merrill and Co., 1879.

R 1879 Harris, Rickoff, Bailey — Harris, William T., Andrew J. Rickoff, and Mark Bailey. *The Fifth Reader*. New York: D. Appleton and Co., 1879.

R 1879 McGuffey — McGuffey, William H. *McGuffey's Fourth Eclectic Reader*. New York: American Book Co., 1879. (1879 copyright date, but from internal evidence could not have appeared before 1890; stamp in front indicates that this copy was used in Gloster, Miss.)

R 1880 Harris, Rickoff, Bailey — Harris, William T, Andrew J. Rickoff, Mark Bailey. *The Fourth Reader*. New York: D. Appleton and Co., 1880.

R 1880 Swinton and Cathcart — Swinton, William and George R. Cathcart. *Easy Steps for Little Feet.* New York: American Book Co., 1880.

R 1881 Monteith — Monteith, James. *Popular Science Reader . . .* New York: American Book Co., 1881.

R 1881 Willson — Willson, Marcius. *The Fourth Reader of the Popular Series.* Philadelphia: J. B. Lippincott Co., 1881.

R 1882 Gourley and Hunt — Gourley, H. I. and J. N. Hunt. *The Modern Third Reader.* New York: Taintor and Co., 1882.

R 1883 Barnes — Barnes, Charles J. *New National First Reader.* New York: American Book Co., 1883.

R 1883 Swinton-4 — Swinton, William. *Swinton's Fourth Reader.* New York: American Book Co., 1883.

R 1883 Swinton-5 — Swinton, William. *Swinton's Fifth Reader and Speaker.* New York: Ivison, Blakeman, Taylor and Co., 1883.

R 1884 Barnes — Barnes, Charles J. *New National Fourth Reader.* New York: American Book Co., 1884.

R 1884 Campbell-4 — Campbell, Loomis J. *The New Franklin Fourth Reader.* New York: Sheldon and Co., 1884.

R 1884 Campbell-5 — Campbell, Loomis J. *The New Franklin Fifth Reader.* New York: Taintor Bros. and Co., 1884.

R 1884 Monroe — Monroe, Lewis. *Monroe's New Fifth Reader.* New York: American Book Co., 1884.

R 1885 McGuffey — McGuffey, William H. *McGuffey's New Fifth Eclectic Reader.* Cincinnati: Van Antwerp, Bragg and Co., 1885.

R 1885 Monroe — Monroe, Lewis B. *Monroe's New Primer.* Philadelphia: E. H. Butler and Co., 1885.

R 1885 Monroe-2 — Monroe, Lewis B. *Monroe's New Second Reader.* Philadelphia: Cowperthwait and Co., 1885.

R 1885 Monroe-3 — Monroe, Lewis B. *Monroe's New Third Reader.* New York: American Book Co., 1885.

R 1886 Cyr — Cyr, Ellen. *The Interstate Primer and First Reader.* Boston: Lothrop Publishing Co., 1886.

R 1888 McGuffey — McGuffey's *Alternate Fifth Reader.* Cincinnati: Van Antwerp, Bragg and Co., 1888.

R 1890 Davis — Davis, Eben H. *The Third Reading Book.* Philadelphia: J. B. Lippincott Co., 1890.

R 1893 Scudder	Scudder, H. E. *Verse and Prose for Beginners in Reading*. Boston: Houghton, Mifflin and Co., 1893.
R 1894 Columbian	*Columbian Fifth Reader*. Chicago: The Werner Co., 1894.
R 1895 Hazen	Hazen, M. W. *Hazen's Third Reader*. Philadelphia: E. H. Butler and Co., 1895.
R 1895 Taylor	Taylor, F. Lillian. *The Werner Primer for Beginners in Reading*. Chicago: Werner School Book Co., 1895.
R 1895 Todd and Powell	Todd, Emma J. and W. B. Powell. *The Normal Course in Reading*. Boston: Silver, Burdett and Co., 1895.
R 1896 Baldwin	Baldwin, James. *Fifty Famous Stories Retold*. New York: American Book Co., 1896.
R 1896 Holmes and Hill	Holmes, George F. and Frank A. Hill. *Holmes' Fifth Reader*. New York: University Publishing Co., 1896. (Also sold in New Orleans.)
R 1896 McGuffey-1	McGuffey, William H. *McGuffey's First Eclectic Reader*. New York: American Book Co., 1896.
R 1896 McGuffey-2	McGuffey, William H. *McGuffey's Second Eclectic Reader*. New York: American Book Co., 1896.
R 1896 McGuffey-3	McGuffey, William H. *McGuffey's Third Eclectic Reader*. New York: American Book Co., 1896.
R 1896 McGuffey-5	McGuffey, William H. *McGuffey's Fifth Eclectic Reader*. New York: American Book Co., 1896.
R 1896 Smythe	Smythe, E. Louise. *A Primary Reader*. Chicago: Werner School Book Co., 1896.
R 1897 Arnold and Gilbert-4	Arnold, Sarah Louise, and Charles B. Gilbert. *Stepping Stones to Literature: a Fourth Reader*. New York: Silver, Burdett and Co., 1897.
R 1897 Arnold and Gilbert-5	Arnold, Sarah Louise, and Charles B. Gilbert. *Stepping Stones to Literature: a Reader for Fifth Grades*. New York: Silver, Burdett and Co., 1897.
R 1897 Arnold and Gilbert-6	Arnold, Sarah Louise, and Charles B. Gilbert. *Stepping Stones to Literature: a Reader for Sixth Grades*. New York: Silver, Burdett and Co., 1897.
R 1897 Baldwin-3	Baldwin, James. *School Reading by Grades: Third Year*. New York: American Book Co., 1897.

R 1897 Baldwin-4 Baldwin, James. *School Reading by Grades: Fourth Year*. New York: American Book Co., 1897.

R 1897 Baldwin-5 Baldwin, James. *School Reading by Grades: Fifth Year*. New York: American Book Co., 1897.

R 1898 Arnold and Gilbert Arnold, Sarah Louise, and Charles B. Gilbert. *Stepping Stones to Literature: a Reader for Seventh Grades*. New York: Silver, Burdett and Co., 1898.

R 1898 Black Black, S.W. *Fifth Reader*. Chicago: Eaton and Co., 1898.

R 1898 Williams G-1 Williams, Sherman. *Choice Literature: Book One for Grammar Grades*. New York: Butler, Sheldon and Co., 1898.

R 1898 Williams P-1 Williams, Sherman. *Choice Literature: Book One for Primary Grades*. New York: Butler, Sheldon and Co., 1898.

R 1898 Williams I-1 Williams, Sherman, *Choice Literature: Book One for Intermediate Grades*. New York: Butler, Sheldon and Co., 1898.

R 1898 Williams G-2 Williams, Sherman. *Choice Literature: Book Two for Grammar Grades*. New York: Butler, Sheldon and Co., 1898.

R 1898 Williams I-2 Williams, Sherman. *Choice Literature: Book Two for Intermediate Grades*. New York: Butler, Sheldon and Co., 1898.

R 1899 Holmes and Anderson Holmes, George F. and L. W. Anderson. *Holmes' Third Reader*. New York: University Publishing Co., 1899.

R 1899 Holmes and Hill Holmes, George F. and Frank Hill. *Holmes' Fourth Reader*. New York: University Publishing Co., 1899.

R 1899 Judson and Bender Judson, Harry Pratt, and Ida C. Bender. *Graded Literature Series: Second Book*. New York: Charles E. Merrill Co., 1899.

R 1899 Kirk Kirk, May. *The Baldwin Primer*. New York: American Book Co., 1899.

R 1899 Perdue and LaVictoire Perdue, H. Avis, and Florence E. LaVictoire. *The New Century: Second Reader*. Chicago: Rand, McNally and Co., 1899.

R 1899 Shaw — Shaw, Edward Richard. *Fairy Tales for the Second School Year.* New York: University Publishing Co., 1899.

R 19— Pratt-Chadwick — Pratt-Chadwick, Mara L. *Little People's Sound Primer.* Boston: Educational Publishing Co., 19—.

R 1900 Aldrich and Forbes-I — Aldrich, George I., and Alexander Forbes. *The Progressive Course in Reading: Fifth Book.* Part I. New York: American Book Co., 1900.

R 1900 Aldrich and Forbes-II — Aldrich, George I., and Alexander Forbes. *The Progressive Course in Reading: Fifth Book.* Part II. New York: American Book Co., 1900.

R 1900 Collard-I — Collard, Thomas T. *The Beginner's Reader.* Part I. New York: Maynard, Merrill and Co., 1900.

R 1900 Collard-II — Collard, Thomas T. *The Beginner's Reader.* Part II. New York: Maynard, Merrill and Co., 1900.

R 1900 Demarest and Van Sickle — Demarest, A. J., and William M. Van Sickle. *New Education Readers: Book Two.* New York: American Book Co., 1900.

R 1900 Holmes and Anderson-1 — Holmes, George F., and L. W. Anderson. *Holmes' First Reader.* New York: University Publishing Co., 1900.

R 1900 Holmes and Anderson-2 — Holmes, George F., and L. W. Anderson. *Holmes' Second Reader.* New York: University Publishing Co., 1900.

R 1900 Judson and Bender-3 — Judson, Harry Pratt, and Ida C. Bender. *Graded Literary Readers: Third Book.* New York: Charles E. Merrill Co., 1900.

R 1900 Judson and Bender-4. — Judson, Harry Pratt, and Ida C. Bender. *Graded Literary Readers: Fourth Book.* New York: Maynard, Merrill and Co., 1900.

R 1900 Lane — Lane, Abby E. *Lights to Literature: Book Five.* Chicago: Rand, McNally and Co., 1900.

R 1900 Monroe — Monroe, Lewis. *The Fourth Reader.* New York: American Book Co., 1900.

R 1900 Taylor — Taylor, Frances Lillian. *The Taylor School Readers: First Reader.* New York: American Book Co., 1900.

R 1900 Williams — Williams, Sherman. *Choice Literature: Book Two for Primary Grades.* New York: Butler, Sheldon and Co., 1900.

SPELLERS

Key	*Publication*
S 1779 Benezet	Benezet, Anthony. *The Pennsylvania Spelling Book, or Youth's Friendly Instructor and Monitor.* Philadelphia: Joseph Cruikshank, 1779.
S 1782 Peirce	Peirce, John. *The New American Spelling Book.* Philadelphia: Joseph Cruikshank, 1782.
S 1783 Webster	Webster, Noah. *A Grammatical Institute of the English Language. Part I.* Hartford, Conn.: Hudson and Goodwin, 1783.
S 1789 Perry	Perry, W. *The Only Sure Guide to the English Tongue.* Worcester, Mass.: Isaiah Thomas, 1789.
S 1797 Barry	Barry, John. *The Philadelphia Spelling Book.* 3rd ed. Philadelphia: Ormrod and Conrad, 1797.
S 1797 Peirce	Peirce, John. *The New American Spelling Book.* Philadelphia: Joseph and James Cruikshank, 1797.
S 1798 Child	*The Child's Spelling Book.* Hartford, Conn.: Printed by John Babcock, 1798.
S 1799 Fenning	Fenning, Daniel. *The Universal Spelling Book.* Philadelphia: G. Douglas, 1799.
S 1799 Heaton	Heaton, Benjamin. *The Columbian Spelling Book.* Wrentham, Mass.: Printed for the author, 1799.
S 1802 Alexander	Alexander, Caleb. *The Young Ladies' and Gentlemen's Spelling Book.* Hudson, N.Y.: Sampson, Chittenden and Croswell, 1802.
S 1802 Snowden	Snowden, Richard. *The New Jersey Spelling Book.* Baltimore (?): Joseph Lippincott, 1802.
S 1803 Fiske	Fiske, John. *The New England Spelling Book.* Brookfield, Mass.: E. Merriam and Company, 1803.
S 1804 Alden	Alden, Abner. *An Introduction to Spelling and Reading. Volume I.* 3rd ed. Boston: Thomas and Andrews, 1804.
S 1807 Carey	Carey, Matthew. *The Columbian Spelling and Reading Book.* 10th ed. Philadelphia: Matthew Carey, 1807. (Recommended by head of a Roman Catholic school.)

S 1807 Kneeland — Kneeland, Abner. *A Brief Sketch of a New System of Orthography*. Walpole, N.H.: Printed for the author by Nichols and Hale, 1807.

S 1808 Peirce — Peirce, John. *The New American Spelling Book*. 6th revised ed. Philadelphia: Joseph Cruikshank, 1808.

S 1809 Parlour — *The Parlour Spelling Book*. Philadelphia: Benjamin Johnson, 1809.

S 1809 Perry — Perry, William. *The Only Sure Guide to the English Tongue*. 10th ed. Worcester, Mass.: Isaiah Thomas, 1809.

S 1810 Webster — Webster, Noah, Jr. *American Spelling Book*. Boston: John West and Company, 1810.

S 1812 Barry — Barry, John. *Philadelphia Spelling Book*. 10th ed. Philadelphia: David Hogin, 1812.

S 1814 Pike — Pike, James. *An English Spelling-Book*. 2nd ed. Boston: Munroe and Francis, 1814.

S 1815 Bradley — Bradley, Joshua. *An Improved Spelling-Book or Youth's Literary Guide*. Windsor, Vt.: Printed by Oliver Farnsworth, 1815.

S 1815 Picket — Picket, Albert. *The Juvenile Spelling-Book*. Newburyport, Mass.: E. Little and Company, 1815.

S 1816 Webster — Webster, Noah. *American Spelling Book*. Boston: West and Richardson, 1816. (Advertisement states that 3 million copies of this work have been sold to date.)

S 1818 Webster — Webster, Noah. *American Spelling Book*. Brattleborough, Vt.: Holbrook and Fessenden, 1818.

S 1819 Alden — Alden, Abner. *An Introduction to Spelling and Reading. Volume II*. 8th ed. Boston: Thomas and Andrews, 1819.

S 1819 Bingham — Bingham, Caleb. *The Child's Companion, being an Easy and Concise Reading and Spelling-Book*. 17th ed. Boston: Caleb Bingham and Company, 1819.

S 1819 Perry — Perry, William. *The Only Sure Guide to the English Tongue*. Brookfield, Mass.: E. Merriam and Company, 1819.

S 1819 Pike — Pike, James. *The Columbian Orthographer or, First Book for Children*. Boston: R. P. and C. Williams, 1819.

S 1820 Kneeland — Kneeland, Abner. *The American Definition Spelling-Book.* Boston: George Hough and Nathan Burrill, 1820.

S 1821 Alger — Alger, Israel, Jr. *Elements of Orthography.* Boston: James Loring, 1821.

S 1821 Hull — Hull, Joseph. *A Guide to the English Language.* Utica, N.Y.: William Williams, 1821.

S 1821 Perry — Perry, William. *The Only Sure Guide to the English Tongue.* Boston: J. H. A. Frost, 1821.

S 1822 Cummings — Cummings, J. A. *The Pronouncing Spelling Book.* 3rd ed. Boston: Cummings and Hilliard, 1822.

S 1822 Hazen — Hazen, Jasper. *The Primary Intructer* [*sic*] *and Improved Spelling Book.* 2nd ed. Windsor, Vt.: Printed by Simeon Ide, 1822.

S 1822? New York — *The New York Spelling-Book: or Fourth Book.* New York: Samuel S. and William Wood, 1822?

S 1823 Cummings — Cummings, J. A. *The Pronouncing Spelling-Book.* Boston: Cummings, Hilliard and Company, 1823.

S 1823 Lee — Lee, Thomas J. *A Spelling Book Containing the Rudiments of the English Language.* Boston: Munroe and Francis, 1823.

S 1823 Marshall — Marshall, Elihu F. *A Spelling Book of the English Language; or, the American Tutor's Assistant.* Concord, N.H.: Jacob H. Moore, 1823.

S 1823 Picket — Picket, A. *Picket's Juvenile Spelling Book or, Analogical Pronouncer.* New York: J. Milton Ferry, 1823.

S 1824 Bentley — Bentley, Rensselaer. *The American Instructer* [*sic*]. Hudson, N.Y.: Printed by A. Stoddard for the author, 1824.

S 1824 Guy — Guy, Joseph, Jr. *Guy's Exercises in Orthography.* Boston: George Gardner, 1824.

S 1824 Picket — Picket, A. *Picket's Juvenile Spelling Book or, Analogical Pronouncer of the English Language.* Wheeling, Va.: A. Picket, Jr., 1824.

S 1825 Alger — Alger, Israel. *The Orthoepical Guide to the English Tongue.* Boston: Richardson and Lord, 1825.

S 1825 Bolles — Bolles, William. *A Spelling Book containing Exercises in Orthography, Pronunciation, and Reading.* New London, Conn.: Printed by Samuel Green for the author, 1825.

S 1825 Torrey — Torrey, Jesse, Jr. *Familiar Spelling Book.* Philadelphia: J. Grigg, 1825. ("And for sale by booksellers and county merchants generally, in the Southern and Western States.")

S 1826 Alden — Alden, Abner. *An Introduction to Spelling and Reading.* 10th ed. Boston: James Loring, 1826.

S 1826 Cobb — Cobb, Lyman. *Cobb's Spelling Book.* Brattleborough, Vt.: Holbrook and Fessenden, 1826.

S 1826 Kelley — Kelley, Hall J. *The American Instructor, Second Book.* Boston: Lincoln and Edmands, 1826.

S 1826 Kneeland — Kneeland, Abner. *The American Definition Spelling Book.* Concord, N.H.: George Hough, 1826.

S 1826 Marshall — Marshall, Elihu. *A Spelling Book of the English Language; or, The American Tutor's Assistant.* Plymouth, Mass.: Ezra Collier, 1826.

S 1826 Principal — By the Principal of the Charles Field St. Academy, Providence. *Exercises in Orthography.* Providence, R.I.: Coible and Brown, 1826.

S 1827 Picket — Picket, A. *Picket's Juvenile Spelling Book or Analogical Pronouncer of the English Language.* New York: Caleb Bartlett, 1827.

S 1827 Webster — Webster, Noah. *The American Spelling-Book.* Baltimore: Cushing and Jewett, 1827. (Note in front leaves states that 5 million copies of this book had been sold by 1818.)

S 1828 Emerson — Emerson, B.D. *The National Spelling Book and Pronunciator.* Boston: Richardson and Lord, 1828.

S 1828 Webster — Webster, Noah. *The American Spelling Book.* Concord, N.H.: Manahan, Hoag and Co., 1828.

S 1829 Bentley — Bentley, Rensselaer. *The American Instructor.* 4th ed. Bennington, Vt.: Darius Clark, 1829.

S 1829 Cobb — Cobb, Lyman. *Cobb's Spelling Book.* New York: J. C. Riker, 1829.

S 1829 Webster — Webster, Noah. *The Elementary Spelling Book; being an Improvement on the American Spelling Book.* Albany, N.Y.: Webster and Skinner, 1829.

S 1829 S. Worcester — Worcester, Samuel. *A Spelling Book for the United States of America.* Boston: Crocker and Brewster, 1829.

S 1830 Byerly — Byerly, Stephen. *Byerly's New American Spelling-Book.* Philadelphia: McCarty and Davis, 1830.

S 1830 Cardell — Cardell, William S. *The Analytical Spelling-Book; Designed for Families and Schools in the United States of America and for Foreigners Learning English.* Philadelphia: Uriah Hunt, 1830.

S 1830 Marshall — Marshall, Elihu F. *A Spelling Book of the English Language; or, American Tutor's Assistant.* Bellows Falls, Vt.: James F. Cutler and Co., 1830.

S 1830 Mulkey — Mulkey, William. *A Syllabical Spelling Book.* Baltimore: Armstrong and Plashitt, 1830.

S 1831 Bolles — Bolles, William. *A Spelling Book.* New London, Conn.: W. and J. Bolles, 1831.

S 1833 Alger — Alger, Israel. *The Orthoepical Guide to the English Tongue.* Boston: Simpkins, 1833. Based on Perry's Speller.

S 1833 Emerson — Emerson, B. D. *The New National Spelling Book and Pronouncing Tutor.* Claremont, N.H.: Claremont Manufacturing Co., 1833.

S 1833 Russell — Russell, William. *Lessons in Enunciation.* Boston: Carter, Hendee and Co., 1833.

S 1834 Hazen — Hazen, E. *The Speller and Definer; or, Class-Book, No. 2.* New York: M'Elrath and Banks, 1834.

S 1835 Cobb — Cobb, Lyman. *Cobb's Spelling Book.* Ithaca, N.Y.: Mack Andrus and Woodruff, 1835.

S 1835 Hazen — Hazen, E. *The Speller and Definer; or, Class-Book, No. 2.* Philadelphia: Uriah Hunt, 1835.

S 1835 Leonard — Leonard, L. W. *The North American Spelling Book.* Keene, N.H.: George Tilden, 1835.

S 1836 Brandreth — Brandreth, Dr. B. *A New System for the Instruction of Youth.* New York: Published by the author, 1836.

S 1836 Parsons — Parson, J. U. *The Analytical Spelling Book.* 5th ed. Boston: William Peirce, 1836.

S 1836 Webster — Webster, Noah. *The Teacher; a Supplement to the Elementary Spelling Book.* New Haven, Conn.: S. Babcock, 1836.

S 1836 S. Worcester — Worcester, Samuel. *Second Book for Reading and Spelling*. Boston: Carter, Lord and Holbrook, 1836.

S 1837 Chichester — Chichester, Samuel. *The Analytical Speller, Primer and Defining Book*. New York: Published by the author, 1837.

S 1837 Hawes — Hawes, Noyes P. *The United States Spelling Book and English Orthoepist*. Belfast, Me.: John Dorr, 1837.

S 1837 Parsons — Parsons, J. U. *The Analytical Spelling Book*. Portland, Me.: William Hyder, 1837.

S 1838 Marshall — Marshall, Elihu F. *Marshall's New Spelling Book*. Montpelier, Vt.: E. P. Walton and Son, 1838.

S 1838 Parsons — Parsons, J. U. *Analytical Vocabulary or Analytical System of Teaching Orthography*. Concord, N.H.: J. F. Brown, 1838.

S 1839 Cramer — By Sundry Experienced Teachers. *Cramer's United States Spelling Book*. Pittsburgh: Johnston and Stockton, 1839.

S 1839 Crandall — Crandall, Daniel. *The Columbian Spelling Book*. 14th ed. Cooperstown, N.Y.: H. and E. Phinney, 1839.

S 1839 Hazen — Hazen, Edward. *The Speller and Definer; or Class Book No. 2*. Philadelphia: Uriah Hunt, 1839.

S 1839 Williams — Williams, George. *A Critical Pronouncing Spelling Book or Youth's First Literary Guide*. Hamilton, N.Y.: William and Maynard, 1839.

S 1840 Gallaudet and Hooker — Gallaudet, T. H. and Horace Hooker. *The Practical Spelling Book with Reading Lessons*. Hartford, Conn.: Belknap and Hamersley, 1840.

S 1841 Cobb — Cobb, Lyman. *Cobb's Spelling Book*. Watertown, N.Y.: Knowlton and Rice, 1841.

S 1842 Emerson — Emerson, B. D. *The National Spelling Book and Pronouncing Tutor*. Boston: Jenks and Palmer, 1842.

S 1842 Fowle — Fowle, William B. *The Common School Speller*. Claremont, N.H.: Claremont Manufacturing Company, 1842.

S 1842 Sanders — Sanders, Charles W. *Sanders' Spelling Book*. New York: Dayton and Saxon, 1842.

S 1842 Webster	Webster, Noah. *The Elementary Spelling Book.* Utica, N.Y.: Bennett, Backus and Hawley, 1842.
S 1843 Bumstead	By a Friend of Mine [Bumstead, J.F.] *My First School-Book, to Teach Me with the Help of my Instructer, to Read and Spell Words, and Understand Them.* Boston: T. R. Marvin, 1843. (Used in Boston schools.)
S 1843 Cobb	Cobb, Lyman. *Cobb's Spelling Book.* Ithaca, N.Y.: Andrus, Woodruff and Gauntlett, 1843.
S 1843 Fowle	Fowle, William B. *The Companion to Spelling Books.* Boston: William B. Fowle and N. Capen, 1843.
S 1843 New York Sunday	*The New-York Sunday School Spelling Book.* 6th ed. New York: New-York Sunday School Union, 1843.
S 1843 Webster-E	Webster, Noah. *The Elementary Spelling Book.* Watertown, N.Y.: Knowlton and Rice, 1843.
S 1843 Webster-A	Webster, Noah. *The American Spelling Book.* Wells River, Vt.: Ira White, 1843.
S 1844 Clagett	Clagett, R. *The American Expositor, or Intellectual Definer.* New York: Saxon and Miles, 1844.
S 1844 Fowle	Fowle, William B. *The Common School Speller.* Boston: William B. Fowle and N. Capen, 1844.
S 1844 Leonard	Leonard, L. W. *The North American Spelling Book.* Keene, N.H.: George Tilden, 1844.
S 1844 Russell	Russell, William. *Spelling-Book, or Second Course of Lessons in Spelling and Reading.* Boston: Tappan, Whittemore and Mason, 1844.
S 1844 Sanders	Sanders, Charles W. *Sanders' Spelling Book.* Rochester, N.Y.: Sage and Brothers, 1844.
S 1845 Bentley	Bentley, Rensselaer. *The Pictorial Spelling Book.* New York: Sheldon and Co., 1845.
S 1845 Fowle	Fowle, William B. *The Companion to Spelling Books.* 30th ed. Boston: William B. Fowle and N. Capen, 1845.
S 1845 Sanders	Sanders, Charles W. *Sanders' Spelling Book.* Chicago: S. C. Gruggs and Co., 1845. (A note in this copy indicates that 2 million had already been sold.)
S 1845 Tower	Tower, David B. *The Gradual Speller and Complete Enunciator.* Boston: Crosby and Nichols, 1845.

S 1845 Wright — Wright, Albert D. *Elements of the English Language; or Analytical Orthography.* 4th ed. Cazenovia, N.Y.: Henry and Sweetlands, 1845.

S 1846 Butterfield — Butterfield, Consul D. *Lessons in Punctuation.* Albany, N.Y.: J. Munsell, 1846.

S 1846 Fowle — Fowle, William B. *The Common School Speller.* Boston: William B. Fowle and N. Capen, 1846.

S 1846 Kraitsir — Kraitsir, Charles. *First Book of English for Children.* Boston: E. P. Peabody, 1846.

S 1846 Leonard — Leonard, L. W. *The North American Spelling Book.* Keene, N.H.: George Tilden, 1846.

S 1846 McElligot — McElligot, James N. *The Young Analyzer.* New York: Mark H. Newman and Co., 1846.

S 1846 McGuffey — McGuffey, William. *McGuffey's Newly Revised Eclectic Spelling Book.* Cincinnati: Winthrop B. Smith and Co., 1846.

S 1846 S. Worcester — Worcester, S. T. *Sequel to the Spelling Book.* Boston: James Munroe and Co., 1846.

S 1847 ASDUK — American Society for the Diffusion of Useful Knowledge. *The English Spelling Book.* New York: Leavitt, Trow and Co., 1847.

S 1847 Chapin — Chapin, Rev. A. B. *New Classical Spelling-Book.* Philadelphia: W. A. Leary, 1847.

S 1848 Webster — Webster, Noah. *The Elementary Spelling Book.* New York: G. F. Coolidge and Brother, 1848.

S 1849 Leonard — Leonard, Levi Washburn. *The North American Spelling Book.* Keene, N.H.: George Tilden, 1849.

S 1849 Swan — Swan, William D. *The Spelling-Book.* Philadelphia: Thomas, Cowperthwait and Co., 1849.

S 1851 Cobb — Cobb, Lyman. *Cobb's New Primary Spelling Book.* New York: John C. Riker, 1851.

S 1851 Northend — Northend, Charles. *Dictation Exercises.* New York: A. S. Barnes, 1851.

S 1852 Smith — Smith, William W. *The Speller's Manual.* New York: Lewis H. Embree, 1852.

S 1852 Swan — Swan, William D. *The Spelling Book.* Philadelphia: Thomas, Cowperthwait and Co., 1852.

S 1853 Bumstead — Bumstead, J. F. *Spelling and Thinking Combined; or, The Spelling-Book Made a Medium of Thought.* Boston: T. R. Marvin, 1853.

S 1853 Comly — Comly, John. *Comly's Spelling and Reading Book.* Philadelphia: Lippincott, Grambo and Co., 1853.

S 1853 Easy Lessons — *Easy Lessons in Reading and Spelling.* New York: James Egbert, 1853.

S 1853 Northend — Northend, Charles. *Dictation Exercises.* New York: A. S. Barnes and Co., 1853.

S 1853 Vaughan-I — Vaughan, Mrs. S. A. *Vaughan's Speller, Definer, and Reader for Beginners.* Vol. I. New York: Daniel Burgess and Co., 1853.

S 1853 Vaughan-II — Vaughan, Mrs. S. A. *Vaughan's Speller, Definer, and Reader, for Beginners.* Vol. II. New York: Daniel Burgess and Co., 1853.

S 1854 Angell — Angell, Oliver. *The Child's First Book.* Philadelphia: E. H. Butler and Co., 1854.

S 1854 Emerson — Emerson, B. D. *The New National Spelling Book: and Pronouncing Tutor.* Boston: Kidder and Cheever, 1854.

S 1854 Fowle — Fowle, William B. *The Common School Speller.* Claremont, N.H.: Claremont Manufacturing Company, 1854.

S 1854 Sanders — Sanders, Charles W. *Sanders' New Speller, Definer and Analyzer.* New York: Ivison and Phinney, 1854. (Advertisement in front of book notes that this book has been adopted in Wisconsin, Illinois, Iowa, Rhode Island and Minnesota.)

S 1855 Wilson — Wilson, John. *A Treatise on English Punctuation.* 3rd ed. Boston: John Wilson and Son, 1855.

S 1856 Easy Lessons — *Easy Lessons in Reading and Spelling for the Use of the Younger Classes in Primary Schools.* New York: James Egbert, 1856.

S 1856 Gallaudet and Hooker — Gallaudet, T. H. and Horace Hooker. *The Practical Spelling Book with Reading Lessons.* Hartford, Conn.: William James Hamersley, 1856.

S 1856 Sargent — Sargent, Epes. *The Standard Speller.* Boston: Sampson and Co., 1856. 5th thousand.

S 1856 Town — Town, Salem. *Town's New Speller and Definer.* Boston: Sanborn, Carter and Bazin, 1856.

S 1857 Fowle — Fowle, William. *Common School Speller.* Claremont, N.H.: Claremont Manufacturing Co., 1857.

S 1857 McElligot	McElligot, James N. *The Young Analyzer.* New York: Ivison and Phinney, 1857.
S 1857 Parker and Watson	Parker, Richard G. and J. Madison Watson. *The National Pronouncing Speller.* New York: A. S. Barnes and Co., 1857.
S 1857 Stearns	Stearns, Edward. *A Practical Guide to English Pronunciation for the Use of Schools.* Boston: Crosby, Nichols and Co., 1857.
S 1857 Webster	Webster, Noah. *The Elementary Spelling Book.* New York: D. Appleton and Co., 1857.
S 1857 J. Worcester	Worcester, J. E. *A Pronouncing Spelling-Book of the English Language.* Boston: Brewer and Tileston, 1857.
S 1858 Denman	Denman, J. S. *The Student's Spelling Book.* 22nd ed. New York: Pratt, Oakley and Co., 1858.
S 1858 Stearns	Stearns, Edward J. *A Practical Guide to English Pronunciation.* Boston: Crosby, Nichols and Co., 1858.
S 1858 J. Worcester	Worcester, J. E. *A Pronouncing Spelling-Book of the English Language.* Boston: Hickling, Swan and Brewer, 1858.
S 1859 Ormsby, Cushing, and Farnham	Ormsby, R., Rev. Charles W. Cushing, and R. Farnham. *The Vermont Speller; or, Progressive Lessons in the English Language.* 3rd ed. Bradford, Vt.: A. Low, Agent and Co., 1859.
S 1859 Town and Holbrook	Town, Salem and Nelson Holbrook. *The Progressive Speller.* Boston: Bazin and Ellsworth, 1859.
S 1860 Tully	Tully, Joseph B. *Tully's Primary Spelling-Book; an Easy Introduction to the Columbian Spelling Book.* New York: P. O'Shea, 1860.
S 1861 Swan-E	Swan, William D. *An Elementary Spelling Book.* Boston: Brewer and Tileston, 1861.
S 1861 Swan-S	Swan, William D. *The Spelling-Book.* Philadelphia: H. Cowperthwait and Co., 1861.
S 1862 Hazen	Hazen, E. *The Speller and Definer; or Class-Book, No. 2.* Philadelphia: Uriah Hunt and Son, 1862.
S 1862 Watson	Watson, J. Madison. *The National Elementary Speller.* New York: A. S. Barnes and Burr, 1862.

S 1863 W. Adams — Adams, W. T. *A Spelling-Book for Advanced Classes*. Boston: Brewer and Tileston, 1863.

S 1863 Willson — Willson, Marcius. *Willson's Primary Speller*. New York: Harper and Brothers, 1863.

S 1864 Ormsby — Ormsby, R. *Vermont Speller; or, Progressive Lessons in the English Language*. Claremont, N.H.: Claremont Manufacturing Co., 1864.

S 1864 Sargent — Sargent, Epes. *The Smaller Standard Speller*. Boston: John L. Shorey, 1864.

S 1865 Campbell — Campbell, Loomis J. *A Primary Spelling-Book of the English Language*. Boston: Brewer and Tileston, 1865.

S 1865 McGuffey — McGuffey, William. *McGuffey's New Eclectic Spelling-Book*. Cincinnati: Sargent, Wilson and Hinkle, 1865.

S 1865 Mulvany — Mulvany, Edward. *The Practical Dictation Spelling-Book*. New York: P. O'Shea, 1865. (Used by the Brothers of the Christian Schools, 1865.)

Confederate Spellers

S 1865 Chaudron — Chaudron, A. *Chaudron's Spelling-Book, Carefully Prepared for Family and School Use*. 5th ed. Mobile, Ala.: S. H. Goetzel, 1865. 40th thousand. (First edition in 1863.)

S 1865 Confederate — [Smith, Richard McAllister.] *The Confederate Spelling Book, with Reading Lessons for the Young*. 5th ed. Richmond, Va.: George L. Bidgood, 1865.

S 1866 Swan — Swan, William D. *The Spelling Book*. Philadelphia: H. Cowperthwait and Co., 1866.

S 1866 Watson — Watson, J. Madison. *National Elementary Speller*. New York: A. S. Barnes, 1866.

S 1867 Sanders — Sanders, Charles W. *Sanders' Union Speller*. New York: Ivison, Phinney, Blakeman and Co., 1867.

S 1867 Sargent — Sargent, Epes. *A Pronouncing Spelling Book*. Boston: John L. Shorey, 1867.

S 1868 Osgood — Osgood, Lucius. *Osgood's Progressive Speller*. Pittsburgh: A. H. English, 1868.

S 1869 Day — Day, Henry N. *The American Speller*. New York: Charles Scribner and Co., 1869.

S 1871 Edwards and Warren — Edwards, Richard, and Mortimer A. Warren. *The Analytical Speller*. New York: Taintor and Co., 1871.

S 1872 Watson — Watson, J. Madison. *Independent Child's Speller*. New York: American Book Co., 1872.

S 1873 Swinton — Swinton, William. *Word Book of English Spelling*. New York: Ivison, Blakeman, Taylor, and Co., 1873.

S 1874 Monroe — Monroe, Lewis B. *First Steps in Spelling*. Philadelphia: Cowperthwait and Co., 1874.

S 1874 Worcester — Worcester, J. E. *Pronouncing Spelling Book of the English Language*. Boston: Brewer and Tileston, 1874.

S 1875 Monroe — Monroe, Lewis B. *The Practical Speller*. Philadelphia: Cowperthwait and Co., 1875.

S 1875 Sanders — Sanders, Charles W. *Sanders' Union Speller*. New York: Ivison, Blakeman, Taylor and Co., 1875.

S 1875 Swinton — Swinton, William. *Word Book of English Spelling*. New York: Ivison, Blakeman, Taylor and Co., 1875.

S 1875 Worcester — Worcester, J. E. *A Pronouncing Spelling-Book of the English Language*. Boston: Brewer and Tileston, 1875.

S 1876 Swinton — Swinton, William. *Word Book of English Spelling*. New York: Ivison, Blakeman, Taylor and Co., 1876.

S 1876 Warren — Warren, Mortimer. *The Graded Class-Word Speller*. New York: Taintor Brothers, Merrill and Co., 1876.

S 1878 Worcester — *A Pronouncing Spelling-Book of the English Language*. New York: Taintor Brothers and Co., 1878. (No author given; copyright held by L. J. Campbell and S. T. Worcester; "Worcester" on front cover.)

S 1879 Westlake — Westlake, J. Willis. *Three Thousand Practice Words*. Philadelphia: Eldredge and Brother, 1879.

S 1880 Althaus — Althaus, Edward. *The Grammar School Word-Book*. New York: Daniel Slote and Co., 1880.

S 1880 Town — Town, Salem. *Town's New Speller and Definer*. New York: A. C. Armstrong and Son, 1880.

S 1880 New — *The New American Advanced Speller*. Philadelphia: J. H. Butler and Co., 1880.

S 1880 Webster — Webster, Noah. *The Elementary Spelling Book*. New York: American Book Co., 1880.

S 1881 Clarke — Clarke, Charles S., Jr. *The Unique Word-Book*. New York: The Argonaut Publishing Co., 1881.

S 1881 March — March, F. A. *March's ABC Book*. Boston: Ginn and Heath, 1881.

S 1886 Blewett — Blewett, Scott H. and Ben. *A List of the Words in McGuffey's Primer and Readers*. New York: American Book Co., 1886.

S 1888 Shoup — Shoup, William J. *Shoup's Graded Speller*. St. Paul, Minn.: D. D. Merrill, 1888.

S 1888 Watkins — Watkins, William B. *McGuffey's Alternate Spelling Book*. Cincinnati: Van Antwerp, Bragg and Co., 1888.

S 1889 Brothers — Brothers of the Christian Schools. *Pronouncing Speller*. New York: LaSalle Bureau of Supplies, 1889.

S 1890 Kupfer — Kupfer, Lillian. *The Natural Speller and Word Book*. New York: American Book Co., 1890.

S 1896 Dutton — Dutton, Samuel T. *The Morse Speller*. New York: The Morse Co., 1896.

S 1898 Rice — Rice, Dr. J. M. *The Rational Spelling Book*. Part II. New York: American Book Co., 1898.

S 1900 Bowen — Bowen, James A. *English Words as Spoken and Written*. New York: Globe School Book Co., 1900.

GEOGRAPHIES

Key — *Publication*

G 1784 Morse — Morse, Jedidiah. *Geography Made Easy*. New Haven, Conn.: Meigs, Bowen & Dana, 1784.

G 1789 Elements — *Elements of Geography and Astronomy*. Philadelphia: John M'Culloch, 1789.

G 1791 Morse — Morse, Jedidiah. *Geography Made Easy*. 3rd ed. corrected. Boston: Samuel Hall, 1791.

G 1793 Workman — Workman, Benjamin. *Elements of Geography*. 4th ed. Philadelphia: John M'Culloch, 1793.

G 1794 Morse — Morse, Jedidiah. *Geography Made Easy*. 4th ed. Boston: I. Thomas, 1794.

G 1796 Dwight — Dwight, Nathaniel. *A Short but Comprehensive System of the Geography of the World.* 2nd ed. Boston: David West, 1796.

G 1798 Morse — Morse, Jedidiah. *Geography Made Easy.* 6th ed. Boston: I. Thomas, 1798.

G 1800 Davidson — [Davidson, Robert.] *Geography Epitomized.* Chapman Whitcomb, 1800.

G 1800 Morse — Morse, Jedidiah. *Geography Made Easy.* 7th ed. Boston: I. Thomas and E. T. Andrews, 1800.

G 1800 Smith — Smith, Charles. *Universal Geography Made Easy.* 2nd ed. New York: C. Smith, 1800.

G 1802 Morse — Morse, Jedidiah. *Geography Made Easy.* 8th ed. Boston: I. Thomas and E. T. Andrews, 1802.

G 1802 Webster — Webster, Noah, Jr. *Elements of Useful Knowledge. Containing a Historical and Geographical Account of the United States.* Vol. I. Hartford, Conn.: Hudson and Goodwin, 1802.

G 1803 Davidson — Davidson, Robert. *Geography Epitomized.* Morristown, N.J.: Henry P. Russell, 1803.

G 1803 Hubbard — Hubbard, John. *The Rudiments of Geography.* Walpole, N.H.: Thomas and Thomas, 1803.

G 1803 Workman — Workman, Benjamin. *Elements of Geography Designed for Young Students in that Science.* 9th ed. Philadelphia: John M'Culloch, 1803.

G 1804 Goldsmith — Goldsmith, Rev. J. (Sir Richard Phillips). *An Easy Grammar of Geography for the Use of Schools.* Philadelphia: Benjamin Johnson, 1804.

G 1804 Morse — Morse, Jedidiah. *Geography Made Easy.* 9th ed. Boston: Thomas and Andrews, 1804.

G 1804 Webster — Webster, Noah, Jr. *Elements of Useful Knowledge.* Vol. II. New Haven, Conn.: Printed for the author by Sidney's Press, 1804.

G 1805 Dwight — Dwight, Nathaniel. *A Short but Comprehensive System of the Geography of the World.* Northampton, Mass.: S. and E. Butler, 1805.

G 1805 Hubbard — Hubbard, John. *The Rudiments of Geography.* 2nd ed. Walpole, N.H.: Thomas and Thomas, 1805.

G 1806 Cottineau-I — Cottineau, Denis Louis. *Geographical Compilation for the Use of Schools.* Vol. I. Baltimore: Printed for the Compiler by John Butler, 1806.

G 1806 Cottineau-II Cottineau, Denis Louis. *Geographical Compilation for Use of Schools.* Vol. II. Baltimore: Printed for the Compiler by John Butler, 1806.

G 1806 Morse Morse, Jedidiah. *Geography Made Easy.* 10th ed. corrected. Boston: Thomas and Andrews, 1806.

G 1806 Webster Webster, Noah. *Elements of Useful Knowledge.* Vol. III. New Haven, Conn.: Bronson, Walter and Co., 1806.

G 1807 Dwight Dwight, Nathaniel. *A Short But Comprehensive System of the Geography of the World.* 7th Connecticut ed. Hartford, Conn.: Hudson and Goodwin, 1807.

G 1807 Goldsmith Goldsmith, Rev. J. (Sir Richard Phillips). *An Easy Grammar of Geography for the Use of Schools.* Boston: William Norman, 1807.

G 1807 Morse Morse, Jedidiah. *Geography Made Easy.* 11th ed. Boston: Thomas and Andrews, 1807.

G 1807 Parish Parish, Elijah. *A Compendious System of Universal Geography.* Newburyport, Mass.: Thomas and Whipple, 1807.

G 1807 Workman Workman, Benjamin. *Elements of Geography.* 11th ed. Philadelphia: Ebenezer M'Culloch, 1807.

G 1809 Webster Webster, Noah, Jr. *Elements of Useful Knowledge.* Vol. II. Hartford, Conn.: Hudson and Goodwin, 1809.

G 1810 Goldsmith Goldsmith, Rev. J. (Sir Richard Phillips). *A Grammar of Geography for the Use of Schools.* Philadelphia: Johnson and Warner, 1810.

G 1811 Morse Morse, Jedidiah. *Geography Made Easy.* 14th ed. Boston: Thomas and Andrews, 1811.

G 1811 Workman Workman, Benjamin. *Elements of Geography.* 14th ed. Philadelphia: W. M'Culloch, 1811.

G 1812 Dwight Dwight, Nathaniel. *A Short but Comprehensive System of the Geography of the World.* 6th ed. Northampton, Mass.: Simeon Butler, 1812.

G 1812 Morse Morse, Jedidiah. *Geography Made Easy.* 15th ed. Boston: Thomas and Andrews, 1812.

G 1812 Parish Parish, Elijah. *A New System of Modern Geography.* Newburyport, Mass.: E. Little and Co., 1812.

G 1813 Dwight Dwight, Nathaniel. *A Short but Comprehensive System of the Geography of the World.* New York: E. Duyckinck, 1813.

G 1813 Nichols — Nichols, Francis. *An Elementary Treatise of Geography*. Philadelphia: Printed for Francis Nichols, 1813.

G 1813 Webster — Webster, Noah, Jr. *Elements of Useful Knowledge*. Vol. II. 4th ed. Hartford, Conn.: Hudson and Goodwin, 1813.

G 1814 Adams — Adams, Daniel. *Geography; or, a Description of the World*. Boston: West and Blake, 1814.

G 1814 Morse — Morse, Jedidiah. *Geography Made Easy*. 17th ed. Boston: Thomas and Andrews, 1814.

G 1814 O'Neill — O'Neill, John. *A New and Easy System of Geography and Popular Astronomy*. 3rd ed. Baltimore: Fielding Lucas, Jr., 1814.

G 1815 Geographical — *Geographical Exercises Compiled for the Use of the Boarding School*. Wilmington, Del.: Robert Porter, 1815.

G 1815 Willetts — Willetts, Jacob. *An Easy Grammar of Geography*. 2nd ed. Poughkeepsie, N.Y.: Paraclete Potter, 1815.

G 1816 Dwight — Dwight, Nathaniel. *A System of Universal Geography*. Northampton, Mass.: Simeon Butler, 1816.

G 1816 Picket — Picket, A. and J. W. *Geographical Grammar*. New York: Smith and Forman, 1816.

G 1816 Rudd — Rudd, Rev. John C. *A Compendium of Geography*. Elizabethtown, N.J.: Mervin Hale, 1816.

G 1816 Workman — Workman, B. *Epitome of Workman's Geography*. Philadelphia: William McCarty, 1816.

G 1817 Cummings — Cummings, J. A. *An Introduction to Ancient and Modern Geography, on the plan of Goldsmith and Guy*. Boston: Cummings and Hilliard, 1817.

G 1817 Dwight — Dwight, Nathaniel. *A System of Universal Geography*. Northampton, Mass.: Simeon Butler, 1817.

G 1818 Green — Green, Samuel. *A Geographical Grammar*. New London, Conn.: Samuel Green, 1818. (Sold in the North and in Baltimore.)

G 1818 Mann — Mann, Herman. *The Material Creation: Being a Compendious System of Universal Geography and Popular Astronomy*. Dedham, Mass.: W. H. Mann, 1818.

G 1818 Morse — Morse, Jedidiah. *Geography Made Easy.* 19th ed. Boston: Thomas and Andrews, 1818.

G 1818 Smith — Smith, Thomas. *Elements of Geography.* New York: Samuel Wood and Sons, 1818.

G 1818 Vinson and Mann — Vinson, T. and H. Mann. *Universal Geography.* Dedham, Mass.: Printed for the proprietor, 1818. (Exactly the same as G 1818 Mann above [Vinson claims his to be the original].)

G 1819 Adams — Adams, Daniel. *Geography.* 4th ed. Boston: Lincoln and Edmands, 1819.

G 1819 Cummings — Cummings, J. A. *First Lessons in Geography and Astronomy.* 2nd ed. Boston: Cummings and Hilliard, 1819.

G 1819 Morse — Morse, Jedidiah. *Geography Made Easy.* 20th ed. Utica, N.Y.: William Williams, 1819.

G 1819 Willetts — Willetts, Jacob. *An Easy Grammar of Geography for the Use of Schools.* 6th ed. Poughkeepsie, N.Y.: Paraclete Potter, 1819.

G 1819 J. Worcester — Worcester, J. E. *Elements of Geography, Ancient and Modern.* Boston: Timothy Swan, 1819.

G 1820 Cummings — Cummings, J. A. *An Introduction to Ancient and Modern Geography.* 7th ed. Boston: Cummings and Hilliard, 1820.

G 1820 Darby — Darby, William. *Ewing's Geography.* New York: Charles N. Baldwin, 1820.

G 1822 Drury — Drury, Luke. *A Geography for Schools upon a plan entirely new.* Providence, R.I.: Miller and Hutchens, 1822.

G 1822 Morse and Morse — Morse, Jedidiah and Sidney. *A New System of Geography, Ancient and Modern, for the use of Schools.* 23rd ed. Boston: Richardson and Lord, 1822.

G 1822 S. Morse — Morse, Sidney. *A New System of Modern Geography.* Boston: George Clark, 1822.

G 1822 Willetts — Willetts, Jacob. *An Easy Grammar of Geography.* 8th ed. Poughkeepsie, N.Y.: Paraclete Potter, 1822.

G 1822 J. Worcester — Worcester, J. E. *Elements of Geography, Ancient and Modern.* 2nd ed. Boston: Cummings and Hilliard, 1822.

G 1823 Cummings — Cummings, J. A. *First Lessons in Geography and Astronomy.* 4th ed. Boston: Cummings and Hilliard, 1823.

G 1824 Fowle — Fowle, William B. *Practical Geography as Taught in the Monitorial School, Boston.* Boston: T. P. and J. S. Fowle, 1824.

G 1824 Morse and Morse — Morse, Jedidiah and Sidney. *A New System of Geography.* 24th ed. Boston: Richardson and Lord, 1824.

G 1824 Woodbridge and Willard — Woodbridge, William C. and Emma Willard. *Universal Geography, Ancient and Modern.* Hartford, Conn.: Oliver D. Cooke and Sons, 1824.

G 1824 J. Worcester — Worcester, J. E. *Elements of Geography, Ancient and Modern.* Boston: Cummings, Hilliard and Co., 1824.

G 1825 Butler — Butler, Frederick. *Elements of Geography and History Combined.* 2nd ed. Wethersfield, Conn.: Deming and Francis, 1825.

G 1825 Cummings — Cummings, J. A. *First Lessons in Geography and Astronomy.* Boston: Cummings, Hilliard and Co., 1825.

G 1825 Gummere — Gummere, Samuel R. *Elementary Exercises in Geography.* 5th ed. Philadelphia: Kimber and Sharpless, 1825.

G 1825 J. Worcester — Worcester, J. E. *Elements of Geography, Ancient and Modern.* Boston: Cummings, Hilliard and Co., 1825.

G 1826 Blake — Blake, John L. *A Geographical, Chronological and Historical Atlas, on a New and Improved Plan.* New York: Cooke and Co., 1826.

G 1826 Cummings — Cummings, J. A. *First Lessons in Geography and Astronomy.* 5th ed. Boston: Cummings, Hilliard and Co., 1826.

G 1826 E. Willard — Willard, Emma. *Geography for Beginners, or the Instructor's Assistant.* Hartford, Conn.: Oliver D. Cooke and Co., 1826.

G 1827 C. Goodrich — Goodrich, Rev. Charles A. *Outlines of Modern Geography.* Boston: S. G. Goodrich, 1827.

G 1828 Adams — Adams, Daniel. *Geography; or a Description of the World.* 11th ed. Boston: Lincoln and Edmands, 1828.

G 1828 Morse and Morse — Morse, Jedidiah and Sidney. *A New System of Geography, Ancient and Modern.* 26th ed. New York: Collins and Hannay, 1828.

G 1828 Smiley	Smiley, Thomas T. *An Easy Introduction to the Study of Geography*. 6th ed. Philadelphia: Clark and Raser, 1828.
G 1828 Woodbridge	Woodbridge, William C. *Woodbridge's Rudiments of Geography on a New Plan*. 9th ed. Hartford, Conn.: Oliver D. Cooke and Co., 1828.
G 1828 J. Worcester	Worcester, J. E. *An Epitome of Geography*. Boston: Hilliard, Gray, Little and Wilkins, 1828.
G 1829 Percival	Percival, James G. *A Geographical View of the World*. New York: D. M. Jewett, 1829. (Goldsmith's Geography revised, corrected and improved by James G. Percival.)
G 1829 Woodbridge	Woodbridge, William C. *Rudiments of Geography*. 10th ed. Hartford, Conn.: Oliver D. Cooke and Co., 1829.
G 1829 J. Worcester	Worcester, J. E. *Elements of Geography, Ancient and Modern*. Boston: Hilliard, Gray, Little and Wilkins, 1829.
G 1830 Adams	Adams, Daniel. *Geography; or, a Description of the World*. 12th ed. Boston: Lincoln and Edmands, 1830.
G 1830 Bazeley	Bazeley, C. W. *The Juvenile Scholar's Geography*. Philadelphia: Printed for the author, 1830.
G 1830 Fowle	Fowle, William B. *Modern Practical Geography, on the Plan of Pestalozzi*. 3rd ed. Boston: Lincoln and Edmands, 1830.
G 1830 Hale	Hale, Nathan. *An Epitome of Universal Geography*. Boston: N. Hale; Richardson, Lord and Holbrook, 1830.
G 1830 Smiley	Smiley, Thomas T. *An Easy Introduction to the Study of Geography*. 7th ed. Philadelphia: Printed for the author by Joseph Harding, 1830.
G 1831 Blake	Blake, Rev. J. L. *A Geography for Children*. Boston: Richardson, Lord and Holbrook, 1831.
G 1831 Pennell	Pennell, Alice Hart. *A Key to the Questions in Adams' Geography: Together with an Account of the Principal Countries, Kingdoms, States, Cities and Towns . . . of the World*. Baltimore: John J. Harrod, 1831.

G 1831 Woodbridge — Woodbridge, William C. *Woodbridge's Rudiments of Geography*. 15th ed. Hartford, Conn.: Oliver D. Cooke, 1831.

G 1831 S. Worcester — Worcester, Samuel. *A First Book of Geography*. Boston: Crocker and Brewster, 1831.

G 1832 Adams — Adams, Daniel. *Geography; or, a Description of the World*. Boston: Lincoln and Edmands, 1832. (Also issued at Baltimore, Raleigh, Mobile.)

G 1832 Allen — Allen, Joseph. *Easy Lessons in Geography and History Designed for the Use of the Younger Classes in the New England Schools*. Boston: Hilliard, Gray, Little and Wilkins, 1832.

G 1832 Blaisdale — Blaisdale, Rev. Silas. *Primary Lessons in Geography; Consisting of Questions Adapted to Worcester's and Woodbridge's Atlases*. 4th ed. Boston: Marsh, Capen and Lyon, 1832.

G 1832 Olney — Olney, J. *A Practical System of Modern Geography*. 11th ed. Hartford, Conn.: D. F. Robinson and Co., 1832.

G 1833 Clute — Clute, John J. *The School Geography*. New York: Samuel Wood and Sons, 1833.

G 1833 Woodbridge and Willard — Woodbridge, William C. and Emma Willard. *Universal Geography*. 5th ed. Hartford, Conn.: Oliver D. Cooke and Co., 1833.

G 1835 Huntington — Huntington, Nathaniel G. *A System of Modern Geography*. 5th ed. Hartford, Conn.: R. White and Hutchinson and Dwier, 1835.

G 1835 Olney — Olney, J. *Practical System of Modern Geography*. 18th ed. New York: Robinson, Pratt and Co., 1835.

G 1835 J. Worcester — Worcester, J. E. *Elements of Geography, Ancient and Modern*. Boston: Hilliard, Gray and Co., 1835.

G 1836 Olney — Olney, J. *A Practical System of Modern Geography*. 22nd ed. New York: Robinson, Pratt and Co., 1836.

G 1836 Smith — Smith, Roswell. *Geography on the Productive System*. Philadelphia: W. Marshall and Co., 1836.

G 1837 Book of Commerce — *The Book of Commerce by Sea and Land Exhibiting its Connection with Agriculture, the Arts and Manufactures*. Philadelphia: Uriah Hunt, 1837.

G 1837 Smith — Smith, Roswell. *Geography on the Productive System.* Philadelphia: W. Marshall and Co., 1837.

G 1837 Village — By a Teacher. *The Village School Geography.* 3rd ed. Hartford, Conn.: Reed and Barber, 1837.

G 1839 J. Worcester — Worcester, J. E. *A Geography for Common Schools.* Boston: Hilliard, Gray and Co., 1839.

G 1840 Mitchell — Mitchell, S. Augustus. *Mitchell's Geographical Reader; A System of Modern Geography.* Philadelphia: Thomas, Cowperthwait and Co., 1840.

G 1840 Olney — Olney, J. *A Practical System of Modern Geography.* 33rd ed. New York: Robinson, Pratt and Co., 1840.

G 1840 Smith — Smith, Roswell C. *Geography on the Productive System.* Hartford, Conn.: Spalding and Storrs, 1840.

G 1843 Mitchell — Mitchell, S. Augustus. *A System of Modern Geography.* Philadelphia: Thomas, Cowperthwait and Co., 1843.

G 1843 Murray — Murray, Hugh. *The Encyclopedia of Geography.* Philadelphia: Lea and Blanshard, 1843.

G 1844 Edmands — Edmands, B. Franklin. *The Boston School Atlas.* 13th ed. Boston: Robert S. Davis, 1844.

G 1845 Book of Commerce — *The Book of Commerce.* Philadelphia: Uriah Hunt and Son, 1845.

G 1845 Mitchell — Mitchell, S. Augustus. *A System of Modern Geography.* Philadelphia: Thomas, Cowperthwait and Co., 1845.

G 1845 S. Morse — Morse, Sidney. *A System of Geography, for the Use of Schools.* New York: Harper and Brothers, 1845.

G 1845 Woodbridge — Woodbridge, William C. *Modern School Geography.* 2nd ed. Hartford, Conn.: Belknap and Hamersley, 1845.

G 1845 Woodbridge and Willard — Woodbridge, William C. and Emma Willard. *Universal Geography.* Hartford, Conn.: Belknap and Hamersley, 1845.

G 1846 Mitchell — Mitchell, S. Augustus. *A System of Modern Geography.* Philadelphia: Thomas, Cowperthwait and Company, 1846.

G 1846 Woodbridge	Woodbridge, William C. *Modern School Geography*. Hartford, Conn.: Belknap and Hamersley, 1846.
G 1847 Woodbridge	Woodbridge, William C. *Modern School Geography*. 5th ed. Hartford, Conn.: Belknap and Hamersley, 1847.
G 1848 Mitchell	Mitchell, S. Augustus. *An Easy Introduction to the Study of Geography*. Philadelphia: Thomas, Cowperthwait and Company, 1848.
G 1848 Smith	Smith, Roswell C. *Geography on the Productive System*. New York: Cady and Burgess, 1848.
G 1850 Book of Commerce	*The Book of Commerce*. Philadelphia: Uriah Hunt and Son, 1850.
G 1850 Mitchell-P	Mitchell, S. Augustus. *Mitchell's Primary Geography*. Philadelphia: Cowperthwait and Company, 1850.
G 1850 Mitchell-S	Mitchell, S. Augustus. *A System of Modern Geography*. Philadelphia: Thomas, Cowperthwait and Company, 1850.
G 1851 Mitchell	Mitchell, S. Augustus. *A System of Modern Geography*. Philadelphia: Thomas, Cowperthwait and Company, 1851.
G 1851 Smith-G	Smith, Roswell C. *Geography on the Productive System*. New York: Cady and Burgess, 1851.
G 1851 Smith-I	Smith, Roswell C. *An Introductory Geography*. 13th ed. New York: Cady and Burgess, 1851.
G 1853 Mitchell	Mitchell, S. Augustus. *Mitchell's Primary Geography. An Easy Introduction to the Study of Geography*. Philadelphia: Thomas, Cowperthwait and Company, 1853.
G 1853 S. Goodrich	Goodrich, S. G. *A Comprehensive Geography and History, Ancient and Modern*. New York: George Savage, 1853.
G 1853 Smith	Smith, Roswell C. *An Introductory Geography*. 20th ed. New York: Daniel Burgess and Company, 1853.
G 1854 Mitchell	Mitchell, S. Augustus. *A System of Modern Geography*. Philadelphia: Cowperthwait, DeSilver and Butler, 1854.
G 1855 Smith	Smith, Roswell C. *Geography on the Productive System*. New York: Daniel Burgess and Company, 1855.

G 1857 Mitchell	Mitchell, S. Augustus. *A System of Modern Geography*. Philadelphia: H. Cowperthwait and Company, 1857.
G 1859 Mitchell	Mitchell, S. Augustus. *An Easy Introduction to the Study of Geography*. Philadelphia: E. H. Butler and Company, 1859.
G 1860 Smith	Smith, Roswell C. *Geography on the Productive System*. Philadelphia: J. B. Lippincott and Company, 1860.
G 1862 Mitchell	Mitchell, S. Augustus. *A System of Modern Geography*. 38th ed. Philadelphia: E. H. Butler and Company, 1862.
G 1865 Mitchell	Mitchell, S. Augustus. *The New Primary Geography*. Philadelphia: E. H. Butler and Company, 1865.
G 1866 Guyot	Guyot, Arnold Henry. *Physical Geography*. New York: Armstrong, 1866.
G 1866 Guyot-C	Guyot, Arnold Henry, and Mary Howe Smith. *Common School Geography*. New York: Charles Scribner and Co., 1866.
G 1866 Guyot-P	Guyot, Arnold, and Mary Howe Smith. *Primary; or, Introduction to the Study of Geography*. New York: Charles Scribner and Co., 1866.
G 1866 Willard	Willard, Emma. *Ancient Geography* . . . Hartford, Conn.: William James Hamersley, 1866.
G 1866 Woodbridge	Woodbridge, William Channing. *System of Modern Geography*. Hartford, Conn.: William James Hamersley, 1866.
G 1867 Guyot	Guyot, Arnold. *The Earth and Its Inhabitants: Intermediate Geography*. New York: Charles Scribner and Co., 1867.
G 1868 Guyot	Guyot, Arnold H. *Introduction to the Study of Geography*. New York: Charles Scribner's Sons, 1868.
G 1869 Warren-C	Warren, D. M. *The Common School Geography* . . . Philadelphia: Cowperthwait and Co., 1869.
G 1869 Warren-E	Warren, D. M. *An Elementary Treatise on Physical Geography* . . . Philadelphia: Cowperthwait and Co., 1869.
G 1870 Cornell-G	Cornell, S. S. *Cornell's Grammar-School Geography*. New York: Appleton and Co., 1870.
G 1870 Cornell-P	Cornell, S. S. *Cornell's Physical Geography*. New York: D. Appleton and Co., 1870.

G 1872 Hall — Hall, Mary L. *Our World: A Second Series of Lessons in Geography.* Boston: Ginn Brothers, 1872.

G 1873 Guyot — Guyot, Arnold. *Physical Geography.* New York: Scribner, Armstrong and Co., 1873.

G 1874 Guyot — Guyot, Arnold H. *The Earth and Its Inhabitants.* New York: Scribner, Armstrong and Co., 1874.

G 1875 Heermans — Heermans, Anna A. *Hieroglyphic Geography.* New York: E. P. Dutton and Co., 1875.

G 1875 McNally — McNally, Francis. *An Improved System of Geography.* New York: A. S. Barnes and Co., 1875.

G 1875 Swinton — Swinton, William. *Elementary Course in Geography.* New York: Ivison, Blakeman, Taylor and Co., 1875.

G 1876 Comprehensive — *The Comprehensive Geography: Number Three.* New York: P. O'Shea, 1876. (For Roman Catholic schools.)

G 1878 Catholic — By a Catholic Teacher. *Sadlier's Excelsior Geography.* Number Three. New York: William H. Sadlier, 1878.

G 1878 Colton — Colton, J. H. *Colton's Common School Geography.* New York: Sheldon and Co., 1878. (Includes special section at back of book on the geography of Pennsylvania; but this copy was used by a boy in Buffalo, N. Y.)

G 1878 Steinwehr and Brinton — von Steinwehr, A. and D. G. Brinton. *An Intermediate Geography.* New York: Van Antwerp, Bragg and Co., 1878.

G 1878 Swinton — Swinton, William. *A Complete Course in Geography.* New York: Ivison, Blakeman, Taylor and Co., 1878.

G 1880 Swinton — Swinton, William. *Grammar-School Geography.* New York: American Book Co., 1880.

G 1881 Maury — Maury, M. F. *Manual of Geography.* New York: University Publishing Co., 1881.

G 1885 Houston — Houston, Edwin J. *The Elements of Physical Geography.* Philadelphia: Eldredge and Bro., 1885.

G 1887 Quackenbos — Quackenbos, John D. and others. *Physical Geography.* Appleton's American Standard Geographies. New York: D. Appleton and Co., 1887.

G 1887 Redway — Redway, Jacques W. *Butler's Complete Geography*. Philadelphia: E. H. Butler and Co., 1887.

G 1887 Warren — Warren, D. M. *Warren's Common-School Geography*. Philadelphia: Cowperthwait and Co., 1887. (New England edition with special section at back on geography of that section.)

G 1888 Redway — Redway, Jacques W. *Butler's Elementary Geography*. Philadelphia: Butler, Sheldon and Co., 1888.

G 1891 Morton — Morton, Eliza H. *Potter's Advanced Geography*. Philadelphia: John E. Potter and Co., 1891.

G 1892 Maury — Maury, M. F. *Manual of Geography*. New York: University Publishing Co., 1892.

G 1892 Mitchell — Mitchell, S. Augustus. *A System of Modern Geography*. Philadelphia: E. H. Butler and Co., 1892. (Special section in back on geography of Tennessee.)

G 1894 Frye — Frye, Alexander Everett. *Primary Geography*. Boston: Ginn and Co., 1894. (Special section in back on geography of Middle Atlantic states.)

G 1894 Harper — *Harper's School Geography*. New York: American Book Co., 1894. (Special section in back on geography of New England.)

G 1894 Maury — Maury, M. F. *Manual of Geography*. New York: University Publishing Co., 1894.

G 1897 Redway — Redway, Jacques W. *Natural Elementary Geography*. New York: American Book Co., 1897.

G 1898 Carpenter — Carpenter, Frank G. *Carpenter's Geographical Reader: North America*. New York: American Book Co., 1898.

G 1898 Payne — Payne, Frank Owen. *Geographical Nature Studies*. New York: American Book Co., 1898.

G 1898 Redway and Hinman — Redway, Jacques W. and Russell Hinman. *Natural Advanced Geography*. New York: American Book Co., 1898.

G 1899 Carpenter — Carpenter, Frank G. *South America*. New York: American Book Co., 1899.

G 1899 Fairbanks — Fairbanks, H. W. *Stories of Our Mother Earth*. New York: William Beverly Harison, 1899.

G 1899 Tarbell — Tarbell, Horace S. and Martha Tarbell. *The Complete Geography*. New York: Werner School Book Co., 1899.

G 1899 Twombly	Twombly, Alexander S. *Hawaii and Its People.* New York: Silver, Burdett and Co., 1899.
G 1900 Dodge	Dodge, Richard Elwood. *A Reader in Physical Geography.* New York: Longmans, Green and Co., 1900.
G 1900 Kellogg	Kellogg, Eva M. C. *The World and Its Peoples.* Book VIII. *Australia and The Islands of the Sea.* New York: Silver, Burdett & Co., 1900.
G 1900 Morton	Morton, Eliza. *Morton's Elementary Geography.* New York: Butler, Sheldon and Co., 1900.
G 1900 Tarbell	Tarbell, Horace S. *The Introductory Geography.* New York: Werner, 1900.
G 1900 Tarr and McMurry-1	Tarr, Ralph S. and Frank M. McMurry. *First Book: Home Geography and the Earth as a Whole.* New York: The Macmillan Co., 1900.
G 1900 Tarr and McMurry-2	Tarr, Ralph S. and Frank M. McMurry. *Second Book: North America.* New York: The Macmillan Co., 1900.

HISTORIES

Key	*Publication*
H 1804 Webster	Webster, Noah, Jr. *Elements of Useful Knowledge.* Vol. I. Hartford, Conn.: Hudson and Goodwin, 1804. Substantially the same as G 1802 Webster.
H 1814 Cooper	Cooper, W. D. *History of North America.* Hartford, Conn.: W. S. Marsh, 1814.
H 1822 Grimshaw	Grimshaw, William. *History of the United States from their First Settlement to the Cession of Florida in 1801.* Philadelphia: Grigg, Eliot and Co., 1822.
H 1826 Hale	Hale, Salma. *History of the United States.* London: J. Miller, 1826. (In 1825 this book was awarded a $400 prize by the American Academy of Belles Lettres as the best history for use in schools.)
H 1831 S. Goodrich	Goodrich, Samuel. *The First Book of History.* Boston: Richardson, Lord and Holbrook, 1831. (By 1876 he had written or supervised the writing of 170 textbooks, which had sold seven million copies in the United States.)

H 1833 C. Goodrich — Goodrich, Charles Augustus. *A History of the United States of America.* Hartford, Conn.: H. F. Summer and Co., 1833. (This book went through 150 editions, 1823–1873.)

H 1836 Olney — Olney, Jesse. *A History of the United States.* New York: F. Ripley, 1836.

H 1839 Frost — Frost, John. *A History of the United States.* Philadelphia: F. W. Greenough, 1839.

H 1843 Hall and Baker — Hall, Samuel Read and Abijah Richardson Baker. *School History of the United States.* Andover, Mass.: B. B. Mussey, 1843.

H 1851 Guernsey — Guernsey, Egbert. *History of the United States of America.* New York: Cady and Burgess, 1851.

H 1852 E. Willard — Willard, Emma Hart. *Abridged History of the United States or Republic of America.* New York: A. S. Barnes and Co., 1852.

H 1855 Berard — Berard, Augusta Blanche. *School History of the United States.* Philadelphia: H. Cowperthwait and Co., 1855.

H 1856 First Lessons — By a Practical Teacher. *First Lessons in the History of the United States.* Boston: Hickling, Swan and Brown, 1856.

H 1857 Lossing — Lossing, Benson John. *A Primary History of the United States.* New York: Mason Brothers, 1857.

H 1866 Lossing — Lossing, Benson John. *A Primary History of the United States.* New York: Mason Bros., 1866.

H 1867 Goodrich — Goodrich, Charles A. *History of the United States of America.* Boston: Brewer and Tileston, 1867. (This copy used in Chicago schools.)

H 1867 Willson — Willson, Marcius. *History of the United States.* New York: Ivison, Phinney, Blakeman and Co., 1867.

H 1868 Kerney — Kerney, M. J. *The First Class Book of History.* Baltimore: John Murphy and Co., 1868. (From internal evidence, a Roman Catholic textbook.)

H 1868 Willard — Willard, Emma. *Abridged History of the United States or Republic of America.* New York: A. S. Barnes and Co., 1868.

H 1869 Quackenbos — Quackenbos, G. P. *Primary History of the United States.* New York: D. Appleton and Co., 1869.

H 1870 Lossing	Lossing, Benson John. *A Common School History of the United States*. New York: Sheldon and Co., 1870.
H 1872 Lossing	Lossing, Benson John. *A Grammar-School History of the United States*. New York: Sheldon and Co., 1872.
H 1872 Noque	Noque, Oro. *Historicals for the Young Folks*. New Haven, Conn.: Charles C. Chatfield and Co., 1872.
H 1872 Venable	Venable, W. H. *A School History of the United States*. Cincinnati: Wilson, Hinkle and Co., 1872.
H 1873 Anderson-G	Anderson, John J. *A Grammar School History of the United States*. New York: Clark and Maynard, 1873.
H 1873 Anderson-R	Anderson, John J. *The United States Reader*. New York: Clark and Maynard, 1873.
H 1874 Anderson	Anderson, John J. *A Junior Class History of the United States*. New York: Clark and Maynard, 1874.
H 1874 Scott	Scott, David B. *A School History of the United States*. New York: Harper and Brothers, 1874.
H 1875 Higginson	Higginson, Thomas Wentworth. *Young Folks' History of the United States*. Boston: Lee and Shepard, 1875.
H 1876 Doyle	Doyle, J. A. *History of the United States*. New York: Henry Holt and Co., 1876. (Actually contains material to 1885; author is English.)
H 1876 Lossing	Lossing, Benson John. *A Pictorial History of the United States*. New York: Sheldon and Co., 1876.
H 1877 Anderson	Anderson, John J. *An Introductory School History of the United States*. New York: Clark and Maynard, 1877.
H 1879? Campbell	Campbell, L. John. *A Concise School History of the United States*. New York: Taintor Bros., and Co., 1879?
H 1879 Quackenbos	Quackenbos, George Payn. *American History for Schools*. New York: D. Appleton and Co., 1879. (Includes a history of each New England state in a special section.)
H 1881 Armstrong	*Armstrong's Primer of United States History*. New York: A. C. Armstrong and Son, 1884.

H 1881 Eliot — Eliot, Samuel. *History of the United States from 1492 to 1872.* Boston: William Ware and Co., 1881.

H 1881 Steele — [Steele, Joel Dorman.] *A Brief History of the United States.* New York: A. S. Barnes, 1881.

H 1881 Thalheimer — Thalheimer, M. E. *The Eclectic History of the United States.* Cincinnati: Van Antwerp, Bragg and Co., 1881. (Actually includes material to November, 1888.)

H 1885 Donnelly — Donnelly, T. F. *A Primary History of the United States.* New York: American Book Co., 1885. (Actually includes material to 1897.)

H 1885 Ensign — Ensign, S. Laura. *Outlines, Tables and Sketches in United States History.* Chicago: A. Flanagan, 1885.

H 1885 Ridpath — Ridpath, John Clark. *History of the United States . . .* Cincinnati: Van Antwerp, Bragg and Co., 1885.

H 1886 Childs — Childs, Emery E. *A History of the United States.* New York: Baker and Taylor, 1886.

H 1889 Chambers — Chambers, Henry E. *A Higher History of the United States.* New Orleans: University Publishing Co., 1889. (Designed for "youth of the South"; includes material through 1892.)

H 1889 Monroe — Monroe, Mrs. Lewis B. *The Story of Our Country.* Boston: Lee and Shepard, 1889.

H 1889? Steele — [Steele, Joel Dorman.] *A Brief History of the United States.* New York: A. S. Barnes, 1889?

H 1890 Eaton and Foster — Eaton, Seymour and Evelyn S. Foster. *Exercises in American History.* Boston: Educational Publishing Co., 1890.

H 1890 Morris — Morris, Charles. *An Elementary History of the United States.* Philadelphia: J. B. Lippincott, 1890.

H 1893 Creery — Creery, William R. *Catechism of the History of the United States.* Baltimore: William J. C. Dulany Co., 1893.

H 1894 Fiske — Fiske, John. *A History of the United States.* Boston: Houghton Mifflin and Co., 1894.

H 1895 Eggleston — Eggleston, Edward. *Stories of American Life and Adventures.* New York: American Book Co., 1895.

H 1896 Murphy — Murphy, Dawsey Cope. *Flash-Lights on American History.* Harrisburg, Pa.: R. L. Miers and Co., 1896.

H 1897 McMaster	McMaster, John Bach. *A School History of the United States*. New York: American Book Co., 1897. (Actually includes material to 1900.)
H 1898 Chambers	Chambers, Henry E. *A Higher History of the United States* . . . New York: American Book Co., 1898. (Uses three different kinds of type or format, each for a different level.)
H 1898 Steele and Steele	Steele, Joel Dorman, and Esther Baker Steele. *A Brief History of the United States*. New York: American Book Co., 1898/1899?
H 1899 Morris	Morris, Charles. *A Primary History of the United States*. Philadelphia: J. B. Lippincott Co., 1899. (Actually includes material to 1904.)
H 1900 Channing	Channing, Edward. *A Short History of the United States*. New York: The Macmillan Co., 1900.
H 1900 Shaw	Shaw, Edward Richard. *Discoverers and Explorers*. New York: American Book Co., 1900.

ARITHMETICS

Key	*Publication*
A 1784 Dilworth	Dilworth, Thomas. *The Schoolmaster's Assistant*. New York: Hugh Gaines, 1784. (English book.)
A 1788 Gough	Gough, John. *A Treatise of Arithmetic in Theory and Practice . . . Adapted to the Commerce of Great Britain and Ireland. To which are added, many valuable additions and amendments; more particularly fitting the work for the improvement of the American Youth—by Benjamin Workman*. Philadelphia: J. M'Culloch for W. Young, 1788.
A 1789 M'Donald	M'Donald, Alexander. *The Youth's Assistant*. 2nd ed. Litchfield: Printed by T. Collier, 1789.
A 1790 Sterry and Sterry	Sterry, Consider and John. *The American Youth*. Providence, R.I.: Printed by Bennett Wheller, 1790.
A 1795 Chaplin	Chaplin, Joseph. *The Trader's Best Companion*. Newburyport, Mass.: Printed by William Barrett, 1795. (Contains tables for reducing British pounds to Federal currency and to the currencies of the states of New Hampshire, Massachusetts, Rhode Island, Connecticut, and Virginia. From now on all contain such tables.)

A 1795 Pike — Pike, Nicolas. *Abridgement of the New and Complete System of Arithmetic Composed for the Use and Adapted to the Commerce of the Citizens of the United States.* Worcester, Mass.: Isaiah Thomas, 1795.

A 1795 Root — Root, Erastus. *An Introduction to Arithmetic.* Norwich, Conn.: Printed for the author by Thomas Hubbard, 1795.

A 1795 Sterry and Sterry — Sterry, Consider and John. *A Complete Exercise Book in Arithmetic.* Norwich, Conn.: Printed and sold by John Sterry and Co., 1795.

A 1797 Lee — Lee, Chauncey. *The American Accountant. Being a Plain, Practical and Systematic Compendium of Federal Arithmetic.* Lansingburgh, N.Y.: Printed by William Williams, 1797.

A 1797 Kendal — Kendal, David. *The Young Lady's Arithmetic. Published by Request of Several Young Ladies Desirous of Adding to Their Other Mental Accomplishments the Pleasing and Useful Science of Figures.* Leominster, Mass.: Printed by Charles Prentiss for the author, 1797.

A 1797 Milns — Milns, William. *The American Accountant. The Whole Calculated to Ease the Teacher and Assist the Pupil; it will be found likewise extremely useful to American Merchants.* New York: J. S. Mott, 1797.

A 1798 Temple — Temple, Samuel. *A Concise Introduction to Practical Arithmetic.* Boston: Samuel Hall, 1798.

A 1800 Daboll — Daboll, Nathan. *Schoolmaster's Assistant.* New London, Conn.: Samuel Green, 1800.

A 1802 Adams — Adams, Daniel. *The Scholar's Arithmetic or Federal Accountant.* Leominster, Mass.: Printed by Adams and Wilder for the author, 1802.

A 1802 Alexander — Alexander, Caleb. *A New and Complete System of Arithmetic.* Albany, N.Y.: Thomas, Andrews and Penniman, 1802.

A 1802 Merrill — Merrill, Phinehas. *The Scholar's Guide to Arithmetic.* Exeter, N.H.: Printed by Henry Ranlet, 1802.

A 1803 Hawley — Hawley, Daniel. *The Federal Calculator or American Schoolmaster's Assistant and Young Man's Companion, 1803.* (Revision of Dilworth.)

A 1806 Vyse — Vyse, Charles. *The Tutor's Guide*. Philadelphia: Joseph Cruikshank, 1806.

A 1807 Walsh — Walsh, Michael. *A New System of Mercantile Arithmetic*. 4th ed. New Haven, Conn.: S. and E. Butler. 1807.

A 1808 Daboll — Daboll, Nathan. *Daboll's Schoolmaster's Assistant. Adapted to the United States*. 6th Connecticut ed. New London: Ebenezer P. Cady, 1808.

A 1808 Judson — Judson, Adoniram. *The Young Lady's Arithmetic*. Boston: Snelling and Simons, 1808.

A 1808 Temple — Temple, Samuel. *A Concise Introduction to Practical Arithmetic*. 6th ed. Boston: Lincoln and Edmands, 1808.

A 1808 Thompson — Thompson, James. *The American Tutor's Guide*. Albany, N.Y.: E. and E. Hosford, 1808.

A 1809 Grout — Grout, Jonathan, Jr. *The Pupil's Guide to Practical Arithmetic*. Sutton, Mass.: Printed by Sewall Goodrich, 1809.

A 1809 Hutton — Hutton, Charles. *A Complete Treatise on Practical Arithmetic and Bookkeeping—Corrected, enlarged and adapted to the use of schools and men of business in the United States by D. P. Adams*. New York: W. Elliot, 1809.

A 1809 Pike — Pike, Nicolas. *A New and Complete System of Arithmetic*. 7th edition abridged by Nathaniel Lord. Boston: Thomas and Andrews, 1809.

A 1810 Carleton — Carleton, Osgood. *Carleton's Compendium of Practical Arithmetic . . . Containing what is necessary for the Merchant, the Mechanic, the Mariner, and the Farmer*. Boston: Thomas Wells, 1810.

A 1810 Fenwick — Fenwick, George. *Fenwick's Arithmetical Essay or a Plain and Concise Mode of Acquiring in a Short Time, a Complete Knowledge of Arithmetic*. Alexandria, Va.: Cotton and Stewart, 1810.

A 1810 Hendrick — Hendrick, Elijah H. *A New and Plain System of Arithmetic*. Richmond, Va.: Lynch and Davis, 1810.

A 1811 Columbian — By an American. *The Columbian Arithmetician*. Haverhill, Mass.: William B. Allen, 1811.

A 1811 Root — Root, Erastus. *An Introduction to Arithmetic*. Norwich, Conn.: Printed by Russell Hubbard, 1811.

A 1811 Watson, Jaudon, and Addington — Watson, Thomas, Daniel Jaudon, and Stephen Addington. *The Youth's Arithmetical Guide.* 2nd ed. Philadelphia: David Hogan, 1811.

A 1812 Adams — Adams, Daniel. *The Scholar's Arithmetic.* Montpelier, Vt.: Wright and Sibley for John Prentiss, 1812.

A 1813 American — *The American Tutor's Assistant Revised . . . Originally compiled by Sundry Teachers in and near Philadelphia.* Philadelphia: Joseph Cruikshank, 1813.

A 1813 Leavitt — Leavitt, Dudley. *Elements of Arithmetic.* Exeter, N.H.: Timothy Gridley, 1813.

A 1814 Adams — Adams, Daniel. *The Scholar's Arithmetic.* 9th ed. Keene, N.H.: John Prentiss, 1814.

A 1815 Daboll — Daboll, Nathan. *Daboll's Schoolmaster's Assistant.* New London, Conn.: Samuel Green, 1815.

A 1815 White — White, John J. *A Collection of the Most Useful Arithmetical Rules and Tables.* 4th ed. Hartford, Conn.: C. Hosmer, 1815.

A 1816 Adams — Adams, Daniel. *The Scholar's Arithmetic.* Keene, N.H.: John Prentiss, 1816. (In the Preface it states that in 14 years it has sold 40,000 copies.)

A 1816 Loomis — Loomis, Leonard. *The Science of Numbers Made Easy.* Hartford, Conn.: Peter B. Gleason, 1816.

A 1817 Gough — Gough, John. *A System of Practical Arithmetic.* 2nd ed. Baltimore: Printed by William Warner, 1817.

A 1817 Preston — Preston, John. *Every Man His Own Teacher, or, Lancaster's Theory of Education, Practically Displayed; Being an Introduction to Arithmetic.* Albany, N.Y.: Printed and published for the author, 1817.

A 1818 Bennett — Bennett, Titus. *New System of Practical Arithmetic.* Philadelphia: Bennett and Walton, 1818.

A 1818 Patterson — Patterson, Robert. *A Treatise of Practical Arithmetic.* Pittsburgh: No publisher given, 1818.

A 1818 White — White, John. *The Self-Instructor, or a System of Practical Arithmetic.* Philadelphia: Printed for the author, by D. Heartt, 1818.

A 1819 Walker — Walker, N. A. *System of Practical Arithmetic. Adapted from the Arithmetic by Rev. J. Joyce.* Baltimore: N.G. Maxwell, 1819.

A 1846 Mix — Mix, Ebenezer. *Practical Mathematics for the Use of Common Schools and Academies.* New York: Published by the author, 1846.

Key	*Publication*
A 1851 Davies	Davies, Charles. *The Logic and Utility of Mathematics with the Best Methods of Instruction Explained and Illustrated.* New York: A. S. Barnes and Co., 1851.
A 1858 Greenleaf	Greenleaf, Benjamin. *Introduction to the National Arithmetic on the Inductive System.* Boston: Robert S. Davies and Co., 1858.
A 1859 Robinson	Robinson, Horatio. *The Progressive Practical Arithmetic.* New York: Ivison and Phinney, 1859. (Sold also in the North, Chicago, St. Louis, New Orleans.)
A 1862 Ray	Ray, Joseph. *Three Thousand Test Examples in Arithmetic.* New York: Wilson, Hinkle and Co., 1862.
A 1863 Colburn	Colburn, Warren. *Intellectual Arithmetic upon the Inductive Method of Instruction.* Boston: Houghton Mifflin, 1863.
A 1863 Fish	Fish, Daniel W. *The Progressive Practical Arithmetic.* New York: Ivison, Phinney, Blakeman and Co., 1863.
A 1863 Loomis	Loomis, Elias. *The Elements of Arithmetic.* New York: Harper and Brothers, 1863.
A 1864 Eaton	Eaton, James S. —— *Arithmetic.* (Torn title page.) Boston: Taggard and Thompson, 1864.
A 1865 Walton and Walton	Walton, G. A. and E. N. L. Walton. *A Written Arithmetic.* Boston: Brewer and Tileston, 1865.

Confederate Arithmetics

A 1863 Lander-S	Lander, S. A. M. *Our Own School Arithmetic.* Greensboro, N.C.: Sterling, Campbell, and Albright, 1863.
A 1863 Lander-P	Lander, Rev. S. *Our Own Primary Arithmetic.* 2nd ed. Greensboro, N.C.: Sterling, Campbell and Albright, 1863.
A 1864 Johnson	Johnson, L. *Johnson's Common School Arithmetic.* Raleigh, N.C.: Bronson and Farrar, 1864.
A 1865 Browne	Browne, Rev. George. *Brown's Arithmetical Tables Combined with Easy Lessons in Mental Arithmetic for Beginners.* Atlanta, Ga.: Franklin Printing House, 1865.

ACKNOWLEDGMENTS

For sympathetic guidance and thoughtful criticism I am particularly grateful to Merle Curti, whose work inspired mine. The generous assistance of David Lowenthal, Susan Turner, and Elizabeth Collins with various parts of the manuscript were of great help. I am deeply indebted to Patricia Egan for encouragement and perceptive criticism throughout. The staff of Special Collections of the Columbia University Library, and especially Kenneth Lohf, provided invaluable assistance in all of the many years I spent among schoolbooks in the Plimpton Collection. For financial aid I am grateful to Vassar College, Columbia University, and the American Association of University Women, whose generous fellowships made the research possible.

I also wish to express gratitude to my daughter Elizabeth for her forbearance while I was absorbed in the children of another century. Finally, I would like to acknowledge an incalculable debt to my husband, Robert Elson.

RUTH MILLER ELSON

INDEX